THE 1989 1990 PUSHCART PRIZE XIV

BEST OF THE SMALL PRESSES

*Edited by
Bill Henderson
with the
Pushcart Prize
editors.
Introduction by
Tess Gallagher
Poetry editors:
Sandra McPherson
and
Laura Jensen*

PENGUIN BOOKS

PENGUIN BOOKS
Published by the Penguin Group
Viking Penguin, a division of Penguin Books USA Inc.,
40 West 23rd Street, New York, New York 10010, U.S.A.
Penguin Books Ltd, 27 Wrights Lane,
London W8 5TZ, England
Penguin Books Australia Ltd, Ringwood,
Victoria, Australia
Penguin Books Canada Ltd, 2801 John Street,
Markham, Ontario, Canada L3R 1B4
Penguin Books (N.Z.) Ltd, 182–190 Wairau Road,
Auckland 10, New Zealand

Penguin Books Ltd, Registered Offices:
Harmondsworth, Middlesex, England

First published in the United States of America by Pushcart Press, 1989
Published in Penguin Books 1990

10 9 8 7 6 5 4 3 2 1

Note: Nominations for this series are invited from any small, independent, literary
book press or magazine in the world. Up to six nominations—tear sheets or copies
selected from work published in the calendar year—are accepted by the November
15 deadline each year. Write to Pushcart Press, P.O. Box 380, Wainscott, NY 11975
for more information.

ISBN 0 14 01.1700 8
ISSN 0149–7863

Printed in the United States of America

Acknowledgments

Introduction © 1989 Tess Gallagher
A Snapping Turtle in June © 1988 Georgia Review
The Importance of Plot © 1988 Threepenny Review
Playing Chess With Arthur Koestler © 1988 Yale Review
Only One Sky © 1988 American Poetry Review
Strand © 1988 Chelsea
James Jesus Angleton 1917–1987 © 1988 Sulfur
Imagining the Ocean © 1988 Threepenny Review
Learning to Eat Soup © 1988 Antaeus
The Rain of Terror © 1989 Frank Manley from *Within The Ribbons, Nine Stories* (North Point Press).
Interpretation of a Poem by Frost © 1988 Epoch
The Family Is All There Is © 1988 TriQuarterly
Freeze © 1988 New England Review/Bread Loaf Quarterly
Westland © 1988 Paris Review
Five Stories © 1988 Conjunctions
The Summer of the Hats © 1988 Threepenny Review
After the Stations of the Cross © 1988 The Quarterly
Party © 1988 Boston Review
Miss Venezuela © 1988 Seal Press
Island © 1988 Ontario Review
Tangier, 1977 © 1988 Tombouctou Books
Coupon for Safety © 1988 TriQuarterly
The Safety Patrol © 1988 Crescent Review
Housework © 1988 The American Voice
Better Tomorrow © 1988 New England Review/Bread Loaf Quarterly
Mutatis Mutandis © 1988 Crazyhorse
Garbage © 1988 Iowa Review
"By Love Possessed" © 1988 Callaloo
Witness © 1988 Boulevard
"43" © 1988 Ironwood
Song © 1988 Burning Deck
Bill's Story © 1988 Green Mountains Review
Celestial Music © 1988 Ironwood
Against Silence © 1988 Boulevard
At A Motel © 1988 American Poetry Review
The Love of Travellers © 1988 Callaloo
Furious Versions © 1988 Ironwood
Explanations © 1988 Gettysburg Review
His Mother © 1988 New Virginia Review
Incident At Imuris © 1988 Sheep Meadow Press
Nice Mountain © 1988 Poetry East
On the Göta Canal, 1986 © 1988 Blue Unicorn
For You © 1988 Milkweed Editions

This book is in memory of Raymond Carver

INTRODUCTION

by TESS GALLAGHER

IN HIS INTRODUCTION to *Pushcart X*, George Plimpton tells of Raymond Carver's having taken a copy of *The Best American Short Stories* to bed with him because he was so pleased at having one of his stories in it. This glimpse of Ray calls up our affection, probably because it reflects so truly that capacity Ray had for unselfconsciously enacting his delight and amazement at what is often, in fact, a solitary occasion—that moment of finding one's words in print. If this story weren't true, which I'm sure it is, it would become true, as stories do which catch the spirit of a person or a time.

This story predates my life with Ray which began in 1977. It occurs instead at a time during which Ray told me more than once, "If there had been a gun in the house, someone would have been shot." To place this story during a period of domestic violence, of bankruptcies, of lives torn apart by alcoholism is to understand the solace, the depth of self-recognition and the beneficent hope which must have accompanied Ray's entry into that publication. Another thing. Those who knew Ray will realize that he would have read that anthology cover to cover, as he did the Pushcart Prize volumes (where he appeared four times), and in doing so, would have celebrated the company of those fellow writers. Since this volume is dedicated to Ray's memory I would like to tell some stories about him which perhaps have bearing on the spirit of the small press and the small literary magazine enterprise in America. Then I shall veer off into ruminations on Ray's and my relationship with small press life, and speak some toward the general state of publishing and writing as it looks at the moment to me.

But first, I want to take time to remember Ray as a reader of the small magazines, because all too often I sense from my students a

11

rather disdainful attitude toward the very magazines in which they attempt to be published. The idea of "appearing" in a magazine seems to overwhelm the fact that these publications are meant to be read. This was never the case with Ray.

I always enjoyed, during our eleven years together, how faithfully, how eagerly Ray attended the reading of the small magazines in which work of his, work of his friends and students, or the work of writers he would meet only on those pages had appeared. During a time when the sheer volume of small press publications may often reduce them to the totemic, Ray was that rare creature—a writer who reads. He was in the habit of turning down corners on the pages where a poem, story or essay had risen above the others to recommend itself further. In my more rushed days of teaching and householding, I relied heavily on these cues and would browse his enthusiasms, calling out to him when something really hit me. Or at mail time or after a meal I would read aloud to him something I'd discovered myself. Ours was a house in which things often were read aloud, and when I think of it now I realize that such caressing of print into speech was to our daylight hours what sleeping with the anthology must have been to Ray's nights in that former time—that is, more than commemorative, rather a giving of palpable new presence to the discovery of neighboring, intersecting and opposing worlds—what small press publication is all about.

I suspect that in getting to the magazines after Ray did, I missed some of that fresh-snow feeling one experiences in coming upon a piece of writing that announces in unforeseen and compelling language that one has been carried headlong onto a new continent of the imagination. Many of my first meetings with contemporaries, and with poets of the generations ahead of mine, took place in little magazines. I can still feel that gambling hall burr of excitement, of about-to-happenness when I remember how I discovered poems by Linda Gregg, Louise Glück, Bill Knott, Bob Hass, Mark Strand, Stanley Kunitz, Madeline DeFrees, William Merwin—well, the list now reads like a Who's Who of American poetry. These were important meetings and they took place in that intimate space between eye and heart, page and spirit.

For an essentially shy man like Ray, an encounter often had the impact of a meeting. Many things he would have, and in fact did, shut the door on in life, he opened up to on the page, either in his own writing or in the writing of others. And perhaps this is one of those verities about readers in general, that we would often rather witness than carry the spear.

I recall a story about Ray told to me in a letter after his death by the poet Ellen Bryant Voigt, about an instance in which Ray mightily volunteered himself to an encounter which seems now to have stepped eerily towards us, fully fleshed from his own fiction. It epitomizes for me that appetite for the unlikely encounter which Ray's fiction and poetry awakens in us, and for which it seems we hunger in the very act of reading.

As Ellen tells the story, Ray had gone into Plainfield, Vermont for a haircut during a break from teaching in what was then the Goddard Writing Program. I think it was his first teaching job sober. When he came back from town Ellen saw him rather sheepishly ducking into the cafeteria. His head had great nicks and gouges where the scalp stared through in the raw hieroglyphics of mishap. "What happened to you?" Ellen asked, and Ray, grinning and running his hand over the bald patches, tried to tell her. Through the laughter and hilarity of his own enjoyment of the story, he told her how he had seen this sign for a barbershop located above a hardware store. He'd gone up a dusty stairwell into the barbershop and found an eighty-year-old barber with one lone chair and no customers. He'd sat down in the chair and allowed himself to be draped with a towel. During this ritual he chanced to note that the barber's right arm hung limp. An even more disturbing awareness pressed itself upon him as the barber picked up his clippers with his left hand, a hand that was shaking.

The barber, in a somewhat apologetic yet resilient tone explained, as he set to work, that he'd had a stroke a couple of months before which had entirely paralyzed his right arm. So he'd had to learn to cut hair with his left hand. This was Okay. He was doing Okay, managing fairly well, until he'd suddenly been taken with palsy in his left arm. Ray was about to experience the barber's first attempt at cutting hair in this freshly acquired situation of challenge. Ray simply braced himself under the jittery hand of the inexplicable and took what the experience meted out. At this point in his telling of this to Ellen, she writes, "Ray could hardly get the story out, he was laughing so much. Not *at* the man, of course, but at life, at the world, at this amazing turn of events." As Ellen so rightly saw, Ray's innocence had been engaged. He had forgotten to care what his head looked like. The encounter itself had refreshed and astounded him. And thereafter when he retold the story one imagines of him the humility of the appreciator, of one who would recognize in the barber a kinship of hard turns, of unsteady comebacks.

In the richness of a literary life we often bear with each other, sustain, and ride compass for one another in the ungainly explorations we make as writers. And indeed it seems that the small literary magazine is still the format which most allows the exhilaration of watching the metamorphosis *while* it happens. For the most part, the crucial struggles are still lonely ones. As in that searingly acute last line of Louise Glück's "Elms," Ray perhaps understood more than most that "the stationary tree is torment" and that "it will make no forms but twisted forms." He was anything but stationary in his work and in his attentiveness to the work of others. He extended himself, and in doing so left a sign for us all. Out of his torments he worked an alchemy of responsiveness to his characters' dilemmas which brought us out into our yards like half-dressed sleepers aroused to the glow of flames fanning a neighborhood.

Ray's sense of the small press enterprise was a strenuous one. When, at age twenty-five he edited *Toyon*, the literary magazine at Humboldt State College where he was studying, he was rumored to have been so dismayed with the low quality of submissions that he sat down and wrote an entire issue himself, birthing the ubiquitous John Vale, among others. This sort of audacity and fulminating mischief seems a bit missing at the moment on the small press scene, at least when I think of *Kayak's* publication of Robin Skelton's hilarious introduction of the fictitious Algerian poet, Georges Zuk, born to a Hungarian father and a French mother and who practiced his own "cult of invisibility", having survived his experiences of occupied Paris. Nor is there that necrophilic glamour of Bill Knott's *Corpse and Beans*, informed by the suicide of its ultra romantic pseudonym, Saint Gerard. No wonder on a recent trip to the Twin Cities I took to the idea of a group of poets there surviving by their wits, writing mystery novels on the side to support themselves instead of trotting off to the academy. Yes, one occasionally longs for highjinks, for a gnashing at the somber literary veil.

Granta, that British Lilliputian turned giant with a current international circulation of some 100,000, and an editor, Bill Buford, who boldly presents himself as anti-literary, seems to have jumped the tracks of what everyone ploddingly accepted about small press efforts—that they would stay small, more the sanctuaries of art and the coterie than the actual innovative format by which flesh and blood readers in number might be enlivened and delighted. When Buford says he's anti-literary he seems simply to mean that he isn't persuaded by anything except the claims of interest a piece of writing make upon him. Through its active representation of American writing along with British writing, *Granta* has fostered a sense of community between British and American sensibilities and concerns. For those like Ray and myself, recently migrated from the working class, I suspect there has always been that longing, however thwarted by the realities, that we might be read by the very people whose news we carry. Perhaps this was at the bottom of the inexplicable pleasure I felt when my elderly high school teacher called me up and asked, with a tremor in her voice, had I seen this new magazine, *Granta?* The direction of news had been reversed. I hadn't had to proselytize. A literary magazine had found its way into the hands of someone who loved literature but who was not a writer, publisher, bookseller or university educator. It was as if the writer's immigrant status into the world of literature had suddenly been given its green card. And although I'm not one of those brashly populist cads who thinks that what Auden called "the odious public" should get what it wants (meaning possibly, the little it deserves!)—I do think Buford's sense of things (that writing ought, at the very least, not be boring) amounts to the discovery of gold in Peoria. Yes. Yes. Yes.

But, of course, and here's the crux, what's "boring" to some is necessity to others. Note, for instance, the slim-to-none offering of poetry in *Granta*. Poetry, that despicably alien, pock-marked artifact that is more indulged than appreciated. I was amazed when an editor from *Esquire* called recently and proposed that perhaps four to six poems of Ray's might be used in their fiction issue. Alas, order was soon restored and it ultimately developed that one poem would be published with a prose introduction. In the foreword to translations of the poems of the Czechoslovakian poet, Jaroslav Siefert, which I read aloud to my students at Beloit College, we learned that "perhaps fifty times as many books of poetry are bought by Czechs as by Americans." It's at moments like this when strange, impossible yearnings begin to overtake the American poet—the desire to learn Czech, to somehow *become* Czechoslovakian, even for a day or two, or at the very least to be translated into Czechoslovakian. But then,

15

unlike most poets, I have the unaccountable desire to be read not only by the person who delivers my mail, but by my gynecologist and my hair dresser, my druggist and the unflappable waitress at the Black Kettle in Pt. Angeles, Washington where I sometimes breakfast. Out of single-minded ambition I have advanced upon these frontiers in an individual way, in the small press tradition, pressing books of poetry into often baffled hands. Because the caretakers at the Pt. Angeles graveyard, for instance, have been curious about this writer, Raymond Carver, who has come into their care, I left copies of his stories and poems with them, and when they were returned, smudged and with page corners crimped, I supplied them with the "more" they asked for. Ray would like it that I did this.

In thinking about matters of audience, of one thing I'm certain, and this is that if a new and larger readership for the best writing is to be found in America it will be discovered and nourished by the small presses which, at this stage in their genesis, are often more aggressively auxiliary to the ignorance, the outright laziness and waste of conglomerate presses than they are frontally adversarial. With amoebic agility they have scouted up, for reprinting, many books the trade presses have shunted off as unprofitable. What one hopes is that the small presses will continue to perform that risky operation of enlisting new talents rather than simply recycling what once sold. I do sense a conservatism among the larger small presses at the moment towards the content and style of what they're willing to take on, which is probably related to this mostly laudable wish to enlarge circulation. Some maverick energy toward what is being published would be an antidote to any faint-heartedness in this regard. I was encouraged in February to read a fine article in the Associated Writing Programs' *Newsletter* by Ron Wallace detailing how university presses have become the main publishers of poetry in this country, and how they have recently been making a larger commitment to sustaining the work of mid-career writers. He makes an important observation about the retreat of trade publishers from the publishing of poetry. Although it's true they've traditionally held a lukewarm attitude toward anything which doesn't sell, now the trade presses just can't compete with the expertise of the university presses when it comes to publishing and distributing poetry.

The economics of the profit motive for trade presses has inadvertently begun to benefit the small non-profit press. The sale of 10,000 copies of a book isn't terribly important to a trade press, but this has left an opportunity for the small presses for whom it is their bread and butter. Also, many small publishers now sell up to 50% of their books outside the normal trade channels, channels that the trade presses haven't bothered to explore. Readers International, I'm told, now sells 80% of its offerings through the mail. If there's a trend afoot for enlarging small press circulation, this seems to be it—selling through the mail. Another small press maneuver has been to particularize the audience for certain books and to publish more by category: depression era stories, holocaust stories, literature of the twenties and third world literature anthologies, etc. For instance, an anthology of short stories about the elderly entitled *Full Measure* was turned down by several trade publishers before Graywolf Press took it up. It has now sold more than 6,000 copies to date and is being read in homes for retired teachers, in senior citizen centers, in classes on geratology, and was recently reviewed in *Modern Maturity*, a magazine which has the largest circulation outside of *TV Guide*.

This kind of publishing story is a long way from where Graywolf began, in a shed in Irondale, Washington with my book of poems, *Instructions to the Double*, as its first publication, a book which was turned on a hand press (all 1500 copies!) and which supported the press for several years, through various printings. My relationship with Scott Walker, editor of Graywolf, and with his press, (I sometimes slip and think "ours"!) began fourteen years ago in 1975 and has been one of the most enduring and exciting ventures in which I've been lucky enough to continue to participate. Ray joined me in that enthusiasm and served as member of the board of Graywolf from its beginning as a non-profit entity in 1983 until his death in August of 1988.

Not all writers have considered small press publication the small pond out of which they hoped to leap to oceanic fame and fortune with the large presses. During my years at Graywolf I had several opportunities to have my poetry published by trade presses, but I stayed with Graywolf, rightly mistrusting, I think, the turnstyle editing and distribution of poetry by the larger presses. What I wanted as a young writer was an editor who was going to stay with me and my work for the journey, an editor responsive to my particular proclivities both in the content and the presentation of my work. Scott Walker has been that editor and he has no doubt been an inspiration to other small presses in the making. By staying at Graywolf I've continued to have those pleasures that a writer can possibly only experience at the small press level—working with the book designer, in my case Tree Swenson, and being able to suggest cover material, and to follow the book through production stages, right down to the material on the flap cover. Walking into the new Graywolf offices in St. Paul for the first time recently, I felt the kind of pride parents must feel in meeting their children as adults. There was a busy office staffed with a manager, a developer, several interns, a publicist, etc. Our small press was no longer small in the sense that it had been—Scott and his companion Linda Foster handling it all right down to mailing the books out as the orders came in, the woodstove burning in the livingroom, tables stacked with work converging on the couch, and out back in the shed—yes, the hand press, emblem of small press origins in the computer age.

Lunching with Scott in a nearby restaurant I confessed to him that Ray's illness and death had left me somewhat like a person who'd been down in the hold of a ship, bailing, and who had now at last come up to see what the rest of the world had been doing. I had an appetite for news and Scott tried to catch me up. As regards the press, some general directions for small press activity began to emerge as he talked, one of them being that this is an era during which the small presses got savvy to marketing and distribution. Much as writers may grimace at the ad man portent of this, it does seem a hopeful development for dealing with a society which is not only fast becoming illiterate, but one which also contains a large segment which is a-literate—that is, people who could read but who don't. This a-literate population is, at the moment, where the small press innovators are putting their energies. In a democracy as diverse as our own, it appears that there has to be an exertion toward finding and engaging readers, and the small presses have stopped orienting their books towards academia. They have also become less conservative in how they go about locating and developing an audience. Graywolf *Travelers Editions,* for instance, will become available in airports, grocery stores, and bus stations before long. Also, agreements have been struck with small luxury hotels around the country to put more than the family bible into their rooms. Graywolf editions of stories and essays are about to find their ways onto the pillow "beside the foil wrapped mint," Scott Walker tells me and grins. "Small luxury hotels?" I say and give him a wry, cocked eyebrow. "Holiday Inn is next," he assures me.

This new expertise in small press marketing seems on the surface to have revised the large press dictate "But will it sell?" to "But to whom will it sell?" But it goes deeper than this. The small presses, unlike corporate publishers, haven't backed off in their essential support for writing of quality. That is they don't underestimate their actual or potential readership. Ron Wallace in the AWP *Newsletter* voices the ever present fear that wider circulation means that writers will automatically snap onto the greed-channel and start writing the trash that the public supposedly wants. I'm not sure this automatically follows. Or that the presses will turn into trolls under our bridges insisting that we write for saleability. Those of us who want simply to sell have known for a long time where to go and we haven't gone. This four letter word "sell" is one of the reasons, however, among others certainly, that we've been seeing some small presses publishing more fiction and non-fiction, but less poetry. In my travels to Great Britain I have observed quite another climate developing around the publishing of poetry in which trade publishers are actually scrambling to enlist poets. There are still things to be learned about nourishing a readership for poetry in this country.

When I entered the fiction world in 1986 with a book of stories I learned first hand about the chasm which separates the treatment of fiction and poetry in America. And it has a lot to do, I think, with that nasty word "marketing." But the fate of poetry readership in America is also being affected by a phrase we're likely to hear more often, even from the supportive independent bookstores, the phrase "turn-around," that death knell of shelf life that books and bread alike have to answer to more and more pressingly. In the so called "Quality Lit Game" I'm told, where 80% of the books are bought by people who see the book in the store and reach for it, the practice of bookstores ordering only on demand from distributors could, if fears become reality, ultimately banish much contemporary poetry from the shelves. Hello Kahlil Gibran. Reviewing practices for poetry and fiction differ widely. Because of stronger marketing pressures from publishers, trade and small press alike, and perhaps in the interest of serving the larger readership for fiction, fiction is given priority over poetry in both space and quality of treatment in the *New York Times*. My book of stories (published by Harper & Row) was reviewed twice there whereas a volume of poetry, even a collection of twenty years of work could, at the most expect an omnibus review of two paragraphs, in the unlikely event that it were to be reviewed at all. Poets around the country in their conversations with each other about this sad state of affairs drift more and more into a sense of isolation and therefore extremes of rancour and ambivalence toward their lot.

While we're considering reviews, it still seems that too few literary magazines have seriously taken up the job of critically reviewing poetry and what reviews do appear can often be either skimpy or stodgily bloated—largely descriptive rather than aesthetically argued or judgmentally acute. Let one hard-jawed critic raise his or her head and a thousand mallets come down. For a lot of intercommunal reasons the scene stays tepidly non-commital. Behind the scenes there is much gnashing of teeth and the repeated prayer that, dear God, some alternative to Harold Bloom and Helen Vendler be close at hand. On the West Coast the cry of Pinsky, now migrated to Boston, goes up. But it isn't enough. Even the deconstructionists, the structuralists and the Marxist theorists sense perhaps that no reputations are to be made by attending to contemporary poetry so they prefer to gild their hems on fiction and popular culture, put off by the so-called "privileged" stature of poetry. The feminist critics are at least enough in touch with some areas of contemporary poetry to know what they're talking about, when they do talk. But then, too often they need, by definition, to push everything through the sieve of sexuality and it won't always go.

When I think of that story Ray tells in his last book of poems, *A New Path to the Waterfall*, about first discovering *Poetry Magazine* on the coffee table of an elderly gentleman who was that rare animal, a reader, I want to get back to essential matters—to the best writing and publishing possible—*that* as the main endeavor. I think of editors like Michael Cuddihy whose magazine *Ironwood* was, for such a long time, one of those places in which a writer was proud to appear. I think of other editors: the late James Boatwright of *Shenandoah*, Clayton Eschelman of *Sulfur*, Laurence R. Smith of *Caliban*, Howard Junker of ZYZZYVA, John Witte of *Northwest Review*, Salima Keegan of *Hayden's Ferry Review* and Laurence Goldstein of *Michigan Quarterly Review*.

But going back to that fluke of a moment when Raymond Carver spotted that issue of *Poetry* on the coffee table and the old gent gave it to him, it does strike me that it's all too haphazard, the way literary magazines find their ways into the hands of readers, and that the magazines could use the stimulation of a Scott Walker when it comes to getting their magazines to the uninitiated. Ray writes of that moment in which he was handed *Poetry*.

> I was just a pup then, but nothing can explain away such a moment: the moment when the very thing I needed most in my life—call it a polestar—was casually, generously given to me. Nothing remotely approaching that moment has happened since.

Now think of it *not* happening and you know something about the gift of the small literary magazines. Just think. This story is revealing in its emphasis on the spirit of beneficence out of which Ray took his mandates in art and life, a mandate which is similarly at the heart of the small press effort. Generosity was the name of his game and it applied even when he couldn't be sure what might come back in return. This gift beyond expectation from editors and small press magazines is something to be protected and celebrated in America.

Once in Santa Monica, Ray and I had been put up in a noisy but trendy art deco hotel where movie companies were wont to park writers. It was called the Shangri La and it felt like a converted motel. The rooms were approachable without entering a lobby. Anyone could climb the stairs to the open air corridor that ran along the doors to the rooms. At about 11 p.m. on our first night there, a knock came at the door, first softly, then firmly, and when we didn't answer right away, a man's voice began to come through our door explaining, asking. I told Ray not to open the door but he did anyway. He opened the door as far as the chain would allow. So this guy, with Ray peering out through the crack in the door, told Ray how his car had broken down earlier and that he'd taken it to a nearby garage for repairs. Now he'd gone to pick it up and they were charging him twenty dollars over the estimate and wouldn't release the car until they had the cash. He explained that he needed the car to go to work, never mind that he had to get home to sleep that night. Furthermore the guy promised Ray that if he loaned him the money he would personally drive home and get the twenty dollars and slip it under the door in an envelope before morning so as not to disturb him again. Ray asked the man to wait a minute. He shut the door and went to where his slacks were thrown over a chair and took out his billfold. Then he opened the door and gave the man the money.

After Ray had completed this transaction, for which he was to receive sleep in exchange for twenty dollars, I think I probably said something appropriately salty about con men and scams, and Ray half heartedly pretended to have simply paid the man to go away. But it's clear to me now, as it was at the time, that Ray thought there could be something authentic about this man's desperation, his need to knock on the doors of strangers at 11 o'clock at night. Ray wasn't taking any chances. He'd covered his bets, making sure he hadn't turned someone in genuine need away.

The next morning at the Shangri La, I kept an eye on Ray. Sure enough, I caught him, first thing, staring at the patch of blank carpet in front of the door. There was no cash. No envelope with money. He turned to me and we both grinned and then we began to laugh until our eyes smarted. He knew that I knew he had expected to find that envelope of money near the door. And he hadn't. The hilarity of the situation spilled over us in that Hopperesque room attached to a stranger we would never see again. But Ray hadn't lost anything. He'd believed, and that is somehow always to be ahead of anyone's game.

The marvel of such encounters—where I began this essay—asks us to extend ourselves beyond the expected, beyond the easily accessible or simply lucrative, and this is the parameter of the small literary magazine and non-profit press effort represented by the *Pushcart Prize*. It is an effort which, while it asks for our generous involvement without promising fame or even a large readership, insists at the same time, in the words of William Carlos Williams that "You got to try hard". Because the endeavor miraculously sustains itself in an excellence that operates outside the trade publishing world of wins and gains, buying and selling, it can demand and sustain excellence by its very reluctance to answer to these pressures. What these magazines keep alive is the simplicity of questions not so very different from those inflicted on us rather hopefully at the back of our school books: Did you enter the story? the poem?

Does it make you feel something? What are you going to remember about this experience? Was it interesting enough to make you want to share it with anyone?

But perhaps, since we have to end, I should close with something Carveresque, something straight out of his stories: "Sugar, I think I'd better pack it up," or "Who do you know in Egypt?"

THE
PEOPLE WHO HELPED

FOUNDING EDITORS—*Anaïs Nin (1903–1977), Buckminster Fuller (1895–1983), Charles Newman, Daniel Halpern, Gordon Lish, Harry Smith, Hugh Fox, Ishmael Reed, Joyce Carol Oates, Len Fulton, Leonard Randolph, Leslie Fiedler, Nona Balakian, Paul Bowles, Paul Engle, Ralph Ellison, Reynolds Price, Rhoda Schwartz, Richard Morris, Ted Wilentz, Tom Montag, William Phillips, Poetry editor: H. L. Van Brunt.*

EDITORS—*Walter Abish, Ai, Elliott Anderson, John Ashbery, Russell Banks, Robert Bly, Philip Booth, Robert Boyers, Harold Brodkey, Joseph Brodsky, Wesley Brown, Hayden Carruth, Frank Conroy, Paula Deitz, Steve Dixon, Rita Dove, Andre Dubus, M. D. Elevitch, Louise Erdrich, Loris Essary, Ellen Ferber, Carolyn Forché, Stuart Freibert, Jon Galassi, Tess Gallagher, Louis Gallo, George Garrett, Reginald Gibbons, Jack Gilbert, Louise Glück, David Godine, Jorie Graham, Linda Gregg, Barbara Grossman, Donald Hall, Helen Handley, Michael Harper, Robert Hass, DeWitt Henry, J. R. Humphreys, David Ignatow, John Irving, June Jordan, Edmund Keeley, Karen Kennerly, Galway Kinnell, Carolyn Kizer, Jerzy Kosinski, Richard Kostelanetz, Seymour Krim, Maxine Kumin, Stanley Kunitz, James Laughlin, Seymour Lawrence, Naomi Lazard, Herb Leibowitz, Denise Levertov, Philip Levine, Stanley Lindberg, Thomas Lux, Mary MacArthur, Thomas McGrath, Jay Meek, Daniel Menaker, Frederick Morgan, Cynthia Ozick, Jayne Anne Phillips, Robert Phillips, George Plimpton, Stanley Plumly,*

Eugene Redmond, Ed Sanders, Teo Savory, Grace Schulman, Harvey Shapiro, Leslie Silko, Charles Simic, Dave Smith, Elizabeth Spencer, William Stafford, Gerald Stern, David St. John, Bill and Pat Strachan, Ron Sukenick, Anne Tyler, John Updike, Sam Vaughan, David Wagoner, Derek Walcott, Ellen Wilbur, David Wilk, David Wojahn, Bill Zavatsky.

CONTRIBUTING EDITORS—Lee K. Abbott, Sandra Alcosser, Joan Aleshire, John Allman, Philip Appleman, Jennifer Atkinson, Jim Barnes, Rick Bass, Barbara Bedway, John Berger, Linda Bierds, Norbert Blei, Marianne Boruch, Rosellen Brown, Michael Dennis Browne, Christopher Buckley, Richard Burgin, Michael Burkard, Frederick Busch, Kathy Callaway, Henry Carlile, Sandie Castle, Kelly Cherry, Naomi Clark, Andrei Codrescu, Robert Cohen, Peter Cooley, Stephen Corey, Philip Dacey, John Daniel, Susan Stayer Deal, Carl Dennis, Mark Doty, Sharon Doubiago, John Drury, Laurie Duesing, Stuart Dybek, Barbara Einzig, Carol Emshwiller, David Ferry, Jane Flanders, H. E. Francis, Ken Gangemi, Gary Gildner, Albert Goldbarth, Barry Goldensohn, Patrick Worth Gray, Victoria Hallerman, Ehud Havazelet, Patricia Henley, Brenda Hillman, Edward Hirsch, Jane Hirshfield, Marie Howe, Andrew Hudgins, Lynda Hull, Colette Inez, Liz Inness-Brown, Richard Jackson, Josephine Jacobsen, Mark Jarman, Julia Just, Dave Kelly, August Kleinzahler, Yusef Komunyakaa, Dorianne Laux, Melissa Lentricchia, Gerry Locklin, Philip Lopate, D. R. MacDonald, David Madden, Dan Masterson, Cleopatra Mathis, Robert McBrearty, Lynne McFall, Joan McGarry, Thomas McGrath, Heather McHugh, Wesley McNair, Leslie Adrienne Miller, Susan Mitchell, Lisel Mueller, Joan Murray, Fae Myenne Ng, Sharon Olds, Greg Pape, Jonathan Penner, Lucia Perillo, Mary Peterson, Robert Pinsky, Robert Pope, Joe Ashby Porter, C. E. Poverman, Francine Prose, Tony Quagliano, Bin Ramke, Donald Revell, Alberto Ríos, William Root, Vern Rutsala, Michael Ryan, Marjorie Sandor, Sherod Santos, Lloyd Schwartz, Bob Shacochis, Eve Shelnutt, Jim Simmerman, Tom Sleigh, Arthur Smith, Christopher Spain, Elizabeth Spires, Maura Stanton, Pamela Stewart, David St. John, Mary Tall Mountain, Barbara Thompson, Lee Upton, Sara Vogan, Marilyn Waniek, Michael Waters, Gordon Weaver, Bruce Weigl, Anita Wilkins, Harold Witt, Christina Zawadiwsky.

CONTENTS

ISLAND

fiction by ALISTAIR MACLEOD

from THE ONTARIO REVIEW

ALL DAY THE RAIN FELL upon the island and she waited. Sometimes it slanted against her window with a pinging sound which meant it was close to hail, and then it was visible as tiny pellets for a moment on the pane before the pellets vanished and rolled quietly down the glass, each drop leaving its own delicate trickle. At other times it fell straight down, hardly touching the window at all, but still there beyond the glass, like a delicate, beaded curtain at the entrance to another room.

She poked the fire within the stove, turning the half-burned lengths of wood so that they would burn more evenly. Some of the wood lengths were old fence posts or timbers which had been hauled from the shore before being cut into sizes which would fit the stove. Some of them contained ancient nails which were bent and twisted deep into the wood's core. When the fire was very hot, they glowed to a cherry red, reminiscent of a blacksmith's shop or, perhaps, their earliest casting. They would glow in the intense heat while the wood was consumed around them and, in the morning, they would be shaken down with the ashes, black and twisted but still there in the grayness of the ashpan. On days when the fire burned with less intensity because the wood was damp or the drafts poor, they remained a rusted brown while the damp wood sputtered and hissed reluctantly before releasing them from the coffins in which they were confined. Today was such a day.

She went to the window and looked out once more. Beneath the table the three black and white dogs followed her with their eyes but

31

made no other movement. They had been outside several times during the day and the wetness of their coats gave off the odor of damp woolen garments which have been hung to dry. When they came in, they shook themselves vigorously beside the stove, causing a further sputtering and hissing, as the water droplets fell against the heated steel.

Through the window and the beaded sheets of rain she could see the gray shape of *tir mòr*, the mainland, more than two miles away. Because of her failing sight and the nature of the weather she was not sure if she could really see it. But she had seen it in all weathers and over so many decades that the image of it was clearly in her mind, and whether she actually saw it or remembered it, now, seemed to make no difference.

The mainland was itself but another large island although most people did not think of it in that way. It was, as many said, larger than the province of Prince Edward Island and even some European countries and it had paved roads and cars and now even shopping centers and a fairly large population.

On rainy or foggy evenings such as this, it was always hard to see and to understand the mainland but when the sun shone it was clearly visible with its white houses and red or gray barns, and with the green lawns and fields surrounding the houses while the rolling mountains of dark green spruce rose behind them. At night the individual houses, and the communities they formed, seemed to be magnified because of the lights. In the daytime if you looked at a certain spot you might see only one house and, perhaps, a barn, but at night there might be several lights shining from the different windows of the house, and perhaps a light at the barn and other lights shining from hydro poles in the yard, or in the driveway or along the road. And there were the moving lights caused by the headlights of the travelling cars. It all seemed more glamorous at night, perhaps because of what you could not see, and conversely a bit more disappointing in the day.

She had been born on the island at a time so long ago that there was now nobody living who could remember it. The event no longer lived in anybody's mind nor was it recorded with accuracy anywhere on paper. She had been born a month prematurely at the beginning of the spring breakup when crossing from the island to the mainland was impossible.

At other times her mother had tried to reach the mainland before her children were born. Sometimes she would cross almost a month before the expected delivery because the weather and the water in all seasons, except summer, could never be depended upon. She had planned to do so this time as well but the ice that covered the channel during the winter months began to decay earlier than usual. It would not bear the weight of a horse and sleigh or even a person on foot and there were visible channels of open water running like eager rivers across what seemed like the gray-white landscape of the rotting ice. It was too late for foot travel and too early for a boat because there was not, as yet, enough open water. And then too she was born a month earlier than expected. All of this she was, of course, told much later. She was also told that when the winter began her parents did not realize that her mother was pregnant. Her father was sixty at the time and her mother close to fifty and they were already grandparents. They had not had any children for five years and had thought their child-bearing years were past and the usual signs were no longer there or at least not recognized until later in the season. So her birth, as her father said, was "unexpected" in more ways than one.

She was the first person ever born on the island as far as anybody knew.

Later she was brought across to the mainland to be christened. And still later when the clergyman was sending his baptismal records to the provincial capitol he included hers along with those of the children who had been born on the mainland. And perhaps to simplify matters he recorded her birthplace as being the same as that of the other children and of her brothers and sisters or if he did not intend to simplify perhaps he had merely forgotten. He also had the birthdate wrong and it was thought that perhaps he had forgotten to ask the parents or had forgotten what they had told him and by the time he was ready to send in his records they had already gone back to the island and he could not contact them. So he seemed to have counted back a number of days before the christening and selected his own date. Her middle name was wrong too. Her parents had called her Agnes but he had somehow copied it down as Angus. Again perhaps he had forgotten or was preoccupied and he was a very old man at the time, as evidenced by his shaky, spidery handwriting. And, it was pointed out, his own middle name was Angus. She did not know any of this until years later when she sent for her official birth certificate in anticipation of her own marriage. Everyone was surprised that a single document could contain so many errors and by that time the old clergyman had died.

Although hers was thought to be the only birth to have occurred on the island there had been a number of deaths. One of them was that of her own grandfather who died one November from "a pain in the side" after pulling up his boat for the winter—thinking there would be no further need for a boat until the spring. He was only forty when it happened, the death occurring only two weeks after his birthday. His widow and children did not know what to do as there was no adequate radio communication and they were not strong enough to get the boat he had so recently hauled up, back into the water. They waited for two days hoping the sullen gray waves would subside, and stretching his body out on the kitchen table and covering it with white sheets—afraid to put too much fire in the kitchen stove lest it might hasten the body's decay.

On the third day they launched a small skiff and tried to row across to the mainland. They did not know if they would be strong enough to make it so they gathered large numbers of dried cattails and reeds from one of the island's marshes and placed them in a metal washtub and doused them with the oil used for the lamp at the lighthouse. They placed the tub in the prow of the skiff and when they rowed out beyond the shape of the island they set the contents of the tub on fire hoping that it might act as a signal and a sign. On the mainland someone saw the rising funnel of gray-black smoke and the shooting flames at its base and then the skiff moving erratically—rowed by the desperate hands of the woman and her children. Most of the mainland boats had already been pulled up for the winter but one was launched and the men went out to what looked like a burning boat and tossed a line to it and towed it in to the wharf after first taking off the woman and her children and comforting them and listening to their story. Later the men went out to the island and brought the man's body over to the mainland so that although he died on the island, he was not buried there. And still later that evening someone went over to light the lamp in the lighthouse so that it might send out its flashing warning to possible travellers on the nighttime sea. Even in the face of her husband's death, the woman, as well as her family, harbored fears that they might lose the job if the Government realized the lightkeeper was dead. They had already purchased their supplies for the winter and there was no other place to go so late in the season, so they decided to say nothing until the spring and returned to the island after the funeral accompanied by the woman's brother.

The original family had gone to the island because of death or rather to aid in death's reduction. The lighthouse was established in the previous century because of the danger the island represented to ships travelling in darkness or in uncertain weather. It was thought that the light would warn sea travellers of the danger of the island or, conversely, that it might represent hope to those already at the sea's mercy and who yearned so much to reach its rocky shore. Before the establishment of the light there had been a number of wrecks which might or might not have been avoided had there been a light. What was known with certainty was that survivors had landed on the island only to die from exposure and starvation because no one knew that they were there. Their skeletons being found, accidently by fishermen in the spring—huddled under trees or outcrops of rock in the positions of their deaths. Some still had the remains of their arms around one another. Some still with tattered, flapping clothes covering their bones although the flesh between the clothing and the bones was no longer there.

When the family first went they were told that their job was to keep the light and to offer salvation to any of those who might come ashore. The Government erected buildings for them which were better than those of their relatives on the mainland and helped them with the purchase of livestock and original supplies. To some it seemed they had a good job—a Government job. In answer to the question of the isolation, they told themselves they would get used to it. They told themselves they were already used to it, coming as they did from a people in the far north of Scotland who had for generations been used to the sea and the sleet and the wind and the rocky outcrops at the edge of their part of Europe. Used to the long nights when no one spoke and to the isolation of islands. Used to seeing their men going to work for the Hudson's Bay Company and the North West Company and not expecting them back for years. Used to seeing their men going to the vast ocean-like tracts of prairie in places like Montana and Wyoming to work as sheepherders. Spending months that sometimes stretched into years, talking only to dogs or to themselves or to imaginary people who blended into ghosts. Startled by the response to their own voices when they appeared, strange and unexpectedly, at the camp or at the store or

35

at the rural trading post. In demand as sheepherders, because it was believed, and because they had been told, that they did not mind the isolation. "Of course I spoke to ghosts," a man was supposed to have said once upon his returning. "Wouldn't you if there was no one else to speak to?"

In the early days on the island, there was no adequate radio communication and if they were in trouble and unable to get across they would light fires on the shore in the hope that such signs would be visible on the mainland. In the hope that they who had gone to the island as part of the business of salvation, might they themselves be saved. And when the Great War was declared, it was said, they did not know of it for weeks, coming ashore to be told the news by their relatives, coming ashore to a world which would be forever changed.

Gradually, with the passage of the years, the family's name as well as their identity became entwined with that of the island. So that although the island had an official name on the marine and nautical charts it became known generally as MacPhedran's Island while they themselves became known less as MacPhedrans than as people "of the island." Being identified as "John the Island," "James the Island," "Mary of the Island," "Theresa of the Island." As if in giving their name to the island they had received its own lonely designation in return.

All of this was already history by the time she was born and she had no choice in any of it. Not choosing, for herself, to be born on the island (although the records said she was not) and not choosing the rather surprised individuals who became her parents after they had already become the grandparents of others. For by the time she was born the intertwined history of her family and the island was already far advanced. And when she was later told the story of the man who died from the pain in his side, it seemed very far away to her although it was not so for her father who had been one of the children in the skiff, rowing with small desperate freezing hands at the bidding of his mother. By the time of her early memories, the Government had already built a wharf at the island which was superior to any on the mainland. The wharf was built "to service" the lighthouse but it also attracted mainland fishermen who were drawn to its superior facilities. Especially during the lobster season months of May and June, men came to live in the shacks and shanties they erected along the shore. Leaving their shanties at four in the morning and returning in the early afternoon to sell their catches to the

36

buyers who came in their big boats from far away. And returning to their mainland homes on Saturday and coming back again on Sunday, late in the afternoon or in the early evening, their weekly supplies of bread and provisions in burlap bags lying at the bottom of their boats. Sometimes lying in the bottoms of the boats there were also yearling calves with trussed feet and eyes bulging with fear who were brought to the island for summer pasturage and would be taken off half-wild in the cold, gray months of fall. Later in the summer the energetic, stifled rams would be brought in the same way, to spend monastic, frustrated months in all-male company before returning to the mainland and the fall fury of the breeding season.

He came to the island the summer she was seventeen. Came before the rams or the young cattle or the buyers' boats. Came at the end of April when there were still white cakes of ice floating in the ocean and when the family's dogs still ran down to the wharf to bark at the approaching boats and to snarl at the men who got out of them. In the time before such boats and men became familiar sights and sounds and odors. Yet even as the boat came into the wharf the dogs seemed to make less fuss than was usual and whatever he said quietened them and caused them to be still. She saw all this from the window of the kitchen. She was drying the dishes for her mother at the time and she wrapped the damp dish towel around her hand as if it were a bandage and then she as quickly unwrapped it again. As he bent to loop the boat's rope to the wharf, his cap fell off and she saw the redness of his hair. It seemed to flash and reflect in the April sun like the sudden and different energy of spring. She and most of her people were dark-haired and had dark eyes as well.

He had come, she learned, to fish for the season with one of the regular men from the mainland. He was the nephew of the man's wife and came from a place located over the mountain. From a distance of some twenty-five miles which was a long distance at the time. He had come early to make preparations for the season. To work on the shanty and repair the winter's damages, to repair the man's lobster traps and to make a few new ones. He told them all of this in the evening when he came up to the lighthouse to borrow oil for his lamp. He brought them bits and scraps of news from the mainland as well although they did not have that many people in common. He spoke in both Gaelic and English although his accent was different from theirs. He seemed about twenty years of age and his eyes were very blue.

They looked at one another often. They were the youngest people in the room.

In the early madness of the lobster season they did not speak to one another although they saw each other almost every day. The men were often up at three in the morning brewing their tea by the flickering lamps, casting their large shadows eerily upon the shanties' walls as they moved about in the semi-darkness. At night they sometimes fell asleep by eight. Sometimes still sitting on their chairs, their heads tilting suddenly forward or backward and their mouths dropping open. She worked with her mother, planting the garden and the potatoes. Sometimes in the evening she would walk down by the shanties but not very often. Not because her parents openly disapproved but because she felt uncomfortable walking so close to so many men. Sometimes they nodded and smiled as all of them knew her name and who she was and some of them were her distant relatives. But at other times she felt uneasy, hearing only bits of the comments and remarks exchanged among them as they stood in their doorways or sat on their homemade chairs or overturned lobster crates. The remarks seemed mainly for themselves, to demonstrate their wit and masculinity to each other. As if they were young schoolboys instead of being mostly beyond middle age. Sometimes they reminded her of the late summer rams, playful and friendly and generally grazing contentedly in *achadh nan caoraich*, the field of the sheep, although sometimes given to spontaneous rages against those who would trespass into their territory or sometimes unleashing their suppressed fury against one another. Rearing and smashing against one another until their skulls thundered and reverberated like the growling icebergs of spring and their pent-up semen ejaculated in spurting jets, leaving them stunned and weak in the knees.

She and her mother were the only women on the island.

One evening she walked to the back of the island, down to the far shore which did not face the mainland but only the open sea. There was a small cove there which was known as *bagh na long bhriseadh*, bay of the shipwreck, because there were timbers found there in the long ago time before the lighthouse was established. She sat on *creig a bhoird*, the table rock which was called so because of its shape, and looked out across the seeming infinity of the sea. And then he was standing beside her. He made no sound in coming and the dog which had accompanied her gave no signal of his approach.

"Oh," she said, on realizing him so unexpectedly close. She stood up quickly.

"Do you come here often?" he said.

"No," she said. "Well yes, sometimes."

The ocean stretched out flat and far before them.

"Were you born here?" he asked.

"Yes," she said. "I guess so."

"Do you stay here all the time? Even in the winter?"

"Yes," she said, "most of the time."

She was defensive, like most of her family, on the subject of the island. Knowing that they were often regarded as slightly eccentric because of how and where they lived. Always anticipating questions about the island's loneliness.

"Some people are lonely no matter where they are," he said as if he were reading her mind.

"Oh," she said. She had never heard anyone say anything quite like that before.

"Would you like to live somewhere else?" he asked.

"I don't know," she said. "Maybe."

"I have to go now," he said. "I'll see you later. I'll come back."

And then he was gone. As suddenly as he had come. Seeming to vanish behind the table rock and the water's edge. She waited for a while, sitting down once more upon the rock to compose herself and then walking up the island's rise towards the lighthouse. Later when she looked down from the kitchen window towards the shanties, she could see him hammering lathes onto a broken lobster trap and readying the bait buckets for the morning. His cap was pushed back upon his head and the evening sun caught the golden highlights of his burnished hair. He looked up once and her hand tightened upon the cloth she was holding. Her mother asked her if she would like some tea.

It was into the next week before she again walked down by the shanties. He was sitting on a lobster crate splicing rope. As she went by she thought she heard him say *Àite na cruinneachadh*. She quickened her step as she felt her color rise, hoping or perhaps imagining that he had said "the meeting place." She went there immediately, down to the bay of shipwrecks and the table rock and waited. She faced out to the sea and sat in such a way that she could not see him *not* coming if that was the way it was supposed to be. The dog sat at her feet and neither of them moved when he came to stand beside them.

"I told you I'd come back," he said.

"Oh," she said. "Oh yes. You did."

In the weeks that followed they went more frequently to the meeting place. Standing and later sitting on the table rock and looking out across the vastness of the sea. Talking more and sometimes laughing and, in retrospect, she could not remember when he asked her to marry him but only that she had burst into tears when she said "Oh yes" and they joined their hands on the flatness of the table rock which was still warm from the retained heat of the descending sun. "Oh yes," she had said. "Oh yes. Oh yes."

He planned to work in a sawmill, he said, after the lobster season was done; and then in the fall or early winter, after the snows began to fall and the ground became frozen, he would go to work in the winter woods of Maine. He would return to fish with the same man the next spring and then in the summer they would marry. They would go then, he said, "to live somewhere else."

"Oh yes," she said. "Oh yes, we will."

It was in the late fall, on the night following a day of cold and slanting rain that she was awakened by the dog pulling at the blankets that lay so heavily upon her bed. She sat up, even as she shivered and pulled the blankets about her shoulders, and tried to adjust her eyes to the darkness of the room. The rain slanted against the window with a pinging sound which meant that it was close to hail and even in the darkness she could see the near-white pellets visible for a moment before they vanished on the pane. The eyes of the dog seemed to glow in the dark and she felt the cold wetness of its nose when she extended her hand beyond the boundary of the bed. She could smell the wetness of its coat and when she moved her hand across its head and down its neck the water filmed upon her palm. She got up then, throwing on what clothes she could find in the darkness of the room, and followed the clacking nails of the dog as it moved down the hallway and past the closed door behind which her parents snored, sometimes snoring regularly and at other times with fitful catches in their sound. She went down through the kitchen and through the tiny puddles caused by the rain slanting through the opened door. Outside it was wet and windy although nothing like a gale and she followed the dog down the darkened

40

path. And then in the revolving cycle of the high lighthouse light the pale beam shone in a straight but moving path. In a single white instant she saw the dark shape of the boat bobbing at the wharf and his straight but dripping form by the corner of the shanties.

The creaky door of the summer shanty yielded easily to his familiar shoulder. Inside it was slightly musty although the wind persisted through some of the unsealed cracks. Their eyes adjusted to the gloom and the few sticks of basic furniture that still remained. The primitive mattresses had been stored away to protect them from mice and the dampness of the sea. They held one another in their urgency and lay upon the floor fumbling with the encumbrances of their clothes. She felt the wet burden of his garments almost heavy upon her although the length of his body seemed light within them.

"Oh," she said, digging her fingers into the dampness of his neck, "when we are married we can do this all the time."

At the moment of explosion their breaths bonded into a single gasp that bordered on a cry.

She thought of this later as she passed the closed door of her parents' room. Thought of how her breath and his had become one and contrasted it with the irregular individual snoring which came from beyond her parents' door. She could not imagine them ever being young.

The same wonder was there the next morning as she watched her father in his undershirt preparing the fire and later going to polish the thick glass of the lighthouse lamp. She watched her mother washing the dishes and then reaching for her knitting needles and the always present ball of yarn.

She went outside and walked down towards the shanties. The door was pulled tight and she had a hard time getting it to move. Inside it all seemed different, probably, she thought, because of the daylight. She looked at the gray boards of the floor thinking she might see the outline of their bodies or even a spot of dampness but there was nothing. She went outside and walked to the wharf, to the spot where the dark boat was moored, but again there was no sign. He had "borrowed" the boat of the man he had fished with and had to have it back before dawn.

The wind was rising as the temperature was dropping. The hail-like rain had given way to stinging snow and the ground was beginning to freeze. She touched her body to see if it had been a dream.

41

As the winter began she was alive with the prospect of marriage. She sent for her birth certificate without ever revealing why and helped her mother with the knitting. As the winter deepened she looked at the calendar more often.

When the ice began to rot and break in the spring she looked out the window more frequently. It seemed like a later spring than usual although her father said there was nothing unusual about it. One day the channel would be clear of ice but the next day it would again be solid. The wind shifted and blew from inconsistent directions. On the mainland they could see, or imagined they could see, men moving about and readying their gear for the opening of the season. Because of the ice they were still afraid to launch their boats into the water. They all looked very small and far away.

When the first boats finally came, the dogs ran down to the wharf barking and snarling and her father went down also, calling to the dogs and welcoming the men and telling them not to be afraid. She looked out the window but did not see him in the boats or on the wharf nor moving about the familiar shanties. But neither did she see the mainland man he fished with nor his boat.

When her father came in he was filled with news and carried some fresh supplies and a bundle of newspapers and a bag of mail.

In the midst of all the newness it was a long time before he mentioned the mainland fisherman's name and added, almost as an afterthought, "That young man who fished with him last year was killed in the woods this winter. Went to Maine and was killed on a skidway. He's looking for another man right now."

When her father spoke he was already looking at a marine catalogue and had put on his glasses. He raised his eyes above the rims of his spectacles as he lowered the catalogue and looked towards them. "You remember him," he said without emotion, "the young fellow with the red hair."

"Oh poor fellow," said her mother. "God have mercy on his soul."

"Oh," was all she could say. Her hands tightened so whitely on the metal knitting needles that the point of one pierced and penetrated the ball of her thumb.

"Your hand is bleeding," said her mother. "What happened? You'll have to be more careful or you'll get blood on your knitting and everything will be ruined. What happened?" she asked again. "You'll have to be more careful."

"Nothing," she said, rising quickly and going to the door. "Nothing at all. Yes I'll have to be more careful."

She went outside and looked down towards the shanties where the newly arrived men were busy preparing for the new spring season. The banter of their voices seemed to float on the current of the wind. Sometimes she could hear their actual words but at other times they were lost and unknown. She could not believe the magnitude and suddenness of change. Could not believe the content of the news nor the method of its arrival. Could not believe that news of such outstanding impact could arrive in such a casual manner and mean so little to all of those around her.

She looked down at her bloodied hand. "Why didn't he write?" she asked herself and considered going back in to recheck the contents of the mailbag. But then she thought that both of them were beyond letters and that in the instant of his death it was already too late for that. She did not even know if he could read or write. She had never thought to ask. It had not seemed important at the time. The blood was beginning to darken and dry upon her palm and between her fingers. Suddenly last winter, although it was barely over, seemed like a long, long time ago. She pressed her hand against her stomach and turned her face away from the mainland and the sea.

When it became obvious that she was expecting a child there was great wonder as to how it came to be. She herself was rather surprised that no one had ever seen them together. It was true that she had always walked "over" or "across" the island while he had walked "around": seeming to emerge suddenly and unexpectedly out of the sea by the table rock of their meeting place. Still the island was small and, especially during the fishing season, there was little opportunity for privacy. Perhaps, she thought, they had been more successful, in some ways, than they planned. It was as if he had been invisible to everyone but herself. She was struck by this and tried to relive over and over again their last damp meeting in the dark. Only the single instant of his dark silhouette in the lighthouse beam was recallable to vision. All the rest of it had been touching in the dark. She remembered the lightness of his body in his dark, wet clothes but it was a memory of feeling rather than of sight. She had never seen him with all his clothes off. Had never slept with him in a bed. She had no photograph to emphasize reality. It was as if in

43

vanishing from her future he had also vanished from her past. It was almost as if he had been a ghost, and as she advanced in her pregnancy she found the idea strangely attractive.

"No," she kept saying to the pressure of their questions. "I don't know. I can't say. No, I can't tell you what he looked like."

She wavered only twice. The first time was a week before her delivery at a time when the approximate date of the conception was more than obvious. They were all on the mainland and the late August heat shimmered in layers above the clear deep water. The shape of the island loomed gray and blue and green across the channel and she who had wished to leave it now wished she might return. They were at her aunt's house and she would remain there until her baby would be born. She and her aunt had never liked each other and it bothered her now to be dependent upon her. Before her parents left to return to the island they came into her room accompanied by the aunt who turned to her father and said, "Well go ahead. Tell her what people are saying."

She was shocked to see the pained embarrassment on his face as he twisted his cloth cap and looked out the window in the direction of the island.

"It is just the way we live," he said. "Some say there was no other man."

She remembered the erratic snoring coming from her parents' room and how she could not imagine that they ever had been young.

"Oh," she said. "I'm sorry."

"Is that all you have to say for yourself?" said her aunt.

She wavered a moment. "Yes," she said. "That's all. That's all I have to say."

After the birth of her daughter, with the jet black hair, she received a visit from the clergyman. He was an old man although not as old as she imagined the one who had confused her own birth records, it seemed to her, so very long ago.

At that time it was in the power of clergymen to refuse to christen children unless they knew the identities of both parents. In cases such as hers the identities could be kept as confidential.

"Well," he said. "Can you tell me who the father is?"

"No," she said. "I can't say."

He looked at her as if he had heard it all before. And as if it were an aspect of his job he did not greatly like. He looked at her daughter and back at her. "We wouldn't want innocent people to burn in hell because of the willfulness of others," he said.

She was startled and frightened and looked towards the window.

"Tell me," he said quietly. "Is it your father?"

She thought for a flash of her own unexpected birth and of how her father was surprised again although the situation was so very much different.

"No," she said firmly. "It isn't him."

He seemed vastly relieved. "Good," he said. "I didn't think he would ever do anything like that. I will stop the rumors."

He moved towards the door as if one answer were all answers but then he hesitated with his hand upon the knob. "Tell me then," he said, "one more thing. Do I know him? Is he from around here?"

"No," she said, gaining confidence from seeing his hand upon the knob. "He isn't from around here at all."

That fall she stayed on the mainland until quite late in the season. It seemed as if her daughter were constantly sick and each time the journey was planned a new variation of illness appeared to stifle the departure. Out on the island her parents seemed to grow old all at once or maybe it was just that she saw them in a different light. Of course they had always seemed old to her and she had often thought of having grandparents for parents. But now they seemed for the first time to be almost afraid of the island and the coming of winter. Never since the first year of their marriage had they been there without a child. When her father fell from the ladder leading up to the lighthouse lamp it was almost as if the fall and the resulting broken arm had been expected.

Ever since her grandfather's death from "a pain in the side," the Government had more or less left them alone. It was as if the officials had been embarrassed by the widow's reluctance to tell them of her husband's death and by her fear that she might lose, in addition to her husband, the only income the family possessed. It was as if the officials had understood that "some MacPhedran" would always be on the island that bore the name and that no further questions ever would be asked. The check always arrived and the light always shone.

But when her father fell it brought a deeper seriousness. He could neither climb to the light nor navigate the boat across the channel, nor manage, quite, to look after the house and buildings and the animals. It seemed best that they should all try to stay on the mainland for the winter.

Her brother came home from Halifax, reluctantly, and manned the light deep into fall. He was a single man who worked on construction crews and who drank quite heavily at times and was given to moods of deep depression. He was uneasy about the island although he understood it and was regarded as "an excellent man in a boat." At the beginning of the winter he said to his father who stood in the departing boat, "I don't want to stay here. I don't want to stay here at all."

"Oh," said his father, "you'll get used to it," which was what they had always said to one another.

But it seemed he did not get used to it. Deep in the blizzards of February one of the island dogs crossed on the ice to the mainland and came to a familiar door. It was impossible to see or move for three days because of the severe temperatures and the force of the wind-driven snow. Impossible for a man to stand upright in the wind or, as they said, for one "to see the palm of his hand in front of his face." When the storm abated four men started across the vast white landscape of the ice. They could feel parts of their exposed faces freezing and the exhaled moisture of their breath froze upon their eyebrows and they could see their eyelashes drooping heavily with ice. As they neared the island's wharf they could see that it was almost buried under gigantic pans of ice. Some of the pans had been pushed so far up on the shore that they almost tilted against the doors of the summer shanties. There was no smoke from the chimney of the house. The dogs came down snarling and circling at first, but the one who had crossed to the mainland had returned and had a calming effect upon the others. The door of the house was open and the stove was cold. The water in the crockery teapot had frozen causing the teapot itself to split into two delicate halves. There was nobody in any of the rooms and no answer to their calls. Outside, the barn doors were open and swinging in the wind. The animals were all dead, still tied and frozen in their stalls. The frozen flesh of some of them had been gnawed on by the dogs.

It seemed his coat and cap and winter mitts were missing but that was all. A loaded rifle and a shotgun were hanging in the porch. The men started a fire in the stove and made themselves something to eat from the store of winter provisions. Later they went outside again. Some walked across the island and some walked around it.

They found no tracks other than their own. They looked at the dogs for a signal or a sign. They even spoke to them and asked them questions but they received nothing in return. He had vanished like his tracks beneath the winter snow.

The men remained for the night and the next day crossed back to the mainland. They told what they had found and not found. The sun shone and although it was a weak February sun it was stronger than it had been a week earlier. It melted the ice upon the window panes and someone pointed out that the days were getting longer and that the winter was more than half way over.

Under the circumstances they decided to go back but to leave the baby behind.

"There seems almost more reason to go back now," said her father, looking through the melting ice on the windows. His broken arm had healed although he knew it would never be the same.

She was often to think of why she went back although at the time there seemed little conscious thought surrounding the decision. While her parents were willing to leave the island to the care of their son they were not willing to abandon it to others. They had found life on the mainland not as attractive as it sometimes seemed when viewed from across the water. They also seemed bothered by complicated shafts of guilt concerning their lost son and their head-strong daughter and while these shafts might persist on the island there would be no people to emphasize and expose them. She, herself, as the child of their advanced years seemed suddenly willing to consider herself old also and to identify with the past now that her future seemed to point in that direction.

She went back with almost a bitter gladness. Glad to leave her carping aunt and her mainland family behind although worried about leaving her sickly daughter in their care. Still, she knew they were right to say that the winter island was no place for a sick child and she felt also that if she did not go her parents could not manage.

"Who will climb up to the light?" asked her father simply. They viewed her youth as their immediate salvation and thought of her as their child rather than as someone else's mother.

It seemed a long time since the red-haired man had asked her to marry him and to share his life in the magical region of "somewhere else." In her persistent refusal to identify him she had pushed him so far back into the recesses of her mind that he seemed even more ghostly than before. She thought sometimes of his body in the dark

17

and of his silhouette by the sea. She was struck by the mystery of his age—if he had an age she thought it had suddenly "stopped" and he had become part of a kind of timelessness—unlike the visible deterioration she witnessed in her father.

In the winter cold of February they returned with a certain sense of relief, each harboring individual reasons. Because of her youth she did most of the work, dressing in her father's heavy, shapeless clothes and following easily the rituals and routines that had become part of her since childhood. More and more her parents remained close to the stove, talking in Gaelic and sometimes playing cards.

When March came in with its howling blizzards it seemed that they had been betrayed by the fickle promise of the February sun and although her father's will was strong his aging body seemed also to contribute to a pattern of betrayal. He was close to eighty and it seemed that each day there was another function which his body refused to perform. It was as if it had suddenly grown tired and was in the process of forgetting.

One day when there was a lull in the storms some of their relatives crossed the ice with a horse and sleigh. They were shocked at the condition and appearance of her father, seeing him changed "suddenly" after an absence of weeks while those who were with him had seen him change but gradually. They insisted that he return with them while the weather was good and the ice still strong. Reluctantly he agreed on the condition that his wife go with him.

After years of isolated permanence he was aware of all the questionable movement.

"Sometimes life is like that," he said to his daughter as he sat bundled in the sleigh at the moment before departure. "It goes on and on at a certain level and then there comes a year when everything changes."

Suddenly a gust of wind passed between them, whipping their faces with fine, sharp granules of snow. And suddenly she knew in that instant that she would never ever see him again. She wanted to tell him, to thank him or perhaps confess now that their time was vanishing between them. The secret of her own loneliness came down upon her and she reached towards his bundled body and his face which was muffled in scarves except for his eyes which were filled with water converting to ice.

"It was," she said, "the red-haired man."

"Oh yes," he said but she did not know with what degree of comprehension he said it. And then the sleigh moved off with its runners squeaking on the winter snow.

Although she was prepared for the death of her father she had not anticipated the loss of her mother who died ten days behind her husband. There was no physical explanation for her death and it seemed not unlike that of certain animals who pine away without their mates or who are unwilling or unable to adjust to new surroundings. As wild birds die in captivity or those who have been caged die from the shock of unexpected freedom or the loss of familiar boundaries.

Because of the spring breakup she was unable to attend either of their funerals and on the respective days she looked across the high gray waves and the grotesque icebergs that rolled between. From the edge of the island she saw the long funeral processions following the horse-drawn coffins along the muddy roads to the graveyard by the mainland church. She turned her face into the wind and climbed up towards the light.

That spring and summer she continued to tend the light although she had little to do with the mainland fishermen and never walked down by the shanties. She began to sign the requisition slips for government supplies with the name "A. MacPhedran" because her initial and that of her father were the same. After a while the checks came in the name of "A. MacPhedran" and she had no trouble cashing any of them. No one came to question the keeper of the light, and the sex of A. MacPhedran seemed ambiguously unimportant. After all, she told herself, wryly, her official birth certificate stated that her given name was Angus.

When the fall came she decided to remain on the island for the winter. Some of her relatives approved because they wanted "some MacPhedran" to remain on the island and they cited her youth and the fact that she was "used to it" as part of their reasoning. They were interested in "maintaining tradition" as long as they were not the ones to maintain that specific part of it. Others disapproved and towards them she was, secretly, most defiant. Her aunt and her aunt's family had grown attached to her daughter, had "gotten used to her" as they said and regarded the child as their own. When she visited them she experienced a certain fearful hostility on their part, as if they feared that she might snatch the child and flee while they were busy in another room.

Most of her relatives, however, either willingly or unwillingly, agreed to help her with the island, by assisting her with supplies, by doing some of the heavier autumn work or even by visiting occasionally. She settled into the life with a sort of willful determination tempered by the fact that she was still waiting for something to happen and to bring about the change.

Two years later on a hot summer afternoon, she was in the lighthouse tower when she saw the boat approaching. She had been restless all day and had walked the length and width of the island twice. She had gone to its edge as if testing the boundaries, somewhat as a restless animal might explore the limitations of its cage. She had walked out into the cold salt water feeling it move gradually up and through and under the legs of her father's coveralls which had become, for her, a sort of uniform. She walked farther out feeling the water rise as she felt the rocks turning beneath her feet. She looked downward and saw her coveralled limbs distorted in the green water, shot through by the summer sun. They seemed not to be a part of her but to have become disembodied and convoluted and to be almost floating away from her at a horizontal level. When she closed her eyes she could feel them intensely but when she looked at them they did not appear the way they felt. The dogs lay on the shore, just above the water line, and watched her. They were panting in the summer heat and drops of water fell from the extended redness of their tongues.

She returned to the shore, still dripping, and walked among the shanties. The lobster fishermen had departed at the end of the season leaving very little of themselves behind. She walked among the deserted buildings looking at the few discarded objects, sometimes touching and turning them with her toes: a worn woolen sock, a length of spliced and twisted rope, a rusted knife with a broken blade, tobacco packages with bleached and faded lettering, a rubber boot with a hole in it. It was as if she were walking through the masculine remnants of an abandoned and vanished civilization. She went back to the house to put on dry coveralls and to hang the wet ones on the outside clothesline. As she left to climb to the lighthouse she looked over her shoulder and was startled by the sight of the vertical coveralls. Their dangling legs rasped together with the gentlest of frictions and the moisture had changed their color up to the waist. Droplets dripped from them onto the summer grass which was visibly distorted by their own moving shadow.

There were four men in the approaching boat and she realized that they were mackerel fishing and did not have the island in mind as a specific destination. The boat zigzagged back and forth across the stillness of the blue-green water stopping frequently while the men tossed their weighted lines overboard. They jerked their lines up and down rhythmically hoping to attract the fish by the movement of the lures. Sometimes they dipped their hands into pails or tubs of *gruth*, dried cottage cheese, and flung the white handfuls onto the surface of the water, waiting and hoping for the unseen fish to strike. She turned her head and looked towards the back of the island. From her high vantage point she could see, or thought she could see, pods or schools of mackerel breaking the surface, beyond the meeting place and the table rock, and beyond the bay of the shipwreck. They seemed like moving, floating islands, changing the clear, flat surface into agitated areas that resembled boiling water.

She hurried down from the lighthouse and shouted and gestured to the men in the boat. They were still far offshore and, perhaps, saw her before they heard her but were still unable to comprehend her message. They directed the boat towards the island. As they approached she realized that the movement of her arm, which was intended as a pointing gesture to the back of the island, was also a beckoning gesture, as they might understand it.

When they were within earshot she shouted to them, "The mackerel. At the back of the island. Go around."

They stopped the boat and leaned forward trying to catch the meaning of her words. One of the younger men, probably the one with the best hearing, understood her first and relayed the message to the others.

"Behind the island?" shouted the oldest man, cupping his hands to his mouth.

"Yes," she shouted back. "By the bay of the shipwreck."

She almost added, "By the meeting place" before realizing that the phrase would be meaningless to them.

"Thank you," shouted the oldest man. He took off his cap and tipped it to her and she could see the whiteness of his hair. "Thank you," he repeated. "We'll go around."

They changed the course of the boat and began to go around the island.

She rushed up to the house and changed out of her coveralls and put on a summer dress which she found in the back of a closet. She walked across the island accompanied by the dogs and went down to the meeting place where she sat on the table rock and waited. The rock was hot from the heat of the day's sun and burned her thighs and the backs of her legs. She could see the floating islands of frenzied mackerel beyond the mouth of the bay. They were deep into their spawning season and she hoped they would still be there when the men in the boat arrived.

"They seem to be taking an awfully long time," she said to no one in particular. And then she saw the prow of the boat rounding the island's end.

She stood up and pointed to the boiling, bubbling mackerel but they had already seen them and even as they waved back they were in the process of readying all their available lines. The boat glided silently towards the fish and by the time the first one struck it was almost completely stilled. The mackerel seemed to surround the boat, changing the water to black by their own density. Their snapping mouths fastened on anything thrown their way and when the men jerked up their lines there were sometimes two or three fish on a single hook. Sometimes they broke the surface as if they would jump into the boat and sometimes their bodies were so densely packed that they became "snagged" as the hooks went into their bellies or their eyes or their backs or their tails. The scent of their own blood spreading within the water spurred them to an even greater frenzy and they fell upon their mutilated fellows, snapping the still living flesh from the moving bones. The men moved in their own frenzy as if to keep pace. Hooks snagged in their thumbs and the singing, sizzling lines burned through the calluses on their hands. The fish filled the bottom of the boat and began to rise in a blue-green, flopping, snapping mass to the level of the men's knees. And then, suddenly, they were gone. The hooks brought back nothing but clear drops of water or shreds of mutilated seaweed. There was no indication of them anywhere either on the surface of the sea or beneath. It was as if they had never been, apart from the heaving weight which caused the boat to ride so low within the water. The men wiped the sweat from their foreheads with swollen hands, sometimes leaving other streaks behind. Some of the streaks contained a mixture of fishblood and their own.

The men looked towards the shore and saw her rise from the table rock and come towards them until she reached the water's edge. They guided the boat across the glass-like sea until its prow grounded heavily on the gravelly shore. They tossed the painter rope to her and she caught it with willing hands.

All afternoon they lay on the table rock. At first they seemed driven by the frenzy of all that had happened and not happened to them. By all the heat and the loneliness and the waiting and all the varied events that had conspired to create their day. The clothes of the men were sprinkled with blackening clots of blood and the golden spawn of the female fish and the milky white semen of the male. She had never seen fully aroused men before, having known only one man at one time, and having experienced in that damp darkness more of feeling than of sight.

She was to remember, for the rest of her life, the oldest man with the white hair. How he took off his cap and then pulled his heavy navy-blue jersey over his shoulders and folded it neatly and placed it on the rock beside her. She was to remember the whiteness of his skin and arms compared with the bronzed redness of his face and neck and that of his bleeding and swollen hands. As if, without clothes, his upper body was still clothed in a costume made of two different materials. The whiteness of his skin and the whiteness of his hair were the same color but totally different as well. After he had folded his jersey he placed his cap neatly upon it. It was as if he were doing it out of long habit and was preparing to lie down with his wife. She almost expected him to brush his teeth.

After the first frenzy they were quieter, lying stretched beneath the sun. Sometimes one of the younger men got up and skipped flat stones across the surface of the sea. The dogs lay above the waterline panting and watching everything. She was later to think how often she had watched them in the fury of their own mating. And how she had seen their surplus young placed in burlap bags, weighted down with rocks, and tossed over the boat's side into the sea.

The sun began to decline and the tide began to fall, the water receding from the heavy boat which was in danger of becoming beached. The men got up and adjusted their clothes. Some walked some distance away to urinate. They came back and all four of them put their shoulders to the prow and prepared to push the boat back into the water.

"One, two, three, heave!" they said, moving in concentrated unison on the last syllable. Their bodies were stretched out almost horizontally as they pushed, the toes of their rubber boots scrabbling in the loose beach gravel. The boat began to move, grudgingly at first, and then more rapidly as the water took its weight. The men scrambled over the prow and over the sides. Most of them were wet up to their waists. They seized their oars to push the boat farther out so there would be room to turn it around and face it towards home.

She watched them leave, standing on the shore. As the boat moved out, she noticed her undergarment crumpled and discarded by the edge of the table rock. The boat moved farther out and farther away and the men waved to her. She felt her arm rising in a similar gesture, almost without her willing it. The man with the white hair tipped his cap. She knew in one of those intuitive flashes that they would never say anything to anyone or scarcely mention the events of the day among themselves. She also knew that they would never be back. As the boat rounded the island's end, she scrunched up her undergarment and threw it into the sea. She began to walk up towards the lighthouse. She touched her body. It was sticky with blood and fishspawn and human seed. "It will have to happen this time," she thought, "because there was so much of it and it went on so long." Comparing the afternoon to her one previous brief encounter in the dark.

When she reached the lighthouse she heard the cries of the scavenging gulls. She looked in the direction of the sound and saw the boat cutting a "v" in the placid water on its way to the mainland. The men were bent double grasping their fishforks and throwing the dead mackerel back into the sea. The gulls swooped and screamed in a whitened noisy cloud.

Two years later she was in a mainland store ordering supplies to take back to the island. Usually she made arrangements with one of her relatives to take the supplies from the store to the water's edge and then ferry them across to the island but on this day she could not find the particular young man. One of the items was a bag of flour. As she stood paying her bill and looking out the door in some agitation, she saw, out of the corner of her eye, the white-haired man in the navy-blue jersey.

"This is too heavy for you," he said. "Let me help," and he bent down and picked up the hundred pound flour sack and threw it easily onto his shoulder. When it landed some of the flour puffed out, sprinkling his blue jersey and his cap and his hair with its fine white powder. She remembered the whiteness of his body beneath the blue jersey and the frenzied afternoon beneath the summer sun. As they were going out the door they met her young relative.

"Here, I'll take that," he said, relieving the man of the bag of flour.

"Thank you," she said to the man.

"My pleasure," he said and tipped his cap towards her. The flour dust fell from his cap onto the floor between them.

"He is a real nice fellow," said her young relative as they moved towards the shore. "But of course you don't know him the way we do."

"No," she said. "Of course I don't." She looked across the channel to the stillness of the island. Her expected child had never arrived.

The years of the next decade passed by in a blur of monotonous sameness. She realized that she was becoming more careless of her appearance and that such carelessness was regarded as further evidence of eccentricity. She came ashore less frequently preferring to try to understand the world through radio. She found her teen-age daughter to be foreign and aloof and embarrassed by her presence. Her aunt's family harbored doubts about their decision to rear the girl and, one day, when she was visiting, suggested that she might want to live on the island with her "real mother." The girl laughed and walked into another room.

Gradually during the next years things changed even more, but so quietly that, in retrospect, she could not link the specific events to the specific years. Many of them had to do with changes on the mainland. The Government built a splendid new wharf and the spring fishermen no longer came to inhabit the shanties which began to fall into disrepair, their doors banging in the wind and the shingles flying from their roofs. Sometimes she looked at the initials carved by the absent men on the shanties' walls but his, as she knew, would never be among them.

Community pastures were established, with regular attendants, and the bound young cattle and the lusty rams no longer came to the summer pasturage. The sweeping headlights of cars became a regular feature of her night vision, mirroring in a myriad manner the beam from her solitary lighthouse. One night after a quarrel with her aunt's family, her daughter left in such a car, and vanished into the mystery of Toronto. She did not know of it until weeks later when she came ashore for the purchase of supplies.

The wharf at the island began to deteriorate and the visitors came less often. She found herself often dealing with members of a newer generation. Many of them were sulky and contributed to the maintaining of island tradition with the utmost reluctance and only because of the badgering of their parents.

Yet the light still shone and the various missives to and from "A. MacPhedran" continued to travel through the mails. The nature of such missives also changed, however gradually. When the first generation of her family went to the island it had been close to the age of sail when captains were at the mercies of the winds. In her own time she had seen the coming of the larger ships and the increasing sophistication of their technology. There had not been a wreck upon the island in all her time of habitation and no freezing, ice-caked travellers had ever knocked upon her midnight door. The "emergency chest" and its store of supplies remained unopened from one inspection to the next.

One summer she realized with a shock that her child-bearing years were over and that that part of her life was past.

Mainland boat operators began to offer "trips around the island," taking tourists on circumnavigational voyages. Very often because of time limitations they did not land but merely circled or anchored briefly offshore. When the boats approached the dogs barked, bringing her to her door or sometimes to the water's edge. At first she was not aware of the image she presented to the tourists with their binoculars or their cameras. Nor was she aware of how she was described by the operators of the boats. Standing at the edge of the sea in her dishevelled men's clothing and surrounded by her snarling dogs, she later realized, she had passed into folklore. She had, without realizing it, become "the mad woman of the island."

It was on a hot summer's day, some years later when, in answer to the barking of the dogs, she looked out the window and saw the big boat approaching. The men wore tan-colored uniforms and the Canadian flag flew from the mast. They tied the boat to the remnants of the wharf and began to climb towards the house as she called off the dogs. The decision had been made, they told her quietly, while sitting in the kitchen, to close the lighthouse officially. The light would still shine but it would be maintained by "modern technology." It would operate automatically and be serviced by supply boats which would come at certain times of the year or, in emergency, they added, by helicopter. It would, however, be maintained in its present state for approximately a year and a half. After that, they said, she would have "to live somewhere else." They got up to leave and thanked her for her decades of fine service.

After they had gone she walked the length and width of the island. She repeated all the place names, many of them in Gaelic, and marvelled that the places would remain but the names would vanish. "Who would know?" she wondered that this spot had once been called *achadh nan caoraich*, or that another was called *creig a bhoird*. And who she thought, with a catch in her heart, would ever know of *Àite na cruinneachadh* and of what had transpired there. She looked across the landscape repeating the phrases of the place-names as if they were those of children about to be abandoned without knowledge of their names. She felt like whispering their names to them so they would not forget.

She realized with a type of shock that in spite of generations of being people "of the island" they had never really owned it in any legal sense. There was nothing physical of it that was, in strict reality, formally theirs.

That autumn and winter her rituals seemed without meaning. There was no need of so many supplies because the future was shorter and she approached each winter task with the knowledge that it would be her last. She approached spring with a longing born of confused emotions. She who had wanted to leave and wanted to return and wanted to stay felt the approaching ache of those who leave the familiar behind. She felt, perhaps, as those who leave bad places or bad situations or bad marriages behind them. As those who must look over their shoulders one last time and who say quietly to themselves, "Oh I have given a lot of my life to this, such as it was, and such was I. And no matter where I go I will never be the same."

That April as the ice broke, for her the final time, she was drying the dishes and looking through the window. Because of her failing eyesight she did not see the boat until it was almost at the remains of the wharf and the dogs did not make their usual sound. She saw the man bending to loop the boat's rope to the wharf and as he did so his cap fell off and she saw the redness of his hair. It seemed to flash and reflect in the April sun like the sudden and different energy of spring. She wrapped the damp dish towel around her hand as if it were a bandage and then she as quickly unwrapped it again.

He started up the path towards the house and the dogs ran happily beside him. She stood in the doorway uncertainly. As he approached she realized that he was talking to the dogs and his accent was slightly unfamiliar. He seemed about twenty years of age and his eyes were very blue. He had an earring in his ear.

"Hello," he said, extending his hand. "I don't know if you recognize me."

It had been so long and so much had happened that she did not know what to say. Her hand tightened on the cloth she was still holding. She stepped aside to let him enter the house and watched as he sat on a chair.

"Do you stay here all the time?" he asked, looking around the kitchen, "even in the winter?"

"Yes," she said. "Most of the time."

"Were you born here?"

"Yes," she said. "I guess so."

"It must be lonely," he said, "but I guess some people are lonely no matter where they are."

She looked at him as if he were a ghost.

"Would you like to live somewhere else?" he asked.

"I don't know," she said. "Maybe."

He raised his hand and touched the earring as if to make certain it was still there. His glance travelled about the kitchen, seeming to rest lightly on each of the familiar objects. She realized that the kitchen had hardly changed since that other April visit so long ago. She could not think of what to say.

"Would you like some tea?" she asked after a moment of awkward silence.

"No thank you," he said. "I'm pressed for time right now but perhaps we'll have it later."

She nodded although she was not certain of his meaning. The dogs lay under the table, now and then thumping the floor with their tails. Through the window she could see the white gulls hanging over the ocean which was still dotted with cakes of floating ice.

He looked at her carefully, as if remembering, and he smiled. Neither of them seemed to know just what to say.

"Well," he said getting up suddenly. "I have to go now. I'll see you later. I'll come back."

"Wait," she said rising as quickly, "please don't go," and she almost added the word "again."

"I'll be back," he said, "in the fall. And then I will take you with me. We will go and live somewhere else."

"Yes," she said and then added almost as an afterthought, "Where have you been?"

"In Toronto," he said. "I was born there. They told me on the mainland that you are my grandmother."

She looked at him as if he were a genetic wonder which indeed he seemed to be.

"Oh," she said.

"I have to go now," he repeated, "but I'll see you later. I'll come back."

"Oh yes," she said. "Oh yes we will."

And then he was gone. She sat transfixed not daring to move. Part of her felt that she should rush and call him back and another fearful part told her she should not know what she might see. Finally she went to the window. Halfway across to the mainland there was a single man in a boat but she could make no clear identification. She did not say anything to anyone about the visit. She could think of no way she could tactfully introduce it. After years of secrecy it seemed a dangerous time to bring up the subject of the red-haired man. Perhaps, again, no one else had seen him? She did not wish to add further evidence to her designation as "the mad woman of the island." She scanned the faces of her relatives carefully but could find nothing. Perhaps he had visited them, she thought, and they had told him not to come. Perhaps they considered themselves in the business of not disturbing the disturbed.

Now as the October rain fell she added yet another stick to the fire. She was no longer bothered by the declining stock of wood because she would not need it for the winter. The rain fell turning more to the consistency of hail and she knew this by its sound as well as by her sight. She looked away from the door as she had so many years ago, the first time at the table rock. Deliberately not looking in the direction of his possible coming so that she could not see him *not* coming if that was the way it was supposed to be. She waited, listening to the regular pattern of the rain, and wondered if she were on the verge of sleep. Suddenly the door blew open and the hail-like rain skittered across the floor. The wet dogs moved from beneath the table and she heard them rather than saw. Perhaps she should mop the wet floor she thought but then she remembered that they planned to tear the house down anyway and its cleanliness seemed like a minor virtue. The water rippled across the floor in rolling little wind-driven waves. The dog came in, its nails clacking across the floor even as little spurts of water rose from beneath its padded paws. It came and lay its head upon her lap. She got up not daring to believe. Outside it was wet and windy and she followed the dog down the darkened path. And then in the revolving cycle of the high lighthouse light she saw in a single white instant the dark shape of the boat bobbing at the wharf and his straight but dripping form by the corner of the shanties.

They moved towards each other.

"Oh," she said, digging her fingers into the dampness of his neck.

"I told you I'd come back," he said.

"Oh," she said. "Oh yes. You did."

She ran her fingers over his face in the darkness and when the light revolved again she saw the blueness of his eyes and his red hair darkened by the dripping water. He was not wearing any earring.

"How old are you?" she asked, embarrassed by the girlish triviality of the question which had bothered her all these years.

"Twenty-one," he said. "I thought I told you."

He took her hands and walked backwards while facing her, down to the darkness of the bobbing boat and the rolling sea.

"Come," he said. "Come with me. It is time we went to live somewhere else."

"Oh yes," she said. "Oh yes we will."

She dug her nails into the palms of his hands as he guided her over the spume-drenched rocks.

"This boat," he said, "has to be back before dawn."

The wind was rising as the temperature was dropping. The hail-like rain had given way to stinging snow and the ground they left behind was beginning to freeze.

A dog barked once. And when the light revolved, its solitary beam found no MacPhedrans on the island or the sea.

Nominated by ONTARIO REVIEW, *Joyce Carol Oates, and Robert Phillips*

A SNAPPING TURTLE IN JUNE

by FRANKLIN BURROUGHS

from THE GEORGIA REVIEW

Aʟʟ ᴛʜᴀᴛ ᴄᴀɴ usefully be said about New England weather has been said. It is arbitrary, precipitate, and emphatic, less certain than a baby's bottom. Like the mind, it isn't necessarily bound by chronology. April can suddenly hearken back to February; a few hours in January will be as balmy as a May afternoon—that is, as one of those rare May afternoons that aren't recollecting March or day-dreaming about September. Here on an overcast Tuesday morning late in June, it is summer sure enough, yet we must depend more upon the floral calendar than the thermometer for corroboration. We've had one spell of hot weather—temperature into the 90's, high humidity, bread going moldy in a day, crackers limp as old lettuce— but that was two weeks ago, and it has been cool since then, either rainy and chill or bright and breezy and autumnal.

But the flowers keep their seasons. Our fields, especially the poorer one that lies between the house and the river, are rich in buttercup and vetch, lesser stitchwort, fragrant bedstraw, and blue-eyed grass. From the standpoint of agriculture, these plants are weeds, and therefore absolutely reliable. Cold, wet, and drought do not deter them; the only way to thwart them is by herbicide or fertilizer. The buttercups are long-stemmed and grow in all but the lushest pastures. Vetch (called partridge-pea in South Carolina) grows in little tangles of vine, like untrellised morning glories, as do stitchwort and bedstraw, and so they fare best in a thin, ledgy, or sandy soil, where the grass is meager. On a moist, unsummery summer morning, these flowers make soft clots and smears of color throughout the watery green of the pasture grasses. Thriving amid the adversities of soil and climate, their inconspicuous beauty seems reflective of rural New England, and it is pleasing to learn that people here once found more than aesthetic solace in them. Stitchwort was so named because it was thought to cure "stitches"—pains in the side, of the sort that runners get—while bedstraw was used to lie upon, back when a bed was a board, covered with straw, covered with a sheet. Fragrant bedstraw is quite odorless in life, but reputedly grows savory in death, when sufficiently dried.

Except for the vetch, we had nothing in South Carolina like these field flowers or the daisies and hawkweed that populate the road shoulders at this season of the year, and there is not a great deal in the Maine summer that particularly recalls the summers of my Southern boyhood. But that strange Wordsworthian hunger for landscape, growing out of an individual and cultural maturity, is complexly regressive and involves much attempted calling back of things that probably exist only in the echo of the caller's voice. Fewer and fewer of us have Wordsworth's privilege of inhabiting as adults the landscape we inhabited as children—and of learning to recognize in it what he called "the language of my former heart." Even if luck and resolution enable us eventually to live in places of great beauty and interest, there is some quality of internal exile that shadows our relation to them.

This is a particular problem if you are a non-New Englander who comes to live in New England. New England is an image readymade for you, no matter where you come from. It has so defined the American conception of landscape, and of the ideal human response to landscape, that it is not easy to arrive at a direct relation to it. It's rather like being married to a celebrity—your own response responds to a simplified and magnified public perception, as well as to the thing itself. Or, as a friend of mine, a tough-minded New Yorker, observed to me one November day, while we sat in a skiff in Broad Cove, looking across blue water that glinted and sparkled as though it were already full of ice shards, through crystal air and toward the shore with its patchwork of fields, woodlots, and bleak, bone-white houses gleaming in the sun: "Who are they trying to kid? This is the most *derivative* goddamned landscape I've ever seen in my life."

Boyhood was once almost as distinct a part of the American terrain as New England is, and, like New England, it had its heyday in the nineteenth century, and continued to be valued because, until fairly recently, it went on evoking the life of that century. There is the image of a sandy or a dusty road, the feel of the road under the feet, the cane pole carried over the shoulder, the drone of cicadas, the hair warm from the sun: the barefoot boy with cheeks of tan, the etchings and engravings of Winslow Homer, and supremely and inevitably, *Tom Sawyer* and *Huckleberry Finn*. In contrast, *girlhood* does not seem to generate this mirage. It doesn't evoke the same semitribal life, the living in a world rather closer to the wordless world of smells, itches, and yapping contentions of the unregulated dogs of small-town America than to the world of adults, or even to the world of the sort of regimented, housebroken, neurotic, pedigreed canines that one finds in the houses of one's friends.

There is of course much compensatory distortion in this image of boyhood, but I do not think it is altogether false. The boredom was as thick as the heat in Conway, South Carolina, and one learned to relish both in the summers. In our neighborhood, which is now an attractive suburban network of streets overhung with water oaks and sycamores, the streets were not yet paved—there was still a lot of unpaved road in the South at that time—and that gave, in a small way, texture and variety to life. In rainy seasons, the roads were slick and the puddles would turn to bogs, rutted out and mucky; occasionally a car, ineptly driven by one of the ladies of the neighborhood, would get stuck. But by summer the sun would have baked the roads hard beneath the dust that powdered them, and boys wore shoes only under compulsion. That is not possible where the streets are asphalt, and the tar sticks to your feet like napalm. I think girls wore shoes more regularly, in the fashion of their sisters in cities, but many of my impressions of girlhood must have been taken from my own sister, who was four years older and that much more aware of the world beyond the doorstep. In any event, I tended to associate femininity with paved streets, and knew for a fact that it was the ladies of the neighborhood, my own mother not excepted, who were most insistent that the roads be paved, so that they would not get stuck in the rainy weather, or have their children tracking mud into the house or getting their feet full of ringworm. From listening to them, you would have thought that they were the Victorian wives of British colonials, suddenly finding themselves in the Burmese or Australian outback, amid conditions of an appalling primitiveness.

At that time, the paved road stopped at the railroad tracks, about a quarter mile from our house. Then one day my great friend Ricky McIver and I walked down to the railroad tracks, preparing to follow them (which we were forbidden to do) along the causeway that ran through the swamps and eventually reached the trestle over Kingston Lake. But there, where the pavement ended, was a roadblock and a detour sign, apologizing for the inconvenience and announcing that this section of the road was to be surfaced. It was the beginning of a lifetime of symbolic Luddite resistance. We pushed over the roadblock, which was no more than a sawhorse, and threw the sign into the ditch beside the road. To no avail, needless to say: the road got paved anyway. History does not leave the backwaters of boyhood alone, and Ricky would soon enough find himself personifying it to barefoot villagers, who liked it no better than he had, in dusty hamlets full of yapping dogs outside Da Nang.

We were not, of course, thinking of pavement in terms of abstractions like History or Progress. It might have crossed our minds that its coming would mean that we had to wear shoes—or that more dogs would be run over, because cars would travel so much faster on the asphalt, and the dogs, like the children, thought of the streets as places of concourse and recreation. But probably nothing even that theoretical occurred to us. I think it was that we were mostly considering the snapping turtles that would, some time in the middle of every summer, appear in the road—sturdy little fellows, their shells not much bigger than a silver dollar. Paving the road would be the end of them.

All these things came to mind on this Tuesday morning in Maine, with the fields full of flowers and late June imitating early May, because, as I started out down the gravel road that connects our house to the highway, and drew abreast of the little quarter-acre pond that sits to the left of the road, here was, large as life and squarely in my way, a big mama snapping turtle, excavating herself a hole to lay her eggs in. I was in no particular hurry, and so I stopped and got out to investigate. Snappers are the most widely distributed of North American turtles, and they are by no means uncommon in Maine, but they are normally reclusive, and when one makes a public appearance it is not an event to be passed over lightly. This particular one certainly had no intention of being passed over lightly: if she had intended to blockade the road, she couldn't have chosen a better spot.

Several things distinguish them from other freshwater turtles, most obviously their size. The one at my feet was about two feet long, from the tip of her snout to the tip of her tail. When I eventually picked her up by the tail (and that is another distinguishing feature of snapping turtles—you pick up an ordinary turtle by the rim of its shell, but a snapper's neck is remarkably long and flexible, so you grab the creature by the tail and hold it well out from your body), I guessed she weighed a good twenty pounds.

The general proportions of a snapping turtle are wrong. The head is far too big; the shell is too little. The plastron, or undershell, is ridiculously skimpy—it seems barely adequate for the purposes of decency, and as useless as a bikini would be as far as anatomical protection is concerned. Consequently a snapper cannot withdraw into itself as other turtles do. It retracts the head enough to shield its neck and doesn't even attempt to pull in its legs and feet. The legs and tail are large in relation to the body: when a snapper decides to walk it really *walks;* the bottom of the shell is a couple of inches off the ground, and, with its dorsally tuberculate tail, long claws, and wickedly hooked beak, it looks like a scaled-down stegosaur.

A snapper compensates for its inadequate armor in a variety of ways, the most immediately apparent of which is athletic ability combined with a very bad temper. It can whirl and lunge ferociously, and, if turned over on its back, can, with a thrust and twist of its mighty neck, be upright and ready for mayhem. If you approach one out of water, it opens its mouth and hisses; if you get closer, it lurches at you with such vehemence that it lifts itself off the ground, its jaws snapping savagely at empty air. Archie Carr, whose venerable *Handbook to Turtles* (1952) is the only authority on these matters I possess, states that the disposition to strike is innate, and has been observed in hatchlings "not yet altogether free of their egg-shells." An adult can strike, he reports, "with the speed and power of a big rattlesnake." Although Carr does not explicitly say so, the snapper appears to be one of those animals, like the hognose snake, that makes the most of its resemblance to a poisonous snake. Its pale mouth gapes open like a moccasin's, and its aggressiveness involves a certain exaggerated and theatrical posturing. Its official name specifically and subspecifically suggests the highly unturtlelike impression that this creates: *Chelydra serpentina serpentina*. But the snapper, unlike the hognose, can back up its bluff. Its first-strike capability isn't lethal, but it isn't trivial either. According to boyhood folklore, a snapper can bite a broomstick in two, but I have seen the experiment conducted. It took a great deal of goading to persuade the turtle to seize the broomstick at all—it plainly would have preferred the hand that held it—but it finally took it, held it, and crushed and pulped it. Mama's broom handle came out looking like a piece of chewed-over sugarcane. Putting your hand in range of a big snapper would not be like putting it under a guillotine or axe; it would be more like putting it under a bulldozer: a slow, complete crunching.

The shell and skin are a muddy gray; the eye, too, is of a murky mud color. The pupil is black and shaped like a star or a spoked wheel. Within the eye there is a strange yellowish glint, as though you were looking down into turbid water and seeing, in the depths of the water, light from a smoldering fire. It is one of Nature's more nightmarish eyes. The eyes of dragonflies are also nightmarish, but in a different way—they look inhuman, like something out of science fiction. The same is true of the eyes of sharks. The snapper's eye is dull, like a pig's, but inside it there is this savage malevolence, something suggesting not only an evil intention toward the world, but the torment of an inner affliction. Had Milton seen one, he would have associated it with the baleful eye of Satan, an eye reflecting some internal hell of liquid fire—whether in Paradise or here on a soft June day, with the bobolinks fluttering aloft and singing in the fields. Snapping turtles did in fact once inhabit Europe, but they died out by the end of the Pleistocene, and so were unknown to what we think of as European history. But they look, nevertheless, like something that Europeans had half-imagined or dimly remembered even before they came to the New World and saw them for the first time: a snapper would do for a gargoyle, or a grotesque parody of a knight on his horse, a thing of armored evil.

Snappers feed on about anything, dead or alive: fish, flesh, or fowl. The fish they catch by luring them into range with their vermiform tongues, which may have something to do with the role of trickster that they assume in the mythology of North American Indians. But they can also be caught in a trap baited with bananas. They are not fastidious: "Schmidt and Inger (1957) tell the grue-

66

some story of an elderly man who used a tethered snapping turtle to recover the bodies of people who had drowned."* We do not learn what this sinister gentleman fed his useful pet to encourage its predilection for waterlogged cadavers. I know on my own authority that snappers are death on ducks, and will rise like a shadow from the oozy muck of the bottom, under the jocund and unsuspecting drake as it briskly preens and putters on the surface of the pond, lock sudden jaws around one suspended leg, one webbed foot, and sink quietly back to the depths, their weight too much for the duck to resist, their jaws a functional illustration of necessity's sharp pinch. There in the darkness the duck is ponderously mauled, mutilated, and eaten, right down to the toenails. We watched a hen mallard and a brood of ducklings disappear from the little pond beside the road one summer—two or three inexplicable deductions per week—until at last only the very nervous hen and one trusting little duckling remained. Then there was only the duckling. It peeped and chirped and swam distractedly around the pond in a most heart-rending fashion. I tried to trap it so we could rear it in confinement and safety, but there was no catching it, and the next day it was gone too.

The law of tooth and nail is all right with me when it involves hawks and mice, or foxes and geese, or even sharks and swimmers—there is a redeeming elegance in most predators, a breathtaking speed and agility. If I thought I could tempt an eagle to stoop, I'd gladly stake my best laying hen in the yard to see it happen. But a snapper is an ugly proposition, more like cancer than a crab is. If one grabs your finger, you do not get the finger back— that too is boyhood folklore, but I have never tested it. Some propositions call for implicit faith, even in these post-theological and deconstructing days.

Unlike most of the other freshwater turtles, snappers never emerge to bask on rocks or logs. They come out in late spring or early summer; their emergence here coincides with the vetch, the stitchwort, bedstraw, and hawkweed. They need sandy soil to lay their eggs in, and such soil isn't always close to the sorts of boggy, miry waters they inhabit. They will often go overland a surprising distance before finally deciding on a spot to dig. Roadbeds and railway embankments can provide good sites that are reasonably

*Turtles: Perspectives and Research, ed. M. Harless and H. Morlock (New York: John Wiley and Sons, 1979), p. 289.

convenient to their usual habitats. Creatures of darkness, cursing the light, they lumber up from pond or river, and one morning you awake to the frantic yapping of dogs and go out, and there, foul and hissing, like some chieftain of the underworld at last summoned to justice and surrounded by reporters and cameras, stands a great gravid snapper. The flesh of her neck, legs, and tail—all the parts that ought to fit inside the shell but don't—has, on the underside, a grimy yellowish cast to it, is podgy, lewd, wrinkled, and soft. In Maine there will normally be one or two big leeches hanging onto the nether parts. These portions of the animal seem to have no proper covering—no scales, feathers, hair, or taut, smooth epidermis. It looks as though the internal anatomy had been extruded, or the whole animal plucked or flayed.

I'm not sure how much of this natural history Ricky McIver and I understood when we were nine or ten; we only knew that, trekking down a sandy road in midsummer, we would suddenly come upon a baby snapper, bustling along with remarkable purpose, as though on its way to catch a train. Of course we would catch the turtle, and one of us would take it home and put it in a dishpan with a little water and keep it under the bed, where all night long there would be the tinny scraping of little claws, as the turtle went round and round inside the pan. Sometimes one would escape, instigating a general panicky search of the room and the house. It would turn up far back under a sofa or cabinet, covered with dust and weakened by dehydration, but still able to muster a parched snap and hiss. Finally we would let it go into a drainage ditch. We never came upon a mother laying her eggs—given the heat, perhaps they did that at night down south. Up here I seem to come across one or two of them every year, and have learned to look for them along road shoulders in late June.

I backed the car up to the house to get Susan and Hannah—the older girls were still asleep—and our old pointer Jacob roused himself and walked down with us, conferring by his stiff-jointed, wheezing Nestorian solemnity an air of officialdom upon the occasion, as though we were a commission sent out to investigate an unregistered alien that had showed up in Bowdoinham. Hannah went along grudgingly, with a five-year-old's saving sense that any time the parents promised to show you something interesting, they probably had concealed motives of one sort or another. When we got to the turtle, Jacob hoisted his hackles, clapped his tail between his legs, and circled her a few times, then sat down and barked once. The turtle raised herself on her forelegs, head up, mouth agape; her hostility did not focus on any one of us so much as on the whole situation in which she found herself. Hannah looked at all of this and pronounced it boring; could she have a friend over to play? The dog seemed to feel that he had discharged his obligations by barking, and shambled over to the edge of the field, pawed fretfully at the ground, then settled himself, curled up, sighed, and went to sleep. The whole thing was beginning to take on the unpromising aspect of Nature Study, an ersatz experience.

We walked around behind the turtle, and there did make a discovery of sorts. Through all of the commotion that surrounded her anterior end, her hind legs were methodically digging. Their motion was impressively regular and mechanical—first one leg thrust down into the hole, then the other, smooth and steady as pistons. Whatever the snapper felt or thought about her situation plainly did not concern the legs, which were wholly intent on procreation. It seemed an awkward way to dig, the hind foot being a clumsy and inflexible instrument anyway, and having to carry on its operations huggermugger like that, out of sight and out of mind too, if the turtle could be said to have a mind. We could not see down into the hole, only the legs alternately reaching down, and a rim of excavated sand that was slowly growing up behind the rim of the turtle's shell. I was later to learn that the digging action, once begun, is as involuntary as the contractions of a mammal giving birth, and even a turtle missing one hind leg will dig in the same fashion, thrusting down first with the good leg, then with the amputated stump, until the job is done.

Hannah, an aficionado of the sandbox, permitted herself a cautious interest in this end of the turtle's operations, and wanted to inspect her hole. I wasn't sure about the ethics of this. It is a general law that you don't disturb nesting creatures; it was, after all, no fault of the snapper's if she failed to excite in us the veneration that generally attaches to scenes of maternity and nativity. On the other hand, she had chosen a bad place. I could see where my neighbor Gene Hamrick had carefully driven around her, going well over onto the shoulder to do so. Other neighbors might be less considerate, and the nest itself would, in any event, be packed hard by the traffic in a few weeks, rendering the future of the eggs and hatchlings highly uncertain. So I grasped her tail and hoisted her up. Aloft, she held herself rigidly spread-eagle, her head and neck parallel to the earth, and hissed mightily as I took her over and put her in the little ditch that drains the pond. Because of the recent rain, the ditch was flowing, and as soon as her front feet touched the water, all of her aggression ceased, and she seemed bent on nothing but escape. She had surprising power as she scrabbled at the banks and bottom of the ditch; it was like holding onto a miniature bulldozer. I let her go and she surged off down the ditch, head submerged and carapace just awash. She stopped once and raised her head and fixed us with her evil eye; the mouth dropped open in a last defiance. Then she lowered her head again and waddled out of sight.

We examined the hole. It looked as though it had been dug with a tablespoon—shapely and neat, a little wider at the bottom than at the top. There were no eggs. Hannah set methodically about refilling the hole, out of an instinct that seemed as compelling as the one that dug it. As she disturbed the sand, I caught a strong musky scent where the turtle had lain. That scent, which was also on my hand, recalled something that the sight of the turtle had not recalled, and that was a peculiar memory connected to the biggest snapping turtle I ever saw, or ever intend to see.

In my high-school summers, I worked for the Burroughs Timber Company, which was owned by a group of my father's first cousins. My immediate boss was Mr. Henry Richards; the crew consisted of the two of us and two cousins, Billy and Wendell Watson. Mr. Richards was not an educated man, and had in his younger days been something of a drinker and a fighter, but he had straightened himself out and gotten some training in forestry. He was good at his job, as far as I could judge—his job largely consisting of cruising and marking timber, overseeing logging operations, and generally keeping track of the company's woodlands. These were mostly small tracts, seldom more than a few hundred acres, scattered from one end of Horry County to the other. Mr. Richards was handsome: lean and weathered, with dark wavy hair, sleepy eyes, and the sort of indolent rasping voice that conveyed the authority of someone who had not always been perfectly nice. He was in his forties. Billy and Wendell were younger by ten or fifteen years, and both were countrymen, from the vicinity of Crabtree Creek.

I am not sure what degree of cousinage joined Billy and Wendell. The Watsons, like the Burroughses and a great many other families in the county, were an extended and numerous clan, and such clans generally divided into what religion had taught us to regard as the children of promise and the children of perdition, or sheep and goats. The binary opposition would express itself in terms of whatever general station in life the family occupied. Thus my Burroughs cousins tended to be either sober, quietly respectable merchants and landowners concerned with tobacco and timber—or drunkards, wastrels, and womanizers, men notorious in Horry County for the frequency with which they married and divorced.

Wendell belonged to the reputable branch of the Watson family— small farmers who held onto their land and led hard, frugal lives. In town, such people were referred to, somewhat inscrutably, as the salt of the earth. Billy came from the other side—poachers, moonshiners, people likely to be handy with a straight razor, who kept six or eight gaunt and vicious hounds (half of them stolen and all of them wormy) chained in the yard, along with a few unfettered chickens and a ragged mule, but who could hardly be called farmers. Their style of life and economy had probably been formed by the county's long history as a demifrontier, and had changed only minimally to accommodate the twentieth century when it eventually arrived.

Wendell was one of those rare county people who, out of some reaction to the dirt and despair of agriculture, had a highly developed fastidiousness. His face was bony, angular, and prim around the mouth; he always wore a dapper straw hat instead of the usual cap, so that his brow was never browned or reddened by the sun. His work shirt and pants were neatly creased, and I never saw them stained with sweat. He would stop for a moment in the resinous, stifling heat of a pine wood, extract a red bandanna handkerchief from his pocket, unfold it, and delicately dab at his brow, removing his hat to do so. Then he would look at the moist handkerchief the way you might look at a small cut or blister, with a slight consternation and distaste, and then fold the handkerchief, first into halves, then into quarters, then into eighths, until it fit back into his hip pocket as neatly as a billfold.

He was lanky, with comically large feet and big, bony, lightly freckled hands and wrists, and you would have expected him to have no strength or stamina at all. But he could use any of the tools we used—bushaxe or machete or grubbing hoe—with no sign of strain or fatigue, all day long, holding the tool gingerly, so that you expected him to drop it at any moment, but keeping a pace that the rest of us could not sustain. He had a crooked, embarrassed grin and said little. In the midday heat, sometimes we would take our lunch to an abandoned tenant house, to eat on the porch and catch whatever breeze funneled through the doorway. Then three of us would stretch out on the warped floorboards, hats over our faces, and doze for half an hour. Wendell never did. He would sit with his back to one of the rough timbers that held up the porch, pull out his pocket knife, and set about pruning his fingernails; then he would stick the knife into a floorboard with an air of finality, lift his head and stare out over the fields with the intense, noncommittal scrutiny of a poker player examining his cards, or of what he was, a countryman watching the big banks of cumulus clouds pile up on a July afternoon. Or he might whittle himself a toothpick and ply it carefully between his teeth, or study a map of the tract we were to cruise in the afternoon. He always kept a watch over himself, as though he feared he might otherwise grow slack and slovenly. He did not own a car, and was permitted to use the company truck to go to and from his house, and to keep it over the weekend. On Monday mornings it would be all washed and cleaned; Mr. Richards would ask him whether he'd been courting in it or was he just planning to sell it. Wendell would only laugh awkwardly at himself, and at his inability to think of a smart retort.

Billy Watson, to hear him tell it, was chiefly proud of having spent six years in the fourth grade, at the end of which time he was sixteen and not legally obligated to go to school anymore. Mr. Richards could not get over it. "Damn, Billy," he said more than once, "don't seem like you're *that* stupid." He'd say it because he relished Billy's invariable answer, always delivered in the same tone of pious resignation, as though he were speaking of some cross that the Lord had, in His ungovernable wisdom, given him to bear: "Oh, I wa'n't stupid. Just ornery." He was a big man, about six foot three, with powerful, rounded shoulders. He had a peculiar sort of physical complacence with himself, was loose and supple as a cat, and could squat or hunker longer and more comfortably, it seemed, than the average man could sit in an armchair. His hair was lank and reddish brown, and was usually seconded by a four- or five-day growth of stubble beard, stained with tobacco juice at the lower right corner of the mouth. It was a big, misshapen mouth, distended by the pouch in one cheek that is the outcome of a lifetime of chewing tobacco—Day's Work or Sun Apple. His teeth were few and far between, worn and yellowed as an old mule's. He had certainly never been to a dentist in his life, and might have been surprised to learn that such a profession existed.

Billy was a river rat; if he could have, he would have lived by doing nothing but trapping and fishing. He sometimes fished for sport: he could handle his stubby casting rod as though he had a kind of intelligence in his hands, placing each cast, cast after cast, far back under overhanging trees, with no pause, no hesitation, no calculation of the risks of getting the plug hung on a branch or snag. There was so much rhythm in it that you'd find yourself patting your foot if you watched him long enough. But he wasn't particular about how he caught fish or what fish he caught: redbreast, bream, goggle-eye, stumpknocker, warmouth, bass, catfish, eel, mudfish, redfin pike, shad, Virginia perch—even the herring that ran upriver in the spring.

If early on a Saturday morning in the spring you happened to be down by Mishoe's Fish Market, a little frame building perched by the edge of Kingston Lake, you might see Billy slipping easily along the near bank of the lake, in a ridiculously undersized one-man paddling boat. He'd give you a look before he drew up to the landing, ask you if there was anybody there. You'd look around for only one thing, a yellow car with a long antenna, because that might be someone from the state fish and game department, which kept an eye on Mr. Mishoe. Not seeing it, you'd say no, nobody here but old man Mishoe. There was a strange, watery peace to it. All the drab, ordinary life of the town was just a few hundred feet away, but here was Billy gliding silently up to the landing, dropping the paddle with muffled reverberation into the boat bottom, then stepping out, shackling the little boat to a cypress, and bending over to lift from it two moist croker sacks, each squirming with his night's work. You'd want to follow him through the fish market to the back, where Mr. Mishoe and one or two helpers would be cleaning and filleting fish. They'd stop to watch Billy empty his sacks into a cleaning sink—the secret, active ingredients of river and river swamp, wriggling, flapping, and gasping there in the back room of a store. The catfish, mudfish, eels, and shad were classified as nongame species and could, within certain limits, be fished and marketed commercially. The rest were pure contraband, which presumably increased their market value. Whatever their cash value was, Billy would receive it in a few greasy bills, walk up to the drugstore on Main Street, and buy himself a cup of coffee and a doughnut. Townspeople who did not know him would edge away from the counter: he was a dirty, rough-looking man, unlaced boots flapping open at his ankles. His eyes, which were small and deep-set, reflected light strangely; they were green, and, in the strict sense of the word, *crazed*, as though the surface of the eye were webbed with minute cracks. You could not tell where they focused.

But Billy wasn't crazy or violent either, as far as I ever heard. Education is liberating in ways it does not always intend, and, by keeping Billy in the fourth grade, surrounded, year after year, by an unaging cohort of ten-year-olds, it liberated him from most notions of responsibility, foresight, or ambition. He had successfully learned how to avoid promotion, a lesson that ought to be learned and taught more often than it is. He had worked out at the plywood mill, upriver from Conway, and told me he had also done some house painting. But working for Mr. Richards and Burroughs Timber suited him best, and he was a valuable employee. He probably knew more about the company land than the company did, having hunted, fished, or trapped on most of it. When we would cruise timber, one of us would set the compass course for him, and then he could follow it, keeping careful count of his paces, marking each of the stations where we would stop and inventory all the timber in a quarter-acre plot, while Billy went ahead to the next station and marked the next plot. Often we would end the day on the back line of a tract, a long way from the truck. The logical thing in thick woods was to plot a course back to the truck and follow the compass out, but Billy would drop the compass into his pocket and strike off through the woods as nonchalantly as a man going across a parking lot. We'd follow. He did everything in such a headlong, unconsidering way that those of us who had gotten beyond the fourth grade could never bring ourselves to trust him entirely, and sooner or later somebody would call out: "Billy, you *sure* this is the right way?" "Time'll tell, boys; time'll tell," he'd call back. Time always did, and we would suddenly emerge from the woods, and there would be the road, and there would be the truck. Townspeople who knew Billy lost no occasion to point him out to you: "That's Billy Watson. Ain't got a lick of sense, but you won't find a better fisherman in this county."

We were working down toward the Pee Dee River, on a low, sandy ridge at the edge of the river swamp. The company had cleared the

74

ridge two or three years earlier and planted it in pine seedlings, but now the hardwoods, regenerating from the stump, threatened to reclaim it for themselves. The smaller hardwoods we chopped down with machete or bushaxe; the larger ones we girdled—gouged a ring around the trunk, half an inch deep, which cut off the tree's supply of food and water, and left it to die on its feet. For this we had a machine called the Little Beaver. It consisted of a four-cycle Briggs and Stratton engine mounted on a packframe, with a flexible hydraulic hose, at the end of which was a notched disk that did the girdling. The machine seemed to have no muffler at all—it was louder than a chainsaw, hot on the back, and the noise and vibration of it were stunning. It was late July, and that sandy patch of scrub oak and seedling pine afforded no protection from the sun. We would trade off the Little Beaver at thirty-minute intervals; not even Wendell volunteered to take any more of its hammering than that.

At noon, as was the custom, we knocked off. Mr. Richards drove out to the Georgetown highway. He knew of a country store across the river, over in Georgetown County, and proposed to take us there for lunch. It was owned by a man named Marlowe. I'd seen it often enough, the usual little mean, flat-topped cinder-block building, painted white, with a screened door for ventilation, within which you could expect to find the standard items: canned goods, bread, a bit of fishing tackle, and one or two coolers full of soft drinks and milk. As we drove, Mr. Richards talked about the Marlowes, and we learned that they were an infamous clan, divided into two subspecific groups which intermingled freely: the regular Marlowes and the murdering Marlowes. If you insulted a regular Marlowe—for example, by catching him stealing your boat—he would, within a week or ten days, set your woodlot on fire, slash your tires, or shoot your dog. But if you did the same thing to a murdering Marlowe, why then your troubles were over—instantly and permanently. That is what Mr. Richards said, but he was something of a talker and not above hyperbole. We didn't take it seriously and probably weren't meant to. Wendell didn't say much—he never did—but he had a tight little grin and plainly didn't believe what he was hearing. Billy was keeping his eye on the swamp and river as we crossed over them—the Pee Dee was outside his usual territory, and he'd been talking all morning about how he aimed to fish her this fall, from Gallivant's Ferry clear down to Yauhannah Bridge, where we were now. When we pulled off the highway and parked in the thin shade of an oak beside Marlowe's store, Mr. Richards said for us to remember to act polite; we didn't need any trouble with these folks, and neither did Burroughs Timber.

When you walk out of the dazzle of noon into a little roadside store like that, it is almost like walking into a movie theater, the darkness seems so great. By the door was a counter with a cash register on it and a man behind it, and there was a shadowy figure in the back of the store, who turned out to be a boy younger than myself, sweeping the single aisle between the shelves. And there was a figure seated to the left of the door as I came in, and on the floor, at my feet, there was a sudden lunging rush.

If you have gotten this far, you have the advantage of knowing that it was, of course, a snapping turtle, but I did not. In the South Carolina woods in the summertime, snakes are never far out of your mind, and, for the first hour of the day, you watch your step. Fatigue and distraction set in soon enough, and you forget about snakes, and you could easily go two weeks without having any particular reason to remember them. But sooner or later you would come upon one, usually a little copperhead, neatly coiled at your feet, and so perfectly merged with the shadow-dappled floor of the forest that you'd begin to worry about all the ones that you hadn't happened to see. So when I heard the hiss and the rush I jumped.

The man in the chair laughed: "Scared you, didden he? I be goddam if you didden *jump*, boy. Don't believe I ever knew a white boy to jump like that." By this time I could see what it was, a snapping turtle stretched out there on the cement floor. It was a huge one—the carapace was matted with dried algae; the head was about the size of a grapefruit. The whole creature could not have been fitted into a washtub. It looked, once I had calmed down enough to look at it, ancient and tired, as though oppressed by its own ponderous and ungainly bulk. The room was thick with a swampy, musky smell, which at the time I did not realize came from the turtle. When I smelled it again in Maine, it did not specifically recall the physical scene—the turtle, the Marlowes, the dark little store. Instead, it brought back directly a sensation of alarm, confusion, and disorientation, in about the same way that the smell of ether does not bring back the operating room so much as it brings back the vertiginous feeling of the self whirling away from itself.

The others came in right behind me. I was too mortified by my own embarrassment and disgrace to see how they reacted to the whole scene, but I think they must have enjoyed it. It had been a good joke, to place the turtle just inside the threshold like that; if it had been played on anyone else, I would have laughed myself. Billy looked down at the turtle and said he'd never seen one that big. In the corner of the evil mouth, which was gaping open, was a big hook, with a piece of heavy line attached to it. "Caught him on a trotline, I see," said Billy.

Trotlines—a short length of line tied to a branch that overhangs the water, so that the baited hook is just below the surface—were and are a common way of fishing, and they were perfectly legal for catching certain species of fish at certain times of year. But they were so widely used by poachers that to call a man a *trotliner* might, if the man were sufficiently thin-skinned, seem tantamount to an indictment. I don't know. I only know that when Billy said "trotline" the man in the chair gave him a sudden look and got up.

When he stood, he lurched and swayed, and we could see that he was ruinously drunk. He was wiry, short, and grizzled, wore knee-high rubber boots with the swamp mud still on them. He glared at Billy: "Your name ain't *McNair*, is it?" Billy said it wasn't and tried to ask the man if anything besides turtles had been biting that morning, but the man kept on: "You sure it ain't *McNair?* You sure you ain't some of them wildlife boys come down here? What you got that aerial on your truck for if you ain't?" He was right about at least that much. The company truck did have a two way radio, and it was painted yellow, which gave it an official look, but it seemed not simply ridiculous but perverse for the man to take the four of us— hot, dirty, and dressed in ordinary work clothes—for some kind of undercover squad from the Department of Fish and Wildlife.

The man behind the counter told him to shut up and sit down, but he spoke in a half-hearted way, as though he knew it were useless. The boy in the back of the store, where I'd gone to get some crackers, had stopped sweeping and gone up to the front to watch the fun. The drunk man was telling Billy exactly what he'd do to McNair if McNair ever stuck his nose in here; he got louder and louder, and seemed to be working himself into the conviction that Billy really was McNair. I got my crackers and came up to the counter. It did not occur to me that anything serious was going on, and even if it was, there was no reason to worry. The drunk man's head scarcely came to Billy's shoulder. It seemed that all of this might in some way still be part of the joke; if not, it would make a good joke to tell, how Billy Watson, of all people, had been mistaken for a game warden.

I was paying for my crackers when the man said: "Let McNair come in here and I'll show him *this*," and I looked up and he had a pistol in his hand. It came from under the counter, as I later learned—the drunk man had reached over and grabbed it when the man behind the counter had turned to the cash register.

It changed everything; the world began to slip away. I had no impulse to act, and did not exactly feel fear. It was more an instinct to call out to everybody, to say *wait a minute; how did we get here? what's going on? let's talk this over and see if we can't make sense of it.* Billy's back was to me. The pistol was a snub-nosed revolver—a heavy, ugly, blunt thing. It was as though I could see through Billy's eyes the rounded noses of the cartridges in the open ends of the cylinders. Everything was utterly distinct and utterly unreal: we were under water, or had fallen asleep and were dreaming and were struggling mightily to waken ourselves from the dream before it reached the point it was meant to reach. Nobody moved to interfere. The thing was going to take its course.

The drunk man had the pistol right in Billy's face, shaking it. His own face was white with rage. "I'd show him *this*," he said, "and *this* is what I'd do with it." He reached down so abruptly and savagely that I winced, and he snatched the turtle by the tail and dragged it out the door, onto the concrete pad beside the gas pumps. The weight of the turtle was great; the man straightened himself slowly, as though only his wrath had enabled him to haul it this far. The turtle seemed weary, deflated, too long out of water. The man nudged its head with his boot, and the turtle hissed and struck feebly toward him. The man glared down at it, letting his rage recover and build back in him. He looked like a diver, gathering to plunge. The turtle's mouth hung open; when it hissed again the man's arm suddenly jerked down with the pistol and he shot it, shattering the turtle's head. "That's what I'd do to that goddamned McNair."

The man came back in and sat down heavily, spent, and the world returned to its ordinary focus. Blood had spattered onto the man's boot and pant leg. By the time we finished buying lunch and were ready to leave, he was snoring easily. The man behind the cash register told the boy to tote that thing off into the bushes, and the boy did, dragging the turtle by the tail, the blood still welling from the smashed head. When we got back to the truck I glanced over there, not wanting to, and could see the head swarming with flies, the big feet limp in the sand.

As we were getting into the truck, Wendell (who seldom said anything) said, "Well." We looked at him. He elaborated, his face perfectly deadpan: "Well. Good thing none of them *bad* Marlowes happened to be in today."

Hannah finished filling the hole, tamped the sand smooth, and brushed her palms briskly against each other, signifying that the job was done. The dog roused himself and we all walked back up toward the house. A yellow warbler flew across in front of us a quick flash of color—perched on a willow branch, sang its hurried, wheezy song, and dropped from sight. Birdsong lasts longer into the morning on these cool, overcast days. The bobolinks were still busy about it, a song that sounds something like an audiotape being rewound at high speed. A robin in a clump of sumacs sang its careful phrase, as though for the edification of less gifted birds, then listened to itself a moment, head cocked appreciatively, then sang the phrase again. A meadowlark whistled from a fencepost. New England seemed, as it often does, more perfect in the intensity of its seasonal moment, and in the whole seasonal cycle that can be felt within the moment, than any place has a right to be. I felt the fatal parental urge, wanting to point out to Hannah all the richness that surrounded her. But to Hannah such familiar sights and sounds were equivalent to presuppositions, invisible until disturbed.

Animals fit themselves enigmatically into the secondary ecology of human thinking. "They are all beasts of burden, in a sense," says Thoreau, "made to carry some portion of our thoughts." Turtles are especially burdened. In Hindu myth, Vishnu, floating on the cosmic sea, takes the form of a tortoise and sustains the world on his back. North American Indians, unacquainted with any sizeable tortoises, nevertheless had the same myth of turtle as Atlas. The Senecans told how the first people lived in the sky, until a woman, whose transgression involved a tree, was thrown out. Below her—very far below—there was only water. A few water birds were there, and these, seeing her descending, hurried to prepare a place for her. They dived to the bottom, found mud and a turtle, and persuaded the turtle to let them place mud on its back, and make a dry spot for her to land on. The woman landed; vegetation grew up out of the mud; and the familiar world we know came into being.

But the Indians weren't through with the turtle, or vice versa. Turtle turns trickster and, disguised as a young brave, seduces the daughter of the first woman. When the daughter realizes what her lover is, she dies, and from her body, as she prophesies in dying, grow the first stalks of corn and the equivocal blessings of agriculture. Among other tribes, in other myths, Turtle continues his depredations. Many tribes tell of his going on the warpath against the first people, who at last catch him and prepare his death. They threaten him with fire; he tells them that he loves fire. They threaten him with boiling water; he begs to be put immediately into the kettle, because he so relishes being boiled. They threaten to throw him into the river. "Anything but that," says Turtle, and so they throw him in. He sticks out his snout and laughs; they curse him and throw sticks, but he easily avoids them. And so Turtle takes up,–one would surmise, the life of a snapper, coming ashore only briefly each year, seeming about as old as the earth, and spreading consternation. God knows what burden of thought the big snapper had borne for the drunk man at Yauhannah Bridge—he symbolized, I believe, a good deal more than the man's adversary, McNair.

I found myself wishing that Hannah had stumbled upon this morning's turtle herself and had confronted the potent oddity of the beast without having it all explained away for her. It might have stood a better chance then than it did now of becoming a fact in her imagination: something she would eventually remember and think about and think with from her days as a country girl. But what any child will think or remember is beyond anybody's knowing, including its own. The turtle had disappeared down the ditch; its hole had been filled. Meanwhile, Hannah let us know that we had on our hands a Tuesday morning in June, which was, with kindergarten over, a problem to be solved. Could she have a friend over? Could we go to town?

Nominated by Stanley Lindberg

AGAINST SILENCE

by MARILYN HACKER

from BOULEVARD

FOR MARGARET DELANY

Because you are
my only daughter's only grandmother,
because your only grandchild is my child
I would have wished you to be reconciled

to how and what
I live. No name frames our connection, not
"in-laws." I hoped, more than "your son's ex-wife."
I've known you now for two-thirds of my life.

You had good friends,
good books, good food, good manners, a good mind.
I was fifteen. I wished this were my home.
(None of my Jewish aunts read *I. F. Stone's*

Weekly, or shopped at Saks
Fifth Avenue, none of them grew up Black
working poor, unduped and civilized.)
I know you were unpleasantly surprised

when, eighteen, we
presented you with the *fait accompli*

81

of court-house marriage in one of two states
where no age-of-consent or miscegenat-

ion laws applied.
Your sister's Beetle—bumps knife-thrusts inside
after a midnight Bellevue D & C—
brought me uptown. You took care of me,

a vomit-green
white girl in your son's room. Had I been
pregnant? Aborted? No. Miscarried? Yes.
You didn't ask. I didn't tell, just guessed

what you knew. You
asked my mother to lunch. I'd "had the flu."
She greeted me, "Your hair looks like dog shit.
Cut it or do something to it!"

I burned with shame
you saw what kind of family I came
from. Could you imagine me more
than an unacceptable daughter-in-law?

When, fortified
I went home to the Lower East Side,
my new job, art school at night and my queer
marriage, you were, understatedly, there.

For a decade's
holidays, there was always a place
set for me, if I was in New York.
Your gifts groomed me: a dark green wool for work,

pinstriped Villager
shirts. I brought books, wine, an Irish mohair
shawl laced with velvet ribbons. I came back
from London with a kangaroo-pouch pack

containing your
exuberant golden granddaughter.

You never asked me why I lived alone
after that. Feast-days' invitation

stopped—Iva went
with her father. Evenings you spent
with friends, but normal Sundays you'd be in.
I'd call, we'd come a little before noon.

Because you did
that, Sundays, there'd be fried liver or shad
roe, or bacon, hot rolls, hash, poached eggs.
We ate while Iva tugged around our legs

the big plush bear
you gave her. From the pile beside your chair
I picked over, passed you the book reviews
in exchange for White Sales and the *News*

of the Week in
Review. Your mother, ninety-eight, deep in
somnolent cushions, eighty years' baker of rolls,
wakened by child-noise, called the child, and told

her stories
nine decades vivid, liking the rose-gold three
year old. British born, Black by law
and choice as she was, with diaspora

Virginia, Harlem;
linking me, listening beside them
with you. She died at one hundred and two
and I, childlike, took it for granted you

would certainly
be bad-mouthing Republicans with me
for two more decades' editorial page.
Seventy-four was merely middle age.

The question some
structuralist with me on a podium,

exalted past politeness, called *"idiote"*
(a schoolyard-brawl word) "For whom do you write?"

I could have answered
(although it wouldn't have occurred
to anyone to ask after that),
"I write for somebody like Margaret"

—but I'd written
names for acts and actors which, by then,
reader, you'd read, and read me out, abhorred
in print lives you'd let live behind closed doors.

You wouldn't be
in that debate, agree to disagree.
We would need time, I thought. This can resume,
like any talk, with fresh air in the room

and a fresh pot
of coffee, in the Fall. But it will not.
Some overload blocked silence in your brain.
A starched girl starts your syllables again.

You held your tongue
often enough to hear, when you were young,
and older, more than you wanted to discuss.
Some things were more acceptable, nameless.

You sometimes say
names amidst the glossolalial
paragraphs that you enunciate
now, unanswerable as, "Too late."

Baffled between
intention and expression, when your son
says, "Squeeze my hand, once for 'no', twice for 'yes',"
you squeeze ten times, or none, gratuitous.

A hemisphere
away from understanding where you are,

mourning your lost words, I am at a loss
for words to name what my loss of you is,
what it will be, or even what it was.

Nominated by Josephine Jacobsen

THE SAFETY PATROL

fiction by MICHAEL MARTONE

from CRESCENT REVIEW

IF YOU LOOK on page 253 of the New College Edition of *The American Heritage Dictionary*, there, in the right margin toward the bottom of the page, you will find an aerial photograph of a cloverleaf interchange at Fort Wayne, Indiana.

Of the six cloverleaf interchanges in Fort Wayne, I am reasonably sure I know which one this is. It is not my favorite. That one is down the road. There, there was a small country cemetery right where the new interstate was going to go. I was on the citizen's committee that saved the place. You can still see it buried beneath the loops and ramps as they detour, twisted out of the way like a spring sprung. On some Sundays, I drive out there, drive around the place, entering and exiting. The interchange spreads for miles. I catch glimpses of the headstones—they're old, from before the Civil War—the patch of prairie grass and wild flowers, the picket fence. It is in the middle of the storm of concrete and cars. Saved. But there is no way to drive to it. All access limited, the site undisturbed. Like clouds the shadows of trucks sail over the plots, change the color of the stones.

The cloverleaf pictured in the dictionary is a perfect specimen. There has been no finagling with the curving lobes of the ramp as they coil from one dual lane to the other. If you look closely you can see snow in the ditch defining the mathematical berms, shading the grade, giving it depth and perspective. A beautiful picture, one the children are proud of.

When we do dictionary drills I include the word *cloverleaf* as a kind of crackerjack prize for the students. They cut into the big book as I've taught them, into the first third. Some feel comfortable using the finger tabs scooped out along the edge. They turn chunks of pages, getting close, getting to C. They peel each page back, then read the index words *close call* and *clown*, saying the alphabet for each letter. And then, one by one, they arrive at the right page. Fingers go up and down columns. One or two gasp, then giggle. They point and whisper. They say things like wow. They can't wait to tell me what they've found.

The cloverleaf is there with pictures of a clothestree, a clown licking an ice cream cone, a clover—the plant and its buds—the cloister of San Marco in Florence, Italy, an earthworm with a clitellum, and the clipper ship *Lightning*. The pictures seem to make the words they represent more important.

The lights on the television and radio towers are always on even during the day when you can barely see the flush of the red lights. The newer towers have bright strobing lights too. You see sharp simultaneous explosions all along the edges. There are revolving lights at the very tip. Guy wires angle down so taut as to vibrate the heavy air around the towers. There are a dozen at least now, and more going up. The neighborhood is zoned for towers.

I like to play games while I look at the towers. Which one is taller? Which is furthest away? Coming up State Street on my way to teach, I watch the towers as I drive. They are solid lines, the lights slowly coming into sychronization. I am waiting for a red light, watching over the cars ahead of me down the road. Each tower is beating its own red pulse. Two or three pulse together a time or two. Then they drift apart, align with other tower lights. I know if I watch long enough, if I am lucky enough and happen to glance at the right time, I'll see all the lights on all the towers switch on and off at the very same moment.

The closer I get to the towers, the more lacey they become. The lattice is like a kid's picture of lightning shooting down the sides. I've been to the root of some of the towers, and they are balanced at a single point on a concrete slab. There the metal flares out in an inverted pyramid, then up slightly, tapered really, but coming together anyway past the red twirling light at the top of the lone antenna pointing to a distant vanishing point.

The closer I get to the towers the more air they become. They disappear. The red and white curtain of color where they are painted in intervals hangs in the air. The lights are nearly invisible in the sun. At that certain distance, when they disappear, it is like the red line of mercury in a thermometer held slightly off center.

I used to worry about the houses that have been built beneath the towers. They are starter homes, small, shaped like monopoly houses, the colors of game tokens, glossy blues and reds and greens and yellows with trim a shade darker but the same color. The trees are puny and new, fast-growing ginkos and Lombardy poplars quaking in the breeze and spraying up like the towers way above them. The houses are scattered and crowded onto cul-de-sacs and terraces like an island village. The addition is called Tower Heights. The guy wires from the towers anchor in backyards in dead eyes and turnbuckles the sizes of automobiles. They are fenced off and landscaped with climbing flowers. The lines of one tower can slip beneath the lines of another, over still another so that the houses and yards are sewn up in a kind of net of cables arriving from the sky.

My students say the towers groan sometimes in storms. The wires twang. They tell me they like to lie looking up at the clouds sailing above the towers. The towers move against the clouds. They sway and topple. On a clear day, the shadows cast by the towers sweep over the houses in single file. My students take to geometry, all the lines and angles, acute, right, obtuse, the triangles, the compass point of the towers, the parallel lines. When I pull the blinds up on the window of my classroom, there, off in the distance, are the towers and wires. The roofs of their houses are just visible, a freehand line drawn beneath the proof.

The children this year have been very well-behaved. It is something we've all noticed and commented on in the lounge. The women think it's me. I am the only man. I teach sixth grade and take most of the gym classes. I have the basketball team. The Safety Patrol is my responsibility.

It is crazy but I am in love with all of these women in the school. Miss A, Miss B, Miss C, Miss D, Miss E, Miss F, Miss H, Miss I, Miss J, Miss K, and Miss L who teaches kindergarten. The principal, Miss M. The nurse, N, who visits twice a week, I first met during hearing tests this fall. The children were listening to earphones, curling and uncurling their index fingers in response to the pure tone. The music teacher Miss O. The art instructor Miss P.

How did I get here? It is difficult to say. But with each it seemed natural enough. Each relationship has a life of its own.

There is a lot of locker room talk in the lounge and during staff meetings. When we meet in a group I'm ignored, taken for granted, as they search around inside their brown bags for the apple, rinse the flatware in the sink. They talk about their boyfriends. In all cases that would be me they are talking about. None knows of my other affairs. When they yak about love they do so casually so as not to let on to the others, to tease me with this our inside joke. Their candor protects them, renders me harmless; their wantonness deflects suspicion from the room.

It is exciting. I share a preparation time with Miss D. We smooch for the half hour in the lounge. The coffee perks. Our red pens capped. On the playground Miss C chases me playfully, jogging, then sprinting. The children are playing tether ball, box ball. They're screaming. She always almost catches me. Our classes in the lavatory, I hold hands for a second with Miss G as we lean against the yellow tile brick in the hall. She turns her body around, presses her face against the cool wall. I haven't been compromised since none of them wants to be discovered. If am alone with one, the others leave us alone because the only time any one of them wants to be with me is when she can be alone with me. I love the moment when we all step out in the hall, look at each other and step back in the classroom drawing the door behind us to begin teaching that day.

I am the only man, but I don't think that has much to do with the discipline of the children. Perhaps there is something in the air. It's history I think. I like teaching history, geography, health, the big wide books which contain all of the pictures. You know the old saying about history: study history or you're doomed to repeat it. That's all wrong I think. You study it *and* you are doomed to repeat it. Maybe even more so because you study what's happened. Get to know it and it's like it's already happened. It is the same story over and over. It is time once again for kids to raise their hands, part their hair, say please and thank you, follow directions. That's all.

The Safety Patrol is in the rain. The streets are slick with oily rainbows, pooled. The gutters are full, flowing. The rain is soaking, steady. They are wearing bright yellow slickers. The water sheets down them. The bills of their yellow caps are pulled down flat between their eyes, hard against their noses like the gold helmets of heavy cavalry. Then snaps are snapped beneath their chins. Their chins are tucked into their dryer chests. The flaps cover their ears, cheeks, necks. The claw fasteners shimmer down the fronts of their coats. They've polished them. They wear black rubber boots over their shoes. They stand in puddles, take the spray from passing cars without moving, their arms fixed at the proper angles, holding back the antsy students pressing to cross the streets into school.

The belts are orange, cinched tight over the shoulder, tight across the chest, over the heart, all buckled at the waist. The pools in the street turn red with the traffic light's light. The orange belts ignite as the headlights of the cars strike across them. For the instant it is just the belt floating without a body like the belt is bone in an x-ray.

The bells ring. We close the doors. Outside the patrol stays on the corners in case someone is tardy. Their heads pivot slowly checking all directions. Their faces sparkle. There are worms everywhere on the sidewalks. The tower lights are juicy. Then from somewhere I can't see, I hear the clear call of the Captain. "Off do tee." He calls again in the other direction, fainter. "Off do tee." Each syllable held a long time. Then the lieutenants at the far ends of the school repeat the same phrasing. The patrols leave the corners one by one, covering each other's moves as they all safely cross the wet streets and come into school.

Each year I do a sociogram of my class. It helps me get a picture of how it all fits together, who the leaders are, who follow, which ones are lonely or lost, who are forgotten. I ask questions. Who in the class is your best friend, your worst enemy? Who is most like a sister, a brother? Who would you never tell a secret to? Who would you ask for help? Who is the strongest? Who would you help? If a boy and a girl were drowning who would you save if you could only save one? Who would you give part of your lunch to? Who would you pick to be on your team in gym class? Who would you want to pick you? Who makes you laugh? Who makes you mad? If someone told you a secret and told you not to tell it to anyone in the class who would you tell it to? Who do you miss during summer vacations? Who would you want to call you on the telephone? Who do you walk home with? Who would you walk home with if you could? If you could rename the school who would you name it after? If you are a girl, which boy would you like to be just for a little while? If you are a boy, which girl would you like to be just for a little while? If something has to be done in class, who would you ask? Who would you want to do your homework? Who would you want to teach you a new game? Who ignores you? If you ran away, who would you send a letter to? If you were in the hospital, who would you want to see most? If you were afraid and by yourself in the dark, who would you call out for? The children like this test because they know the answers. They sneak looks at each other as they work. Their pencils wag.

I collect the data, assign values, note names. I graph responses, plot intersections. I never question their honesty. I can map out grudges and feuds, old loves, lingering feelings, all the tribal bonds and property disputes, the pecking order, the classes in the class.

And then I have conferences with the parents. We sit on the downsized chairs. I cast out the future for their son or daughter in the language of talk shows. I dissect the peer pressure, explain the forces at work. The parents want to know about change. Is this set in stone? Can my son be a leader, a professional? Will my daughter grow up to like men? I tell them that it's hard to say, that the children are all caught up in a vast machine of beliefs and of myths. It is of this group's own making. These responses are almost instinctual now, I tell the parents. Each class has its own history, its own biology, its own math and logic. I'm just presenting what's what.

I know now who leads the class and who operates in the shadows. I know where the power is and the anguish, who shakes down who, what favors are owed, who might turn a gun on his friends, on himself.

I ask those same questions of myself. I answer Miss A, Miss B, Miss C, Miss D, and so on. Who do I trust? Who would I want to go home with? I wish I could ask the women as well, but the results would be skewed.

There is no place to stand, no distance. Skewed.

The Safety Patrol is in the hallway of the school before and after classes and at lunchtime. Inside, they wear the white cloth belts they launder. A bronze pin, given by the Chicago Motor Club is attached where the belt begins to arch over the shoulder, the collar bone.

There is no running in the hall. The Patrol patrols up and down, one stationed every two or so classrooms. Stay on the right side of the hall. There is a red dashed line painted on the floor. The Patrol stands at ease, straddles the line. The small children move along cautiously, try not to look around. There is a bottleneck near the piano on rollers that moves from classroom to classroom with the music teacher, Miss O. The piano is pushed, keys first, against the wall. The bench is flipped on top of the upright. The legs point up like a cartoon of a dead animal. Handles are screwed on the side for easier moving. Something spills out of the intercom only the teachers can understand. Loose squares of construction paper stapled on the bulletin boards lift and fall as kids pass by.

A Safety Patrol will speak. "What's your name?" and everyone in the hall will stop. "Yes, you," the Safety Patrol will say. Each member of the Safety Patrol can always see at least two other members. Their bright white belts cut across plaids and prints. They are never out of each other's sight.

They have arrayed themselves this way on their own, without my help. The Captain and his lieutenants have posted schedules, worked out posts and their rotation. The Safety Patrol is on the corners of Tyler and State and on the corners of Tyler and Rosemount, and one is at the crossing on Stetler with the old crossing guard who has the STOP sign he uses as a crook. A Patrol walks with a passel of kindergarteners all the way to Spring Street, almost a mile, to push the button on the automatic signal. He eats his lunch on the corner and walks the afternoon students back to school. A lone Patrol guards the old railroad tracks that separate the school from Tower Heights. There are Patrols at each door into the building. They are strung through the halls. There, I've seen them straightening the reproductions of famous paintings the PTA has donated. They watch over the drinking fountains. They turn lights out in empty classrooms. They roust stragglers from the restrooms.

I want my students to copy each other's work. It is a theory of mine. I've put the slower ones in desks right next to the ones who get it. I've told them that it is all right by me if they ask their neighbors for the answers, fine too for the neighbors to tell.

They want to know if they own their answers.

They want to know what happens if they don't want to tell.

Fair questions. I see them covering their papers with their hands and arms as they go along, turning their backs on the copier.

"What are you protecting?" I ask them. Students can't break the habits they have of cheating. They look out of the corners of their eyes. They whisper. They sneak. They drop pencils on the floor.

They don't get this, my indifference. My indulgence. If they would ask me I would tell them the answers but it never occurs to them to ask me.

We are doing European Wars—The Peloponnesian. The Punic. The Sackings. The One Hundred Years, The Thirty Years. We are studying an Eskimo girl and a boy from Hawaii. Our newest states. We are doing First Aid. We are doing the Solar System. We are doing New Math. We spell every Wednesday and Friday. We read "A Man Without a Country."

We have taken a field trip to one of the television stations to appear on the Engineer John Show, a show that airs in time for the kids coming home from school. Engineer John dresses like a railroad engineer—pin striped bib overalls, red neckerchief, crowned hat, a swan-necked oil can, big gloves. Really he is the other type of engineer who works with the transmitters, the wires, the towers, the kind in broadcasting, during the rest of the day. As a personality, he is cheap. He introduces Sgt. Preston movies and Hercules cartoons and short films provided by the AFL-CIO called *Industry on Parade* that show milk bottles filling on assembly lines or toasters being screwed together. There are no people in the films. The students love the show, especially the factories of machines building other machines. They think Engineer John is a clown like Bozo, who is on another station, since they don't know what the costume means. To us in the studio audience he talked about electricity while the films ran on the monitors. He talked about the humming we heard.

Later, we wound through the neighborhood in a yellow bus dwarfed by the towers, dropping students at their houses. I sat in the back of the bus next to the Emergency Door with Miss J. holding her hand and rubbing her leg. We both looked straight ahead. Squeezed.

The Safety Patrol made sure the windows did not drop below the lines, that hands and heads and arms stayed inside. The Captain whispered directions to the driver. The STOP sign arm extended every time we stopped. All the lights flashed as if we had won something.

Every year there is a city-wide fire drill. All the schools, public and parochial, evacuated simultaneously. An insurance company provides red badges for the children, the smaller children wear fire hats. They are sent home with a checklist of hazards and explore their houses. Piles of rags and papers. Pennies in the fuse box. Paint cans near the water heater. I know they watch as their parents smoke. They inventory matches. They plan escapes from every room, crawl along floors. They touch doors quickly to see if they are hot before they open them. Extension cords. They set fire to their own pajamas.

In school they discuss their findings with each other, formed up in circles of chairs. They draw posters. They do skits.

On the day of the drill a fire company visited. Their pumper was in the parking lot gleaming. A radio station, WOWO, broadcast messages from the Chief and the Mayor and the Superintendant. These were piped through to our classroom. A voice counted down the time to the moment when a little girl in a Lutheran elementary school this year would throw the switch and all the buzzers and bells in every other school would ring. Of course, this drill is never a surprise. That's not the point. Usually the alarm just sounds, and those assigned to close the windows close the windows. They turn out the lights. They leave everything. My students form into a single file, are quiet for instructions, no shoving, no panic, know by heart where to go, what area of the playground to collect in, how to turn and watch the school, listen for the all clear or the distant wail of sirens.

I arrive at school in the dark. The Safety Patrol is already sowing salt along the sidewalks. Their belts quilt their heavy overcoats. They are scooping sand from the orange barrel that is stored at an angle in a wooden frame on the corner with the little hill. The Captain watches over the dim streets as others spread the sand in sweeping arcs. Going by, the few cars crush the new snow. In the still air, I can clearly hear them chopping ice and shoveling the snow.

* * *

I gave all the women sample-sized bottles of cheap perfume I bought at the Woolworth's. Their desks were covered with tiny packages wrapped in color comics and aluminum foil, gifts from their students. I smelled the musky odor everywhere in the school for months later.

Miss I sent me a note one day. A fifth grader, one size too small, handed it up to me. It was on lined notebook paper. Three of the five holes ruptured when she pulled it from the ringed notebook in the beautiful blue penmanship many of the women have. *Do you like me? Yes or No.* She had drawn in little empty squares behind yes and no. The fifth grader waited nervously just outside the door. My class in the middle of base two watched me as I filled in the yes square and folded up the paper. I sealed it with a foil star, sent the child back to the room. My own students watched me closely. I knew they were trying to guess what what I did meant.

I thought I saw them all blink at the same time. I couldn't be sure since I can't see all the eyes at once but it was a general impression, a feeling, a sense I had, a moment totally my own in my classroom when what I did was not observed.

In the lounge the smell of the perfume is strongest, overpowering the cool purple smell of mimeograph, the gray cigarette smoke, the green mint breath, the brown crushed smell of the wet Fort Howard paper towels.

Miss A has drawn our initials, big block printing, in her right palm, stitched together with a plus sign. Her hands are inscribed with whorls and stars, marks against cooties and answers to problems. If I just touch her she thrills and titters, runs and hides, rubbing her body all over with her streaked hands.

In Fort Wayne we say there are more cars *per capita* than in any other city in the United States except Los Angeles. I believe it when I am caught in traffic on State Street. Up ahead are the school and the axle factory and a little beyond them the towers. We creep along one to a car through a neighborhood built after the War. All the houses have shutters with cutouts of sailboats or moons or pine trees.

I drive a Valiant. I shift gears by pushing buttons on the dash, an idea that didn't catch on.

In the middle of the intersection I am waiting to turn across the oncoming lane. The Safety Patrol watches me, knows my funny old car. It has no seat belts. The way they hold their hands, their heads, it's like a crucifixion. Their faces are fixed.

I am stopped again by the crossing guard in the street. He leans heavily on the striped dazzling pole. I have seen him swat the hoods of cars that have come too close. The Safety Patrol is behind him funneling the children along the crosswalk of reflecting paint smeared in slashes on the street.

The guard has told me a story that may be true. He says when he was a boy he saw his kid brother die at the first traffic light in Fort Wayne. The light had no yellow, only the green and red flags snapping up and down. The boys knew what it meant, crossed with the light, but the driver came on through, peeled the one brother from the other. It was a time, the guard has said, when signs meant nothing.

He has played in the street. When he was a boy, he told me, he played in the street, Calhoun, Jefferson, highways now, throwing a baseball back and forth with his brother. They didn't have to move all day. He drove cattle down Main Street, cows home to be milked twice a day, then back out to pasture.

He remembers when all the land the school is on and all the land around was a golf course, and before that a swamp. All of this was a swamp, he says.

I like old things. I like the old times. It doesn't take long for things to get old. Everything seems to have been here all along but often it is not old.

Our principal tells us one day there will be no students, the neighborhood is aging, running out of babies, but there is no evidence of that. The school is teeming every year, spontaneous generation. We do that old experiment each year in the spring. The cheesecloth over the spoiled and the rotting meat grows its fur of maggots, the children love this.

Getting out of my car in the parking lot I am almost hit by something. It zips by my ear. Something skitters across the pavement. Nearby Miss F flings acorns my way, brazils, cashews, mixed nuts. When we're alone she pinches me long and hard, won't let up, kicks me on the shins. She bites when we kiss. She says she likes me, she doesn't mean to hurt me. She wants me so much she wants to eat me up.

This is an elementary school. The sprawling one story was built in the 1950's with Indiana limestone, a flat roof, and panels in primary colors. Its silhouette is reminiscent of the superstructures of the last luxury liners—The SS United States, the *France*—streamlined with false ledges and gutters trailing off the leeward edges giving the illusion of swift movement.

The Safety Patrol makes a big deal of raising and lowering the flag. Three or four members and always an officer parade out in the courtyard. There are salutes and an exaggerated hand-over-hand as the flag that flew over the Nation's Capitol goes up and down. They fold the flag in the prescribed way, leaving, when done properly, that pastry of stars which one of them holds over his or her breast.

Finally you can never be emotionally involved with any of this. That's a fact, not a warning.

This is an elementary school. The children move on. I have their homeroom assignments for junior high school. It's all alphabetical from now on. I come to the school believing it is some kind of sacred precinct. Teachers are fond of saying how much we learn from the children, how when we paddle, it will hurt us more than it will hurt them. Tests test what? What was learned or how it was taught? Children are like any other phenomenon in nature.

The first steps in the scientific methods according to the book are to observe, collect data. An hypothesis would be an intimate act. All the experiments would be failures. I know my job. I am supposed to not know more than I do now. No research. I repeat each year the elemental knowledge I embody, the things I learned a long time ago.

I watch the seasons change on the bulletin boards. I take down the leaves for the turkeys and the Pilgrims, and the leaves leave a shadow of their shapes burned into the yellow and orange and brown construction paper. The sun faded the background. The stencils and straight pins, colored tacks and yarns, the cotton ball snow, the folded doily flakes, no two alike. The eggshell flowers are in the spring. The grass cut into a fringe on a stripe of green paper is curled bluntly through the scissors. The summer is cork.

* * *

The Safety Patrol folds its belts like flags. At the end of the school day they are sitting at their desks folding their belts to store them away. The other children have already been ferried across the streets. It is like a puzzle or trying to fold a map. The trick is to master the funny angle of the crossing belt, the adjusting slides, the heavy buckle. It's like folding parachutes. They leave the packets in the center of their desktops the bronze pin on top of each.

I go home and watch the Engineer John Show. There are so many kinds of people that exist now only on TV—milkmen, nuns in habit, people who live in lighthouses, newsboys who yell "Extra". Engineer John arrives with the sound of a steam engine.

We know that tornadoes when they happen are supposed to sound like freight trains. It is spring and the season for tornadoes, which Fort Wayne is never supposed to endure according to an old Indian belief, still repeated, that the three rivers ward them off. We will drill. The students sit Indian fashion under their desks, backs to the windows. Or in the hall the bigger children cover their smaller brothers and sisters.

During our visit, Engineer John told us about the ground. How electricity goes back to it, finds it. I thought of the towers as a type of well. These pictures gushing from the field, a rich deposit. The electrons pump up and down the shafts.

In storms, the children say they watch the lightning hit the towers. They turn their sets off and watch. The towers are sometimes up inside the clouds. The clouds light up like lampshades. I think a lot of people watch the towers, know which windows in their houses face that way. They sit up and watch when the storm keeps them awake. Or when they can't sleep in general, maybe they stare out at all the soothing, all the warning lights.

The sixth grade girls are gathered in one room to watch the movie even I have never seen. I have the boys. They are looking up words in the dictionary. I tell them that dictionaries have very little to do with spelling but with history, with where the word comes from, how long it has been used and understood.

Miss K calls me out in the hall. The doors are closed and she leads me to the nearest girls' restroom and pulls me inside. I always feel funny in the wrong washroom, hate to open the door even to yell in "Hurry up" to my girls who are just beginning to use makeup and are dawdling over the sinks and mirrors.

We cram into the furthest stall, and Miss K unbuttons her dress which has her initials embroidered on her collar—AMR. We have played doctor before in the nurse's room where there are screens, couches, and gowns. There are even some cold metal instruments ready on a towel. She is in her underwear when we hear the doors wheeze, and someone comes in. A far stall door clicks closed and we hear the rustle of clothes and the tinkle. Miss K worms around me, crouches down to look beneath the partition. Elastic snaps.

The flush. We hear hands being washed in the sink, dried on paper towels.

When we're alone again Miss K finishes undressing. She clutches pieces of her clothes in each hand, covers her body and then quickly opens her arms. She lets me look at her, turns around lifting her hands over her head, clothes spilling down, taking rapid tiny steps in place. She tucks her clothes into the wedge of her elbows, hugging the bundle next to her breast, her bronze nipple. She reaches down between her legs with her other hand watching me as she does so, trying not to giggle. Then she shows me her hand. There is some blood on her fingers, she thinks it is so funny. She couldn't sit through the movie.

Perhaps all of the women in the school are bleeding at the same moment, at this moment, by chance or accident, through sympathy, gravity, vibration. It's possible. It could be triggered by suggestion, by a school year of living out blocks of time, flow sheets, periods of periods, drinking the same water, breathing the same air. And what if it had happened, is happening? Would it be any worse if the planets all aligned or if everyone in the world jumped up in the air at the same time. The school, a little worse for wear a few days each month, tense, cramped, even horny, a word my students always giggle at. And now that some of them are alone with dictionaries I know they are looking up all the words they've never said and know they should never say.

The bright yellow tractors are back cutting the grass around the school. The litter in the lawn is mulched and shot out the side with the clippings. The driver takes roughly a square pattern, conforming to the shape of the lawn, the patches fitting inside each other. The green stripe is a different shade depending upon the angle of the light—flat green, the window of cut grass and the bright lush grass still standing. The tractors emit those bleating sounds when they back up, trimming around trees.

I see all of this through my wall of windows. The Safety Patrol on their corners cover their ears as the tractors come near. I can see them shouting to the other children, waving at them, yanking them around. Their voices lost in the roar of the mowers. They mean to take the shrapnel of shredded branches, stones, crushed brick, the needles of grass into their own bodies. An heroic gesture they must have learned from television.

The word carnival means the putting away of flesh according to *The American Heritage Dictionary.* I feel as if no one knows this as I thread through the crowded school halls.

Parents and neighbors and high school kids have come to the carnival. We're just trying to raise money for audio visual equipment, tumbling apparati, maybe buy a few more trees. The students are here, many with their faces painted like clowns, one of the attractions. Some fifth graders are following me around since they have learned I'll be their teacher next year.

They're drinking drinks that a fast food place donates. Their lips and tongues are orange or purple or red or a combination of those colors. Underfoot a carpet of popcorn pops where we walk. The floors are papered with discarded spin art and scissored silhouettes. People are wearing lighter clothes, brighter clothes. They form clots in the hall, push and shove. Children are crying or waving long strips of the blue tickets above their heads, hitting others as they go by. It is a job, this having fun.

Each room has a different game run by the teachers and room mothers. I am floating from one place to the other, bringing messages and change, tickets and cheap prizes. One room has the fish pond. I see the outline of Miss B working furiously behind the white sheet attaching prizes to the hooks. Children are on the other side of the sheet holding long tapering bamboo poles. In another room is the candy wheel. Another has a plastic pool filled with water and identical plastic ducks. There are rooms where balls are tossed at hoops and silver bottles. There is the cake walk. One room is even a nursery where mothers are nursing or changing their babies. In all the rooms are the cards of letters—Aa Bb Cc Dd Ee some in cursive Aa Bb Cc Dd Ee with tiny arrows indicating the stroke of the pen. There are green blackboards, cloak rooms, the same clock, the drinking fountain and the illuminated EXIT sign over the door.

In the cafetorium adults are having coffee. Children are rolling in the mats. Pigs in Blankets are being served, beans, Jello. Up on the stage behind the heavy curtains is the Spook House. Four tickets. There is a long line.

In the dark you are made to stumble and fall. Strings and crepe streamers propelled by fans whip your face. There are tugs on your clothes, your shoes, your fingers. There are noises, growls, shrieks, laughs. Things are revealed to you, such as heads in boxes, spiders, skulls, chattering teeth. All the time you can hear the muttering of the picnic outside damped by the curtain, the thrumming of conversation. And your eyes just get used to the dark when you come upon a table set with plates each labeled clearly: Eyeballs, Fingers, Guts, Hearts, Blood, Brains. You can see clearly now the cocktail onions, the chocolate pudding, the ketchup, the Tootsie rolls, the rice, everything edible. The tongue, tongue. Someone is whispering over and over "touch it, touch it." And it's hard to, even though you know what these things really are. Or you want to because you know you never would touch the real things.

I go outside up on the roof, I have the key, to sneak a smoke. The Safety Patrol is out in the parking lot. The towers are sputtering off in the distance. For a couple of tickets you take a couple swings with a sledge hammer at an old car. The car looks very much like mine.

The glass is all removed, the sharp edges. It only looks dangerous. The sound reaches me a heartbeat after I see the hammer come down. People like the thin metal of the roof, the hood and trunk, the fine work around the head and tail lights. The grill splinters. The door that covers the gas cap is a favorite target.

The Safety Patrol rings the crumpled car holding back the watching crowd a prudent distance. Their belts together are a kind of Hounds Tooth pattern. In the moonlight the metal of the car shines through the dented enamel and catches fire. The car has been spray painted with dares and taunts. A blow takes the hammer through the door and there is chanting. Again. Again. Again. And the Safety Patrol joins hands.

Nominated by Marianne Boruch

THE IMPORTANCE
OF PLOT

by DIANE JOHNSON

from THE THREEPENNY REVIEW

THOSE OF US who are serious readers or writers are apt to share a certain guilty feeling about reading an engrossing novel, if indeed we can find one. There are certainly people who feel no such guilt. One sees them on trains and planes, raptly absorbed in something by Sidney Sheldon or Stephen King, oblivious to the social and intellectual condescension they have invited by this shameless reading. It's irrelevant whether we would strike up a conversation with someone reading Sidney Sheldon—the question is would they want to break off their clearly great enjoyment of a good read to talk to us. No. We, tensely clutching our Nadine Gordimer, our collected letters of Flaubert, leaf fitfully through our books, eyes restively darting up, hoping the movie will come on, looking for the drinks cart.

Writers are told not to consider the reader. Think of art or money. Yet surely every writer asks herself, himself, what the secret is of engrossing the reader. I know as a writer I ask myself that. However much we may construe the purpose of writing as being to express, or to comment, or to create a formal whole, it is inevitably also to be read and, somehow, liked. Oh dear yes, as Forster said: the novel tells a story, but Forster was almost the last person to say so, and one hears his tone of apologetic regret, while educated readers regularly complain that novels aren't as wonderful, or something—they hardly know what—as they used to be. Someone told me, of my recent novel *Persian Nights,* that he had admired it, adding "and it's also good!" I was complimented, of course, but also sympathetic, for as a reader I'm happy to find something good, or, as I suppose as he meant, readable. It tells a story. It's true that the more we read, the more sophisticated we are as readers, the more we are unable to enjoy certain clumsy or obvious airplane novels. It takes more to please us—more intelligence from the writer, basically— but that doesn't stop us from wanting to be pleased. Walter Benjamin has pointed out that "the greater the decrease in the social significance of an art form, the sharper the distinction between criticism and enjoyment by the public." As a novelist, you know what he means, and you'd like to find a way of being enjoyed, and with enjoyment there might be some hope of restoring the novel to its influence.

I think the novel's loss of influence has to do with the loss of plot. How is it that the idea of story, and particularly of plot, has become so discredited that a respectable novelist denies having one? Here's an excerpt from a recent interview with Wright Morris:

Interviewer (Olga Carlisle): To this day your fiction is considered experimental. Critics have never had an easy time fitting you into any particular group or movement. How do you see yourself? Do you consider yourself a story teller?

Morris: I can tell a story and often do, but it has never occurred to me to "plot" one. If I'd taken writing courses, as is done today, someone would surely have instructed me in plotting, but I doubt that the advice would have been taken. In practice I had discovered that a narrative could be sustained without plotting, and I have held to that practice.

Interviewer: Since you don't plot, what is it that carries you forward in the narrative?

And Morris goes on to explain how he arrived at the story—we might say plot—of Bundy and his dog. It is the word "plot" which he has learned to abhor. "There is a narrative line, but no plot," he insists. "I accept what happens—what occurs to me—and imagine an appropriate resolution."

Is there some way that the serious writer can acknowledge and go back to plot; and the serious reader can find, again, enjoyable books in the sense that the books of childhood were enjoyable, in the days when one found oneself wrapped up, heart nearly stopped, in the excitement and suspense of a wonderful story? To try to answer this, I found myself turning to—reading engrossedly—some readable popular nineteenth-century novels, hoping to get at the mystery of plot, to ask what it is, and why it has fallen into disrepute, and whether or not it might be a more essential component of fiction than we have been thinking. I'm going to suggest—but am by no means able to prove—that plotting is *the* essential artistic activity in fiction, and an important, innate ingredient—a dynamic property generated, as it were, in the spaces between the words, invisible but powerful, and something that happens to the reader. Without plot, fiction is collapsing into smaller and smaller units—it's starving to death. Each generation of little story gets smaller and smaller, like plants grown in poor soil, or fleas left in the carpet.

E. M. Forster, in his influential *Aspects of the Novel*—still one of the few books about writing that is written from what one might term the writer's point of view—made a well-known and I think misleading distinction between plot and story: story is sequential and plot emphasizes causation. In the process Forster perpetuates attitudes which are implicit in the two words "plot" and "story." A story is an innocent tale, such as those we began to hear at our mother's knee (and only incidentally a little lie), and goes "and then, and then, and then," while plot smacks of the illicit, over-complicated, unnaturally contrived. To tell the story of what happened implies historical truth while to tell the plot is to separate out the elements of gratuitous ingenuity from the character interest, beautiful language, or whatever else. I wish to contend that the activity of plotting, the ingenuity of the writer, is as essential an artistic activity as the selection of the *mot juste* or the supplying of, say, motivation to the character, and may be more important.

In this connection, I am going to talk about, among others, Wilkie Collins, the nineteenth-century detective story writer, and his use of plot in the disapproved sense of a story with whatever elements of gratuitous ingenuity the writer can devise. Collins, talking of his own work, made another distinction that may be helpful in trying to get at, first of all, what plot is. Most novels, he said, were studies of the effect of events on character. His sort of novel—he didn't call it a novel of plot, but others did, or called them "sensational novels"— was interested in the effect of character on events. Upon examination, this probably flippant inversion does serve to describe something more about the novel of plot. Collins is alluding to a debate that raged among the Victorians themselves, and among the French dramatists, and indeed has raged since Aristotle, between the sensationalists, so called, and the anti-sensationalists. Aristotle of course was a sensationalist. He believed foremost in plot—"action," as he called it.

The classical novel of character, anti-sensational—we'll think of *Emma*—describes the effect of events, of misunderstandings and embarrassments, on the character of an immature, rather bossy young woman. To be sure she has herself caused some of the events: the relation of character and event is inevitably circular. But the direction of the action is toward Emma's change in character. She learns to be better. The novels of Collins (he is right) and the novels of Trollope, Charles Reade, Sheridan LeFanu, some of Dickens, and of other nineteenth-century novelists we classify as readable, plotted, and probably, except for Dickens, minor, have the opposite propensity. A character, evil or stubborn or honorable or fiercely independent, because of this trait, sets in motion a series of events. Think of the rigid Jeanie Dean's religious scruples, in *The Heart of Midlothian*, which do not permit her to stretch the truth to save her condemned sister's life. Or, to take less familiar examples, I'll be talking about Wilkie Collins' novels *The Dead Secret*, a bad novel, and *No Name*, quite a good one. (*The Moonstone* would be a familiar example; but I wish to begin with the bad novel of plot, these bad relations that have given the good novel of plot a bad name.) The novel of plot seems more apt than the novel of character (if I may persist with this old-fashioned distinction) to go awry, and the point is that while good characters cannot rescue a book that has a ridiculous plot, the reverse is not true: a good plot can carry a book where the characters are pale or conventional.

In *The Dead Secret*, Sarah, a maidservant with prematurely white hair, is entrusted with a secret at the deathbed of her mistress, who compels her to promise, under the threat of being haunted forever, to deliver a letter to her husband, after her death, which will reveal a dreadful secret. The maidservant, for reasons we do not know (but soon can, alas, imagine all too easily), is unwilling to disclose the secret, and she finds a reason, in the wording of the promise to her dead mistress, to hide the document rather than deliver it by hand. She hides it in some floorboards of the house, hides the key, and vanishes. Collins would have us believe that events are set in motion by the defects in Sarah's intelligence and understanding: "the oath which had been proposed by Mrs. Treverton under no more serious influence than the last caprice of her disordered faculties, had been accepted by Sarah Leeson as the most sacred and inviolable engagement to which she could bind herself. The threat of enforcing obedience to her last commands from beyond the grave, which the mistress had uttered in mocking experiment on the superstitious fears of the maid, now hung darkly over the weak mind of Sarah, as a judgment which might descend on her, visibly and inexorably, at any moment of her future life." Riddled with superstitious fears and later by other scruples— "under no circumstances could she have expected to remain in her situation, now that the connection between herself and her mistress had been severed by death. . . . could she accept protection and kindness at the hand of the master whom she had been accessory to deceiving still?"—Sarah disappears. Time passes. Rosamund, the little daughter of Captain and Mrs. Treverton, is now eighteen and has just married her childhood sweetheart, Leonard Frankland, despite his having been recently blinded. His family has bought the house where Rosamund grew up, and where the secret letter is still hidden. A mysterious nurse appears, her head always covered with a veil or scarf. She tries to warn the young couple away from the house, naturally strengthening their resolve to go back. . . .

Collins' contemporaries complained that the mystery is not mysterious: "The book has sufficient interest to make you read it, but not sufficient to make you regret the revelation of the secret when it comes at last." "He makes his secret as if it were a pancake, and keeps tossing it about from one pan to the other, and hiding it, and seeking it, and missing it, and getting nearer to it, and farther from it again, till at last the poor thing is scrabbled over with incident and description, as if it had been raked with a small-toothed comb, and still we do not know what it is, and when we do know, we feel inclined to say 'Oh, is that all?' "

The Dead Secret is an unsuccessful novel because the plot, to the modern reader at least, is absurd. You have guessed that Rosamund turns out to be the daughter not of the dead Mrs. Treverton but of the servant Sarah, the babies having been exchanged at birth. Rosamund is thus not the heiress her husband took her for—though this makes no difference, as it proves, and the secret, when revealed to a reader obtuse enough not to have guessed it from the clumsy clues throughout, is anticlimactic.

The plot has let us down. Other plots may let us down in several ways: plots can be boring—insufficient conflict—or implausible: coincidence, unexpected good fortune, acts of God, unbelievable motivations. Plots can for one reason or another be too distressing to continue with. If, as I imagine, Victorians were more like us than it would appear from their literature—one sometimes glimpses reality through the cracks of their melodramas—it is a question how their toleration grew for reading about events, situations, and denouements which had so little to do with reality, which were simply expressive of moral destiny, like the convention by which the unwed mother or fallen woman must die in the course of the fiction, situations as stylized as the Noh drama or the Chinese opera. Perhaps this is only a matter of literary fashion, but it may be that the actual circumstances of Victorian life were bound by the melodrama which issues from the conflict of law or custom with impulse. Hans Sachs, the analyst and critic, has told us "the basic subject matter of fiction is the struggle between impulse and inhibition."

Certainly the circumstances of Wilkie Collins' own life were such as to make him believe in melodrama. We have the rough outlines of the story: when he was walking one night with his brother and the painter Millais, they were accosted by a frightened young woman in white who pleaded with them for protection. She was fleeing from a man who had been holding her prisoner. Collins took this lady under his protection, as the phrase went, and lived with her, and her daughter, a number of years. When, finally, at her ultimatum, he refused to marry her, she married the plumber. But she returned, mysteriously, to Collins when her venture into married life did not work out; he in the meantime had taken up with a second lady who bore him three children. . . . These irregularities were secret, of course, to everyone but Collins' most intimate friends, Dickens and a few others.

We complain about the looseness of ties, the anomie of modern life. In the nineteenth century, you really had an uncle who might leave you out of his will. Your cousin was at hand to hate you. What you did or didn't do had effects, like the effects of a pebble in a pond; the literary character had the hard instrumentality, therefore, of a thrown pebble. People were sustained by their plots—while modern life is plotless, and has rendered us suspicious of the will, the secret, the shadowed birth.

Above all, the conflicting social classes of Victorian England ordained plots now unavailable to us. All conflict engenders plot, but consider how many of the most elaborate Victorian novels concern mysteries of social class or origins—everywhere in Collins and Dickens—the mystery of Estella's birth, or of Rosamund's, in *The Dead Secret:* will the husband, Lenny, still love Rosamund when it is known that she is not the child of the Trevertons but of the servant? And above all, now that she does not inherit?

There was a law in England that the subsequent marriage of the parents of illegitimate children did not make them legitimate, a law Collins, of course, had reason to condemn on behalf of his three children. His novel *No Name,* then, is the story of Magdalen Vanstone, a beautiful young woman who, angry at finding that her illegitimacy deprives her of her father's estate, determines to cheat the heir out of it by marrying him under an assumed name. The heir, a selfish, foolish invalid, is protected by a sinister housekeeper, and the point of the story, as one reviewer described it, is "the contest between these two deceitful, wicked, obstinate women."

We can imagine, from this, that the rise of the plot in Victorian times has something to do with the fall of God. Without a divine sense of direction, each person must act on her own, and this may make a girl like Magdalen watchful, secretive, in competition with others. The secret is, above all, the salient feature of the Victorian plot—and, I would hold, of all plots, a matter I'll return to.

On the other hand we can see how the fall of the plot since then is connected to the rise of Freud. It is easy to find the origins of plot in the Gothic novel of the late eighteenth century. The mainstream eighteenth-century novel was with some exceptions a realistic, picaresque, burlesque affair—a novel of quest. But our Victorian novelists also read, in their youths, *The Castle of Otranto,* or *The Mysteries of Udolpho,* finding in them the rusty keys, the lost will, the prisoner in the attic; and taking these creaking but symbolic articles out of the castle into the daily lives of people living at Barchester or Richmond Park was their great achievement. *Wuthering Heights,* published in 1849, is a beautiful example of a Siamese twin of a novel concerned to fuse the Gothic with the everyday world. In the novels of Anthony Trollope, it is not a desperate monk but a friendly cleric who secretly hides the fatal letter. The idea of a secret, so essential to Freud's view of character, gives some clue to why the plot gave way in respectability to character. That is, after Freud the emphasis shifts from what the person does to protect his secret to why he has got the secret in the first place: did he get it from his unhappy childhood, or the sordid conditions of his society? Forster manifests the post-Freudian preference, perfectly orthodox for a novelist of his day: "We believe that happiness and misery exist [not in Action, as Aristotle would say] but in the secret life which each of us leads privately and to which the novelist [and, he might have added, the analyst] has access." It is not to be revealed by action at all, not so much as by a speech or a sigh. It is tempting to say that it is with this pronouncement, when the secret was denied expression in action, that things begin to go wrong with the modern novel.

Did not many of us feel that our Victorian grandparents had something hidden in the attic? At any rate, the secret accompanied by action was a feature in Victorian life. People didn't confess, they concealed. We might think of Matthew Arnold burning biographical evidence—probably in particular the evidence of his French affair— or Dickens' trips "oystering and roystering" to Paris. The secret was as tangible a possession for the Victorian as a locket containing the strand of hair. And the secret is a metaphor for the mysteries of life—the particular inner thing each of us holds away from others, as Forster saw, but also the secret which destiny refuses to reveal, the secret of our fate. So productive of anxiety in real life, fictional secrets can be unwound, revealed, life can unroll before the characters like a safe road. And this, I think, is the satisfaction of the plot which consists of a mysterious secret: it can be solved.

So to tell a great story requires an understanding of secrets as well as an unusual degree of candor. To return to *No Name*, the Victorians were consternated by the character—in the old-fashioned sense—by the bad character of Magdalen. They were disgusted, particularly, in a day when heroines should be passive, at her instinct for self-preservation. "A career of vulgar and aimless trickery and wickedness, for which it is impossible to have a shadow of sympathy, but from all the pollutions of which he intends us to believe she emerges, at the cheap cost of a fever, as pure, as high-minded, and as spotless as the most dazzling white of heroines," writes Mrs. Oliphant. "Hard and coarse elements which deprive her of our sympathy," writes *The Atheneum*. It's a measure of Collins' boldness and his modernity that he rewards his bad heroine with a change of heart and a rich, good husband at the end of the tale, even if he did have to resort to the feeble device of having her fall into a fever, from which she recovers reformed.

The novels of Collins brought up a critical discussion on the whole subject of the plotted novel versus the novel of character, and, as I've said, "character" was universally preferred as somehow more moral, reflecting the romantic interest in individuality—a shift in Freud's direction even before Freud. In general, the disparagement of plot was so widespread that it alerts us to the fact that Collins was on to something close to the heart of literature, to the way novels work. Character is safe, but plot is dynamite. The influential *Westminster Review* deplores the fact that "Mr. Wilkie's productions sell by thousands of copies, *Romola* with difficulty reaches a second edition." (Which would you rather read, *Romola* or *The Moonstone?*) The *London Review* goes so far as to say that plot causes crime: "the tendency of the multiplication of these tales is to create a class of such criminals [as Collins' characters] if they do not already exist. Writers . . . scatter impressions calculated to shake that mutual confidence by which societies, and above all families are held together, to abate our love of simple, unpretentious virtue." Only one reviewer, in the *Saturday Review,* feels that "all that criticism has to say against this reduction of fiction to a rule and a contest of low artifices is too obvious and has been said too often . . . it is more important to notice the merits of this sort of book. Criticism says that Mr. Wilkie Collins invents a puzzling plot and does nothing more. This is true; but then it is so very difficult to invent a puzzling plot. Anyone who has ever tried to sketch a story will remember that there were many things that came at once . . . the descriptions of scenery, the moral reflections, the colour of the heroine's eyes . . . all these welled up spontaneously in the breast of the fertile dreamer. But between him and an embodied dream there was the great barrier of an unimagined plot. Who was the heroine to be, and why was she to be unhappy; and who was to bring in the philosophy; and how on earth was it to come in naturally? A good plot—a plot that interests, excites, and properly balances bewilderment and explanation—is a very considerable effort of the mind and one which demands great practice, patience and inventiveness . . . but if art means something which requires labour and foresight, and a sub-ordination of parts to the whole, then we can understand how it is that Mr. Collins . . . boldly claims to be an artist." And anyone who has ever tried to write a novel (I read somewhere that ninety per-cent of college-educated women try it sometime or other) can attest that it is very hard and slow.

The reviewer who said that plot was an attack on simplicity has simple-mindedly struck at the heart of one objection to plot: plot as a very metaphor for complication produces anxiety, moral fear; the reader takes pleasure when complications are resolved in the plot the way they rarely are in life. By the experience of fear or suspense and reassurance, we can be reassured that life's situations, however complicated, can also work out—and this is why we read fiction. A third Victorian reviewer senses this unconscious operation the way Freud might have described it later: "the tale is very powerful; the poison is distilled so subtly that the evil is wrought almost before suspicion is awakened; the art with which the whole is managed is so complete, that the mind unconsciously drifts on into an acquies-cence in a state of things which, were it free from the glamour which the author throws over the mental vision, it would at once condemn."

This concern for the moral poison of plot came up in the case of *No Name*. Reviewers attacked the ending because it didn't conform to poetic justice. The bad girl should have been punished, but was allowed to reform and marry: "after all her endless deceptions and horrible marriage it seems quite right to the author that she should be restored to society, have a good husband and a happy home," Mrs. Oliphant objects.

The novelist of plot, then, by the third quarter of the nineteenth century, was facing suspicion and critical disapproval. The novel was reverting to a mode which we saw in the eighteenth century, the novel of quest. It seems to me that plots, when looked at closely, resolve themselves into not forty-nine basic ones, or even seven, but two: there are the quest and the secret, or puzzle, or mystery—different words are used. Tom Jones's was a quest for his birthright. Ernest's quest in the next century—in a novel, *The Way of All Flesh*, whose modernity has struck us all—is for maturity, but now the concern is his inner life. He has to "adjust." We do not experi-ence quest novels as being highly plotted; they are stories, in For-ster's sense. The novel of elaborate plot combines the quest and the secret. *Emma,* as we've noticed, is partly a quest, Emma's for maturity, but there are also secrets galore—Harriet's paternity, Jane Fairfax's piano, and so on. In fact, the novels of the seemingly so natural Jane Austen are models of plotty complication.

As the "serious" novelist began to eschew secrets, other forms sprang up which specifically require them, above all the detective story. Here a character, the detective, quests for an answer to a secret. The detective story is also, in Wilkie Collins' sense, a novel of the effect of a character upon events—the resolute character of the detective and the defective character of the criminal. These are the opposite of novels of character in that the personages of the narrative are by definition capable of doing anything, so that we cannot be sure which of them has committed the crime. It's only the detective—resolute, judgmental, equivocal, or compromised—who generates the denouement. It's no surprise that Collins in his masterpiece, *The Moonstone,* should in effect invent this form.

Any novelist is conscious of having in her workbasket two sorts of disparate materials, let us say yarn and paint. The yarn will knit up into the plot, the paint is for painting the portraits. But what form can you arrive at with yarn and paint but a strange sort of messy construction like the gods-eyes the Greeks wind up out of yarn and paint, or like Kachina dolls? One of the qualities we respond to in any work of art is a sense of making, of craft, of pain and ingenuity on the part of the artist; we like to see the wrapping and tying, and this is as true in fiction as in woodcarving. Style is one kind of painstaking, up to a point compelling the same admiration, but better lavished on a short form, a poem or story. The novelist must lavish pains on structure and plot, which contain within them a dynamic of conflict and solution which we find eternally pleasing. We will look briefly at other reasons why this might be so.

Simon O. Lesser, in his notable *Fiction and the Unconscious,* published in the Fifties, has suggested that "fiction provides us with images of our emotional problems expressed in an idiom of characters and events." We have always found this easy to see in the case of characters; events are less easy to discuss because, simply, they are more powerful. It is they that make us anxious or reassured or cautioned. It wouldn't matter what the inner lives of Emma Bovary or Anna Karenina were if they had not taken poison or thrown themselves under trains. Lesser goes on to add that fiction "provides a forum in which the positions of the id, the ego, and the superego all receive a hearing—compromise formations whereby repressed and repressing forces obtain expression in the same work. For this reason the latent and manifest content are often contradictory." A work which seems to say you must respect your elders, say, can also argue powerfully for the ascendency of self. Plot is the place where the narrative expresses these ambivalent messages: a woman yearns for love and freedom, and rebels against the strictures of marriage. These things are covertly permitted by the vitality of the art at the same time that the cautionary endings would seem to warn against them.

If you've ever taken a book off that small shelf of books about how to write fiction, you will have noticed that few discuss plotting, though many discuss the plots of novels after the fact. The activity is mysterious. The effort, the considerable effort of the mind, is akin to a very hard acrostic, or algebra, as anyone knows who has tried it. A novel must have an action, and it must be rendered in some order. A body of complex information must be presented; the reader must know some things before he can know others. Most of us have learned from childhood the principles of rudimentary narration— the "and then, and then" of Forster's "story." But this seldom suffices to render a universe freighted with thematic and moral significance, psychological nuance, suspense, sadness, comedy, whichever of these things the writer is striving for (one always hopes to get them all). These chaotic and often contradictory impulses must be gathered and ordered, we must resort to a plan, and that's a plot. So the greatest novels are really deeply plotted. The writer turns to her chart, her list, her calendar. The serial writer, like Dickens and Trollope or Collins had also to fit the work into the format of the monthly installment. Sometimes writers look at the plots of other works. Someone once pointed out to me that *Gatsby* has the plot of *Wuthering Heights*.

It has always seemed curious to me that Anthony Trollope, another innate story-teller and good spinner of plots, should have denied that he did anything of the kind. Indeed, he said, no author, impatient to get on with the story, could be expected to spend much time on such an exhausting aspect of composition: "The plot is the most insignificant part of a tale." Yet, in *Orley Farm*, Lady Mason forges a will. In Barchester, Mr. Slope schemes for episcopal power. In *He Knew He Was Right* Emily and Louis Trevelyan and Colonel

Osborne are locked into a drama occasioned by their respective characters. Louis Trevelyan is from the outset a jealous, overbearing husband: "he liked to have his own way." When he cannot domineer over his wife Emily in the matter of whether or not she should allow the old family friend, Colonel Osborne, to the house ("Emily also liked to have her own way," Trollope tells us) Louis Trevelyan will not apologize for his unjust suspicions, and so it must end in madness and death. The characters do not change; the imperatives of their natures sweep them into cataclysms of misery. It's a riveting plot.

However many pains he may or may not expend on the plot, evidently the great storyteller cannot help himself from making things interesting. In the face of whatever current fashion for plotless narrative, his view of the world is as a series of events connected by strange quirks, coincidences, the desires of people and their consequences. Trollope was a great storyteller. It was Dorothy Sayers, herself a great story-teller, who said that the gift is innate and compulsive: "it is mightiest in the mighty," she said, "and by itself it can produce the minor immortality of a *Sherlock Holmes* or a *Three Musketeers*. In the hands of a great poet it produces the major immortality of an *Odyssey,* a *Paradise Lost,* or a *Divine Comedy*." And another great storyteller, Somerset Maugham, believed this too. He defended the plot more forthrightly than anyone in this century: "the novel of incident . . . has as much right to exist as any other. The plot is a lifeline thrown to the reader, to help him through the tale." What Maugham calls a lifeline, Forster called a tapeworm: "the lowest and simplest of literary organisms" but also the "highest factor common to all the very common literary organisms known as novels."

Sayers' mention of Dumas is endearing. The speakers in this lecture series were asked to speak of their own literary responses, so this is the place to confess my early and abiding love for the works of Alexandre Dumas (*père*). At any rate we must add Dumas to our list of nineteenth-century readable novelists. *The Count of Monte Cristo* is a perfect example of an enduring, beloved, eternally pleasing tale in which the plot is the most important thing. The means by which the implacable count gets revenge on those who blighted the life of the young Edmond Dantes forever gratifies our sense of justice and tells us, contrary to what we know of the world, that wrongs are righted, that the wicked are punished, that a person may be reborn into more favorable circumstances as a fabulously wealthy nobleman, say, and that one's enemies may yet be brought to tremble. But, lest we dismiss this as mere wish-fulfillment, too easily gratifying to be "serious," we learn also that what is past is past: Mercedes is grown old, alas, and has slept with another man; the dead are dead (Edmond's old father cannot be brought back); wealth does not bring happiness. Many and serious are the lessons of *The Count of Monte Cristo*. It is not a trivial but a perfect work, whose fascination arises from action, from what happens, not from character or form. There is a curious sense in which the happening in a novel is free of the words, exists in a third dimension, is an invisible dynamic generated by words but *not* them, where character descriptions or brilliant dialogue lie upon the page in one dimension. To say, as people frequently do, that such and such springs to life off the page is to express just this sense of insubstantial reality, a third or invisible dimension where the action lives, different from the words which are used for it. And in this dimension is the essence of plot, and it needs to be returned to its rightful dominion.

Nominated by Michael Ryan and The Threepenny Review

FOR YOU

by JIM MOORE

from THE FREEDOM OF HISTORY (Milkweed Editions)

I know it sounds too much like poetry,
but it was dusk that made me a felon,
a winter evening in Moline, Illinois.
The next day I quoted Whitman
to my draft board, "Dismiss
whatever insults your own soul,"
and sent my draft card back to them.
I can still feel the cold metal
on the mailbox, see the park
with its oaks, the black winter sky
so close, so distant,
as I dropped the letter inside
and turned quickly away.

For two years I'd argued the War,
drinking instant coffee with a man
who wore the same blue velour shirt so often
it's all I remember of him now.
We took turns arguing one way,
then another about "what to do."
We sat in the basement kitchen
of a boarding house.
Sometimes we yelled,
sometimes we sat silently, our hands
around our mugs of coffee,
our hearts confused. Deferments

from the draft meant we were the men
who could afford to choose a future.
And we had so wanted to go on drifting,
floating on the moment's shifting current
as we learned to give the poems we tried to write
a chance to rise, waveringly,
into their own shapes, existences
born of dreams, not arguments. I didn't want
to chant slogans. I didn't want
to be "right." To judge.
And these were more than choices,
these were entire lives, futures
that could never be redeemed—
or so we felt then in the midst
of a slaughtering time.
Back and forth we went, the guy
in the blue velour shirt and I,
all of us who read Emerson and Thoreau,
ate frozen dinners, drank
3.2 beer, played pinball or pool—
any game at all that would give us
a few hours away from ourselves,
those of us who underlined
CIVIL DISOBEDIENCE and wrote excited comments
in the margins late at night,
rather than actually take to the streets.

I lived alone in Moline, Illinois,
one dusty and dimly lit flight
above a greeting card shop
run by a likeable red-faced
John Bircher. It was the first year
I got paid for teaching, paid
for being excited
about what I believed in,
for having opinions
I couldn't give away
to my friend in the velour shirt.
Then two students quit school
and within months were dead

117

in Vietnam. A working class
college, our basement classroom
was in an old pentecostal church.
The mix of Sunday School
and poverty was too much
on Monday mornings, the students
almost asleep, sprawled
on the freshly waxed floor,
huddled near their classrooms
like refugees waiting for their morning soup
rather than for classes to begin.

I was the razzle dazzle guy
from the Big U
in Iowa City. I didn't
own a tie, I lived
in a VW bus all fall,
I had opinions that gave off
the glitter of newly minted
funny money. To the students
I was a classy eccentric
and I had them with me from the first,
those future postal clerks
and nurses, mechanics
and would-be writers
with their mixed bag of Sartre
and letter jackets, hickeys
and acid and—finally—
of life and death.

The second student who died
had sat in the back of the room,
chair tilted against the wall,
his long hair spread out behind him
like a scraggly fan. He often
brought his guitar to class
in a black case, and wrote his poems
on cheap yellow paper. He wanted
to know about mileage
from my bus: these

118

were the only details I remembered
when his girlfriend told me he had been killed.

It was winter by then
and I was living alone
above the greeting card shop.
After that second student's death
I spent the week-end by myself.
I was reading Suzuki at the time
and wanted to believe in something,
even if it was only the pull
and release of my own breath
as I sat cross-legged, meditating
best I knew how. I liked Zen.
For someone raised an Anglican
it seemed the closest thing
to all that upper class tastefulness, so
lovely, so earnest in its own careful way.
While I sat, meditating, I felt
even lonelier: all my enthusiasm
in the classroom, my voluble
and spontaneous love of poetry
that fit itself so nicely
into the 50 minute school hour,
my a la mode hiking boots.
I thought of that dead boy
with his guitar and his questions,
and the careful but wasted economy
of his cheap yellow paper
and I felt sick to my soul,
for all my talk of Thoreau and Whitman.
I wanted to be a citizen again, to Pledge
Allegiance to something with the faith
I'd felt in 4th grade, facing
the flag behind Miss Rodger's desk.
It was my country, too,
not just the John Bircher's downstairs
with his saccharine greeting cards
and his private gun collection.

That weekend I drank green tea,
believing it more Japanese than Lipton Orange.
I stared at the gray clouds
of dust under the bed, I followed
the flow of my breath
in and out of my stomach—
like a golden river, Suzuki said.
For two days I did nothing
but alternately sit and then hobble
on legs permanently sore
from being crossed so much.
I quit thinking about everything: the draft,
my dead students,
the future, the past. Was it
a spiritual state? I don't know,
but I felt as if I'd grown 3 inches overnight
and everything I saw
looked slightly different,
smaller and further away,
the way a dream does
as you wake up
and it begins to leave you.
Towards evening of the second day
I'd had enough of the hush,
pause, hush, of my own breath
and the shooting pain of ankles
and knees. I wanted out
and away from those motionless dust balls.
It felt wonderful to walk into evening
alone in Moline, Illinois,
in the middle of America,
the weightless center
of a centerless country.

I walked and I looked.
I saw some men sitting at a bar.
I stood outside, staring
through the small pane of glass
at the top of the door.
Everything moved so slowly:

my breath still deep
and even, holding me rooted
in the evening air like an anchor
when men fish from a boat and seem to drift,
but are only rocking back and forth
between one known place and another.
I saw the men, heads bent
toward the neon light of a beer sign
behind the bar: a man with a lasso
in one hand and a beer in another.
The lasso was red, the beer golden.
A bartender stood beside the sign,
white-aproned, holding a pencil.
I watched as he gestured
towards the bent heads of the men
sitting before him. One of them
nodded up and down and that simple,
barely noticeable sign of agreement
brought tears to my eyes
and an assent of my own
where I stood anchored
by my own steady breath.
I walked on, went up the hill
that rose steeply away from the river
near where I lived. A sled
had been left out for the night
on a front yard's thin crust of snow.
I saw this ordinary sight
framed in a deepening gray
like a letter in a phrase,
still undeciphered, but so important
that once I understood it
it would change the meaning of all other words.

As I walked slowly up the hill,
other objects I saw seemed part
of the same phrase:
a porch swing drawn up on its two chains
waiting near the roof for spring;
a car with a broken windshield

121

glittering under a streetlight
like the traces of a phosphorescent map;
the corner of an old newspaper
frozen into an iced-over sidewalk.

"For you," I found myself saying
over and over as I neared the top of the hill.
My breath came in short gasps now,
"For you, for you."
It became a kind of greed.
I couldn't get enough
of the men with their bent heads in the bar,
the sled, the swing. They gave
and I took.
I wanted it to go on forever,
this greed for the world. I knew
that it was for the sake of a sled
left behind in the moment of impatience
for dinner that I would go to prison.
Not just for political reasons,
not even for moral ones:
not for reasons at all,
or not the kind I could explain
to a draft board. For you,
sled. For you, bent heads.
For you, for you.

If, in a moment of peace, the world
could yield up such signs,
then I wanted an inner peace,
both permanent and casual.
But I could not begin
until I settled with the War.
It was that dusk, that walk, that sled
that convinced me their world could sustain me
if only I could abandon my soul-searching
and endless arguments over what to do,
like a character in a Chekhov story
so busy talking outside
on a cold winter's night

he almost dies of frostbite
while trying to prove the existence of God.
If it meant going to prison,
so be it. There, too, there would be
ordinary sights that would sustain me.
Or so I told myself
in that moment when I believed so deeply
in the strangely calming power
that came from seeing clearly
into the heart of everyday life.
I stood at the top of the hill, alone,
surrounded by what I loved.
I looked down towards the Mississippi,
black except where a bridge curved
through the night, and I did not know
what the future would bring
or what it was inside me
that would not let go
of my two new words, "For you."

Nominated by Rosellen Brown, Michael Dennis Browne and Maura Stanton

MISS VENEZUELA

fiction by BARBARA WILSON

from MISS VENEZUELA (Seal Press)

THERE WAS A boardwalk once, surfacing through the sand only to disappear if you tried to follow it. Gray rough timber made porous by the salt air, it was hotter than ordinary wood, much hotter, Rhonda and Eric agreed, jumping on and off with tender young feet, and screaming loudly if they caught a splinter.

The boardwalk belonged to an earlier time; if you looked up at the mural over the entrance to the Long Beach Municipal Auditorium, you could puzzle out which era—unless you were a child, that is, and could ask your mother everything.

"Why are those girls wearing shorts in the water?"

"They're not shorts, they're bathing costumes."

"They're funny," said Eric, but Rhonda always looked and wondered. She liked the mural very much; it was faded but still colorful, like an old advertisement painted on a barn. It depicted a crowded seaside scene, all blues and yellows. Two young women with strong thighs and muscular arms disported in the shallow waves. Their hair was clipped around smiling faces and the costumes were sheer and black, looking painted on, as indeed they were.

"Bathing beauties," said Helen, their mother, and laughed a little, possibly because neither woman was particularly beautiful.

That was left to a few gorgeous creatures in the background who waved parasols with bamboo handles and Chinese fans against the summer heat. Modishly wasp-waisted and refined from every angle, the women still looked pale and droopy to Rhonda compared with the frolicking swimmers in the water.

"I bet the ones in the long dresses wish they could take everything off and go in the water," she observed once.

"Oh, I doubt it," said Helen.

"But they're not going to have any fun like that."

"Beauty never does," sniffed her mother. "That's not what it's there for."

Dolores María Angelus Otero was born in Caracas in 1940. Her father, Rafael Otero, was a *mestizo* from the Sierra Nevada de Mérida. For helping to organize a student strike he had been exiled with hundreds of others in 1928 under the dictatorship of Juan Vincente Gómez. He fled to Costa Rica, where he married the daughter of a butcher, Eva López Angelus. The two of them, with Eva pregnant, returned to Caracas in 1940. There they worked with Rómulo Betancourt and Acción Democrática until 1948, when Major Marco Pérez Jiménez brutally took power. Rafael Otero was jailed for the political crime of trade unionism and sent to the infamous Guasina Island camp in the jungles of Orinoco. He may have been tortured to death, though the certificate read that malaria was the cause.

Dolores Otero grew up after 1948 in a squatter's shack on the hills around the capital. They had a dirt floor and no running water, but Dolores had a good education. Her mother read her the novels of Gallegos, the poetry of Martí and Darío and Neruda, and gave her the oral history of resistance in Venezuela, starting with Simón Bolívar, the Great Liberator. Eva told her daughter that when Betancourt came to power again the foreign oil companies would pay for what they had done to Venezuela. Meanwhile, in Cuba, a group of bearded men and brave women were fighting in the Sierra Maestra against their dictator. Eva, though not Dolores (who was by this time attending the university), was among the crowd that stoned Richard Nixon, American vice-president, in 1958, during his visit to Caracas.

Eva died shortly after, of tuberculosis, ironically just months before Pérez Jiménez was driven from office and Betancourt, her old friend from exile and Acción Democrática, formed a new, democratic régime.

Dolores had no brothers or sisters, and only a few relatives she had never met in Mérida and Costa Rica. She was a brilliant and independent girl, however, strikingly beautiful and something of a troublemaker. She wanted both to make a lot of money and to change the world. She was also fatally unsophisticated, and before she was nineteen had had two abortions and had lost her place at the university.

Near the Municipal Auditorium there was a long pier, where you could walk out and have clam chowder or fritters or buy abalone ashtrays or shell-studded box purses. It was lined with people in windbreakers, fishing, hooking their lines with raw bait from a tin bucket and catching tires and bottles and sometimes sea bass. There was a smell of oil and tar, a tang so fierce and fresh it almost burned. Sunsets, seen from the pier, were orange and red in winter, pastel in summer. And sometimes you could see Catalina Island, a low dinosaur on the horizon. There were no large waves anymore, though Long Beach was once known for its surf. The word "breakwater" used to confuse Rhonda, for how could water break?

The ocean water was always a little dirty and hardworking from the port and navy base, and full of bits of wood and big kelp bubbles. Rhonda and Eric, with Helen watching from the shore, still swam and bobbed in it, talking about sharks to scare each other, but never seeing any, seeing only jellyfish, rounds of white transparency, like slices of albino fruit. At intervals along the shore, as they walked back to the car, were the longlegged lifeguard stations, chapped by the wind and deserted in winter.

There was the Pike, before they cleaned it up, when it was still adult and rough and smacking of war. In later years Rhonda and Eric would dare each other to go there, among the tattoo parlors and the blood banks and the side shows of freaks and animals and the fun houses, among the pawn shops and cardhalls and shops selling souvenirs for wives and girlfriends of the sailors, to the rickety calligraphy of the roller coaster, the one they said threw people off into the ocean as if they were dead fleas flying from the coat of a running dog.

Helen and Bob, their parents, had met at the Pike during a wartime dance, but they avoided the place now. Helen explained that the water in the pool called The Plunge was half pee and half spittle. And as Helen and Bob were themselves moving up in the world, so they all moved up geographically from the low life of the pier and the Pike to the fresh glamour of the bluff and Ocean Boulevard, with its divider of green grass, tall palms, its half-timbered mansions interspersed with neat little pink and yellow hotels called SeaView and Ocean Breeze.

They moved up to the Pacific Coast Club.

Dolores' first lover was the son of an oilman. Eva would have been shocked if she had known. Ever since the oil deposits had been discovered in the Lake Maracaibo basin and Gómez had awarded lucrative contracts to foreign developers, Venezuela had been in the hands of Gulf, Standard Oil and Royal Dutch Shell. The native Venezuelans who embezzled with them grew rich too, built villas around Caracas and vacationed in Europe on the graft money. Hermann's father was white, a *caudillo* turned businessman who had gone to Yale and who knew the Rockefellers intimately. Hermann had grown up mostly in New York, attending private schools, and had spent his summers in Maine and his winters in Switzerland.

To be honest, Hermann was not as bad as he might have been. A short, rather serious boy, he was too romantic, too generous, to be a good playboy. He was genuinely intrigued by Dolores, whose rich dark beauty had attracted him from a chauffeured car on a Caracas street. He was only eighteen, a year older than Dolores, and this was his first real foray into Venezuelan life. The fact that Dolores' father had been a member of the Generation of '28 and that he had been persecuted by Pérez Jiménez, the same man who had helped make his father rich, gave her additional glamour in his eyes. Without the knowledge of his family, he arranged meetings with her in a highrise apartment building and began to tutor her in the ways of the wealthy.

Dolores took to the life immediately. She was old enough to have a contempt for everything Hermann represented and young enough to long for it desperately. While arguing politics with him she consumed four-course meals; with money discreetly left in a drawer she bought clothes and took English lessons. To assuage her guilt she also bought presents for her classmates and handed out dozens of bolivars every day to beggars.

In the end she grew fond of Hermann who, after all, was always so kind to her. When she became pregnant, Hermann said he would go to his father and ask to marry her. That was the last she ever saw of Hermann. A woman who said she was his mother came to the luxury apartment, welcomed Dolores into the family and said she was taking her to the doctor for a check-up. Under anesthesia, the baby was aborted. When Dolores woke up she was in a dark room and bleeding. Hermann's mother was gone. Her own mother she never told.

Dolores was more careful with her next lover, a businessman who traveled frequently. She continued attending the university and decided on a career in law. She did not live with Ricardo, even after her mother died, but she accepted willingly his gifts and dinners. When she became pregnant again she knew what to do and did it. But something changed inside her after that: there were complications, an infection set in, and when it was cured, the doctor said she was sterile.

It was 1959 and Castro and his fellow revolutionaries had just overthrown Batista, but Dolores's university career was cut short by her inability to explain her long absence from class.

The Pacific Coast Club was a brown sandcastle of rather fantastic appearance, built on the side of a bluff. It had a turret, stained glass windows, a red carpet leading from the sidewalk through the gold-leafed doors and a lobby complete with doorman, leather book to sign in and huge fireplace. Off the lobby was a patio restaurant, with a marbled pond owned by three very large old carp and supervised by waiters in white jackets who didn't like children.

Though the lobby was plush with old leather and humidors, the beach at the base of the club was strictly tropical. A bamboo fence surrounded it; there was an outdoor cafe where people in bright sarongs and polo shirts sipped tall pink and orange drinks. There were umbrellas and striped lounge chairs laid out in rows. Here you could see older women the color of walnuts and oily as fish lying hour after hour in their bikinis, with two little white half eggs shielding their eyes.

Although they, Bob, Helen, Rhonda and Eric, passed through this private beach on their way to the ocean, it wasn't a place any of them lingered in, any more than they did the lobby.

"Too fancy," sturdy Helen said, while privately yearning. Both Helen and Bob were nondrinkers as well as a little pale and stout. They looked best in their roles as Mother and Father, and sought out those like themselves at the club, rather than the heirs to oil fortunes and orange groves around Disneyland.

No, their sphere was the level in between lobby and beach, the physical family world of the Ladies' and Men's Locker Rooms, pool and gym. The pool, Olympic-sized, was ostensibly the reason for joining the club in the first place. Helen and Bob, who were bringing up their children in California as if it were their own Midwest, on canned vegetables, snowflecked Christmas trees and tales of hardship, religion and struggle, nevertheless insisted early that their children learn to swim—not as they had, fearfully dipping and plunging in summer waterholes and rivers, or later, by the shores of Lake Michigan, learning the awkward, head-elevated breaststroke— but really learn to swim. This did not mean an occasional dip in the urinated, snotty waters of Pike's Plunge, but special swimsuits and classes—beginner, intermediate, advanced—and for Rhonda, fi- nally, the swim team. It meant that Saturdays were swim days at the club—eyes smarting from chlorine, ears clogged and muscles pleas- antly heavy. It meant, eventually, dozens of boring laps, swim meets with whistles blowing and terrifying views from the high dive. But it also meant, always, the Ladies' Locker Room.

Dolores Otero had both a common and a distinctive beauty. She was on the short side, with large breasts and a nipped-in, curva- ceous figure. Slightly bowed legs only gave her a more provocative stance, as she habitually leaned on one hip to compensate. Her hair was black, her skin was gold. All this was attractive and very Ven- ezuelan. Where she differed was in the high cheekbones and the great Egyptian eyes, accented with a curling wave of eyeliner. Her nose was straight and delicate; her lips formed a naturally red ridge over small white teeth.

"Elegant, but sexy," approved several judges.

"Nefertiti," said another.

Dolores, in the course of looking up a professor who she hoped would intercede for her in the matter of her dismissal, had wan- dered into a beauty contest.

The ten other young women, one of whom, an almost natural blonde, had thought she had it in the bag, watched carefully as Dolores sauntered through the room.

"They told me Professor Carlos Guerrera was here?"

"Name?"

"Dolores María Angelus Otero . . . have I made a mistake?"

"Not the daughter of Rafael?" exclaimed one man, jumping up to embrace her. "We were in Costa Rica together. And Eva?"

"Eva's dead. . . . "

Such sympathy in the room. Daughter of a hero—in '59 you could say it—a distinctive Venezuelan beauty—an orphan now. All at once the men began to explain the advantages of being Miss Venezuela.

129

The money, the chance to travel, the opportunity to represent the new democratic Venezuelan state to the world. She was a patriot certainly, the daughter of Rafael couldn't be anything else. But it was the promise of a scholarship that swayed Dolores most. For if she had a scholarship, surely she would be able to return to law school.

To Rhonda, at seven, the Ladies' Locker Room was huge, as big as an underground city, with streets and avenues of tiny rooms, cubicles for dressing and undressing, each one with a shower and six lockers. The ceiling was high, though the walls dividing the rooms were low; the floor was entirely cement, drained at intervals by sieved holes. There were no doors, only white cloth curtains that never quite closed.

The Ladies' Locker Room had a very special smell, the combination of ripe femaleness and water. It was the odor of women undressing in small spaces, struggling with their girdles and stiff brassieres, panting a little, giving off eddies of perfume, talcum powder and deodorant as they got into their wire-stiffened cotton swimsuits and tucked their hairdos under elastic caps, stiff white helmets embossed with sea-floral designs or softly shirred pastel wigs. It was the smell of women coming back from the pool, chlorinated water dripping from between their legs, from their fingertips. As they got into the showers there was the smell of hot water, soap, complete cleanliness dried by fresh rough towels—then more perfume, deodorant, hairspray, cosmetics, but never enough to completely eliminate the smell of chlorine and of wrinkled dampness.

It wasn't just the smell that fascinated Rhonda. It was also the sight of women. Eric, being younger, dressed with Helen and his sister if Bob didn't come along. Those were the times he and Rhonda liked to go crazy, running up and down the little streets of white curtains, tugging them back, twitching them, pretending to push each other inside, generally being bad, and sometimes, as a kind of reward, getting a glimpse of a huge, pink, wrinkled ass half-congealed into a girdle, or a pair of brown-nippled breasts falling out of a rigid ivory brassiere.

Eric eventually moved on permanently to the male world of jock straps and Brill Cream—the Men's Locker Room—while Rhonda remained, with her fantasies that grew both more circumspect and more daring. By the time she was eleven she no longer raced through the streets and alleys of the locker room, flicking aside curtains in the hope of surprising a woman's body. Instead, she practiced posing, shoulder strap casually falling off to reveal a small bud of breast, or towel draped artistically over her hipless form. She flung back her head, straddled the wooden bench and squirmed pleasantly. She stared at the two pubic hairs around her soft pink petals. And she waited.

Waited, not for some creepy kid to run up and down the corridors, but for a woman to make a mistake and come in.

Meanwhile, up in the lobby, Helen, so heavy now that she never bothered to come downstairs, tapped her foot and eyed Rhonda penetratingly.

"It seems like it's taking you longer and longer to get dressed."

"Señor Columbus made his discovery in 1498 and also chloromycetin was discovered by a Venezuelan. We have thirty-two species of eagle and eighty percent of the goods made by Sears, Roebuck and Co. are made here. The River Orinoco is one thousand six hundred miles long and has a big mouth at the Atlantic Ocean. The highest uninterrupted waterfall in the world is here. It is Angel Falls and is named for Jimmy Angel, an American pilot who crashed in it. Caracas is our main city and it is three thousand one hundred and thirty-six feet high. Its average temperature is seventy degrees so it is very pleasant. . . ."

Dolores paused, discouraged less by her bad memory and worse syntax than by the complete irrelevance of what she was reciting. These English lessons, these facts to be memorized, all useless, watered down to be picturesque and nonthreatening. When she tried to do research on her own, into how much control the foreign oil companies exercised over the political situation, into why Bethlehem Steel and U.S. Steel had gotten such a foothold on the iron ore industry, she was told she was being provocative and ungenerous. Venezuela had the highest per capita income in South America and all this was due to American development. It was true that certain industrialists had sometimes misused their power . . . but times were changing. Betancourt was in power again.

It was curious. A month ago she'd been both ignorant and powerless, a nineteen-year-old ex-student and ex-mistress. Now she was suddenly viewed as the representative of the country. She'd met

Betancourt, exchanged platitudes about her father. All her life she'd been taught to revere this president, as a man who'd spent twenty-one years either in exile or in prison in defense of his ideals. But now, he was in power and he was so frightened of the military on the Right, the Americans in the middle, and Fidel Castro on the Left, that he hardly dared take a step in any direction. He was a shrunken, tired-looking man who couldn't help letting his hand slip accidentally from her shoulder in friendly greeting to her full breast.

"The per capita income of Venezuela is the highest in South America. Besides oil and iron ore our principal income derives from the export of cacao and coffee. Along the coastal zone production is bananas, fish, and there are beach resorts. In the *llanos* or middle plains there are many goats and cattles. Coffee grows in the Andes as well as some wheat and potatoes. The government is in the process of di-ver-si-fying, what is called 'sowing the petroleum'; meaning we like to put our money into other things to make more money some day. . . . "

There was something very wrong with all this, but Dolores wasn't quite sure what to do about it, other than to follow, with greater than usual interest, the triumphs and problems of the new government in Havana.

Every year, at least since 1952 when Catalina Swimsuits had set up its own alternative to the Miss America Pageant, the far more exotic Miss Universe Contest had taken place in Long Beach, California. Rhonda's family was a great supporter of the pageant. Not only did they sit on the curb of Ocean Boulevard and watch the parade, but they followed the events on television as well, from the very first national anthem introductions through the swimsuit and evening gown competitions, right up to the final palpitating moments when the announcer opened the last envelope, the music surged expectantly and the newest Miss Universe burst into happy tears.

Nobody thought there was anything strange about this spectacle at the time. Rhonda's family certainly didn't. They used to compare the women fiercely at dinner and in front of the TV, both physically and geographically. Bob, a former information specialist in the Army and now the owner of a carpet store, liked to drop in bits of history and anthropology, perhaps to disguise his natural interest in

132

the beauties' figures. Helen could be a little cruder; she sometimes made jokes about the sizes of their busts. Rhonda's own was hardly developing, a fact which seemed to please Helen, so obsessed these days with weight. "I never had this problem before I married," she would sigh, over the two huge mounds that covered her chest. "I was as flat as Rhonda."

When Rhonda looked at the foreign women she felt a glow and a wonder. What were they like, each one of them? What were the places like that they came from, that round, chin-tilted one from the Philippines, for instance, that tall lithe one from Iceland, that strapping freckled redhead from Australia.

Most years she got a chance to mingle with them in person, for there was always an overflow from the Lafayette Hotel into the Pacific Coast Club. Some years, damp and fresh, she'd run up from the Ladies' Locker Room and find the lobby full of mysterious women in suits and corsages, wearing wide ribbons: Miss Uruguay, Miss Canada, Miss India.

When she had been a child, they had sometimes stopped and smiled at her, stroked her head. At twelve Rhonda was awkward and yearning, with too much intensity.

Her mother found a picture of a naked woman in Rhonda's room. From now on, she said, Rhonda was too old for slumber parties.

If only she were beautiful—not Miss America, but something else, someone else. In school they offered Spanish or French as an elective. Rhonda signed up for both.

Dolores' roommate was from Sweden and could not have been more opposite, both in looks and in temperament; leggy, fair, careless and cheerful, Brigitte claimed she had starved her healthy body for weeks to win the contest, but that the money was worth it. She wanted to continue her medical studies in London and afterwards open up a clinic for women in Africa.

She introduced Dolores to Miss Portugal and Miss Sierra Leone, both of whom she'd met on the plane. Miss Portugal, a dimpled, satin-cheeked eighteen-year-old from Oporto, was the only one who was not anti-American or embarrassed at being in a beauty contest. Carmen ate her steak and salad at the welcoming lunch, wide-eyed and quiet, as the others discussed the de Beers diamond mines in Sierra Leone and Standard Oil in Venezuela. Brigitte mentioned that Long Beach, California, was an oil town too.

133

It was true. After lunch that first day the contestants were taken about the city on a tour bus. They saw the beaches and the amusement park, the harbor, the Douglas Aircraft plant and the new state college. They were even taken up to Signal Hill, an unincorporated outpost in the middle of the city that looked like a huge disheveled refuse heap. It had no wide boulevards fringed with palm trees or pink-and-green-stuccoed houses covered with bougainvillea, only row upon row of oil derricks and funny machines pumping up and down like rocking horses. The roads here were rough and dirty, the very air smelled of petroleum.

In spite of Dolores' late consuming interest in the oil industry, this was the first time she had seen a working oil field. She wanted to stop and walk around, to take pictures with her new camera. The chaperone, the former Miss California and now a stylish matron in a little blue hat and white gloves, masked her disapproval with trilling laughter.

"Well, just for a moment. . . . "

She watched helplessly as Dolores scampered about, photographing and thinking about industry's place in a socialist society.

Rhonda got up stiffly. The last float had gone by, the last white-gloved waving hand. She must be getting older; she felt a little silly this year as she made her way along through the crowds, evading Helen and her brother. Who in their right mind would wear long white gloves and high heels with a one-piece bathing suit? And you had to admit, the whole international thing was pretty hokey: having Miss Holland pose in wooden shoes, a white winged cap and a striped apron, while a tape recorder whined out a little dance.

All the same, it was still the one place where it was okay to stare. Ever since her mother had found that picture, Rhonda had been self-conscious. Her mother wouldn't even understand that they'd all been looking at it at the slumber party. It was Nancy's brother's, from his *Playboy* magazine. They'd spread it out on the floor in the middle of the night and practiced the same pose, draping bits of sheet over *that place*. It was a *joke*, Mom, Rhonda wanted to say. All the same it was Rhonda who'd taken the *Playboy* picture home with her, nobody could deny that; and maybe it was only Rhonda out of all the girls who had that funny feeling when she looked at the woman lying there smiling, smiling with her nice soft breasts, as if she were inviting Rhonda to touch them. Her mother had looked so funny when she found the photo: "*What* are you using this for?" she asked. Not even, Where did you get this?

And she'd snatched it from the drawer and torn it right in half, right through the breasts.

She didn't understand that Rhonda needed to know . . . what? Well, what they giggled about in gym class. That story about the woman who found the mouse in her closet, but it was really something to do with a hole in the wall and a man next door. She never understood that. And some girls talked about other girls who went all the way, like Jean who wore the thick lipstick and whose mother still let the older boy next door babysit because she didn't know what he and Jean were doing. But Rhonda didn't like boys very much. She just liked looking at women, even though she now knew that somehow it was bad.

She returned to the Pacific Coast Club, went downstairs to the Ladies' Locker Room. It was quiet today, for a Saturday. All the changing rooms stood open, their white curtains slack and sad in the thick, moist air.

Dolores was explaining the Cuban Revolution to Brigitte. It was the night after the swimsuit competition and they both needed to erase from their minds how it had felt to walk through the middle of a crowded auditorium, elevated on a runway like a turkey on a conveyor belt, wearing nothing but a white swimsuit, long white gloves and high heels.

"For some reason it's the gloves I hate most of all," said Brigitte. "Why cover up the hands, except to make us look like we can't resist, that we're clean goods as well?"

"Have you heard of a woman Celia Sánchez?" asked Dolores. "No? But she was up in the mountains, the Sierra Maestra, with Fidel Castro and the others. Knowing the way, leading and fighting. That is what I would like, *sabes?* I read their speeches now and the doctor's too, Che Guevara, and I am so happy, excited. For a people to be taking control. Soon they say they nationalize the industries, and give the land to the *gente* back from the *latifundistas*. And make everyone learn to read. What work there is to be done there, if one has the will to struggle. But struggle with others, not against them."

"When I become a doctor," said Brigitte, inspired, "I'll go there and work for them."

"Is it possible?" said Dolores. "To give up everything and start again? Better this time?"

Rhonda had escaped from her mother and Eric for a few moments, claiming that she had dropped her small purse on the beach and needed to retrieve it. It was the end of a boring day spent with the family, an entity she was coming more and more to despise. If it wasn't her brother kicking and pinching her, it was her mother remarking on everything with that sour smirk of unhappiness and condemnation. Why was she so unhappy, why so suspicious that everyone was cheating them or lying? And why did her father ignore her or believe what Helen said about her? Helen had probably told him about the *Playboy* picture. . . .

Rhonda walked along the edge of the water. It was getting on late afternoon; the sky had that white, blowsy feeling it got sometimes before sunset, when the ocean turned skittish and cold, the sand flared up under your feet. Seagulls cried hopelessly, callously.

She was thinking about the woman whose breasts her mother had torn in half. She couldn't help it, she still thought about them. And that funny feeling kept coming into her *place;* lately she had taken to rubbing it, not just on a bench or with a towel, but with her hand. She would die if anyone ever saw her, she knew that no one else ever did it, but more and more she wanted to. It felt so good, it felt like something built up, she didn't know what, because nothing ever happened. She would do it for a while, until she almost started to feel uncomfortable or in pain from the tingling and the want. And then she would stop, feeling unsatisfied and strange but also excited.

And now she was doing it again in her mind, thinking of the breasts and wondering how whatever happened, happened. But what? But what? And suddenly Rhonda was overcome by the immense weariness of being a child. It wasn't fair never to understand, and to be pushed around and made to feel bad about everything.

She was approaching one of the lifeguard stations. Having completely forgotten, though perhaps intentionally, about Helen and Eric waiting in the lobby of the Pacific Coast Club, Rhonda decided it would be fun to climb the wooden ladder to the platform and to sit for a while. And think.

Dolores had escaped from the pageant temporarily, from her chaperone and the various officials. She was definitely not interested in the planned trip to Disneyland and so, during the flurry of boarding the bus, she had slipped away, back to her room to grab a scarf, dark glasses and coat. Thus disguised she'd come down to the beach to walk and to wonder what would happen if she suddenly flew straight from Los Angeles to Havana. Miss Venezuela was a full-time job; they had appearances scheduled for her all year in Caracas and around the country. A life waited for her there, though it was not, if it had ever been, her life.

She had climbed onto the platform of the lifeguard station and was sitting against the wind with her back to the warm, weatherworn door, when she saw the head of a young girl pop up over the side. The girl's eyes widened so comically that Dolores had to laugh.

"Don't be afraid, *chiquita*," she said. "I won't eat you."

The girl hesitated, then bashfully continued her climb. She was a gangly, awkward thing with big brown eyes and cowlicky hair. Her arms were rather muscular; she had a scrape on her knee, and elbow as well. She was wearing a skirt and sandals and carrying a white cardigan sweater. She seated herself at the far end of the platform and asked, "Are you in the contest?"

Dolores shrugged and with some embarrassment, then decided to be sophisticated. "Miss Venezuela, Dolores María Angelus Otero, at your service."

"Gee," said the girl slowly, staring hard and turning away, beet red. "Gee," she repeated.

"Please," said Dolores, a little impatiently, but also kindly, "What is your name?"

"Uh. Rhonda. Rhonda Metcalfe. Wow," she said. "You're really from Venezuela?" And she seemed suddenly to have recovered the use of her tongue. "What's Venezuela like? I don't know anything about it. I mean, I know about Mexico, we went to Tijuana once anyway. I'm taking Spanish, you know. I mean, how could you know, but I am. *Cómo estás?* See, that's because I want to travel and do everything when I'm older. I can hardly wait, I can't stand being twelve, I mean, sometimes I don't feel like I'm twelve. I don't know, I feel so old sometimes but they treat me like a baby all the time. I wish I was as old as *you*. I wish I could be like you, it must be so *neat* to wear all those dresses and maybe get to be Miss Universe and meet everybody from other countries. . . . " Rhonda broke off. Dolores was staring at her in bewilderment. "Do I talk too fast?" she exclaimed solicitously.

Dolores burst out laughing and removed her dark glasses. To Rhonda she looked less like Nefertiti than Sophia Loren, redolent of sex and mystery and luxury. Dolores said, "It is just that, I am not so much used to, you are talking about very many things all at once. But you are a nice girl," she added.

Rhonda sighed and dropped her eyes for a moment, breathing hard. Her mind was busy with impossible schemes: asking Miss Venezuela to dinner, seeing if she could stay with them during her visit; dropping in on her someday in Venezuela. She was so excited that she could hardly think straight. "Do you have a little sister?" she burst out.

"I have no one," Dolores said, and her gaze swept the sea tragically. "I am now planning to be a revolutionary."

"Can I be your little sister?" Rhonda asked and then was aware of how ridiculous this sounded. She blushed again, up to the roots of her cowlick.

Yet for the first time Dolores really seemed to look at her and a soft yet spirited expression came into her large painted eyes. "I will be your sister, little one," she said, as if making a promise. "In my heart I will think of you. That we will both have better lives from this day forward."

It was so wonderful, her saying that, that Rhonda could hardly believe Miss Venezuela was talking to her. Perhaps Dolores was just being friendly, perhaps she was making some deeper vow to herself alone. At any rate Dolores suddenly reached over and took Rhonda's hand and squeezed it.

"Just be careful, my young friend, with the boys. Watch out," Dolores said, eyes narrowed.

It was on the tip of Rhonda's tongue to exclaim that she didn't even like boys anyway, but she didn't want to spoil the moment. She yearned into Dolores' lovely face, murmuring, "Okay."

This was the scene, then, that met Helen's eyes as she approached the lifeguard station in the course of looking for Rhonda all over the beach and fearing the worst: her twelve-year-old daughter holding hands with some dark, foreign-looking woman in a raincoat and scarf.

"My lands!" she gasped, standing stock-still in the windy sand.

"Who's that lady with Rhonda?" Eric said, and his piercing young voice carried over to the lifeguard station so that Rhonda turned around with a jerk of horror.

"My mother," she muttered to Dolores.

"Rhonda, you come right down off of that platform. Right now."

"Good-bye," said Rhonda, tortured, to Dolores, with one last look. Dolores put her sunglasses back on and looked mysterious. "Good-bye, Rona," she said, squeezing the girl's hand. *"Que tengas una vida muy feliz."* She ignored Helen and the yapping Eric at her heels.

"Who is that woman?" Helen hissed when Rhonda crossed slowly over the sand to them. "Just who is that woman you were holding hands with, Rhonda Metcalfe?"

"Miss Venezuela," sighed Rhonda. *"Just* Miss Venezuela, that's all." And for once her mother had nothing to say.

For years afterward, long after she could quite remember Dolores' liquid gaze and firm grasp, Rhonda cultivated a special fascination for the country of Venezuela. She dressed up as a cowgirl from the *llanos* for a skit on different countries once; she wrote a paper or two on Venezuela in school. She continued taking Spanish all the way through college. And naturally she nursed a secret preference for dark-eyed women who looked like Sophia Loren, though she ended up with a perfectly nice woman from Kansas, a freckle-face named Mary Sue.

When Rhonda went into the Peace Corps she was stationed in Bolivia. She managed to visit Venezuela several times, to sit on a bit of beach overlooking the sea, to smell the strong, familiar tang of salt and oily water, to feel a little silly but somehow at home.

Of course she never ran into the former Miss Venezuela. Dolores had jumped bail as the country's queen long ago and had moved to Cuba. She became a lawyer, married, and adopted three children, one of whom she named Rona. It might have been coincidence. It might have been how she kept her promise.

Nominated by Seal Press

PLAYING CHESS WITH ARTHUR KOESTLER

by JULIAN BARNES

from THE YALE REVIEW

Game 1

WE play not on a board but on a curious rubber traveling mat. Perhaps it was originally magnetized to make the pieces hold firmly to their squares, but if so, the magnetism has long worn off. The mat has been rolled up for many years and does not flatten out properly, despite Arthur's smoothings. The surface dips and sways like undulating meadowland: bishops look even more threatening as they cant toward you at twenty degrees to the perpendicular. Those who play chess know how in the course of a game that bland grid of sixty-four squares becomes charged with lines of energy, pockets of power, backwoods domains of stagnancy and despair. As the isobars of control and vulnerability develop, this ruckled mat throws in some extra uncertainties, some distracting bits of dream and surrealism.

We begin cautiously: neither of us has played for some time. Every so often I am interrupted by the thought, *I'm playing chess with Arthur Koestler!* While it's normal to imagine how your opponent is assessing your game (will he buy that bluff? does he know I prefer bishops to knights?) it's less helpful to start worrying about what your opponent will think of you off the board because of what you do on it. But these considerations are hard to put aside when playing someone you have long admired, whose work spoke with a personal clarity during your intellectually formative years—and someone, after all, who reported the Fischer-Spassky match in Reykjavik for the London *Observer*. What does such a man think as I swap knights to double a pawn on his KB file? Is he judging this a crude maneuver that achieves a petty, vulgar advantage when one ought to be aiming for elegance, beauty, and finesse? Or is he saying to himself—like any other normal chess-playing human— "Oh damn, why did I let this whippersnapper double my pawns like that?"

Our rustiness, the joke "board," and the normal half-ludic, half-social uncertainties of playing an unfamiliar opponent are compounded by Arthur's physical condition. He is now seventy-seven, and known to be suffering from Parkinson's disease. When I arrive he remarks, in front of his wife Cynthia, how much he has deteriorated in the last twelve months. "Zis Parkinson's—it knocks me sidevays," he says in that almost parodic Middle European accent which still comes as a surprise because you somehow expect mastery of written and spoken English to go together. (But of course they don't. See Nabokov: "I think like a genius, I write like a distinguished author, and I speak like a child.") Arthur's hand movements have lost their precision, and perhaps his eyesight is not so good anymore, because occasionally during our five games he starts to put a piece down on an impossible square, awarding himself, for example, two bishops on the same diagonal. Usually he notices; once or twice I have to point it out (and do not like to ask whether the fault is one of hand or eye). Each time, he apologizes courteously: "Zis Parkinson's, it knocks me sidevays."

The game is tedious and barely competent until I get a useful pawn pin. He struggles to shift it and loses another pawn, then I rack up the pin, he semi-blunders, and I win rook for bishop. This, I know, is the key breakthrough: queens are already off, and my two rooks look unstoppable. Then it's my turn to blunder. Like many average players, I have a visceral fear of the opponent's knight. Bishops, queens, and rooks move in that straightforward, undeceitful way of theirs; the knight—well, the opponent's knight—is sneaky and treacherous. Predicting the piece's behavior more than two moves ahead is almost impossible. So suddenly, without any decent notice at all, Arthur's whinnying horse is right in where it shouldn't be, forking my rook and king. All that hard work wasted, I think. "Analyzing the position" (as we describe sitting there and worrying a lot), I see that when he takes my rook, I recapture the knight, and we're level on material again. A long, grim struggle to come. So I move my king and *bang*, his next move is not, as I expect, to take off my rook, but to contrive a very neat mate with two bishops and knight. Ouch. You do like at least to be allowed to foresee the manner of your impending defeat. Oh well. 1-0.

Game 2

It's the summer of 1982, and I am down at the Koestlers' farmhouse in Denston, Suffolk, for a week. I seem to be writing two novels at the same time, one of which is about Flaubert. Writers divide into those who happily talk about their work in progress and those who squirm in embarrassment at the prospect. I am a squirmer (of course, it's not just embarrassment; it's also caution that someone might steal the idea for your book, plus sheer vanity—however good you make it sound you probably won't be able to convey the full originality, daring, and brilliance of the project). Three or four times over the last year or so Arthur has asked me what I am working on, and each time I answer, with tight-lipped paranoia, "A book about Flaubert." Each time—preferring, as is his style, the challenging question to the molifying expression of interest—he responds, "Why not Maupassant?" I never really find an answer. I suppose I should just say "Flaubert's better."

I stay in the visitor's flat at the end of the farmhouse. I write in the morning, have lunch, read, play chess with Arthur, and go for a run in the early evening (I am in what I hopefully refer to as "training" for the London Marathon, which is a safe nine months away). The weather stays fair, and a satisfying balance is held between work, exercise, and pleasure. The only bogus thing about my day is the "training." I have decided to avoid an overhasty build up to the twenty-six miles, and so jog around the unfrequented Suffolk lanes for twenty minutes or so, each day making it to a slightly more distant tree, a different patch of cow parsley. All kinds of mental stratagems have to be employed (dreaming up dinners, playing through sexual fantasies) to keep my legs moving, to rebuff the tempting voice which says, "What are you doing this for, you don't need this running shit, nobody can see you, come on, give up. . . ." But I just about don't give up in my low-level quest for a certain healthiness.

Arthur, as it later turns out, is worse than he lets on: he has leukemia as well as Parkinson's. Both diseases are to some extent controllable, though one or the other will get him in the end. One example of his "deterioration," he says, is that his voice is no longer reliable. It tires quickly and he can't always control the register; recently he's been turning down requests for radio and television interviews, and won't do any more. I fail to notice any fluctuations in his voice over two and a half hours the first evening, so am only half-convinced of his supposed decline, but he knows better. As it transpires, he is already planning his suicide. He has always been a firm and public believer in what is—either euphemistically or accurately, I can never quite decide—referred to as "self-deliverance." EXIT, the British organization founded to promote the cause of euthanasia, has produced a booklet offering practical advice. Arthur, in his methodical way, has already annotated his copy with a précis of what to do: "1. An hour and a half before your meal. . . . " He summarizes the amounts of drink and drugs specified, and notes for future use the shelf life of barbiturates (eight years).

The second game lasts longer than the first, about an hour and three-quarters. Playing white, I open with a fianchettoed bishop. There is occasionally some mild surprise value in this beginning though I use it mainly because it tends to lead to open, attacking chess. I hate and fear those clogged games with a great ball of pawn tension in the middle of the board; one minor miscalculation and the whole thing will suddenly unravel in your face. I remind myself that Bent Larsen, the Danish grand master famous for his attacking style, frequently opens with a fianchettoed bishop. As I play p-QN3 followed by B-N2, I dream of a pair of bishops on neighboring diagonals aiming their crossbows into the heart of black's defensive nest. But it seems I am not as good a chess player as Bent Larsen. A lot of pins and semi-pins hinder the bold maneuvers I have imagined. My diagonal threats peter out. Another loss. 2-0.

Game 3

After the second game, I mention to Arthur that I've never played the King's Gambit. Whenever I try it out by myself, it always seems to lead to a lost position for white: it is suicidal. I only know one person—a reckless, pressing daredevil on the board—who ever plays this sharp, aggressive, old-fashioned gambit. So I ought to be less surprised when Arthur, as white, opens p-K4, p-KB4. I think, *Oh shit, the King's Gambit? I should never have told him how unfamiliar I am with it.* I picture him sneaking off the previous evening to his chess manuals and running through all the subtleties of this violent opening. Such thoughts don't help black's defenses; also, the suicidal tendencies implicit for white whenever I rehearse the King's Gambit seem mystifyingly absent for my opponent.

Now, toward the very end of his life, Arthur is mellowed by weakness. In the three or four years I have known him, he has become much less combative. I met him first at his house in Montpellier Square, at one of those London dinners at which most of those present have two houses and yet (and therefore) spend a lot of time complaining about the trade unions. It seems *de rigueur* on these occasions to have in your wallet a cutting from the *Daily Telegraph* about some obscure restrictive practice whereby workers with metal-boring drills are bringing the country to its knees by refusing to use their drills for boring wood. I was working for the *New Statesman* at the time (and living in a bed-sitter), so was unsusceptible to the inference that if only these recalcitrant workers would allow themselves to be pushed around a bit more, then people with two houses could afford a third house (which conclusion has been well borne out as Mrs. Thatcher's Britain continues). There was much disgust and dismay expressed that evening about the behavior of the National Graphical Association—the printers then being the particular object of fashionable odium among right-thinking people. (Quite by chance, I had spent that day at a small printing works in Southend, supervising the going-to-press of the *Statesman's* back half. Everyone there had been hardworking, cooperative, and entirely lacking in a forked tail.) Not long after Mrs. Thatcher became leader of the Conservative Party, she paid a visit to Arthur. A previous prime minister, Harold Wilson, had recruited two famous Hungarian economists, Balough and Kaldor, to his staff of special advisors. Arthur recalled that he was flattered by Mrs. Thatcher's attention but declined her casting: "I will not be your Hungarian guru."

Now he sits in the sunshine, with Mozart on the radio and a bottle of Moselle in a wine cooler before him, looking rather like a wise squaw. He walks with a stick and seems weary of his reputation for belligerence. I have recently read a new biography of Camus, and mention—thinking it might amuse him—that the historical record is confused. Some authorities maintain that he gave Camus a black eye only once; others assert that it was twice. But he is not particularly amused. "Only once," he says wearily. "It was a drunken brawl."

Despite my trepidation when faced with the King's Gambit, I seem to have chances at first; then Arthur establishes a strong center. A potential weakness is that he leaves his queen and knight on the same diagonal. But how to exploit this without being obvious? Gratifyingly, the weakness exploits itself: a forced defensive pawn-push on my part sets up a square for my bishop, which leaps out from the back rank into a killer pin on knight and queen. The queen falls. Some peril remains, as Arthur has two attacking rooks, two bishops, and a knight, plus a pawn on the sixth rank, but once all chances of a breakthrough are headed off he gently topples his king. 2-1.

Afterwards, I go for a run, light-headed and light-hearted. Hey, I've beaten Arthur Koestler at chess! There is nobody, alas, to tell; but I run for twenty-eight minutes nonstop, the longest for ages, without feeling too bad. When my calves begin to ache, I imagine lush country wives with throbbing décolletages who drive up alongside and implore me to take a lift; then I don't think of my calves for a while. But reality being what it is, there are no beckoning *chauffeuses;* I seem to have chosen a road driven only by careless and surly males.

Game 4

While we are on the subject of literary brawls, there's something else to clear up. That famous occasion Arthur threw a bottle at Sartre, was it the same brawl as when he gave Camus a black eye, or a separate one? "I *never* threw a bottle at Sartre," he replies. The record on that, he insists, is false. He adds that his friendship with Sartre was "poisoned" by "Simone."

I open p-QB4, which Arthur says he has never played against (can this be true? well, it will be in this sense, that my first few moves are always divertingly ungrounded in opening theory). After a tense beginning, Arthur gradually puts on the K-side pressure and establishes—revenge for the last game—an unbreakable pin on knight and queen. For a while, I am forced into a mixture of last-ditch defense and a series of waiting moves (never good for morale). Then I see the chance of a possible breakthrough: I give up the pinned knight for two central pawns, which opens routes to his isolated king which he has overconfidently neglected to castle. Gradually, I increase the pressure and cram him into back-row submission. After an hour and a half of unremitting tension, I pummel my way to victory. 2-2.

With the game over, Arthur puts the pieces back on the board and dismisses one of his moves as a blunder—or rather, given his joke-shop pronunciation, "a blonder." If I hadn't mated him, he points out, he would have mated me. So far we have played four times, he has won twice and "blondered" twice. Tomorrow will be the decider.

Afterwards, another record-breaking run: a whole thirty minutes nonstop. Arthur's postmatch exercise is of a different nature. If he sits down for too long he gets dizzy; so while I glide puffingly past the cow parsley dreaming of delinquent wives he walks slowly twice round the house to clear his head. "Zis Parkinson's, it knocks me sideways." His attitude to his illness seems mainly one of interest. He mentions other famous people who have suffered from Parkinson's. It is a distinguished disease (a disease for people with two houses, perhaps). His response to old age is also scientific and practical. The brain needs exercise like any other muscle. He writes five hundred words a day. He does the *Times* crossword. No doubt his chess games with me are designed not just for pleasure.

Domestically, he is a frail dictator. The telephone rings while he is in the house and Cynthia is gardening. Arthur gets up and walks slowly to the front door. "Ooo-oo," he goes, an Indian brave's call now reduced, in old age, to a squaw's call. "Telephone, angel." And Cynthia comes running from the garden. Neither seems to find this system unusual. One year, my wife and I are staying at Denston on Arthur's birthday. The telephone rings several times; Cynthia screens the callers. Perhaps he takes one birthday greeting out of six. Nor is there, for the rest of that day, any acknowledgement of the date. He is devoid of sentimentality or nostalgia. In the same way, he is interested only in what he is working on now, not what he wrote thirty years ago. In another writer this might spring from irritation at being praised for your blacklist while doubts are raised about your current preoccupations; with him it seems quite genuine. He once showed me a garage at Denston which he mockingly referred to as his "archive": I remember rows of steel shelving and large numbers of foreign editions. "Do you have a copy of your first book?" (I remembered it as an encyclopedia of sex written under a rather transparent pseudonym.) "Of course not," he replied, "that would be an enormous vanity."

He is a very courteous man. I quiz him about his name being on a board outside the local church: there is "Arthur Koestler" amidst a lineup of English officers, gentry, and clergymen appealing for funds. "It is expected," he replies defensively and a little stiffly, as if I should not be so openly surprised at an agnostic Hungarian Jew taking up his squirearchical responsibilities. At dinnertime he always rises to pour the first glass of wine for everyone—with however trembling a hand. His courtesy, however, should not be mistaken for indulgence. "You won't mind if I slip away after dinner?" he inquires most evenings, almost as if it were your house and his tiredness were making him a bad guest. But when, after dinner, you attempt to bid him good-night as it is only a quarter past nine and your glass has just been refilled, he responds with a slightly firmer emphasis, "I think we all go to bed now, yes?" Yes, Arthur. He needs Cynthia to help him: he has a contact lens, for instance, which he is no longer able to handle himself; she puts it in and takes it out for him. No doubt he doesn't want you sitting up and discussing him with his wife.

Game 5

Six in the morning. High cloud and light summer air. Moorhens are processing from the pond to the cornfield; two young rabbits are rolling on their backs in a dustheap where an elm has been removed; tits and sparrows are already in overdrive, all motion and babble and fighting. I stand there sniffing, a city dweller charmed by the simplest country sights; and the sound of Arthur's voice in my head as I watch the exuberant, carefree, normal scenes. "Zis Parkinson's, it knocks me sidevays."

It is our final game of the series, the decider. I am thirty-six and in full health; he is seventy-seven and very ill; the score is 2-2. Perhaps he will never play chess again. Perhaps I should lose, perhaps I should make a deliberate blunder. Like every chess player, Arthur delights in victory and loathes defeat: surely, out of gratitude for his writing, and out of affection, I should throw this last game?

Such reflections seem patronizing and irrelevant after only a couple of moves. Has any chess player *ever* thrown a match? Chess is a game of courteous aggression—and therefore very suitable for Arthur—but the courtesy and formality only serve to sharpen and focus the aggression. As Arthur's first attack develops, he immediately stops being a seventy-seven-year-old invalid who may never move p-K4 again; he becomes a ferocious assailant trying personally to damage me, to overthrow and humiliate me. How dare he! Gradually, I neutralize his first thrust, then begin a dogged pawn-march of my own. At first the maneuver is purely defensive—I push a pawn, he is obliged to retreat a piece—but its nature slowly changes. I realize that a huge advancing arrowhead of pawns with one's pieces undeveloped behind them is hardly recommended by any reputable chess strategist, but in this particular game the ploy seems unfaultable: with every pawn-move he is getting more and more cramped. His pieces are pushed back until they have barely a single square left to go to: in one corner, for instance, he has a rook's pawn, doubled pawns on the knight file, plus a knight in the corner square, all of which are locked up by a mere two pawns of mine. His queen darts out, but I lay a trap and plan my final push. I move a knight, which discovers a double attack on his queen. He must resign—yes, he must lose his queen, and then he must resign! I've got him beaten!

At this point an alarm clock goes off somewhere in the house. It is set for regular intervals throughout the day and designed to remind Arthur to take his medicines. Cynthia has gone out, so we set off around the house looking for the alarm, which is still buzzing. For some reason this proves difficult; eventually we track it down in Arthur's study and turn it off. He dutifully swallows a pill and we return to the board.

My inevitable feelings of pity and tenderness during this interruption do not affect my planned ruthlessness on the board. The game, after all, is serious (on move 7 Arthur attempts to vault one of his bishops over the top of a pawn; he doesn't spot the illegality,

148

I point it out, he apologizes—"It's my eyes, you know"). Now we settle back into our chairs again. Yes, that's right, his queen is attacked by two of my pieces. There is no free square for it to run to. I must win! But then, quite unexpectedly, Arthur finds a place for his queen: on a square currently occupied by one of my pawns. Fuck! Damn! A blonder! Worse, I'm clearly due to lose another pawn (in fact, the two pawns cementing down his K-side corner). Ah well, nothing to do but push on. Arthur, having prized away one little finger of my stranglehold, is able to begin an attack; I counter by grubbing out some of his seventh-rank pawns with my rook. Queens are now off, we have one rook each, I have bishop for knight (good), but am two pawns down. Even so, I have chances, incredibly strong chances: a pawn on the seventh rank, defended by a rook, and with its queening square covering my bishop. Yes, I must surely queen, and then win his rook. How can this not happen? Victory soon! And yet, somehow, I don't manage to queen (I can't quite work out why not—his king just lolloped over and fucked me up, I should never have allowed it). I lose rook and pawn for rook, and though I still have bishop for knight I'm three pawns down. Nothing for it. *Resigns.* 3-2.

Afterwards, despite the result, I don't feel as depressed as I normally would: it has been a fluctuating, violent, eccentric game in which we both had chances, and I played as well as I could. That Arthur won makes me feel, in the circumstances, a more or less grudgeless admiration. An hour and a half, a titanic struggle, and I feel shattered: what a testament to the old fighter that he overcame the young (well, youngish) whippersnapper. . . . But this magnanimity in defeat is not allowed to lie undisturbed. Arthur has the true chess victor's talent for rubbing things in: over dinner, an hour or so later, he changes the conversation to remark wistfully, "Of course, I am only fifty percent vot I vos at chess." I'm not exactly cheered by this not exactly tactful remark. But a little later I am partially restored. Cynthia says she can't remember when Arthur last had a series of daily games like this—surely not since he played George Steiner at Alpbach. That must have been interesting; what, I ask, was Steiner's game like? Arthur, a small man, has a way of puffing up his chest like a pouter pigeon at moments of pride. "He played like a *schoolboy.*" Well, that's some consolation. Oh, and did you tend to beat him, Arthur? More puffed chest: "Alvays."

Analysis

We oscillate, Koestler recognized, between *la vie triviale* and *la vie tragique*. I was preparing to run the marathon; he was preparing to die. I failed (well, the winter snow interfered with my training schedule—and besides, in the end my application was rejected, probably because I put "journalist" on the form and they decided they had far too many journalists running already and didn't need any more coverage); he succeeded. We met over chess, that trivial pursuit which refers to nothing else in life, to nothing significant, and yet which engages our full seriousness. George Steiner, who like Koestler covered the Fischer-Spassky match, strove in his report to convey the powerful emotions involved in a chess match. What he wrote is certainly unforgettable:

> The poets lie about orgasm. It is a small, chancy business, its particularities immediately effaced even from the most roseate memories, compared to the crescendo of triumph in chess, to the tide of light and release that races over mind and knotted body as the opponent's king, inert in the fatal web one has spun, falls on the board.

Steiner had the grace (and humor) to add: "More often than not, of course, it is one's own king." Without this rider, sated Casanovas would probably have been rushing to the local chess club to try out a more passionate sport.

Later that year my wife and I went down to Denston. Arthur said to us quietly, "Here is a conundrum which I cannot express to Cynthia. Is it better for a writer to be forgotten before he is dead, or dead before he is forgotten?" We nodded, and I remember thinking, *Well, that's hardly a conundrum for you, Arthur, obviously your work is going to survive your death.* . . . Except, of course, that this was not his question. He was asking which was *better*.

In late February of the following year Cynthia telephoned. We had a long-standing arrangement to take them to a Hungarian restaurant; she was canceling for the second time in a fortnight. She said Arthur had the flu, and whenever he got mild secondary illnesses it made his Parkinson's worse. She sounded nervous and apologetic, but no more so than usual; we agreed to fix a new date when Arthur was feeling stronger. "We're not going to let you get out of this, Cynthia," I said.

They did get out of it. Four days later Arthur and Cynthia killed—or delivered—themselves. I was standing in the newsroom of the *Observer*, one Thursday after lunch, and saw it on a television routinely emitting Ceefax news. A journalist standing nearby glanced at the screen and commented with casual knowledgeability, "He killed her and then did himself in." I wanted to knock the journalist down, or at least insult him violently, but said nothing. There wasn't any point in being angry with the fellow himself (saying the first thing that comes into our heads on such occasions wards off the reality, denies that death will call for us too in due course); what made me angry was the realization that Arthur was finally passing into untender hands (FAMOUS AUTHOR IN SUICIDE PACT, etc.), that he would no longer be there to correct things, get annoyed, or even just laugh. He had moved from "Arthur" to "Koestler," from present to past tense. He had been handed irretrievably into the care of others: how well would they treat him? (No more accurately than he would have predicted.) All his life Arthur had been sternly opposed to having children: the *Times* obituary, in its final paragraph, invented a daughter for him and Cynthia.

The note Arthur left was dated the previous June—before I played chess with him. In it he spoke of his clear and firm intention to commit suicide before he became too enfeebled to make the necessary arrangements. He reassured his friends that he was leaving them in a peaceful frame of mind, and "with some timid hopes for a depersonalised after-life beyond due confines of space, time and matter and beyond the limits of our comprehension."

His death was exemplary, well-managed, and, from the evidence, easy. Cynthia's death was, from the evidence, difficult, and causes problems. That she lived entirely for him nobody doubted; that he could be tyrannical was equally clear. Did he bully her into killing herself? This was the unmentionable, half-spoken question their friends came up against. I did not know him very well, but I seldom met anyone with less obvious romanticism or sentimentality; I would judge that a suicide pact would strike him as foolish, vulgar, and anachronistic. Indeed, I can imagine him getting irritated with Cynthia for wanting to join him: if his death, like his life, was to be part of a campaign, if it was intended to change people's minds about self-deliverance, what could be more counterproductive as propaganda than for his healthy fifty-five-year-old wife to kill herself as well? Which provokes the slimy follow-up question: if he didn't bully her into it, why didn't he bully her out of it? It seems to me that at this point speculation becomes impertinent, unless you can imagine yourself as a seventy-seven-year-old suffering from Parkinson's and leukemia and no longer able to rely on prolonged spells of lucidity. If you can do that, then I'll listen to you.

Cynthia, in the note she left, said that she didn't think much of double suicides as a rule. She wasn't a dramatic woman; she was shy, nervous, birdlike, capable of seeming in the same day both twenty-five and fifty-five. She moved awkwardly, like an adolescent unhappy with her body, who expects at any moment to knock over a coffee table and be sent to her room for doing so. I liked her, but her character evaded me: it was as if she would not show you what she was like for fear that something (what?) might happen to make her realize she'd been a fool for showing herself to you. On warm summer afternoons at Denston she used to clear the pond of weed, with a dog occasionally and unhelpfully at her heels. She had a long garden rake with a piece of rope attached to the end of the handle. She would throw the rake into the pond, haul it out with the rope, scrape the weeds off the teeth of the rake, pile them on the bank, and throw the rake back in. It looked a slow and awkward business. She herself looked awkward, liable to overbalance into the pond at any moment; but she kept at it with what looked like a childlike doggedness. Splash, pull, scrape, pile; splash, pull, scrape, pile; splash, pull, scrape, pile. That last summer I played chess with Arthur she didn't clean the pond.

Nominated by The Yale Review

43

by JIMMY SANTIAGO BACA

from IRONWOOD

6:00 a.m.
awake and leave to fish
the Jemez.
Coronado rode
through this light, dark
green bush,
horse foaming saliva,
tongue red and dry
as the red cliffs.
Back then the air
was bright and crisp
with Esteban's death
at the hands of Zuni warriors.
Buffalo God, as he was called,
was dead, dead, dead,
beat the drums
and rattled gourds.
The skin of the Moor
was black
as a buffalo's nose,
hair kinky
as buffalo shag-mane.
No seven cities
of Cibola gold were found.
Horses waded the Jemez,
white frothing currents

banking horse bellies,
beading foot armor,
dripped from sword scabbards.
Even as I wade in
up to my thighs
in jeans,
throw hooked
salmon egg bait
out in shadowy shallows
beneath overhanging cottonwood,
I realize
I am the end result
of Conquistadores,
Black Moors,
American Indians,
and Europeans,
bloods rainbowing
and scintillating
in me
like the trout's flurrying
flank scales
shimmering a fight
as I reel in.
With trout
on my stringer
I walk downstream
toward my truck.
"How you do?" I ask
an old man walking past,
          "Caught four—biting pretty good
          down near that elm."
I walk south
like the Jemez and Pecos pueblos
during the 1690 uprisings,
when the Spanish came north
to avenge their dead.
Indians fled
canyon rock shelters,
settling in present day
open plains.

Trout flails like a saber
dangling from scabbard stringer
tied to my belt,
chop-whacking long-haired weeds.
Peace here now. Bones
dissolved, weapons rusted.
I stop, check my sneaker prints
in the moist sandy bank.
Good deep marks.
I clamber up an incline,
crouch in bushes,
peer at vacation houses
built on rock shelves,
nestled in pine trees,
sunning decks and travel trailers—
the new invasion.

Nominated by Alberto Ríos

AFTER THE STATIONS OF THE CROSS

fiction by PETER TYSVER

from THE QUARTERLY

[1]

I was the definition of toast in the aisle with all the cereals and I had
my fixing goggles on the sweet ones when I heard some dude go,
Robbie. This is my name, so I of course checked it out, but all that
was there was this one dude stamping price tags on boxes of Cheerios, so I was ready just to bag it and think it was just my brutal
toastedness and my ears fucking with me, when I saw that the dude
stamping price tags on boxes of Cheerios was looking like I was
supposed to say something back to him, so I figured it was him who
said it, even though I didn't have a shit's clue as to who this dude
was. It fucking took forever to figure it out, too, and this all because
of his feathery blow-dry neat-look hair job, and the apron and tie and
fashion-tight pants, and the pointy-toed pimp shoes that made him
look like some whole different type of dude altogether. So here I
was, about to try to say something back to some dude who looks like
he knows me when I know I don't know him, when I notice he's got
this tattoo hanging out on his arm, where he's got his sleeve rolled
up, of some dude hanging casual on one of those one-seater mini-
cartoon floating desert islands with one palm tree, and he's sipping
with a straw from a cut-in-half coconut. This tattoo I hadn't seen
since shop class senior year, on a dude named Chuckie Goldman,
and I can tell you right now it's the only thing that's stayed the same.

See, back then he was a textbook burnout, with the biker boots and the bell-bottoms and the big-mother black leather wallet the size of a payroll check that he chained to his belt with the bottle-opener buckle. Really, the only difference between Chuckie Goldman and every other burnout dude was where when every other burnout had his black concert T-shirt with *Black Sabbath* or *Judas Priest* on it, Chuckie Goldman and his buddies had something different, because of this gang they had they called The Sons of Satan, so that they custom-printed *The Sons of Satan* on the backs of their black T-shirts, and so that they got this iron-on of a black leather biker dude and a nude foxy mama on a floating Harley surrounded by clouds and by big Bible letters that said, SWORN TO FUN, LOYAL TO NONE on the front. Chuckie Goldman and his buddies all had that scummy heavy-metal burnout hair and the chocolate-milk mustaches, and on the backs of the black leather jackets they wore, it said *The Sons of Satan*, too. Chuckie Goldman also had this big black van with bubble windows in back, and he cruised all The Sons of Satan around in it, and so I just always figured he was Big Cheese with The Sons of Satan, even though I really never had a shit's clue what The Sons of Satan ever did besides hanging behind the boiler room by the Bio pond before school and at lunch, blowing the doobage with all the other burnouts. Really, if you want to know the truth, all I ever really knew about Chuckie Goldman was that he made a metal bong in my shop class senior year, and that he sold my buddy Spooge smokables like he still does now, and that he had the same tattoo then as he did when I saw him stamping price tags while I was such toast in the grocery store.

So when I knew who he was, I went, Hey, dude, what's the hap?

He went, Having a bash at my place tonight.

This bash at his place, I figured would be to the fucking gills with the type of dude like Chuckie Goldman is, who were burnouts then but now are all decked out and filling bags for somebody's mother, or collecting carts in the parking lots, or whatever the shit ex-burnouts working at grocery stores have to do—since, besides Spooge, the only other dudes I know of around here that didn't go away someplace to school are the type of dude like Chuckie Goldman is.

I went, Big bash?

He stamped another price tag on another box of Cheerios and went, Well, sort of, but it's bring-your-own. Need directions?

Since Spooge has been buying smokables from the dude, I went, Spooge knows how to get there.

Chuckie Goldman went, Cool.

Then he went right on back to stamping more price tags, so I figured he was as much of a toast bandit as I was and couldn't think of jackshit to say, so I went back to the sweet-cereal scene and copped myself some Lucky Charms and chucked them in the cart and went, Check you out later, dude. Then I cruised my cart to the checkout line when I really should have checked out the Beauty and Health Aids and Feminine Needs aisle to get some sunscreen and Chap Stick for the Claw, which was the big reason I was there in the first place, since the Claw was running late and still packing and didn't have time to get it herself before the airport limo came, and she was crawling up my ass, calling me lazy lummox and having a fucking cow and making me go shopping for her sunscreen and Chap Stick, and also for chow for me and the Embryo for when she and the Old Man booked on vacation. So the Claw gave me cash, and since the fake-wood wagon was in the shop, the Claw gave me the Old Man's BMW keys, which I took and booked, cruising along in luxury, cranking tunes and blowing some of the mind-stop that Spooge got from Chuckie Goldman, all of this explaining why I was such serious toast in the grocery store and forgot to get the sunscreen and Chap Stick after hearing about the bash, and was completely clueless about it until the Claw blew me the major pies when I got home.

[2]

The Claw went, Selfish, thoughtless, good-for-nothing! What *is* this! Sweet cereal and frozen *pizza*? You do this to *spite* me! You can't even do me this *one thing*! Let me see your eyes! *Let me see them!* So, how many puffs of marijuana smoke *today*, Robbie? How many puffs from that water pipe that I happen to know that you're hiding? Oh, your *father* will be *very* happy to hear about *this* when I meet him at the airport. How does it *feel* to know you've ruined our whole vacation, *hmmn*? I should just call it *all* off, just *call* it off! How would you feel about *that*, hmmn? *Oh*, of *course*, I forg*ot*, you're *far* too drugged on that marijuana smoke to feel *anything*, aren't you? Oh, to *think* I could be so *foolish* as to trust *you* to watch over your little sister! It's *she* who should be doing the watching!

Well, I guess that's about enough of the Claw's rag treatment action. Besides, she had to finish varnishing her hair dome, and then got distracted when the Embryo came squealing down the stairs, going Mother! Mother! Look at me! Look! and spinning around like the Barbie doll she is in her peach-puke cotton-candy Homecoming dress, and it's of course the exact type of Easter egg afterbirth the Claw eats right up.

The Claw was going, Oooooo! *Don't* you look *nice*! That is *just* the *cutest* little *dress*!

You can bet there was too much cheese flying around for me to deal on, so I booked to the kitchen and copped myself some Lucky Charms and milk and cruised with it into the TV room, where I cooked through the channels, with it mostly just news on, until I found a rerun of *The Flying Nun*, which I hung with and got casual. During this part I was watching where the Flying Nun needed to take off and cook around but couldn't because of her flying powers being fucked somehow, I heard this car horn honking outside the TV room window. I looked out and saw this big-mama black stretch job of a limo hanging out there in the half-circle driveway, and whoever the fuck the lame-assed dude behind the smoked glass was was laying on the goddamn horn like he just drove up in a cab. I yelled in to the Claw, going, You pay this dude to come honk his horn?

The Claw went, Shut your smart mouth, young man, and take my bags out there. Pronto!

Now, I could've tried to crawl up her ass, just to do it, but I figured she'd only blow me some more pies, so I swallowed my pride and went and got her three heavy-as-shit suitcases from the front hall and booked with them out to the big black stretch job honking in the driveway. Let me tell you, it was cold enough out there to make your scrotal sac shrivel up and goose-pimple, and whoever the lame-assed dude behind the smoked glass was seemed to know it, because he didn't even get out to give me a hand, he just popped the trunk open from inside. I gave the smoked glass a fuck-you look and chucked the Claw's shit in the trunk and shut it. I started cruising in when the Claw cruised out, looking something fierce in her foofy fur coat and giving me the silent business like she thought it would break my heart. Then she just got in and slammed the door behind her and was gone to the airport, where she and the Old Man would fly away to where I wouldn't have to see them for a week.

Don't think this upset me, it was extremely suitable, but still, when I stood there in the driveway with it almost completely dark out and my arms folded in that brutal nip-chilliness in just jeans and a T-shirt, I couldn't help getting boged-out, because I was feeling like I was stuck down in this stupid house in this little dinky island of a town with nothing but some mind-stop for this whole fucking week off I got from flipping meat at one of the Old Man's Sizzlers to babysit the Embryo. Then I started getting boged-out about the fact that winter and snow and shit were coming soon, ever since the leaves got orange and fell, and I got boged-out about it being so shiver-assed cold, which made me think what the fuck was I doing standing in the driveway in just jeans and a T-shirt and freezing when I'd be much better off inside, where it was at least warm, so I started heading back in, and I put my hands in my pockets, and I just about shit my pants, because in my one pocket I still had the keys to the BMW that the Claw forgot to ask for back.

[3]

All fired up about the keys like I was, I figured I'd go in and ring up Spooge and tell him about it, which I tried to do, but the Potato picked it up and told me she'd have him call back, because he was hanging on the throne, which was what I half expected, seeing as half his waking hours are spent trying to lay some cable and he's always at it whenever I call.

So I hung up and got casual again with *The Flying Nun* and picked up my Lucky Charms to finish them off, but they'd been hanging so long they'd turned to mush, and I had to bag the whole idea and torch up a square instead, which I was smoking while I watched the last part of *The Flying Nun* when the Embryo came in and stood right in front of my view of the TV, going, Where is my lipstick? Where did you put my lipstick?

I went, What the fuck do I look like here. Mr. Encyclopedia King? Get out of my face, I'm trying to watch the TV.

160

So the Embryo went, Fine, A-hole, how about I just tell Mother I caught you smoking in the house? How would you like that, you big fat jerk?

I went, Eat my shorts, tight-assed bitch. Then I expectorated with vigor, without letting it fly, just as a warning so she'd think I had a good juicy greenie coming and she'd get the fuck out of my way.

She went, Gross! You fat pig! But she moved out of my way and I thought it did the trick until she went to the phone behind me and called up some tight-assed bitch friend of hers and started walking around the room with the phone in her hand in her peach-puke cotton-candy Homecoming dress, making these swishing noises and going off in her loud-assed stupid whiny fuck socialite voice, like all of a sudden she's turned into a Jewish chick.

Let me tell you, when the Embryo gets into this action, it's way beyond the valley of unacceptable, where she's going, Omi*god!* I mean, I'm like, omi*god!* I like, *totally* can't even *believe* that! I mean, Todd is like *way* cute. I mean, he's like, *so* totally cute, he's like, totally *way cute.* for *sure.* Wait, you *did?* Omi*god!* I *know!* Totally! Omi*god! Missy,* you're like, *so* totally *lucky!* I *swear,* I'm like, *totally* like, omi*god!*

I hope you get the idea of how brutal that can be, and how it's hard to keep yourself from projectile yacking, and how you have to shout, Shut the fuck up! which I did and she didn't, but instead made the nearly fatal mistake of trying to wedge her way even deeper up my ass by putting her puke assed dress right in my line of watching the end part of *The Flying Nun,* on purpose, which I wasn't about to sit there and deal on, so this time none of this nice-guy fake hocker bluffing action, this time I let a really truly vicious hunk of brutal lung cheese come cooking up my throat and wing out end over end like those good heavy ones always do, and she was fucking lucky she got out of the way, too, because when it slapped against the TV and went gooping down the Flying Nun's face, it didn't look like something you'd want hanging out on your Homecoming dress, and that's for fucking sure.

And so of course the Embryo had to start going, *Eeeeew! Eeeeew! Gross!* You're *sick!* You gross *pig!* It's my fat a-hole brother, and he like, *spit* at me! You're lucky you missed, A—hole, you're just *lucky!* Missy, I'm like, wearing my dress? Yeah, and my A-hole brother *spit* at it! Isn't that the *grossest*? Get out of here, gross *pig*! I'm telling Mother on you!

I cashed my square in my Lucky Charms and went, Go ahead you little ax wound. Then I booked into the kitchen and chucked the bowl into the sink, and I looked up and saw the picture hanging there above it of the Claw and the Old Man in their stupid-looking ski outfits, smiling at the camera, with their arms around each other and the mountains big behind them. I went, Fuck you, too.

[4]

Right then the doorbell went off in the front hall, and I could hear the Embryo on the phone in the TV room going, Omig*od*! He's *here*! I'm so totally *psyched*! Gotta *go*! Then I could hear her puke-assed dress swishing toward the front door, and I could hear her shout, Clean off the TV, fat pig! Then I heard her open the door, sounding just like the Claw when she answers the phone with her velvet voice. Then the phone in the kitchen started ringing and I picked it up and it was Spooge.

I went, Hey, dude, how'd it go?

Spooge went, How'd what go?

I went, Weren't you eating a rat?

This was a big hairy fat-assed boner on my part, because I was forgetting that Spooge takes his ka-kas very seriously, getting all into a fucking sweat about the shapes and sizes and textures of things, and going off about them like they're his parents or something. Like he'll go, Today my stool was a kind of a dark yellow and kind of like soft serve and it had whole pieces of corn in it that I ate last night. Or he'll go, Today I had really bad Hershey squirts and the upshot is, it gave me ring of fire and now it hurts like hell to walk. And he'll go on and on, too, if you don't stop him and go, Spooge, listen, I know you like to stand up after laying some cable and look at it in fine-assed detail and let it tell you all about what kind of day you're going to have, but really, I really wouldn't be all that offended if you decided you wanted to keep that part of your life a secret from me. Like right then, when I'd pulled the boner and asked him how his rat-eating session went, Spooge went, Well, I've been feeling rather costive lately, so today after my psychology class, when I was downtown at school, I went into the cafeteria and bought

162

a bran muffin, because it's said that bran muffins increase your regularity, and so when I got home here and took my shit, it was really very painful, and it looked just like this hard little bran muffin, only it was quite a bit darker.

I went, Spooge, that's nice. Thanks for sharing. Now listen. Then I told him about seeing this Chuckie Goldman dude earlier at the grocery store and how he told me he was having a bash and how the Claw booked without taking the keys to the BMW with her. So Spooge said to come on over to do some bongs, since we couldn't do them here because of the Claw crawling up my ass about the goddamn things ever since I got the boot from Culver Military Academy sophomore year for getting caught smoking one in my room. Spooge doesn't have to worry about getting caught smoking his, because his units are casual and their bedroom is downstairs and Spooge's is up and they never go up there, and even if they did and caught him tooting on the thing, they probably wouldn't care.

I asked Spooge if he had any drinkables and he said he didn't, so I hung it up and booked up the back stairway to my bedroom and got my half-full bottle of Jack from the rain gutter outside my window. I put it in my coat pocket and put on my coat and was about to book down the front stairway when I saw what was standing there down at the bottom in the front hall, looking at this framed-certificate thing the country club gave the Old Man when they made him the Big Cheese hanging on the wall. It was this dude who I figured must've been the Embryo's date for the dance, and he was looking at the framed-certificate thing like he thought it was hot shit. This dude was a serious dweeb, looking just like one of those dudes that was going to grow up to be one of those dudes that I used to caddy for when I used to caddy, the type of dude that wears super-bright green pants and a bright red sport shirt and shiny like-new white shoes, the type of dude that tips you only a dollar fifty for eighteen holes and gets you a hot dog instead of a hamburger at the halfway house. He was holding this little white box, which I figured must've been the Embryo's flower, and he looked like such a weenis with his hair slicked back and his little bow tie that I almost felt sorry for him in the same way that I feel sorry for my little brother, thinking about him marching around in those brutal stiff black uniforms and twirling his rifle in the air and standing like at attention with a pole up his ass and dying to please. So you can see why I didn't want to talk with this dude. He looked to me like the kind of dude that would call you big guy, and to be called big guy would've been a bit too much for me to deal on.

So I went around and down the back stairway instead, booking out the back door by the covered swimming pool, cruising along the back of the house and through the back door of the garage, where the Old Man's BMW was waiting with its stupid-assed custom-job license plates that say EAT OUT in reference to the six Sizzler Steak Houses that the Old Man owns. It's hard to believe the Old Man could be so clueless and not know what people will take it to mean. They might as well just say 12 INCHES. The fake-wood wagon that was in the shop has custom-plate jobs, too, saying SKI BUM, which is what the units have flown off to be for the week. But even though the plates on the BMW are much more brutal, it's a much more suitable car, and I never get to drive the fucking thing, either. So I had a seat and sunk down in the furry white bucket dealies, shutting the door behind me and popping the engine, pressing the garage-door opener clipped to the sun shield and booking backward out the driveway, pressing it to Shut as I cruised down the street.

Like it always is with these expensive foreign jobs, it's so vacuum-packed quiet that you can't hear a thing, not even the engine, and there were no streetlights and it was black outside and I hadn't even popped the headlights yet, so it was like floating fast in a big black hole. When I popped them on, everything got grounded, and it looked pretty spooky out there, with these fucked-up shadows flying around the trees as I booked past, and these black shapes of houses floating by so smooth and quiet, and not jackshit in sight. I must've still been kind of toasted, because it was spooking me out in a weird-assed way, so I popped on the radio and cranked some tunes and concentrated on the orange glow of the dashboard lights until things seemed suitable again, and the next thing I knew, I was cruising up Spooge's driveway.

[5]

I threw it in park by the garage behind the house and got out and walked up to the back door. There was a window in the door, and I looked inside through it, and the whole downstairs looked dark, but then I saw this orange-tipped square burning off in the distance, so

164

I knocked and the orange tip got up and came to the door and let me in, and I shut the door behind me. It was the Potato, and she went back to where she was, toward the table in the kitchen in the dark.

The Potato went, Hey, Robbie.

I went, Hey, what's the hap?

The Potato went, Nothing. Bored. Then she had a seat again at the kitchen table in the dark and kept on smoking her square and not saying anything. She's always there, smoking in the dark, when I come over, just like Spooge is always upstairs doing bongs and cranking tunes, and just like their units are always in the front room by the front door that nobody ever uses, watching the TV.

I went, Bored, huh?

The Potato just sort of laughed, like she was doing it in her sleep, which is exactly how she talked, too. Maybe it had something to do with what Spooge told me about some buddy of hers going down to Mexico and bringing back a shitload of prescription Valiums for her, but that might only be part of it, because she'd seemed like that ever since she'd dropped out of school a few months before that. Spooge told me that mostly she'd just hang out all day, stoned shitless and watching soaps and fingering peanut butter out of the jar in her sorority T-shirt and sweats, and then at night hanging at the kitchen table in the dark, smoking squares and smoking squares.

What's fucked up about all this is that she used to be pretty hot, and that there she was that night, looking like death and getting all fat, and all because of this one dude she did the boyfriend scene with for almost six years, this dude from around here named Bruno Pasquarelli, better known as Bruno I'm an Idiot Pasquarelli, of the Pasquarelli Construction family fame, the studly gold-chain guido pimp-shoes type of Italian dude that you'd figure his type of name would make him. She started doing the boyfriend scene with him back in high school, and then they went away to school together, and they ended up going out for almost six fucking years, until right when the Potato dropped out, which Spooge told me happened because of this Bruno dude selling blow.

Spooge told me this Bruno dude sold blow to most of the frats there, and that he used to hose a good number of the sorority chicks, too, but that the Potato didn't really give a shit, as long as he kept her blowhound tooter full. Thing was, she was such a blowhound that she started looking like one of those starving little African dudes that you always end up seeing if you come home late and toasted and you pop on the TV, and there they are, the kinds with the fucking flies hanging out on their lips. Apparently Bruno didn't get into that look, so he dropped her, and because he dropped her, she dropped out of school, and only two months from graduation, which is something even I wouldn't do if I'd gotten that far. I figured she must've had her reasons, though, because when I saw her when she came home after Bruno dropped her and she dropped out, she was pretty major fucking spooky action, like those brutal-looking dudes you see in those pictures of concentration camps.

[6]

It took her about a month to start looking normal again, and right about the time she did and started looking hot before she started getting fat, she and Spooge and me went out to this lame-assed bar they have around here called the Cattle Company, where all the ex-burnout grocery dudes hang out, and where all the swinging divorced chicks hang out, and where all the chicks wear their pants so tight that their crotches look like camel toes. I don't have a clue why we were there, because we'd been there once before and we knew it was beyond the valley of being unsuitable, but there we were, hanging, drinking beers in this one part that's supposed to look like a corral or some such shit, watching all these pathetic weenises doing the boogie-shoes scene like the hurting units they were on this dinky little lit-up-from-under dance floor while the lame-assed DJ played this tortured elf music with a disco beat. By the time we booked out of there, we were all pretty much toast bandits, but especially Spooge, because when we went back to Spooge's room for a bong session, Spooge took one down that would've made a house explode, and as he let the smoke fly and it hung above our heads, he fell back on his bed with the bong in his hand and was passed-out toast just like that. I had to cook over there and grab the bong from him, because he was about to spill the soup from it all over himself. If you've ever smelled bong soup, you'd thank me if you were Spooge, because the shit smells worse than the crust on your underwear.

So it was me and the Potato, laughing about Spooge sawing wood like a banshee, like the lightweight he was. When we finally stopped

166

laughing, we just sat there and didn't say a thing, I guess because we couldn't think of anything to say. What was wigging me out, though, was that the Potato was hanging there on the floor next to me and smiling like I was Bruno I'm an Idiot Pasquarelli and not me. Obviously this wasn't the case, though, because then she started talking to me about him, and it was out of bounds, because out of the blue she started telling me about the first time she and Bruno hosed, when they were in their senior year of high school, in the other bedroom up there, on the Potato's pink-cotton candy canopy bed, while Mrs. Spooge was downstairs cooking up dinner. She told me neither of them had hosed before, and that neither of them had a shit's clue what to do, and that Bruno had such a humongous husker that it hurt, and this whole time she was going off, I was hanging there with this shit-eating grin and not saying jackshit, because what the fuck do you say, and plus I was such toast I thought this was some kind of an invitation, even when she started saying that she never really even liked having sessions anyhow, even though she looked kind of bummed.

When she was finished talking about it, she just sat there like a wet puppy hanging out in the middle of a road, waiting for a truck to come and run it over. There wasn't anything I could think of to say, and besides, she all of a sudden moved over closer to me and put her head on my shoulder, right there on my fucking shoulder, and what else was there I was supposed to do? So I of course took her head in my hands and started playing kissy face with it, and it was fine, too, it was suitable, and it went on for a pretty good long time, with the only sound being Spooge sawing wood, until I tried to go for the old titty action and knew I'd fumbled the ball in a big way.

She pulled away from me like she all of a sudden realized who the fuck I was, and that I sure as shit wasn't Bruno I'm an Idiot Pasquarelli, and she went, No.

I went, Are you sure?

She didn't say anything then, just sat there fixing her goggles on her hands in her lap like she was autistic, and I looked at her and listened to Spooge sawing wood, which sure as shit didn't help my chances any in the romantic-mood department.

Finally she went, I think you better go.

I went, Sure about that?

She just kept on staring at her hands and didn't say jackshit, and I, not being the type of dude that will beg just to get his end wet, booked.

[7]

When I got outside, though, I for some reason didn't feel much at all like hopping in the old fake-wood wagon with the SKI BUM plates and cruising home. I instead, for some reason, walked over to the fence that runs alongside Spooge's driveway and jumped it to where the Infant Jesus of Prague School playground is, the playground for where me and Spooge used to go to grade school, where I went until seventh grade, when my units made me go to Culver. When I landed on the ground on the other side, I cruised over to the swings and hung out there by them, looking up at the Potato's bedroom window until I saw the light go out there. Then I took out a square and torched it, and went around and had a seat on the middle swing facing Infant Jesus of Prague with my back to Spooge's house. Across the softball field from the playground, Infant Jesus of Prague sort of looked like it was a castle on an island, because of the fact that it stood alone on a hill, and that the street curved around it and surrounded it like a moat, and that the fence that went alongside Spooge's house separated it from everything else, and that on that night, it looked so huge in the darkness, even though it still didn't look so huge as when we were little dudes and were so wigged out by the Nazi nuns that we called it International Japanese Prison because of the initials being the same. It's a pretty ruthless building, an old brownish-red brick three-story job with black metal fire escapes and big-mother windows, and they shut it down just last year, I guess because of a shortage of Catholic kids or something. I heard last week that they're tearing it down to the ground soon, heard it when the Claw was reading *The Star* to the Old Man at breakfast before they booked for their golf game and before I went to toss meat around at the Old Man's Sizzler. The Old Man just about popped a hemorrhoid when he heard that, because he grew up around here and went to grade school there just like me, and he started going off about how he was going to protest it at the next Jaycees meeting, while he salted his eggs with his elephant salt shaker. I have to admit I was kind of wigged when I heard about it, too, but probably not for the same reasons as the Old Man. He probably misses the nuns winging erasers at him and trying to peg him with their long-assed rulers, where I'm just going to miss the building. It's a pretty suitable building.

Like that night when the Potato told me to book and I was hanging on the swings, that night Infant Jesus of Prague was looking like a castle in a very big way. That night I was hanging on the swings and smoking a square, the sky behind Infant Jesus of Prague was this kind of orange color, like this kind of a black-orange color, because of the lights from the city way off making it that way, and it pretty much drowned out the stars. Infant Jesus of Prague was like this jumbo black shadow against this blackish-orange sky, and the only detail of it you could see was that part of the fire escape sticking out on that one side, that same part of the fire escape that Sister Thomas Annette took a gravel dive off of when I was in third grade.

It was when Roy Spitzig, who was my best buddy at that time, was tossing Spooge's Twinkie as a joke around the gym where we ate lunch, and Spooge got all bent out of shape and went and told on him to Sister Thomas Annette, who was our lunch guard or something like that, hanging out all the time in her black robed nun getup, and she caught Roy by the collar and took Spooge's Twinkie from him and shoved the fucking thing in his face, and it had this white cream shit coming out of it by this time from it being tossed around, and she was shoving it in his face, going, Eat it! Eat it! And Roy wigged and slugged her in the gut and booked out of the lunchroom, and Sister Thomas Annette didn't seem to be hurt by that punch, because she booked right out of there after him.

Roy told me that Sister Thomas Annette finally cornered him in this one classroom on the third floor with that fucked-up Twinkie still in her hand, and she was still going, Eat it! Eat it! Roy told me that he was right next to the door to the fire escape, and so he opened it and went out there and started going down it. Sister Thomas Annette followed him out there, and if you don't believe that, believe it, because Sister Thomas Annette had flaming orange hair and a face like Ernest Borgnine with a potato chip wedged up his ass. Roy told me that when he got down to the bottom of the fire escape and had no place else to go but to jump, he turned around and looked up and saw Sister Thomas Annette coming down at him with that fucked-up Twinkie still in her hand, coming down that final flight, when the heel of one of her little black nun boots got sucked right down in between the rungs, and she screamed, Holy Jesus! loud enough that we could hear it from the lunchroom, where we were wondering what was going down up there, where it turned out it was Sister Thomas Annette, because it was then that she fell one flight down right on her flaming orange head.

Roy told me that the way it looked to him, it looked like Sister Thomas Annette was being pulled down to the ground really slow, or like she was a big black bomb he was watching fall through the sky from a plane high up, and that after that he would have these brutally bad dreams about falling nuns calling out his name. I'll tell you, I can't say I wouldn't either if I were him, because when Sister Thomas Annette took that gravel dive right down on her flaming orange head, she was turned right into a vegetable not too much different from what the Potato turned into when she dropped out of school and started smoking squares in the kitchen in the dark, there where I was hanging with her that night, listening to her laugh like she was laughing in her sleep.

[8]

I went, Spooge upstairs?

The Potato kind of nodded and made this grunting type of noise, like she was holding back a really good ta-fa, and just sat there looking at the square in her hands on the kitchen table, glowing in the dark, and I stood there, too, for a little while, with my goggles fixing on the orange tip of it there. Then I went, Yeah, well, check you out later, and booked out of there through the dark dining room, being not noisy so Spooge's units wouldn't hear me and I wouldn't have to get sucked into a flying-cheese session with them. I cracked open the door to the upstairs part, and it was all dark there, too, but I could hear the cranking of tunes from up there, so I took a grab at the railing and made my way up like a blind dude, stepping over all the piles of folded clothes and shit until I made it to the top, where down at the end of the hall I saw light from inside Spooge's room falling out into the darkness. I took my half-full bottle of Jack out of my coat pocket and walked down and into his room, sloshing it around in the air, but when I got in there, I saw Spooge hanging on the floor in his fucking undies with the big bong

170

between his legs and the long round tube going up to his mouth, where he was working on woofing a lungful of mind-stop that was bubbling through the bong soup from the bowl he was torching. The dope glowed to ash as he slipped his thumb off the carb and the smoke slammed out of sight, Spooge taking away his mouth and squinting up his eyeballs and turning sort of purple as he popped the bowl off and cashed it in the ashtray.

I went, Bonging savage!

Spooge jerked up quick and coughed like he was yacking, and a mind-stop cloud came at me like those time-lapse clouds you see cooking across the sky in those encyclopedia science flicks that they showed us when we were in high school. When the smoke stopped coming, Spooge kept on coughing, and when he stopped that he went, Hey, dude.

He didn't say jackshit after that, he just was hanging there with a vicious case of bottle mouth, picking with his fingers at the red, white, and blue shag carpeting on his floor, so I had a seat on his bed and went, Toasting out, dude. Got a grip. Then I unscrewed the Jack and had a couple visits with it.

After a while, Spooge looked up and went, What? with this palsy-lipped smile, making this noise like somebody stirring macaroni and cheese.

I went, Check it out, sort of sloshing the half-full bottle of Jack around in the air in front of the toast bandit, just to check out if he was still alive, sort of like I used to hold up slices of pizza and other human food in front of my good old now-dead dog Taffy, with the scabs on the back, just to see if it was still kicking there in its plaid basket in the laundry room. I could tell Taffy still had it when it made some noises like its lungs were full of mud, just like I could tell Spooge still had it when he talked about his turds again, going, I can't drink that stuff, it gives me burning shits.

I went, Fucking everything does. Just fill me a bong.

[9]

So he did, a couple in a row from the little pile of mind-stop on the LP between his legs, the whole time flapping his jaw with those little things of foamy shit at the corners of his mouth, so that you get your fixing goggles on them and they're all you ever end up paying

171

any attention to. But he kept on going off the whole time he was filling bongs about how these Cattle Company grocery dudes were all going to be at Chuckie Goldman's bash full force to the gills, and about the kinds of Trans Am Corvette kinds of cars these dudes cruise around in, and about how these cars are really just extensions of their penises that they use to subliminally impress the camel-toed chicks at the Cattle Company, and on and on about all this other related bogus mind-action shit from some stupid-assed psychology class he was in at the time.

I woofed down bong three and tuned right out, my mind floating off and my body feeling pulled down to the bed, with Spooge as far off as the Claw when I'm toast at home and she's blowing down the major pie sessions on me, and I'm couched and out to lunch, except with Spooge I every once in a bong session will pick up on some sentence blowing out his ass that sounds worth calling him on, like when I heard him go, I like to have sex, sort of, except for the part where you actually start to do it.

That I heard, and had to go, What in fuck's sake are you talking about?

So Spooge had to fill me in, going, *You* know, like when you're kissing with a girl, and then you're rubbing her breasts, and then you're squeezing her buttocks, and then next thing you know, you're both unzipping and fondling each other's things, and how that's all just so great and just all so much fun?

I went, Yeah, so?

So Spooge went, Well, like, then you decide to get down to the gravy and go for the goods, and so you moisten up and penetrate, and then you're in there for about a second and you blow your wad right off and you get all depressed, and your thing, your thing, you know, it goes all soft and you get all depressed, and then you just end up wondering, you wonder, what's the point to it all?

So I went, Spooge, ever stop to think that if you could just control your husker from coughing up the mayo at the drop of a hat and just get a little more stamina action in there, that then it might just become a little more enjoyable for you? So Spooge went, Don't talk to me about stamina! I'm here beating off nightly to try to get stamina! It's completely different when there's a girl there! It sucks! Stamina doesn't even come into play! I could beat off forever, but if a girl's there, forget it! Stamina's out the window! I know what I'm talking about!

So I went, Spooge, there's no way you can know what you're talking about, because you're sitting here in your fucking undies and you're not talking about jack, except maybe that you like boxing your clown more than you like having sessions.

So Spooge went, Well, maybe I do! I happen to enjoy it, okay? Big deal!

So I went, Cut this shit, dude. I can deal on your always talking about eating rats, and I can deal on your penis-extension talk, but when you start going off about boxing your clown, I'm sorry, I don't think I can deal, all right?

Spooge got all huffy-puffy at that, going, Oh, I see! So you're trying to tell me that you don't masturbate, is that it? Or is it that you just can't handle the fact that I'm more enlightened than you and willing to admit it, while you just sit there all repressed and pretend like it isn't true.

He gave me this I-just-cashed-you-under-the-table-with-my-genius mind smile then, like he'd just beat the shit out of me at thumb wrestling or something.

So I went, I'm not pretending jackshit. I just don't want to hear about it. Far as I'm concerned, if you shake it more than three times, you're playing with it, and you can keep it to yourself.

Spooge went, Are you trying to tell me you don't? Anybody who says they don't is a liar.

So I went, And anybody who talks about it all day long is a fucking butt pirate.

Don't go thinking I'm out of bounds here, because you haven't heard some of the fucking brutal shit Spooge thinks makes him enlightened, because he's flapping his jaw to me about it, shit I not only wouldn't do, but shit I sure as fuck wouldn't be going off at the mouth about if I had.

Like check this one out: when Spooge decided to share with me about the time when he was cruising to class in his units' car on the expressway, and he unzipped and whipped out his husker right there while he was driving and started shaking hands with the fucking thing. He was telling me it was pretty intense, until he started getting all wigged out that a truck was going to come cruising alongside him, and that the truck-driver dude was going to look down and see Spooge hanging there and boxing his clown like a banshee, and think he was a turd burglar and run him off the road.

173

That's the exact type of thing that gets me calling Spooge a butt pirate, and then that's the exact type of thing that gets Spooge acting like he's all hurt feelings and shit, like he did when I called him one, and so I had to go, Spooge, listen. Don't be such a weenis. We both know we're five-star generals in the celibate army, and we both got our problems, but at least I don't go around talking about boxing my clown the whole fucking day. Now, if you want to box it, go ahead, box it, just don't expect me to sit around here and listen about it. Now, would you get fucking dressed? I want to book.

Spooge just hung there for a while rubbing the mind-stop on the LP between his fingers, while I had a visit with Jack, and then he got up and started changing shirts a shitload of times, because he said he was afraid everything he was putting on was going to make him break out into a rash, and when he was done with that and dressed, we booked down the dark stairs and into the dark kitchen, where Spooge put on his coat. The Potato still had her seat there at the table, torching up a match to light a fresh square, and the light from it made her face all fucked-up shadows and shit, like she was someone we didn't know, as we slipped out the door and she went, Going somewhere? as she blew out the match and we shut the door behind us and headed for the Old Man's penis extension parked there in the driveway.

[10]

We got in, sucked down by the furry bucket seats, and I popped the engine and booked us backward out the driveway and drove to Family Liquors, where we dropped our two twelvers of Coors on the counter while the purple-faced dude standing behind it stood there with his fixing goggles on Spooge's ID, trying to blow us pies by telling us it was fake, which it was, with the name and dates and all the vitals for Bruno Pasquarelli, and the picture pure Spooge, look- ing like anything but a Pasquarelli, hanging there in the picture with his vicious bottle mouth, while the purple-faced dude behind the counter was looking at it and going, You don't look Eyetalian to me. I don't know about this. I know of that Pasquarelli Construction family, and you don't look nothing like them.

So Spooge put on his wading boots and went, Listen, I know,

okay? Don't rub it in. If you have to know, I don't look Italian because of the fact that I was adopted. You had to know. Satisfied?

The purple-faced dude turned purpler and went, Sorry, and rung them up, and we booked with them out to the Old Man's car with the EAT OUT plates, and cruised out to the boonie factors, where all the condos are, where this bash Chuckie Goldman was supposed to be having was supposed to be.

We tore through four Coors each just looking for the thing, because it was all the way out there in butt-fuck land, where nothing's been developed but the streets, everything's just empty lots with FOR SALE signs stabbed in them and sometimes frames of houses that will all be put up looking just like every other one, and there's not even any grass laid down on the ground. It's nothing like behind us, where me and Spooge live, where it's all a lot older and the trees are all jumbo and the houses all look different, and where it's still sucking wind but heaven compared to out here in the boonies, where it's all empty parts of road stretching out between little plopped-down condos that Pasquarelli Construction is busy putting up in the middle of cornfields, but mostly just the blackness and the road cooking under the headlights, which I kept popping off to float through it all in the vacuum-packed no noise of the Old Man's car, while Spooge would freak, make me turn them back on again, bumming that I wouldn't let him crank any tunes.

If he wasn't hanging shotgun, I'd have cashed the fuckers permanently, cruised along without jackshit in sight until the outline of this black road showed itself to me in the dark orange light glowing down from the sky of the city behind me. I would have floated like that, not hearing a sound, not Spooge's talking on the shotgun side, flapping away while I un-huh-ed and yeah-ed just to be social, while the rest of me took off, just took off, really, thinking nothing special and just holding that wheel.

But then Spooge was pointing right across my face to this huge sign in black and white that said, EVERGREEN, A PASQUARELLI CONSTRUCTION DEVELOPMENT PROJECT, and behind it, far off, a dark clump of condos.

Spooge went, This is them, Evergreen. Hang a louie up there, and then you hang a ralph. We cruised into this wide-open parking-lot type of thing, and by then I could see that these Evergreen condo things were just like any other condo things Bruno's old man or anybody else's old man was having put up all over these empty places way out here where nothing is. Just phone lines and dinky trees stuffed in piles of dirt surrounded by just-unrolled grass surrounding these shitloads of exactly the same painted gray things all jammed together in groups and joined at the walls like there's not room out here enough to even keep them separate.

I went, How the fuck're you supposed to tell your place from anybody else's?

Spooge looked at me like I was autistic and went, They've got *numbers.*

Then he was pointing across my face again to this one bunch of condo things where there were all these Trans Am T-Tops and Corvettes and all other kinds of penis extensions parked outside of, and I knew I was in the right place when I saw Chuckie Goldman's big black van with the bubble windows in back. There was an open space next to it, so I took it and cashed the engine, and then me and Spooge just hung there and didn't say a word, with those condo things surrounding us like a big humongous horseshoe. I swear I felt just like that one dude in that one joke where he's in someplace somewhere like hell and he has to look inside all these doors to pick which thing inside one it is he wants to get sucked into doing for the rest of all time, and all that forever kind of shit. So there's this dude, going through all these doors with all this unsuitable shit going on behind them, like gruesome fat chicks sitting on your face, or your toenails getting ripped out in slow motion, or fist-fucking, or whatever it is, I'll leave it up to you, because it's all ruthless, until he comes to the last door, where he sees a bunch of dudes standing knee-deep in big fat turds, and even though it might sound brutal, compared to all the other things behind all the other doors, what's behind this last one seems at least *kind* of suitable, so he goes for it. Thing is, once he's inside and the door's shut behind him, he hears this loud-assed whistle blowing and this loud-assed voice shouting, Okay, everybody, coffee break's over! Back on your heads!

I figured Spooge must've felt about the same way, because he went, This is pretty depressing shit.

I went, That's not the word. I don't even think we should bother.

Spooge popped a Coors and went, What else do you suggest? The Cattle Company? If that's what you're thinking, drop me off at home, because I'd rather be beating off.

I went, Don't start, Spooge.

Then I popped a Coors of my own and we just sat there, steaming up the inside of the windshield with our breath.

Finally Spooge went, Let's do up some more doobage. I need to be more baked if I'm going to go in there.

I went, Casual by me.

So we did up the doobage and slammed down our beers, and that seemed to do it, so we took our two twelvers and got out and locked up and headed for the door with the big number 7, which when we got there we stood outside of and listened to the music and voices coming from inside, and I was thinking how I'd rather be tossing meat around at the Old Man's Sizzler, or listening to the Claw blowing her rag, anything else but right there and right then. I was about to go, Let's book, to Spooge, too, when he made what you might call a decision by knocking on the door. Next thing was this voice coming closer to the other side while I looked down, watching the knob turning and pulling away, leaving me with my fixing goggles on a black T-shirt with a white iron-on of the burning Hindenburg and the big red words LED ZEPPELIN underneath.

Then there was this big raspy-lunger voice that went, Robbie?

I looked up, and there was this huge dude a head or two huger than me, holding out his hand that wasn't holding his twelver. He had pizza face severely and a laid-out-flat type of boxer nose, and except for the fact that he'd gotten much huger and had taken to dressing like the old type of burnout, he looked just like my buddy from Infant Jesus of Prague, my good old best buddy, Roy.

I went, Roy?

Roy went, Fuckin' Robbie dude man! holding out his huge hand for me to shake, and I did. I looked down and saw my hand there in his and felt like a dinky little dude, like my old best buddy, Roy, was going to lift my little hand and my whole body attached to it, shake my hand so I'd cook up into the air, and whip back down fast, cracking cement and shooting underground like a dude in a cartoon, or maybe just rip my whole fucking arm off right at the shoulder altogether.

He then did the same routine with Spooge, going, Spooge man!

Good to see you! Good to see both of you two dudes! Come on inside!

He walked in, and we walked in and shut the door behind us. Roy was already cutting through the crowd toward the back of the room, and me and Spooge cruised along behind him. This room was packed with the ex-burnout grocery dudes, all ironed and blow-dried and dancing to this Cattle Company tortured-elf disco shit, with their mall-rat cosmetology-school dropout girlfriends with the flared-back-hair syndrome and the camel-toe pants, and it seemed to me like Roy cruising up in front of us with his twelver in one hand was the only dude left in the black concert T-shirt and the frayed-at-the-heels bell-bottoms. Roy up ahead of us looked like one of those Cro-Magnon dudes, with those big-mother dinosaur-bone exhibit bones, and fucking tall, like his head was above the crowd as he cruised through, heading for the back of the room, going through a darkened door there. We followed, cut through the crowd, and went through it, too, and there we were in Chuckie Goldman's garage with the lights out, except for the light coming in from the room we were just in, and except for the lights from the glowing tips of squares and doobage, smokables strong-smelling with the garage door closed, the orange tips moving around shapes in the dark, dudes standing smoking with their twelvers at their feet.

Roy was standing right inside the door, smiling and going, Thought you dudes'd wanna come back here where the weed is going around.

I went, You thought right, dude. Thanks.

Spooge scoped the scene for a second and turned to Roy and went, You seen Chuckie around back here?

Roy went, Sure thing, dude. He's right over there. Follow me.

We followed Roy over to where these two dudes were standing, where it was too dark to make out their faces, when one of the dudes torched up his lighter to fire up some doobage rolled like a stogie that the other dude was holding, and in the flame from the lighter we could see that the dude who was stoking on the doobage was the dude who Spooge was looking for. He saw us, too, and went, You dudes are right on time. I'm firing up some of these primo California buds I got in today for the very first time.

Me and Spooge and Roy put our twelvers on the floor and popped one each. Chuckie took a drag and passed it to the other dude, who took a drag and passed it on to Roy, who took a drag and passed it on to me, and it went around the bases like that until it was roached, with none of us talking and lung-blowing coughs. This shit was mind-stop in capital letters, and I was way beyond the valley, with my cheeks fluttering in the wind, while Chuckie Goldman and Spooge went off about what primo bud action the shit we smoked sure was, and Spooge asking what it cost to take some off his hands and then bumming on the price, with Chuckie Goldman going, Shit walks, money talks, and then those two and the dude I didn't know wandering off to do bongs and leaving me the toast bandit I was with three Coors left and one in hand in that dark garage with my old best buddy, Roy Spitzig, hanging there next to me with a beer in his hand, too, not saying anything, and me not saying anything either for I don't know how long, until I took a square out and Roy went, Bum a smoke off you, dude?

After I gave him one and torched them both, and we were just standing there smoking, I all of a fucked-up sudden got this fucked-up idea in my head, this idea in my fucked-up head about Roy there. And it was even though I hadn't even seen the dude since seventh grade when him and me weren't buddies anymore, when Roy was the bad dude of Infant Jesus of Prague, that dude who smoked and spit and swore, that dirty-looking dude with the mean-looking pizza face who never wore his clip-on or combed his hair, that dude who the Claw called the Pagan Baby, with the mom in the kidney machine and the seven no-good brothers, all ex-Marines, and it was even though all that shit, I still got this fucked up idea in my head that Roy had something important that it was important for him to tell me, and I didn't even have a shit's clue what. Not tossing meat or pumping gas or bagging groceries, but maybe something that Roy had to say, maybe just Roy saying something important.

I took out my one-quarter-full bottle of Jack and held it out. I held it out in the dark in the direction of Roy and went, Here. I want you to take this. Have it. It's yours.

He reached for it and took it, and went to me, Thanks.

I watched him unscrew it and have a long visit, cashing his beer as a chaser and copping a fresh one from the twelver at his feet. The Jack was almost gone. I went, Roy?

Roy went, Yeah?

I went, I want to ask you something. That okay?

Roy went, Piece of cake.

I went, I don't really know what I want to ask, just, like, not stupid shit. Something maybe important.

Roy went, Shoot.

I went, I don't know. You've been around here since you've been born, right? Lived here your whole life and shit?

Roy went, Fuckin'-A, dude.

I went, Right, so you know what it can be like, what it gets like when it feels like everything's crawling right up your ass and won't come back down. What are you supposed to do when that happens, you know? What the fuck're you supposed to do?

Roy laughed raspy and took a tug off his beer and went, Fuckin' dude, you tell me, right? He laughed again. He went, Fuckin' you tell me.

I went, Roy, if I could tell you, I wouldn't be asking you.

Roy stood there for a minute and then went, You wanna know what I think, huh?

Roy went, You really wanna know. I'll tell you. Listen. Check this out. Like my one brother. Fuckin' my brother, man, happen you're my brother and you get married and you have two kids like him. My brother's two kids? Check it out, they both came out retarded, *both* of them, fuckin' *both* retarded, and the ugly kind of retarded, too. Happen that's you. What do you do? Or happen you're my *other* fuckin' brother and half your fuckin' foot gets blowed off in the Marines. You ain't got no foot. What the fuck do you do? Roy went, What the fuck, happen you find out some chick you're fuckin' is fuckin' someone else, or happen you're out of weed and can't find none to smoke, or happen you get home late from work and everybody you know is already out and you don't know where. That's all it is, dude.

Roy went, Wait, no, no, say this. Say happen it's nice out someday so you go to Wampum Woods with some whiskey or some Mad Dog 20/20. Happen you see some fuckable chicks there. Happen you fuck a whole bunch of chicks all in one day. It's just like that. Or happen you don't wanna fuck a bunch of chicks all in one day. Happen you don't even like fuckin' chicks. That's something, too. I tell you, dude, it's all just whatever, you know?

Roy tossed down the rest of the Jack and put the empty bottle on the floor next to his twelver, and I finished a Coors and cashed my square with my shoe. I copped a fresh one from the twelver at my feet and popped it open and swallowed some down.

Roy went, I really gotta take a major piss.

I went, Don't let me stop you.

Roy went, Cool. Take it easy, dude. He picked up his twelver and patted me on the arm and went, Lighten up, dude. Take it light. Nothin' ain't that heavy.

Then he booked out of the garage, taking his twelver with him, and I just hung there looking at all the dark shapes of dudes and the orange glowing from their smokables, and I knew right then it was time to be booking, but I kept on hanging there still, to kill off my beers and smoke some more squares, and when I was done and left that dark garage through that lighted door and started cruising through that crowd in that other room, I couldn't find Spooge until I talked to Chuckie Goldman, who said he did one too many bongs of that mind-stop we'd been smoking, and his eyes went up in his head and he booked outside to breathe some air.

[12]

I took it outside to find him and shut the door behind me. I couldn't see Spooge around anywhere, but I sort of heard this far-off goober cough splashing noise like the sound of someone yacking, so I headed for where I heard it in the direction of the Old Man's car, which was where I found him, against Chuckie Goldman's big black van, bent over, hacking and hockering over a pile of his pies.

I went, Spooge, you okay, dude?

Spooge stayed bent over but went, Yeah. He hacked and hockered a little bit more and then stood himself slow until he was standing straight up. He was looking blue and sweaty, with his hair all damp at the edges and stuck to his face. He went, Oh, Jesus, I think I'm finished. I think that doobage was dusted.

I unlocked the shotgun side and went, I hope you can make it home without yacking on the dashboard.

Spooge sawed wood the whole way home, while I tried my hardest to keep my fixing goggles on the black road cooking under the headlights, and to keep my fists on the wheel at ten and two, and to keep my foot on the gas until we hit Spooge's driveway, where I threw it in park and shook Spooge to wake him, going, You're home, dude. You're home.

Spooge grunted and squinted at me like he didn't have a shit's clue who I was, and then he went, Oh.

I went, See you tomorrow.

He went, Tomorrow?

I went, Tomorrow.

He sat nodding like he understood. Then he stopped and stared up his driveway. I hung out, waiting for him to do something, but he never did, so I reached across him and popped the door open for him. Eventually he dropped his feet out to the ground and crawled out and stood up.

He went, Later.

I went, Later.

Spooge shut the door behind him and just stood there squinting into the headlights as I booked backward and the beams shot up into his face. He lifted his arm up to shield the light from his eyes, and in that last second before the lights turned out onto the street, he looked like he would stay like that forever, like a dude breaking free from prison and getting blinded by the searchlight with no fucking place left to go to anymore.

But then the headlights left him behind there as they turned out onto the road, and that quiet-assed car cruised me up and around that curving road, around and surrounding Infant Jesus of Prague, back all the way to the back behind Spooge's house, back by the bike racks and the basketball poles. I stopped the car and parked it, without my thinking why, and I climbed out and jumped those bike racks and headed for those swings.

[13]

Infant Jesus of Prague was a huge deserted shadowy shape, pressed up tight against the black and orange of the sky. I had my seat on the middle swing and looked up at it, at that school of mine that would be torn to the ground soon, and I put my hands upon those cold rusty chains, hanging in tight with my ass in the sling, starting off swinging and pushing back on dirt with my feet, coming back, legs lifted, until picking up on speed, the chains digging rust in my fingers as I tugged, laying back into it and kicking up hard, breathing like the rhythm in the pumping down the poles, tucking under forward before cooking backward fast, like I was going to die if this

182

wasn't what I did, cold out but sweating, the creaking up the chains, my hard exhale at that hang on the backstroke, kicked back forward into a shoot back down.

This was swinging to shoot off like slingshot, and slingshot is what I intended to be, so I shut my eyes tight during a sharp swing backward, to be shot like a stone up and over that school, and on that fast-throwing down-up-forward, I let go of the chains and put my hands to the dark, and I let go blind off and into the air.

[14]

I crack my eyes open to my body gone tiny, dressed up neat in my Catholic school clothes, in my stiff plaid clip-on and my bright red blazer, shiny black dress shoes on my dinky little feet. Infant Jesus of Prague is far down there below me, that building brick-red and shining in the sunlight. My little hand is being held, in a hand warm and pinkish, in a hand much bigger and older than mine is. And it's lifting me up here, up to up above here, and I'm shivers and weightless and lifting through sky, a sky sunny-blue, stretching big up above us, me and this hand holding, lifting, me here. But then the hand lets me go, and floats up off above me, and I can see a shape in black flapping robes against the wind.

It shoots up high against the bright blue sky above me, its black boots kicking air out from underneath black folds. I am floating up and following, cruising quietly behind it. This face is pink and pretty, these eyes are bright and kind, this voice is calling out to guide me, Come along with me now, my children! Come along with me now, my dears!

Nominated by Gordon Lish

FURIOUS VERSIONS

by LI-YOUNG LEE

from IRONWOOD

1.

These days I waken in the used light
of someone's spent life, to discover
the birds have stripped my various names of meaning entire:
the sparrow by quarrel,
the dove by grievance.
I lie
dismantled. I feel
the hours. Do they veer
to dusk? Or dawn?
Will I rise and go
out into an American city?
Or walk down to the wilderness sea?
I might run with wife and children to the docks
to bribe an officer for our lives
and perilous passage.
Then I'd answer
in an oceanic tongue
to *Professor, Capitalist, Husband, Father.*
Or I might have one more
hour of sleep before my father
comes to take me
to his snowbound church,
where I dust the pews, and he sets candles

out the color of teeth.
That means I was born in Bandung, 1958;
on my father's back, in borrowed clothes,
I came to America.
And I wonder
if I imagined those wintry mornings
in a dim nave, since
I'm the only one
who's lived to tell it,
and I confuse
the details: was it my father's skin
which shone like teeth?
Was it his heart that lay snowbound?
But if I waken to a jailor
rousting me to meet my wife and son,
come to see me in my cell,
where I eat the chocolate
and smoke the cigarettes they smuggle,
what name do I answer to?
And did I stand
on the train from Chicago to Pittsburgh
so my fevered son could sleep? Or did I
open my eyes
and see my father's closed face
rocking above me?
Memory revises me.
Even now a letter
comes from a place
I don't know, from someone
with my name,
and postmarked years ago,
while I await
injunctions from the light,
or the dark;
I wait for shapeliness
limned, or dissolution.
Is paradise due, or narrowly missed,
until another thousand years?
I wait

in a blue hour
and faraway sound of hammering,
and on a page a poem begun, something
about to be dispersed,
something about to come into being.

2.

I wake to black
and one sound—
neither a heart
approaching, nor one shoe
coming, but something
less measured, never
arriving. I wander
a house I thought I knew,
I walk the halls as if the halls
of that other
mansion, my father's heart.
I follow the sound
past a black window
where a bird sits like a blacker
question: *To where? To where? To where?*
Past my mother's room where her
knees creak, *Meaning, Meaning.*
While a rose
rattles at my ear, *Where
is your father?*
And the silent house
booms, *Gone. Long gone.*

A door jumps
out from shadows,
then jumps away. This
is what I've come to find:
the back door, unlatched.
Tooled by an insular wind, it
slams and slams
without meaning
to and without meaning.

3.

Moonlight and high wind.
Dark poplars toss, insinuate the sea.
The yard heaves, perplexed
with shadows massed
and shadows falling away.
Before me a tree, distinct
in its terrible
aspects, emerges, reels, sinks,
and is lost.
At my feet, shapes
tear free, separate darknesses
mingle, then crawl to the common
dark, lost.
At the brink
of my own now-here-now-gone
shadow stand three flowers,
or two flowers,
and one's shade.
Impatiens? Alyssum?
Something forbids me to speak
of them in this
upheaval of forms and
voices—voices
now, plaintive, anxious.
Now I hear
interrogation in vague tongues.
I hear ocean sounds and a history of rain.
Somewhere is a streetlamp
and my brother never coming.
Somewhere a handful of hair and a lost box of letters.
And everywhere, fire,
corridors of fire, brick and barbed wire.
Soldiers sweep the streets
for my father. My mother
hides him, haggard,
in the closet.
The booted ones herd us
to the sea.
Waves furl boats

lovingly, and bodies
going out, farther out.
Now my father holds my hand, he says
Don't forget any of this.
A short, bony-faced corporal
asks him politely, deferring to class,
*What color suit, Professor, would you like
to be buried in? Brown or blue?*
A pistol butt turns my father's spit to blood.
It was a tropical night.
It was half a year of sweat and fatal memory.
It was one year of fire
out of the world's diary of fires,
flesh-laced, mid-century fire,
teeth and hair infested,
napalm-dressed and skull-hung fire,
and imminent fire, an elected
fire come to rob me
of my own death, my damp bed
in the noisy earth,
my rocking toward a hymn-like night.
How, then, may I
speak of flowers
here, where
a world of forms convulses,
here, amidst
drafts—yet
these are not drafts
toward a future form, but
furious versions
of the here and now . . .

Here, now, one
should say nothing
of three flowers,
only enter with them
in silence, fear, and hope,
into the next nervous one hundred human years.

4.

But I see these flowers, and they seize
my mind, and I
can no more un-see
them than I can un-dream
this, no more than
the mind can stop
its wandering over the things
of the world, snagged on the world
as it is.
The mind is
a flowering
cut into time,
a rose,

the wandering rose
that scaled the red brick
of my father's house in Pennsylvania.
What was its name?
Each bloom, unsheathed
in my mind, urges, *Remember!*
The Paul's Scarlet!
Paul, who promised the coming
of the perfect and the departing of the imperfect,
Else why stand we in jeopardy every hour?

I thought of Paul
the morning I stepped out my door
and into an explosion of wings,
thudding and flapping, heavenly blows.
Blinded, I knew the day
of fierce judgement and rapture
had come. I thought
even the dooryard rose,
touched by wind, trembling
in anticipation
of first petal-fall,
announcement of death's commencement,
would take back

its flowering, claim glory.
So the rose and I
stood, terrified, at the beginning
of a new and beloved era.

It was pigeons, only pigeons
I'd startled from the porch rafters.
But the dread and the hope
I carry with me
like lead and wings
let me momentarily believe otherwise.

True, none of this
has to do with heaven since the sight
of those heavy birds flying away
reminded me
not so much of what's to come
as of what passes
away: birds,
hours, words, gestures, persons,
a drowned guitar in spring,
smell of lacquered wood
and wax when I prayed as a boy,
a pale cheek cut
by a green leaf,
the taste of blood
in a kiss,
someone whispering into someone's ear,
someone crying behind a door,
a clock dead at noon.
My father's hand
cupping my chin, weighing
tenderness between us,
pressing my mother's hip, weighing desire,
and cleaving a book open.
On the right of his hand the words:
The Song of Songs, which is Solomon's.
Let him kiss me with the kisses of his mouth.
On the left of his hand the words:
For God shall bring every work

into judgement with every secret thing,
whether it be good,
or whether it be evil.
Outside his window, his
rose, aphid-eaten, bad-weather-wracked,
stem and thorn,
crook and bramble groping,
gripping brick, each sickly
bloom uttering, *I shall not die!*
before it's dispersed.

5.

My father wandered,
me beside him, human,
erect, unlike
roses. And unlike
Paul, we had no mission,
though he loved Paul, read him continually
as republic to republic,
oligarchy to anarchy to democracy we arrived.

Once, while I walked
with my father, a man
reached out, touched his arm, said, *Kuo Yuan?*
The way he stared, and spoke my father's name,
I thought he meant to ask, *Are you a dream?*
Here was the sadness of ten thousand miles,
of an abandoned house in Nan Jing,
where my father helped a blind man
wash his dead wife's newly dead body,
then bury it, while bombs
fell, and trees raised
charred arms and burned.
Here was a man who remembered
the sound of another's footfalls
well enough to call to him
after twenty years,
on a sidewalk in America.

America, where, in Chicago, Little Chinatown,
who should I see
on the corner of Argyle and Broadway
but Li Bai and Du Fu, those two
poets of the wanderer's heart.
Folding paper boats,
they sent them swirling
down little rivers of gutter water.
Gold-toothed, cigarettes rolled in their sleeves,
they noted my dumb surprise:
What did you expect? Where else should we be?

6.

It goes on and it goes on,
the ceaseless inventions, incessant
constructions and deconstructions
of shadows over black grass,
while, overhead, poplars
rock and nod,
wrestle *No* and *Yes*, contend
moon, no moon.

To think of the sea
is to hear in the sound of trees '
sound of the sea's work,
the wave's labor to change
the shore, not for shore's sake, nor wave's,
certainly not for me,
hundreds of miles from sea,
unless you count
my memory, my traverse
of sea one way to here.
I'm like my landlocked poplars; far
from water, I'm full of the sound of water.

But sea-sound differs from the sound of trees
in that it owns
a rhythm, almost
a meaning, but

no human story,
and so is like
the sound of trees,
tirelessly building
as wind builds, rising
as wind rises, steadily gathering
to nothing, quiet, and
the wind rising again.
The night grows
miscellaneous in the sound of trees.
But I own a human story,
whose very telling
remarks loss.
The characters survive through the telling,
the teller survives
by his telling; by his voice
brinking silence does he survive.
Yet, no one
can tell without cease
our human
story, and so we
lose, lose.

Yet, behind the sound
of trees is another
sound. Sometimes, lying
awake, or standing
like this in the yard, I hear it. It
ties our human telling
to its course
by momentum, and ours
is merely part
of its unbroken
stream, the human
and otherwise simultaneously
told. The past
doesn't fall away, the past
joins the greater
telling, and is.
At times its theme seems

murky, other times clear. Always
death is a phrase, but just
a phrase, since nothing is ever
lost, and lives
are fulfilled by subsequence.
Listen, you can hear it: indescribable,
neither grief nor joy, neither mine nor yours . . .

But I'll not widow the world.
I'll tell my human
tale, tell it against
the current of that vaster, that
inhuman telling.
I'll measure time by losses and destructions.
Because the world
is so rich in detail, all of it so frail;
because all I love is imperfect;
because my memory's flaw
isn't in retention but organization;
because no one asked.
I'll tell once and for all
how someone lived.
Born on an island ruled by a petty soldier,
he was wrapped in bright cloth
and bound to his mother's hip,
where he rode until he could walk.
He did not utter a sound his first three years,
and his parents frowned.
Then, on the night of their first exile,
he spoke out in complete sentences
a Malaysian so lovely it was true song.
But when he spoke again
it was plain, artless, and twenty years later.
He wore a stranger's clothes,
he married a woman who tasted of iron and milk.
They had two sons, the namesakes
of a great emperor and a good-hearted bandit.
And always he stood erect to praise or grieve,
and knelt to live a while
at the level of his son's eyes.

7.

Tonight, someone, unable
to see in one darkness,
has shut his eyes
to see into another.
Among the sleepers, he is one
who doesn't sleep.
Know him by his noise.
Hear the nervous
scratching of his pencil,
sound of a rasping
file, a small
restless percussion, a soul's
minute chewing,
the old poem
birthing itself
into the new
and murderous century.

Nominated by Marianne Boruch, Patricia Henley, Fae Myenne Ng and Alberto Ríos.

THE SUMMER
OF THE HATS

fiction by SIGRID NUNEZ

from THE THREEPENNY REVIEW

An OVAL HEAD, a long neck, a delicate nose and mouth, and oblique, wide-open eyes: my mother had what the saleswomen called a perfect hat-face.

My mother shopped for her hats in many different stores, but the one I remember best was on Madison Avenue and was owned by an Italian woman. This woman wore a strong, rose-scented perfume and spoke mellifluously-accented English that was like the vocal equivalent of her thick, glossy rolls of hair. She had the nicest name I had ever heard: Ariana. The finest hats in the world were made by Italians, she would have us know. The very word milliner was derived from Milaner. Ariana herself was from Rome. Most of the hats for sale had been designed by Ariana and made by hand in a room divided from the store by a chintz curtain. Sometimes Ariana would be in the back when we came in. As she swept out to greet us, we'd catch a glimpse of several dark chignons and black-draped shoulders hunched at a cluttered table.

Out front, hats of all kinds crowned the bald, featureless busts that I always found dimly disturbing. My mother would try on hat after hat, admiring herself in the ormolu-framed mirror that hung on the wall. Ariana stood by, an elbow in each palm, beaming. "How can you choose, when every hat looks so good on you? You have the perfect face for hats." And then, addressing her own reflection severely: "Me, I cannot wear hats at all." A prominent nose and low forehead were to blame. That Ariana should have chosen to spend her life making and selling hats that she herself could not wear seemed just the sort of baffling, irrational thing a grown-up would do.

We visited Ariana's shop several times a year and never left without buying at least one hat to add to my mother's collection. Hatboxes crowded our closets and towered in the attic, where once it got so hot the millinery fruit melted, doing irreparable damage. A white straw cap was transformed into a half-eaten strawberry sundae.

I could not agree that my mother looked good in all hats. Some that she wore seemed to me just awful. Snoods, for example, that hid all her chestnut hair except her widow's peak and made her look ready to dive in the pool. And there was a chinchilla fez with a red tassel that I used to beg her to throw out. Her dunce cap, I called it. I hated all the fur hats as I hated the fur coats. True, they were alluringly soft, but to touch fur with no hope of life underneath was a disappointment I could not bear. I remember also a lavender pillbox that I could never see without tasting the violet mints I used to like making myself sick on. Hats with veils were all right so long as the veils were not black and did not cling to the face. One of my mother's favorites had this sort of veil, disfiguring her cheeks with horrid, black velvet moles.

In general, I preferred the summer hats: leghorns trimmed with grosgrain streamers, sunbonnets that tied fetchingly under the chin—fanciful, romantic hats of the kind seen in portraits from more opulent days. When my mother stepped out in one of these, chosen to match one of the pastel, chiffon summer dresses that seemed more an emanation of her person than something worn, she drew stares. Seeing how people admired her made up for the times my friends would sneer: Why does your mother always wear those silly hats?

After leaving Ariana's, my mother and I walked four blocks south to a children's shoestore to buy oxfords and T-straps to replace the pairs I'd outgrown. Then, hat- and shoeboxes knocking awkwardly against our hips, we crossed Madison Avenue to a patisserie. My mother was always in a bright mood at these times. I can see her pale, slender-fingered hand with its polished nails resting on her coffee cup. I once made her laugh by saying that she had perfect ring-hands. But, except for her wedding band, she wore no rings, nor any other jewelry, ever.

Tedious as shopping could be, I relished these particular afternoons. The rose-scented hat shop, my spotless new shoes, the custard tarts, Ariana's accent, and the French accent of the patisserie waitress—all this was pure enchantment to me. My mother and I were happy in those days.

As a child, I never thought of my mother as preening or vain. The hours she spent shopping for clothes or getting ready to go out seemed to me part of her duty, no less so than making sure that dinner was served on time, or that my own clothes were ready each morning when I went to school. Surely only duty could have compelled her to make her face up so painstakingly every time she went out. I used to watch her at this and marvel—not at the transformation (she looked pretty much the same to me, only a little slicker, like a woman on a magazine cover), but at the trouble. The whole job took about an hour, and she spent almost that long getting dressed. I often think of these endless preparations of hers when tearing through my own three-minute toilette. But then, I could never have worn my mother's styles. The only hat that doesn't look ludicrous on me is a fedora. I have my father's face.

We spent the summers in the country. Our house, set in a small oak-and-pine wood a few miles from the beach, was nearly a century old and in bad need of repair. My parents always talked about having it renovated but never seemed to get around to this. Me, I would not have changed a board of it. I wished we could live there all year round. Some of the saddest memories of my childhood are associated with draping the summer house furniture in sheets. In winter I was often there in spirit, haunting the icy rooms, where the ghosts of hippos and giant tortoises slept, while the snow made a polar bear den of the yard. Every summer, the first thing my mother did, even if the day was scalding, was to build a blazing fire in the hearth, to absorb every last trace of damp and chill—a habit my father thought absurd.

My father's work kept him very busy, and he was able to join us only on some weekends. Once or twice during the season my mother would return to the city for a few days, leaving me in the care of friends. We had been coming to that village for many years, and we knew several other families who summered there.

It was the beginning of my twelfth summer, a glorious day of June, hot and blue. I came home from school and found my mother upstairs in her room, packing. Clearing a space for myself on the bed, I sat down to watch.

Right away I knew something was up. I could tell by the slapdash way my mother was packing—she was usually so meticulous about her things. And there was a tension about her mouth that bespoke dissatisfaction. I knew this mood of hers and I could not ignore it. Whenever I saw my mother like this I was forced to acknowledge once more how utterly dependent my happiness was on hers, a thought that could at different times fill me with anger, tenderness, or fear. This time it was mostly fear. I sat very still in my corner of the bed, though the silence made me want to jump out of my skin. Then, as if the silence were bothering her too, my mother asked me to tell her about my day. And when I did I realized that she wasn't listening.

Finally she slammed several full suitcases shut and began putting away what had been left out. She had brought the summer hats in their boxes down from the attic, and now to my surprise she asked me to help her carry them back up again.

"Why? Aren't you taking any?"

My mother ran the back of one hand lightly across her forehead. I knew this gesture: it meant that she wanted to seem indifferent. When she spoke, her voice had a false-bright ring, like a coin striking concrete. "I can't wear those hats anymore. I'm too old. They look silly."

So that was it. All that fine blue afternoon my mother had been trying on her summer hats and, studying herself in the mirror, had had this revelation.

I had a classmate in those days named Ricky Howe. His parents were old and it was the curse of his life. They were wrinkled and grey and looked a generation older than everyone else's parents. They were known to have been mistaken for his grandparents. We all knew how ashamed of them Ricky was and how hard he tried to keep us from seeing them. And we sympathized. We knew it was a terrible thing to be old. And now my mother's words struck dread in me. I had a vision of her suddenly aging, turning overnight into withered, dun, dowager-humped Mrs. Howe. I could not bear to think of my mother like that. I could not bear to think she would ever change at all.

But change she did over that summer, if not quite in the way I had feared. The sullen mood I had caught her in while packing visited her many times. She was often irritable, more often bored. She brightened only when my father was around, and that was seldom. She spent long hours alone in her room—reading, supposedly, though I couldn't help noticing what slow progress she was making through *The Group*. Unfortunately, it rained a lot that summer. The sand never really had a chance to dry. My mother grumbled constantly about the weather. Then she caught a cold, which turned into a bronchial infection. I had never seen her so miserable, nor had she ever been so distant to me. Whole days passed in which we exchanged hardly a word. More devastating still were those moments when my mother's eyes would settle on me without seeming to see me. All the pleasure of that vacation died for me. I could not walk the beach without hearing something ominous in the pulse of the waves. I could not believe that I had ever been happy under that dismal roof, which sprang a new leak with every downpour.

By the end of that summer I realized that my mother was not on the verge of turning into Mrs. Howe. The tragedy wasn't being old, it was not being young anymore. So I overheard my mother put it to my father one night soon after we had moved back home. I was a reasonable child. My own eyes told me that my mother had no cause for concern. She looked no different than she had for years. What, then, could have gotten into her? Whatever had given her the idea that she must stop wearing her hats? I figured this for another one of those irrational adult notions—like my father's conviction that, to use my mother's words, the stock market would crash if he took a day off.

And so I was astonished when I opened one of my mother's fashion magazines and read: A woman over twenty-five should never wear heavy eye makeup, broad-brimmed hats, skirts above her knee, or hair past her chin.

So there it was.

Of course, not all of my mother's hats had broad brims. With the cooler weather she got out her winter collection: her sealskin toque, the odious chinchilla, and wool berets in every color.

But the summer mood persisted. An air of brooding clung to her, like one of the gossamer summer dresses. And then she made the intolerable discovery: my father was seeing another woman.

200

"He's so busy, he hardly has time for us, but he has time for—*that*."

By sheer luck, at a pajama party the weekend before, I had been enlightened—not wholly accurately, it would turn out, but at least enough not to be stumped by "that."

They did not divorce. In fact they somehow managed to settle things without even much noise. From the way other people behaved, it seemed to me that I was the only one who noticed anything different about my parents. They had never been uncivil to each other and they were not so now. But from this time on there was a reserve between them, a new politeness, as of people neither hostile nor friendly to each other. My father's presence, though never unwelcome to my mother, no longer lifted her spirits, and she no longer pleaded with him to let the market crash and stay home. He was still doing *that*. We both knew it. But now, instead of seeing signs of his infidelity everywhere, my mother seemed blind to even the most conspicuous ones.

Gradually, over the next few years, my mother changed her style. She dressed more quietly, made up her face only for special occasions, and paid less attention to fashion. Though she was still always carefully turned out, her appearance ceased to be a passion with her. (Older now, I realized that what I'd mistaken for duty had indeed been a passion.)

For a time I was tormented by guilt over how much I missed my mother's younger, prettier self. It had been a source of great pride to me, how she stood out among the other, less attractive mothers. I knew that this was one of her own worst fears, that others—that my father, particularly—did miss her younger self. In a bitter moment she once warned me that women—especially pretty ones—were not permitted to grow old and plain. She used that word: permitted. That was the summer she decided she could no longer appear on the beach in a bathing suit. I remember how I winced for her when she announced this. Something gross and shameful was happening to her body. Something equally unseemly was happening to mine, too, during these same years, and I didn't wish to be seen in a bathing suit, either.

Seeing my mother so downcast, I wanted to drag her to the hat shop and stand her in the sunburst of Ariana's approval. I was certain that Ariana would scoff at the rule about women over twenty-five. She would urge my mother to try on hat after hat, exclaiming how divine she looked in all of them. The chignoned women would emerge for the first time from the back room to join in Ariana's praise.

Oh, why didn't we drop everything and go at once to Ariana's? She would send us home with stacks of hats teetering in our arms, like the beret vendor in the Madeline story.

But my mother said that Ariana's had become too expensive. And I had outgrown the children's shoestore. Nor in those days would you have caught my mother in a patisserie: she was watching her weight.

The spring I graduated from high school, the music students gave a recital. I played the piano. I played Beethoven's *Pathétique* sonata. I told my mother, whose dream of youth had been to be a pianist, and who still clung to the dream that her daughter might be one, that I would do it for her. It was not easy for me. I was never really that good. I practiced arduously, for months. It was a very difficult thing for me, to get up before an audience and play. It was the last thing in the world I was suited for, the last thing I wanted to do. But I did it for her.

I had got through the first movement, not too badly. In the middle of the slow movement I risked a glance into the audience, to the place where I knew my mother sat. I caught her with a tissue at her nose and that finished me. Tears started to my own eyes, and I rushed madly to the end of the piece, heaving and slurring, in the grip of that roiling emotion that is the enemy of art.

My mother came backstage to thank me. She had a tender, anxious look, reminding me of a time when I was small and ill with a soaring fever. She even pressed her palm to my forehead. As she did this, I was acutely aware of the fine deltas at the corners of her eyes and of the deeper creases between her arched brows, which in recent years had given her face such a doleful expression. It was as if I were seeing these lines for the first time, though in fact she had long been in the habit of pointing them out. A moment of perfect understanding passed between us. My mother said, "It's been a long time since I've been a mother to you, hasn't it, darling. I'm ashamed to say it, but it's true. I've been wasting my life away, worrying about things that don't really matter. But I've made up my mind: all that's got to change. Life is too short—" And the tissue was again at her nose.

She was as good as her word. That month my mother began seeing a doctor, a woman whom she always referred to as Hazel. From what I understood, each time she saw Hazel my mother ended up telling her things she had never told anyone—things she had never thought she would or could or should tell anyone. The effect was shattering. I had my doubts about a therapy that reduced my mother to tears three times a week, and it seemed a miracle to me when she began to get better.

I went away to college. Away from home for the first time, I thought constantly about my mother. I had a roommate who bore towards her parents an almost murderous rancor. Late into the night I would listen to her carry on about them. Her mother in particular she denounced, for having always put herself ahead of her children. These bitter harangues struck a deep chord in me. Listening to my roommate, I found myself against my will thinking of those times when my mother would look at me without seeming to know me. I had the sense of tottering near a precipice. Though it was my roommate who spoke, I could not escape the feeling that the words rose from my own heart. Each accusation was like an arrow striking my mother miles away—and who would protect her from these arrows, if not I?

I had to go home often to assure myself that my mother was all right. In fact, I had never seen her so content. She was full of enthusiasm for her new life. She had made up her mind to go for a degree. She charmed my friends with her genteel feminism: "I understand why we want to stop being drudges and sex objects, you know. But why would we want to stop being ladies?"

And then, in the midst of all this enthusiasm and consciousness-raising and hope, she became ill. There seemed hardly cause for alarm at first. She was just a little tired, she just had a little pain.

In the hospital I sat for hours by her bed, rubbing her light, dry hand. That hand made me think of a fallen leaf that withers and curls each day a little more, getting smaller and drier, until one day the wind blows it to dust.

It took even less time than the doctors had said, and they had given her almost no time at all.

After my mother's death I seldom came home, and once I'd finished school I shunned my father completely. He sold the house where I grew up and moved to an apartment in Manhattan. The summer house he rented each year to strangers. At the time, I did not question the rightness or wisdom of my decision to be an orphan. If I was sure of anything in life it was that I would never need my father again.

Two years ago I was in Paris, walking down a street near the Palais-Royal, when a bomb went off in a post office. I had stopped a few doors down from the building and was fumbling in my purse for cigarettes. I didn't know what had happened at first. I was aware only of a boom so loud it took away my hearing. Then my ears popped open to a trumpeting shriek, and I half expected to see, through the cumulous smoke, a wounded elephant sinking to its knees. There followed shouts and a kind of frenzied peeping. My cigarettes lay scattered about my feet. I stooped and mechanically began gathering them up.

A hand gripped my shoulder. Looking up, I saw a man pressing a bloody rag to his cheek. He said something in French that I did not understand. But the harsh, incomprehensible sounds, the rapidly darkening rag, and the frantic pulse of his eyes made me panic. I started to run away from him and tripped over the body of a woman lying face down in a pool of blood. How strange, I thought: one of her legs is much longer than the other. That snapped me out of it. I knew exactly where I was, what had happened, and what I was looking at. I began to cry, and when the man approached and touched my shoulder again, I let him lead me away.

In the *salle des urgences*, I tried the patience of those good French nurses. "*Mais, vous n'êtes pas blessée,*" they assured me. It was true, I was merely shaken. But I clung to their wrists, I did not want to return to my hotel alone.

An English tourist who had come in the same ambulance with me, and who had suffered only scrapes, piped on and on about how lucky we had been. Extraordinary, he said: people quite close to us had been killed. The thought seemed to brace him. He left the hospital in jubilant spirits.

Though I had only just arrived in Paris, I arranged to fly home the next day. That night I could not sleep. At the hospital I had been given a few tablets of Mogadon, but I was afraid to take any. I kept thinking, What if there's a fire in the hotel and I don't wake up?

In those days I was living in Boston, but I took the plane to New York. I dozed off, dreamed we were crashing and flailed awake, upsetting my neighbor's beer into his lap. After that I couldn't fall asleep again.

It was twilight when we landed. I got in a cab and gave the driver my father's address. I had never been to his apartment.

"Young lady says she's your daughter," the doorman announced, in a tone implying that he found this improbable. A glance in the lobby mirror and I understood: my clothes were dishevelled and travel stained, and I had carried away from the bombing with me, in my own eyes, the crazed look of the Frenchman.

My father greeted me with open mouth. In twelve years we had seen each other just twice: at his mother's and father's funerals. I threw down my bag in the front hall and marched past him into the living room. Dropping onto the couch, I demanded a drink. Without a word my father fetched a glass and some bourbon, shock weighting all his movements. He sat down across from me and stared as if he could not believe his eyes. I took a gulp of bourbon and launched into the story about the bombing. My father had heard about it on the news. He named the two different terrorist groups that were claiming responsibility. But I dismissed this. I knew for whom that bomb had been planted. I knew who was really meant to be lying face down in a pool of blood. I described the dead woman to my father: "It could have been me." He frowned and clasped his hands together, I thought perhaps to keep them from trembling. His speechlessness provoked me. I swilled the rest of my bourbon. "You almost lost me." It came out snide, belligerent. At last my father found his tongue.

"Do you always drink like this?"

I didn't. But that night I kept drinking, talking and drinking—as though I believed that if only I drank enough my father would have to understand.

It wasn't long before the bourbon and the lack of sleep got the better of me. I had the delicious sensation of being scooped up in the shovel of an earth-mover. But in fact I was down—flat on my back on the couch, still talking. I remember saying,"You want to know why I came here?" and my father's troubled face drawing near. Then I imagined that we were no longer alone. A woman had entered the room. The last thing I saw was a lovely, wide-eyed face hovering over me.

The next morning, after my father had gone off to work, I studied that face across the breakfast table. She was young—younger than I—with a cleft chin and magnificent, jealous-green eyes. I was still groggy from twelve hours' sleep. "You have a perfect hat-face," I told her.

She laughed. "And *you* have your father's face." Then she added, "I never wear hats. They ruin your hair."

Her name was Dorsey. She was a graduate student in psychology. My father was paying her tuition and part of the rent on her apartment near Washington Square. She announced this without the least hesitation. She believed in being completely honest and open with everyone about everything, Dorsey said. And she quoted Sartre: in the ideal state, no one would have any secrets. She asked me what I did, and because I believed that Sartre's dream pointed the way to total chaos, I told her I was thinking of going to law school, a thought that had never entered my mind. About my struggle to be a writer, which had been going on already for years, I said nothing. Inevitably, Dorsey wanted a history of my relationships ("just the serious ones"), and I was relieved to find that crabbed tale of waywardness and failure simplifying itself into a list: a veteran of Vietnam, a painter, a writer, a pianist, and a doctor.

Had it not been for Dorsey, I don't think I would have stayed long in my father's house. Impulsively storming back into his life, I had not bargained for so much pain. I had not foreseen that being with my father would keep my mother constantly in my thoughts, and that I would begin to miss her as intensely as I had in the period right after her death. And when I learned that Dorsey knew more about my father than I did, that she was closer to him than I had ever been, I felt cheated, as I had felt cheated when my mother died. Nevertheless, week after week, I let Dorsey talk me out of leaving. After all, she said, twelve years is a long time for two people to become strangers to each other. Of course, she knew the truth, that my father and I had been strangers all our lives. But Dorsey would not be discouraged. It wasn't her style. She liked happy endings. She did not like to see people suffer. She was grateful to my father for all he'd done for her and determined to help him now. He needed Dorsey to explain that my surliness masked a welter of remorse. Without Dorsey, I would not have known that, under his air of feckless bewilderment, my father had forgiven all and, like the father in the parable, was ready to kill the fatted calf, now that the child feared lost had come home.

I sit at my desk by the open window, writing. A patch of sun warms the back of my hand. Now and then I glance out the window to the yard below, where my father is working. His face is hidden under the battered Panama he took to wearing after burning his scalp one bright afternoon, weeding the flower beds. He had found the hat hanging on a nail in the garage. Neither of us remembered ever having seen it, and we assume it must have belonged to one of the tenants of the last dozen summers.

A breeze lifts the curtain, wafting in the smell of sea spray and roses—the smell of my childhood.

I drove down from Boston yesterday. My father has been living in the house since early spring. A year ago he shocked his colleagues, who always thought he would work until he dropped, by retiring. He wanted to devote himself full time to renovating the house. All year he has been overseeing workmen. A new roof has been put on, and a Palladian window cut into the west wall of the living room. The living and dining-room ceilings have been raised. The crumbling chimney has been restored. In all the rooms are freshly painted walls and slick new floors. After the thaw, my father moved into the house and turned his attention to the grounds. The lilac and rose bushes had been allowed to grow wild. My father pruned them and planted other flowers: pansies, foxgloves, peonies, and phloxes. He cultivated a small vegetable patch as well, for growing herbs and tomatoes.

The renovations, the flower beds, the vegetable patch—for years my parents talked about doing these things together. After my mother died and I left home, my father had not had the heart to return to the summer house. Now he blesses the intuition that kept him from selling it all this time. He wants the house to be mine one day, and for me to be happy in it as I was when I was growing up. He has not yet given up the hope that someday I will live here with a family of my own.

Yesterday was my birthday. My father took me out for lobster and champagne. He spoke contentedly about the garden's progress. He is proud of his peonies, his herbs. He described how odd but good it felt to be going about in old, soft clothes, working in the open air, getting his hands dirty. Were it not for me, none of this happiness would be his, he has said many times. He would have slogged on at his job till he dropped, as everyone said he would.

The meal was first-rate. My father's eyes shone, his cheeks turned pink with pleasure.

There is no doubt that he has forgiven me absolutely, a burden that at moments lies heavily on me, for I know that the rest of my life will be judged by the light of that forgiveness, that because of it I am obliged to do something worthy.

A muddled expression of this came out over dinner. My father shook his head. "God knows, we've all done things we regret, things that ended up hurting people, though we didn't intend it."

This was the first time he had alluded to—that. Earlier he had told me: "I'm not offering this as an excuse, but the truth is, I never went out looking for it. Women always came after me. Especially since your mother died. Maybe you'll find it hard to believe, but women threw themselves at me—even the young ones."

Nothing hard to believe about that. My father is lavish with his wealth, and, on a man, our face is striking.

I brought up Dorsey, now living in San Diego with someone she hopes to marry.

My father sighed. "I miss her. But an old goat like me doesn't expect to keep a girl like that for long. And Dorsey was always honest, I have to say. She never promised to stay with me. On the contrary, she warned me from the start: as soon as she found some-one she thought she could settle down with, she'd be gone. She wanted to have her first child by the time she was thirty." He took a sip of champagne, and when he spoke again his voice was plain-tive. "Speaking of age, how does it feel to be thirty-five? Not too terribly old, I hope?"

Only later, when I was alone and getting ready for bed, did I understand why, when he asked me this, my father had struck that odd note. He must have been thinking about my mother. He must have been remembering the summer of the hats, the summer she decided she was no longer young, and that her life was over. She was thirty-two.

Glancing out the window, I see that my father is gone. My breath catches—until I hear the rattle of the wheelbarrow and spy him turning the corner of the house, back from the compost heap.

I do not think that I will ever have a family of my own. When I look into the future, I see myself living much as I do now, alone, in a small apartment in a big city, like Boston or New York. Summers, I will be here. Arriving at the house for the first time each season, I will light a fire in the hearth, even if the day is scalding, to absorb every last trace of damp and chill.

Nominated by Julia Just and Pat Strachan

AT A MOTEL

by BRENDA HILLMAN

from AMERICAN POETRY REVIEW

It was almost Christmas and the pink lights of the avenue
battered the curtains quite festively
but with restraint so they looked babyish, cherubic;
we had not been there long, had just dozed off

when I was awakened by a woman's voice outside throwing
the sentence with a sameness like bricks:
"Give me my money, give me my money!" The doors
of the stable sealed by tired numbers in italics—

and our aboveness had a kind of falsity
because of the season or our need: we looked down
into a crèche or the birth of a story, beginnings
having the same stiffness on this earth . . .

We were the only "guests" at the motel
that night besides her and the black
pimp who serenely watched her standing
barefoot, in her slip, the smooth

edge of her non-being so alert that her body pressed
forward as a separate event . . . and the moon
pressed through the nylon
fog the same way, with extra strips of rather

pretty light to spare, surrounding
the two of them so they looked—well, blessed . . .
(Light can be such a liar.)

The pimp said nothing while she shouted.
Looked bored in his suit. Went back to the room below ours
shuffling like a husband after church; the door
closed softly, opened, closed again.

She stood there in the courtyard sobbing—
her long brown hair—she looked a little
like myself. I waited for her to choose for us, but choice
is illusory; if she moved forward, did she choose death?

But the grooms of dawn went about their business;
and she veered down the avenue in a radiant
line that made ropes of my nightgown and her slip
and the daylight suffer the same shine.

Nominated by Henry Carlile, Barry Goldensohn, Jane Hirshfield,
Sharon Olds, Robert Pinsky, Michael Ryan and David St. John.

WESTLAND

fiction by CHARLES BAXTER

from THE PARIS REVIEW

SATURDAY MORNING at the zoo, facing the lions' cage, overcast sky and a light breeze carrying the smell of peanuts and animal dung, the peacocks making their stilted progress across the sidewalks. I was standing in front of the gorge separating the human viewers from the lions. The lions weren't caged, exactly; they just weren't free to go. One male and one female were slumbering on fake rock ledges. Raw meat was nearby. My hands were in my pockets and I was waiting for a moment of energy so I could leave and do my Saturday morning errands. Then this girl, this teenager, appeared from behind me, hands in *her* pockets, and she stopped a few feet away on my right. In an up-all-night voice, she said, "What would you do if I shot that lion?" She nodded her head: she meant the male, the closer one.

"Shot it?"

"That's right."

"I don't know." Sometimes you have to humor people, pretend as if they're talking about something real. "Do you have a gun?"

"Of course I have a gun." She wore a protective blankness on her thin face. She was fixed on the lion. "I have it here in my pocket."

"I'd report you," I said. "I'd try to stop you. There are guards here. People don't shoot caged animals. You shouldn't even carry a concealed weapon, a girl your age."

"This is Detroit," she explained.

"I know it is," I said. "But people don't shoot caged lions in Detroit or anywhere else."

"It wouldn't be that bad," she said, nodding at the lions again.

"You can tell from their faces how much they want to check out."

I said I didn't think so.

She turned to look at me. Her skin was so pale it seemed bleached, and she was wearing a vaudeville-length overcoat and a pair of hightop tennis shoes and jeans with slits at the knees. She looked like a fifteen-year-old bag lady. "It's because you're a disconnected person that you can't see it," she said. She shivered and reached into her pocket and pulled out a crumpled pack of cigarettes. "Lions are so human. Things get to them. They experience everything more than we do. They're romantic." She glanced at her crushed pack of cigarettes, and in a shivering motion she tossed it into the gorge. She swayed back and forth. "They want to kill and feast and feel," she said.

I looked at this girl's bleached skin, that candy bar and cola complexion, and I said, "Are you all right?"

"I slept here last night," she said. She pointed vaguely behind her. "I was sleeping over there. Under those trees. Near the polar bears."

"Why'd you do that?"

"I wasn't alone *all* night." She was answering a question I hadn't asked. "This guy, he came in with me for awhile to be nice and amorous but he couldn't see the point in staying. He split around midnight. He said it was righteous coming in here and being solid with the animal world, but he said you had to know when to stop. I told him I wouldn't defend him to his friends if he left, and he left, so as far as I'm concerned, he is over, he is zippo."

She was really shivering now, and she was huddling inside that long overcoat. I don't like to help strangers, but she needed help. "Are you hungry?" I asked. "You want a hamburger?"

"I'll eat it," she said, "but only if you buy it."

I took her to a fast-food restaurant and sat her down and brought her one of their famous giant cheeseburgers. She held it in her hands familiarly as she watched the cars passing on Woodward Avenue. I let my gaze follow hers, and when I looked back, half the cheeseburger was gone. She wasn't even chewing. She didn't look at the food. She ate like a soldier in a foxhole. What was left of her food she gripped in her skinny fingers decorated with flaking pink nail polish. She was pretty in a raw and sloppy way.

"You're looking at me."

"Yes, I am," I admitted.

"How come?"

"A person can look," I said.

"Maybe." Now she looked back. "Are you one of those creeps?"

"Which kind?"

"The kind of old man creep who picks up girls and drives them places, and, like, terrorizes them for days and then dumps them into fields."

"No," I said. "I'm not like that. And I'm not that old."

"Maybe it's the accent," she said. "You don't sound American."

"I was born in England," I told her, "but I've been in this country for thirty years. I'm an American citizen."

"You've got to be born in this country to sound American," she said, sucking at her chocolate shake through her straw. She was still gazing at the traffic. Looking at traffic seemed to restore her peace of mind. "I guess you're okay," she said distantly, "and I'm not worried anyhow, because, like I told you, I've got a gun."

"Oh yeah," I said.

"You're not a real American because you don't *believe!*" Then this child fumbled in her coat pocket and clunked down a small shiny handgun on the table, next to the plastic containers and the french fries. "So there," she said.

"Put it back," I told her. "Jesus, I hope the safety's on."

"I think so." She wiped her hand on a napkin and dropped the thing back into her pocket. "So tell me your name, Mr. Samaritan."

"Warren," I said. "My name's Warren. What's yours?"

"I'm Jaynee. What do you do, Warren? You must do something. You look like someone who does something."

I explained to her about governmental funding for social work and therapy, but her eyes glazed and she cut me off.

"Oh yeah," she said, chewing her french fries with her mouth open so that you could see inside if you wanted to. "One of those professional friends. I've seen people like you."

I drove her home. She admired the tape machine in the car and the carpeting on the floor. She gave me directions on how to get to her house in Westland, one of the suburbs. Detroit has four shopping centers at its cardinal points: Westland, Eastland, Southland and Northland. A town grew up around Westland, a blue collar area, and now Westland is the name of both the shopping center and the town.

214

She took me down fast food alley and then through a series of right and left ninety-degree turns on streets with bungalows coveted by aluminum siding. Few trees, not much green except the lawns, and the half-sun dropped onto those perpendicular lines with nothing to stop it or get in its way. The girl, Jaynee, picked at her knees and nodded, as if any one of the houses would do. The houses all looked exposed to me, with a straight shot at the elements out there on that flat grid.

I was going to drop her off at what she said was her driveway, but there was an old chrome-loaded Pontiac in the way, one of those vintage 1950s cars, its front end up on a hoist and some man working on his back on a rolling dolly underneath it. "That's him," the girl said. "You want to meet him?"

I parked the car and got out. The man pulled himself away from underneath the car and looked over at us. He stood up, wiping his hands on a rag, and scowled at his daughter. He wasn't going to look at me right away. I think he was checking Jaynee for signs of damage.

"What's this?" he asked. "What's this about, Jaynee?"

"This is about nothing," she said. "I spent the night in the zoo and this person found me and brought me home."

"At the zoo. Jesus Christ. At the zoo. Is that what happened?" He was asking me.

"That's where I saw her," I told him. "She looked pretty cold."

He dropped a screwdriver I hadn't noticed he was holding. He was standing there in his driveway next to the Pontiac, looking at his daughter and me and then at the sky. I'd had those moments, too, when nothing made any sense and I didn't know where my responsibilities lay. "Go inside," he told his daughter. "Take a shower. I'm not talking to you here on the driveway. I know that."

We both watched her go into the house. She looked like an overcoat with legs. I felt ashamed of myself for thinking of her that way, but there are some ideas you can't prevent.

We were both watching her, and the man said, "You can't go to the public library and find out how to raise a girl like that." He said something else, but an airplane passed so low above us that I couldn't hear him. We were about three miles from the airport. He ended his speech by saying, "I don't know who's right."

"I don't either."

215

"Earl Lampson." He held out his hand. I shook it and took away a feel of bone and grease and flesh. I could see a fading tattoo on his forearm of a rose run through with a sword.

"Warren Banks," I said. "I guess I'll have to be going."

"Wait a minute, Warren. Let me do two things. First, let me thank you for bringing my daughter home. Unhurt." I nodded to show I understood. "Second. A question. You got any kids?"

"Two," I said. "Both boys."

"Then you know about it. You know what a child can do to you. I was awake last night. I didn't know what had happened to her. I didn't know if she had planned it. That was the worst. She makes plans. Jesus Christ. The zoo. The lions?"

I nodded. "She'll do anything. And it isn't an act with her." He looked up and down the street, as if he was waiting for something to appear, and I had the wild idea that I was going to see a float coming our way, with beauty queens on it, and little men dressed up in costumes.

I told him I had to leave. He shook his head.

"Stay a minute, Warren," he said. "Come into the backyard. I want to show you something."

He turned around and walked through the garage, past a pile of snow tires and two rusted-out bicycles. I followed him, thinking of my boys this morning at their scout meeting, and of my wife, out shopping or maybe home by now and wondering vaguely where I was. I was supposed to be getting groceries. Here I was in this garage. She would look at the clock, do something else, then look back at the clock.

"Now how about this?" Earl pointed an index finger toward a wooden construction that stood in the middle of his yard, running from one side to another: a play structure, with monkey bars and a swing set, a high perch like a ship's crow's nest, a set of tunnels to crawl through and climb on, and a little rope bridge between two towers. I had never seen anything like it, so much human effort expended on a backyard toy, this huge contraption.

I whistled. "It must have taken you years."

"Eighteen months," he said. "And she hasn't played on it since she was twelve." He shook his head. "I bought the wood and put it together piece by piece. She was only three years old when I did it, weekends when I wasn't doing overtime at Ford's. She was my assistant. She'd bring me nails. I told her to hold the hammer when

216

I wasn't using it, and she'd stand there, real serious, just holding the hammer. Of course now she's too old for it. I have the biggest backyard toy in Michigan and a daughter who goes off to the zoo and spends the night there and that's her idea of a good time."

A light rain had started to fall. "What are you going to do with this thing?" I asked.

"Take it apart, I guess." He glanced at the sky. "Warren, you want a beer?"

It was eleven o'clock in the morning. "Sure," I said.

We sat in silence on his cluttered back porch. We sipped our beers and watched the rain fall over things in our line of sight. Neither of us was saying much. It was better being there than being at home, and my morning gloom was on its way out. It wasn't lifting so much as converting into something else, as it does when you're in someone else's house. I didn't want to move as long as I felt that way.

I had been in the zoo that morning because I had been reading the newspaper again, and this time I had read about a uranium plant here in Michigan whose employees were spraying pastureland with a fertilizer recycled from radioactive wastes. They called it treated raffinate. The paper said that in addition to trace amounts of radium and radioactive thorium, this fertilizer spray had at least eighteen poisonous heavy metals in it, including molybdenum, arsenic, and lead. It had been sprayed out into the pastures and was going into the food supply. I was supposed to get up from the table and go out and get groceries, but I had gone to the zoo instead to stare at the animals. This had been happening more often lately. I couldn't keep my mind on ordinary, daily things. I had come to believe that depression was the realism of the future, and phobias a sign of sanity. I was supposed to know better, but I didn't.

I had felt crazy and helpless, but there, on Earl Lampson's porch, I was feeling a little better. Calm strangers sometimes have that effect on you.

Jaynee came out just then. She'd been in the shower, and I could see why some kid might want to spend a night in the zoo with her. She was in a tee-shirt and jeans, and the hot water had perked her up. I stood and excused myself. I couldn't stand to see her just then, breaking my mood. Earl went to a standing position and shook my hand and said he appreciated what I had done for his daughter. I said it was nothing and started to leave when Earl, for no reason that I could see, suddenly said he'd be calling me during the week, if that was all right. I told him that I would be happy to hear from him.

Walking away from there, I decided, on the evidence so far, that Earl had a good heart and didn't know what to do with it, just as he didn't know what to do with that thing in his backyard. He just had it, and it was no use to him.

He called my office on Wednesday. I'd given him the number. There was something new in his voice, of someone wanting help. He repeated his daughter's line about how I was a professional friend, and I said, yes, sometimes that was what I was. He asked me if I ever worked with "bad kids"—that was his phrase—and I said that sometimes I did. Then he asked me if I'd help him take apart his daughter's play structure on the following Saturday. He said there'd be plenty of beer. I could see what he was after: a bit of free counseling, but since I hadn't prepared myself for his invitation, I didn't have a good defense ready. I looked around my office cubicle, and I saw myself in Earl's backyard, a screwdriver in one hand and a beer in the other. I said yes.

The day I came over, it was a fair morning, for Michigan. This state is like Holland, and nothing drains out of it, resulting in cold clammy mists mixed with freezing rain in autumn, and hard rains in the spring broken by tropical heat and tornadoes. It's attack weather. The sky covers you over with a metallic blue, watercolor wash over tin foil. But this day was all right. I worked out there with Earl, pulling the wood apart with our crowbars and screwdrivers, and we had an audience, Jaynee and Earl's new woman. That was how she was introduced to me: Jody. She's the new woman. She didn't seem to have more than about eight or nine years on Jaynee, and she was nearsighted. She had those thick corrective lenses. But she was pretty in the details, and when she looked at Earl, the lenses enlarged those eyes, so that the love was large and naked and obvious.

I was pulling down a support bar for the north end of the structure and observing from time to time the neighboring backyards. My boys had gone off to a scout meeting again, and my wife was busy, catching up on some office work. No one missed me. I was pulling at the wood, enjoying myself, talking to Earl and Jaynee and

Jody about some of the techniques people in my profession use to resolve bad family quarrels; Jaynee and Jody were working at pulling down some of the wood, too. We already had two piles of scrap lumber.

I had heard a little of how Earl raised Jaynee. Her mother had taken off, the way they sometimes do, when Jaynee was three years old. He'd done the parental work. "You've been the dad, haven't you, Earl?" Jody said, bumping her hip at him. She sat down to watch a sparrow. Her hair was in a ponytail, one of those feminine brooms. "Earl doesn't know the first thing about being a woman, and he had to teach it all to Jaynee here." Jody pointed her cigarette at Jaynee. "Well, she learned it from somewhere. There's not much left she doesn't know."

"Where's the mystery?" Jaynee asked. She was pounding a hammer absentmindedly into a piece of wood lying flat on the ground. "It's easier being a woman than a girl. Men treat you better 'cause they want you."

Earl stopped turning his wrench. "Only if you don't go to the zoo anytime some punk asks you."

"That was once," she said.

Earl aimed himself at me. "I was strict with her. She knows about the laws I laid down. Fourteen laws. They're framed in her bedroom. Nobody in this country knows what it is to be decent anymore, but I'm trying. It sure to hell isn't easy."

Jody smiled at me. "Earl restrained himself until I came along." She laughed. Earl turned away, so I wouldn't see his face.

"I only spent the night in the zoo *once*," Jaynee repeated, as if no one had been listening. "And besides, I was protected."

"Protected," Earl repeated, staring at her.

"You know." Jaynee pointed her index finger at her father with her thumb in the air and the other fingers pulled back, and she made an explosive sound in her mouth.

"You took that?" her father said. "You took that to the zoo?"

Jaynee shrugged. At this particular moment, Earl turned to me. "Warren, did you see it?"

I assume he meant the gun. I looked over toward him from the bolt I was unscrewing, and I nodded. I was so involved in the work of this job that I didn't want my peaceful laboring disturbed.

"You shouldn't have said that," Jody said to Jaynee. Earl had disappeared inside the house. "You know your father well enough

219

by now to know that." Jody stood up and walked to the yard's back fence. "Your father thinks that women and guns are a terrible combination."

"He always said I should watch out for myself," Jaynee said, her back to us. She pulled a cookie out of her pocket and began to eat it.

"Not with a gun," Jody said.

"He showed me how to use it," the daughter said loudly. "I'm not ignorant about firearms." She didn't seem especially interested in the way the conversation was going.

"That was just information," Jody said. "It wasn't for you to use." She was standing and waiting for Earl to reappear. I didn't do work like this, and I didn't hear conversation like this during the rest of the week, and so I was the only person still dismantling the play structure when Earl reappeared in the backyard with the revolver in his right hand. He had his shirt sleeve pulled back so anybody could see the tattoo of the rose run through with the sabre on his forearm. Because I didn't know what he was going to do with that gun, I thought I had just better continue to work.

"The ninth law in your bedroom," Earl announced, "says you use violence only in self-defense." He stepped to the fence, then held his arm straight up into the air and fired once. That sound, that shattering, made me drop my wrench. It hit the ground with a clank, three inches from my right foot. Through all the backyards of Westland I heard the blast echoing. The neighborhood dogs set up a barking chain; front and back doors slammed.

Earl was breathing hard and staring at his daughter. We were in a valley, I thought, of distinct silence. "That's all the bullets I own for that weapon," he said. He put the gun on the doorstep. Then he made his way over to where his daughter was sitting. There's a kind of walk, a little stiff, where you know every step has been thought about, every step is a decision. This was like that.

Jaynee was munching the last of her cookie. Her father grabbed her by the shoulders and began to shake her. It was like what you see in movies, someone waking up a sleepwalker. Back and forth, her head tossed. "Never never never never never," he said. I started to laugh, but it was too crazed and despairing to be funny. He stopped. I could see he wanted to make a parental speech: his face was tightening up, his flesh stiff, but he didn't know how to start it, the

220

right choice for the first word, and his daughter pushed him away and ran into the house. In that run, something happened to me, and I knew I had to get out of there.

I glanced at Jody, the new woman. She stood with her hands in her blue jeans. She looked bored. She had lived here all her life. What had just happened was a disturbance in the morning's activities. Meanwhile, Earl had picked up a board and was tentatively beating the ground with it. He was staring at the revolver on the steps. "I got to take that gun and throw it into Ford Lake," he said. "First thing I do this afternoon."

"Have to go, Earl," I said. Everything about me was getting just a little bit out of control, and I thought I had better get home.

"You're going?" Earl said, trying to concentrate on me for a moment. "You're going now? You're sure you don't want another beer?"

I said I was sure. The new woman, Jody, went over to Earl and whispered something to him. I couldn't see why, right now, out loud, she couldn't say what she wanted to say. Christ, we were all adults, after all.

"She wants you to take that .22 and throw it," Earl said. He went over to the steps, picked up the gun, and returned to where I was standing. He dropped it into my hand. The barrel was warm, and the whole apparatus smelled of cordite.

"Okay, Earl," I said. I held this heavy object in my hand, and I had the insane idea that my life was just beginning. "You have any particular preference about where I should dispose of it?"

He looked at me, his right eyebrow going up. This kind of diction he hadn't heard from me before. "Particular preference?" He laughed without smiling. "Last I heard," he said, "when you throw a gun out, it doesn't matter where it goes so long as it's gone."

"Gotcha," I said. I was going around to the front of the house. "Be in touch, right?"

Those two were back to themselves again, talking. They'd be interested in saying goodbye to me about two hours from now, when they would notice that I wasn't there.

In the story that would end here, I go out to Belle Isle in the city of Detroit and drop Earl's revolver off the Belle Isle Bridge at the exact moment when no one is looking. But this story has a way to go. That's not what I did. To start with, I drove around with that gun in my car, underneath the front seat, like half the other residents of this area. I drove to work and at the end of the day I drove home, a model bureaucrat, and each time I sat in the car and turned on the ignition, I felt better than I should have because that gun was on the floor. After about a week, the only problem I had was not that the gun was there but that it wasn't loaded. So I went to the ammo store—it's actually called the Michigan Rod and Gun Club—about two miles away from my house and bought some bullets for it. This was all very easy. In fact, the various details were getting easier and easier. I hadn't foreseen this. I've read Freud and Heinz Kohut and D. W. Winnicott, and I can talk to you about psychotic breaks and object-relations and fixation on oedipal grandiosity characterized by the admixture of strong object cathexes and the implicitly disguised presence of castration fears, and, by virtue of my being able to talk about those conditions, I have had some trouble getting into gear and moving when the occasion called for it. But now, with the magic wand under the front seat, I was getting ready for some kind of adventure.

Around the house my character was improving rather than degenerating. Knowing my little secret, I was able to sit with Gary, my younger son, as he practiced the piano, and I complimented him on the Czerny passages he had mastered, and I helped him through the sections he hadn't learned. I was a fiery angel of patience. With Sam, my older boy, I worked on a model train layout. I cooked a few more dinners than I usually did: from honey-mustard chicken, I went on to varieties of stuffed fish and other dishes with sauces that I had only imagined. I was attentive to Ann. The nature of our intimacies improved. We were whispering to each other again. We hadn't whispered in years.

I was frontloading a little fantasy. After all, I had tried intelligence. Intelligence was not working, not with me, not with the world. So it was time to try the other thing.

My only interruption was that I was getting calls from Earl. He called the house. He had the impression that I understood the mind and could make his ideas feel better. I told him that nobody could make his ideas feel better, ideas either feel good or not, but he didn't believe me.

"Do you mind me calling like this?" he asked. It was just before dinner. I was in the study, and the news was on. I pushed the MUTE button on the remote control. While Earl talked, I watched the silent coverage of mayhem.

"No, I don't mind."

"I shouldn't do this, I know, 'cause you get paid to listen, being a professional friend. But I have to ask your advice."

"Don't call me a professional friend. Earl, what's your question?" The pictures in front of me showed a boy being shot in the streets of Beirut.

"Well, I went into Jaynee's room to clean up. You know how teenage girls are. Messy and everything."

"Yes." More Beirut carnage, then back to Tom Brokaw.

"And I found her diary. How was I to know she had a diary? She never told me."

"They often don't, Earl. Was it locked?"

"What?"

"Locked. Sometimes diaries have locks."

"Well," Earl said, "this one didn't."

"Sounds as though you read it." Shots now on the TV of Ed Koch, the mayor, then shots of bag ladies in the streets of New York.

Earl was silent. I decided not to get ahead of him again. "I thought that maybe I shouldn't read it, but then I did."

"How much?"

"All of it," he said. "I read all of it."

I waited. He had called *me*. I hadn't called him. I watched the pictures of Gorbachev, then pictures of a girl whose face had been slashed by an ex-boyfriend. "It must be hard, reading your daughter's diary," I said. "And not *right*, if you see what I mean."

"Not the way you think." He took a deep breath. "I don't mind the talk about boys. She's growing up, and you can wish it won't happen, but it does. You know what I'm saying?"

"Yes, I do, Earl." A commercial now, for Toyotas.

"I don't even mind the sex, how she thinks about it. Hey, I was no priest myself when I was that age, and now the women, they want to have the freedom we had, so how am I going to stop it, and maybe why should I?"

"I see what you mean."

"She's very aggressive. *Very* aggressive. The things she does. You sort of wonder if you should believe it."

"Diaries are often fantasies. You probably shouldn't be reading your daughter's diary at all. It's *hers*, Earl. She's writing for herself, not for you."

"She writes about me, sometimes."

"You shouldn't read it, Earl."

Tom Brokaw again, and now pictures of a nuclear reactor, and shots of men in white outer space protective suits with lead shielding, cleaning up some new mess. I felt my anger rising, as usual.

"I can't help reading it," Earl said. "A person starts prying, he can't stop."

"You shouldn't be reading it."

"You haven't heard what I'm about to say," Earl told me. "It's why I'm calling you. It's what she says."

"What's that?" I asked him.

"Not what I expected," he said. "She pities me."

"Well," I said. More shots of the nuclear reactor. I was getting an idea.

"Well is right." He took another breath. "First she says she loves me. That was shock number one. Then she says she feels sorry for me. That was shock number two. Because I work on the line at Ford's and I drink beer and I live in Westland. Where does she get off? That's what I'd like to know. She mentions the play structure. She feels *sorry* for me! My God, I always hated pity. I could never stand it. It weakens you. I never wanted anybody on earth pitying me, and now here's my punk daughter doing it."

"Earl, put that diary away."

"I hear you," he said. "By the way, what did you do with that gun?"

"Threw it off the Belle Isle Bridge," I said.

"Sure you did," he said. "Well, anyway, thanks for listening, Warren." Then he hung up. On the screen in front of me, Tom Brokaw was introducing the last news story of the evening.

Most landscapes, no matter where you are, manage to keep something wild about them, but the land in southern Michigan along the Ohio border has always looked to me as if it had lost its self-respect some time ago. This goes beyond being tamed. This land has been beaten up. The industrial brass knuckles have been applied to wipe out the trees, and the corporate blackjack has stunned the soil, and what grows there—the grasses and brush and scrub pine—grows tentatively. The plant life looks scared and defeated, but all the other earthly powers are busily at work.

Such were my thoughts as I drove down to the nuclear reactor in Holbein, Michigan, on a clear Saturday morning in August, my loaded gun under my seat. I was in a merry mood. Recently activated madcap joy brayed and sang inside my head. I was speeding. My car was trembling because the front end was improperly aligned and I was doing about seventy-five. One false move on the steering wheel and I'd be permanently combined with a telephone pole. I had an eye out for the constables but knew I would not be arrested. A magic shield surrounded my car, and I was so invincible that Martians could not have stopped me.

Although this was therapy rather than political action, I was taking it very seriously, especially at the moment when my car rose over the humble crest of a humiliated grassy hill, and I saw the infernal dome and cooling towers of the Holbein reactor a mile or so behind a clutch of hills and trees ahead and to my left. The power company had surrounded all this land with high cyclone fencing, crowned with barbed wire and that new kind of coiled lacerating razor wire they've invented. I slowed down to see the place better.

There wasn't much to see because they didn't want you to see anything; they'd built the reactor far back from the road, and in this one case they had let the trees grow (the usual demoralized silver maples and willows and jack pines) to hide the view. I drove past the main gate and noted that a sign outside the guards' office regretted that the company could not give tours because of the danger of sabotage. Right. I hadn't expected to get inside. A person doesn't always have to get inside.

About one mile down, the fence took a ninety-degree turn to the left, and a smaller county road angled off from the highway I was on. I turned. I followed this road another half mile until there was a break in the trees and I could get a clear view of the building. I didn't want a window. I wanted a wall. I was sweating like an amateur thief. The back of my shirt was stuck to the car seat, and the car was jerking because my foot was trembling with excited shock on the accelerator.

Through the thin trees, I saw the solid wall of the south building, whatever it held. There's a kind of architecture that makes you ashamed of human beings, and in my generic rage, my secret craziness that felt completely sensible, I took the gun and held my arm out of the window. It felt good to do that. I was John Wayne. I fired four times at that building, once for me, once for Ann, and once for each of my two boys. I don't know what I hit. I don't care. I probably hit that wall. It was the only kind of heroism I could imagine, the Don Quixote kind. But I hadn't fired the gun before and wasn't used to the recoil action, with the result after the last shot, I lost control of the car, and it went off the road. In any other state my Chevy would have flipped, but this is southern Michigan, where there are shallow ditches and nothing drains away, and I was bumped around—in my excitement I had forgotten to wear my seatbelt—until the engine finally stalled in something that looked like a narrow offroad parking area.

I opened my door, but instead of standing up I fell out. With my head on the ground I opened my eyes, and there in the stones and pebbles in front of me was a shiny penny. I brought myself to a standing position, picked up the penny, a lucky penny, for my purposes, and surveyed the landscape where my car had stopped. I walked around to the other side of the car and saw a small pile of beer cans and a circle of ashes, where some revelers, sometime this summer, had enjoyed their little party of pleasure there in the darkness, close by the inaudible hum of the Holbein reactor. I dropped the penny in my trouser pocket, put the gun underneath the front seat again, and I started the car. After two tries I got it out, and before the constables came to check on the gunshots, I had made my escape.

I felt I had done something in the spirit of Westland. I sang, feeling very good and oddly patriotic. On the way back I found myself behind a car with a green bumpersticker.

CAUTION: THIS VEHICLE
EXPLODES UPON IMPACT!

That's me, I said to myself. I am that vehicle.

There was still the matter of the gun, and what to do with it. Fun is fun, but you have to know when the party's over. Halfway home, I pulled off the road into one of those rest stops, and I was going to discard the gun by leaving it on top of a picnic table or by dropping it into a trash can. What I actually did was to throw it into the high grass. Half an hour later, I walked into our suburban kitchen with a smile on my face. I explained the scratch on my cheek as the result of an accident while playing racquetball at the health club. Ann and the boys were delighted by my mood. That evening we went out to a park, and, sitting on a blanket, ate our picnic dinner until the darkness came on.

Many of the American stories I was assigned to read in college were about anger, a fact that would not have surprised my mother,

226

who was British, from Brighton. "Warren," she used to say to me, "watch your tongue in front of these people." "These people" always meant "these Americans." Among them was my father, who had been born in Omaha and who had married her after the war. "Your father," my mother said, "has the temper of a savage." Although it is true that my mind has retained memories of household shouting, what I now find queer is that my mother thought that anger was peculiar to this country.

Earl called me a few more times, in irate puzzlement over his life. The last time was at the end of summer, on Labor Day. Usually Ann and I and the boys go out on Labor Day to a Metropark and take the last long swim of the summer, but this particular day was cloudy, with a forecast for rain. Ann and I had decided to pitch a tent on the back lawn for the boys, and to grill some hot dogs and hamburgers. We were hoping that the weather would hold until evening. What we got was drizzle, off and on, so that you couldn't determine what kind of day it was. I resolved to go out and cook in the rain anyway. I often took the weather personally. I was standing there, grim faced and wet, firing up the coals, when Ann called me to the telephone.

It was Earl. He apologized for bringing me to the phone on Labor Day. I said it was okay, that I didn't mind, although I *did* mind, in fact. We waited. I thought he was going to tell me something new about his daughter, and I was straining for him not to say it.

"So," he said, "have you been watching?"

"Watching what? The weather? Yes, I've been watching that."

"No," he said, "not the sky. The Jerry Lewis telethon."

"Oh, the telethon," I said. "No, I don't watch it."

"It's important, Warren. We need all the money we can get. We're behind this year. You know how it's for Jerry's kids."

"I know it, Earl." Years ago, when I was a bachelor, once or twice I sat inside drinking all weekend and watching the telethon and making drunken pledges of money. I didn't want to remember such entertainment now.

"If we're going to find a cure for this thing, we need for everybody to contribute. It's for the kids."

"Earl," I said, "they won't find a cure. It's a genetic disorder, some scrambling in the genetic code. They might be able to prevent it, but they won't *cure* it."

227

There was a long silence. "You weren't born in this country, were you?"

"No," I said.

"I didn't think so. You don't sound like it. I can tell you weren't born here. At heart you're still a foreigner. You have a no-can-do attitude. No offense. I'm not criticizing you for it. It's not your fault. You can't help it. I see that now."

"Okay, Earl."

Then his voice brightened up. "What the hell," he said. "Come out anyway. You know where Westland is? Oh, right, you've been here. You know where the shopping center's located?"

"Yes," I said.

"It's the clown races. We're raising money. Even if you don't believe in the cure, you can still come to the clown races. We're giving away balloons, too. Your kids will enjoy it. Bring 'em along. *They'll* love it. It's quite a show. It's all on TV."

"Earl," I said, "this isn't my idea of what a person should be doing on a holiday. I'd rather—"

"—I don't want to hear what you'd rather do. Just come out here and bring your money. All right?" He raised his voice after a quick pause. "Are you listening?"

"Yes, Earl," I said. "I'm listening."

Somehow I put out the charcoal fire and managed to convince my two boys and my wife that they should take a quick jaunt to Westland. I told them about Earl, the clown races, but what finally persuaded the boys was that I claimed there'd be a remote TV unit out there, and they might turn up with their faces on Channel 2. Besides, the rain was coming down a little harder, a cool rain, one of those end-of-summer drizzles that makes your skin feel the onset of autumn. When you feel like that, it helps to be in a crowd.

They had set up a series of highway detours around the shopping center, but we finally discovered how to get into the north parking lot. They'd produced the balloons, tents, and lights, but they hadn't produced much of a crowd. They had a local TV personality dressed in a LOVE NETWORK raincoat trying to get people to cheer. The idea was, you made a bet for your favorite clown and put your money in his fishbowl. If your clown won, you'd get a certificate for a free cola at a local restaurant. It wasn't much of a prize, I thought; maybe it *was* charity, but I felt that they could do better than that.

Earl was clown number three. We'd brought three umbrellas and were standing off to the side when he came up to us and introduced himself to my wife and the boys. He was wearing an orange wig and a clown nose, and he had painted his face white, the way clowns do, and he was wearing Bozo shoes, the size eighteens, but one of his sleeves was rolled up, and you could see the tattoo of that impaled rose. The white paint was running off his face a bit in the rain, streaking, but he didn't seem to mind. He shook hands with my children and Ann and me very formally. He had less natural ability as a clown than anyone else I've ever met. It would never occur to you to laugh at Earl dressed up in that suit. What you felt would be much more complicated. It was like watching a family member descend into a weakness like alcoholism. Earl caught the look on my face.

"What's the matter, Warren?" he asked. "You okay?"

I shrugged. He had his hand in a big clown glove and was shaking my hand.

"It's all for a good cause," he said, waving his other hand at the four lanes they had painted on the parking lot for the races. "We've made a lot of money already. It's all for the kids, kids who aren't as lucky as ours." He looked down at my boys. "You have to believe," he said.

"You sound like Jaynee," I told him. My wife was looking at Earl. I had tried to explain him to her, but I wasn't sure I had succeeded.

"Believe what?" she asked.

"You've been married to this guy for too long," he said, laughing his big clown laugh. "Maybe your kids can explain it to you, about what the world needs now." There was a whistle. Earl turned around. "Gotta go," he said. He flopped off in those big shoes.

"What's he talking about?" my wife asked.

They lined up the four clowns, including Earl, at the chalk, and those of us who were spectators stood under the tent and registered our bets while the LOVE NETWORK announcer from Channel 2 stood in front of the cameras and held up his starter's gun. I stared for a long time at that gun. Then I placed my bet on Earl.

The other three clowns were all fat, middle-aged guys, Shriners or Rotarians, and I thought Earl had a good chance. My gaze went from the gun down to the parking lot, where I saw Jaynee. She was standing in the rain and watching her old man. I heard the gun go off, but instead of watching Earl, I watched her.

Her hair was stuck to the sides of her head in that rain, and her cotton jacket was soaked through. She had her eyes fixed on her father. By God, she looked affectionate. If he wanted his daughter's love, he had it. I watched her clench her fists and start to jump up and down, cheering him on. After twenty seconds I could tell by the way she raised her fist in the air that Earl had clumped his way to victory. Then I saw the new woman, Jody, standing behind Jaynee, her big glasses smeared with rain, grinning.

I looked around the parking lot and thought: everyone here understands what's going on better than I do. But then I remembered that I had fired shots at a nuclear reactor. All the desperate remedies. And I remembered my mother's first sentence to me when we arrived in New York harbor when I was ten years old. She pointed down from the ship at the pier, at the crowds, and she said, "Warren, look at all those Americans." I felt then that if I looked at that crowd for too long, something inside my body would explode, not metaphorically but literally: it would blow a hole through my skin, through my chest cavity. And it came back to me in that shopping center parking lot, full of those LOVE NETWORK people, that feeling of pressure of American crowds and exuberance.

We collected our free cola certificates, and then I hustled my wife and kids back into the car. I'd had enough. We drove out of the Westland parking lot, then were directed by a detour sign into a service drive that circled the entire shopping center and re-entered the lot on the north side, back at the clown races. I saw Jaynee again, still in the rain, hugging her American dad, and Jody holding on to his elbow, looking up at him, pressing her thigh against him. I took another exit out of the lot but somehow made the same mistake I had made before, and, once again, found myself back in Westland. Every service drive seemed designated to bring us back to this same scene of father, daughter, and second wife. I gave them credit for who they were and what they were doing—I give them credit now—but I had to get out of there immediately. I don't know how I managed to get out of that place, but on the fourth try, I succeeded.

Nominated by Lee Upton and The Paris Review

THE LOVE OF TRAVELLERS

(Doris, Sandra and Sheryl)

by ANGELA JACKSON

from CALLALOO

At the rest stop on the way to Mississippi
we found the butterfly mired in the oil slick;
its wings thick
and blunted. One of us, tender in the finger tips,
smoothed with a tissue the oil
that came off only a little;
the oil-smeared wings like lips colored with lipstick
blotted before a kiss.
So delicate the cleansing of the wings
I thought the color soft as watercolors would wash off
under the method of her mercy for something so slight
and graceful, injured, beyond the love of travellers.

It was torn then, even after her kindest work,
the almost-moth exquisite charity could not mend
what weighted the wing, melded with it,
then ruptured it in release.
The body of the thing lifted out of its place
between the washed wings.
Imagine the agony of a self separated by gentlest repair.

"Should we kill it?" One of us said. And I said yes.
But none of us had the nerve.
We walked away, the last of the oil welding the butterfly
to the wood of the picnic table.
The wings stuck out and quivered when wind went by.
Whoever found it must have marveled at this.
And loved it for what it was and
had been.
I think, meticulous mercy is the work of travellers,
and leaving things as they are
punishment or reward.

I have died for the smallest things.
Nothing washes off.

Nominated by Rita Dove, Reginald Gibbons and Leslie Adrienne Miller

FIVE STORIES

fiction by LYDIA DAVIS

from CONJUNCTIONS

THE RACE OF THE PATIENT MOTORCYCLISTS

IN THIS RACE, it is not the fastest who wins, but the slowest. At first it would seem easy to be the slowest of the motorcyclists, but it is not easy because it is not in the temperament of a motorcyclist to be slow or patient.

The machines line up at the start, each more impressively outfitted and costly than the next, with white leather seats and armrests, with mahogany inlays, with pairs of antlers on their prows. All these accessories make them so exciting that it is hard not to drive them very fast.

After the starting gun sounds, the racers fire their engines and move off with a great noise, yet gain only inches over the hot, dusty track, their great black boots waddling alongside to steady them. Novices open cans of beer and begin drinking, but seasoned riders know all too well that if they drink they will become too impatient to continue the race. Instead, they listen to radios, watch small portable televisions, and read magazines and light books as they keep an even step going, neither fast enough to lose the race nor slow enough to come to a stop, for according to the rules, the motorcycles must keep moving forward at all times.

On either side of the track are men called checkers, watching to see that no one violates this rule. Almost always, especially in the case of a very skillful driver, the motion of the machine can only be perceived by watching the lowering forward edges of the tires settle into the dust and the back edges lift out of it. The checkers sit in directors' chairs, getting up every few minutes to move them along the track.

Though the finish line is only 100 yards away, by the time the afternoon is half over the great machines are still clustered together midway down the track. Now, one by one the novices grow impatient, gun their engines with a happy racket, and let their machines wrest them from the still dust of their companions with a whip-like motion that leaves their heads crooked back and their locks of magnificently greasy hair flying straight out behind. In a moment they have flown across the finish line and are out of the race, and in the grayer dust beyond, away from the spectators, and away from the dark, glinting, plodding group of more patient motorcyclists, they assume an air of superiority, though in fact, now that no one is looking at them anymore, they feel ashamed that they have not been able to last the race out.

The finish is always a photo finish. The winner is often a veteran, not only of races for the slow, but also of races for the swift, where he has also, usually, been a winner. It seems simple to him, now, to build a powerful motor, gauge the condition and lie of the track, size up his competitors, and harden himself to win a race for the swift. Far more difficult to train himself to patience, steel his nerves to the pace of the slug, the snail, so slow that by comparison the crab moves as a galloping horse and the butterfly a bolt of lightning. To inure himself to look about at the visible world with a wonderful potential for speed between his legs, and yet to advance so slowly that any change in position is almost imperceptible, and the world, too, is unchanging but for the light cast by the traveling sun, which itself seems, by the end of the slow day, to have been shot from a swift bow.

TELEVISION

1.

We have all these favorite shows coming on every evening. They say it will be exciting and it always is.

They give us hints of what is to come and it comes and it is exciting.

If dead people walked outside our windows we would be no more excited.

We want to be part of it all.

We want to be the people they talk to when they tell what is to come later in the evening and later in the week.

We listen to the ads until we are exhausted, punished with lists: they want us to buy so much, and we try, but we don't have a lot of money. Yet we can't help admiring the science of it all.

How can we ever be as sure as these people are sure? These women are women in control, as the women in my family are not.

Yet we believe in this world.

We believe these people are speaking to us.

Mother, for example, is in love with an anchor man. And my husband sits with his eyes on a certain young woman reporter and waits for the camera to draw back and reveal her breasts.

After the news we pick out a quiz show to watch and then a story of detective investigation.

The hours pass. Our hearts go on beating, now slow, now faster.

There is one quiz show which is particularly good. Each week the same man is there in the audience with his mouth tightly closed and tears in his eyes. His son is coming back on stage to answer more questions. The boy stands there blinking. They will not let him go on answering questions if he wins the final sum of a hundred-and-twenty-eight-thousand dollars. We don't care much about the boy and we don't like the mother, who smiles and shows her bad teeth, but we are moved by the father: his heavy lips, his wet eyes.

And so we turn off the telephone during this program and do not answer the knock at the door that rarely comes. We watch closely and my husband presses his lips together and smiles so broadly that his eyes disappear and as for me, I sit back like the mother with a sharp gaze, my mouth full of gold.

2.

It's not that I really think this show about Hawaiian policemen is very good, it's just that it seems more real than my own life.

235

Different routes through the evening: channels 2, 2, 4, 7, 9, or channels 13, 13, 13, 2, 2, 4, etc. Sometimes it's the police dramas I want to see, other times the public television documentaries, such as one called "Swamp Critturs," etc.

It's partly my isolation at night, the darkness outside, the silence outside, the increasing lateness of the hour, that makes the story on television seem so interesting. But the plot, too, has something to do with it: tonight a son comes back after many years and marries his father's wife. (She is not his mother.)

We pay a good deal of attention because these shows seem to be the work of so many smart and fashionable people.

I think it is a television sound beyond the wall, but it's the honking of wild geese flying over the city in the first dark of the evening.

You watch a young woman named Susan Smith with pearls around her neck sing the Canadian National Anthem before a hockey game. You listen to the end of the song. You change the channel.
Or you watch Pete Seeger's legs bounce up and down in time to his Reuben E. Lee song, then change the channel.

It is not what you want to be doing. It is that you are passing the time.
You are waiting until it is a certain hour and you are in a certain condition so that you can go to sleep.

There is real satisfaction in getting this information about the next day's weather—how fast the wind might blow and from what direction, when the rain might come, when the skies might clear—and the exact science of it is indicated by the words "forty percent" in "forty percent chance."

It all begins with the blue dot in the center of the dark screen, and this is when you can sense that these pictures will be coming to you from a long way off.

Often, at the end of the day, when I am tired, my life seems to turn into a movie. I mean my real day moves into my real evening but also moves away from me enough to be strange and a movie. It has by then become so complicated, so hard to understand, that I want to watch a different movie. I want to watch a movie made for TV, which will be simple and easy to understand, even if it involves disaster or disability or disease. It will skip over so much, it will skip over all the complications, knowing we will understand, so that major events will happen abruptly: a man may change his mind though it was firmly made up, and he may also fall in love suddenly. It will skip all the complications because there is not enough time to prepare for major events in the space of only one hour and twenty minutes, which also has to include commercial breaks, and we want major events.

One movie was about a woman professor with Alzheimer's disease; one was about an Olympic skier who lost a leg but learned to ski again. Tonight it was about a deaf man who fell in love with his speech therapist, as I knew he would because she was pretty and he was handsome. He was deaf at the beginning of the movie and deaf again at the end, while in the middle he heard and learned to speak with a definite regional accent. In the space of one hour and twenty minutes, this man not only heard and fell deaf again but created a successful business through his own talent, was robbed of it through a company man's treachery, fell in love, kept his woman as far as the end of the movie, and lost his virginity, which seemed to be hard to lose if one was deaf and easier once one could hear.

All this was compressed into the very end of a day in my life that as the evening advanced had already moved away from me. . . .

KILLED BY MONOTONY

Maupassant writes a story called "The Idyll," in which a hungry young carpenter nurses from the painfully swollen breasts of an older wetnurse to relieve her pain; he writes another called "The Confession," in which a coachman finally has his way, many times over, with a farmer's daughter. Babel includes an account of these two stories in a story he writes called "Guy de Maupassant," in which a poor young writer works with a rich married woman on her translations of Maupassant and finally makes love with her one evening after they have both drunk some excellent wine and he has upset a bookcase containing 29 volumes of Maupassant stories. A young writer, W., gives an account of the Babel story in a story of his called "Chekhov," in which a poor young student comes to spend the evening in the California home of an older man, a professor of Russian, and makes love with him after drinking several bottles of beer and talking about the stories of Babel and Chekhov. In a story of L.'s called "W.," which is about a poor young writer—W., in fact—writing a story about a poor young student and an older professor, L. gives an account of the story by W. along with his account of Babel's story including Babel's account of Maupassant's two stories. L. then describes her story in a letter to R. or K., and lastly, describes to another friend, A., her letter to R. or K. She now turns to her journal and notes down her conversation with A. and all it contained of the rest, though she senses that while one story within a story may add a certain richness to a story, too many cause that richness to fall away.

ALMOST NO MEMORY

A certain woman had a very sharp consciousness but almost no memory. She remembered enough to get by from day to day. She remembered enough to work, and she worked hard. She did good work, and was paid for it, and earned enough to get by, but she did not remember her work, so that she could not answer questions about it, when people asked, as they did ask, since the work she did was interesting.

She remembered enough to get by, and to do her work, but she did not learn from what she did, or heard, or read. For she did read, she loved to read, and she took good notes on what she read, on the ideas that came to her from what she read, since she did have some ideas of her own, and even on her ideas about these ideas. Some of her ideas were even very good ideas, since she had such a sharp consciousness. And so she kept good notebooks and added to them year by year, and because many years passed this way, she had a long shelf of these notebooks, in which her handwriting became smaller and smaller.

Sometimes, when she was tired of reading a book, or when she was moved by a sudden curiosity she did not altogether understand, she would take an earlier notebook from the shelf and read a little of it, and she would be interested in what she read. She would be interested in the notes she had once taken on a book she was reading or on her own ideas. It would seem all new to her, and indeed most of it would be new to her. Sometimes she would only read and think, and sometimes she would make a note in her current notebook of what she was reading in a notebook from an earlier time, or she would make a note of an idea that came to her from what she was reading. Other times she would want to make a note but choose not to, since she did not think it quite right to make a note of what was already a note, though she did not fully understand what was not right about it. She wanted to make a note of a note she was reading, because this was her way of understanding what she read, though she was not assimilating what she read into her mind, or not for long, but only into another notebook. Or she wanted to make a note because to make a note was her way of thinking this thought.

Although most of what she read was new to her, sometimes she immediately recognized what she read and had no doubt that she herself had written it, and thought it. It seemed perfectly familiar to her, as though she had just thought it that very day, though in fact she had not thought it for some years, unless reading it again was the same as thinking it again, or the same as thinking it for the first time, and though she might never have thought it again, if she had not happened to read it in her notebook. And so she knew by this that these notebooks truly had a great deal to do with her, though it was hard for her to understand, and troubled her to try to understand, just how they had to do with her, how much they were of her and how much they were outside her and not of her, as they sat there on the shelf, being what she knew but did not know, being what she had read but did not remember reading, being what she had thought but did not now think, or remember thinking, or if she remembered, then did not know whether she was thinking it now or whether she had only once thought it, or understand why she had

239

had a thought once and then years later the same thought, or a thought once and then never that same thought again.

CONFUSIONS

1.

On my way home, late at night, I look in at a coffee shop through its plate glass front. It is all orange, with many signs about, the counter tops and stools bare because the shop is closed, and far back, in the mirror that lines the back wall, back the depth of the shop and the depth of the reflected shop, in the darkness of that mirror, which is or is not the darkness of the night behind me, of the street I'm walking in, where the darkened Borough Hall building with its cupola stands at my back, though invisible in the mirror, I see my white jacket fluttering past disembodied, moving quickly since it is late. I don't see my head or hands, only my jacket fluttering past, and I think how remote I am, if that is me. Then think how remote, at least, that fluttering white thing is, for being me.

2.

I sit on the floor of the bathroom adjoining my hotel room. It is nearly dawn and I have had too much to drink, so that certain simple things surprise me deeply. Or they are not simple. The hotel is very quiet. I look at my bare feet on the tiles in front of me and think, Those are her feet. I stand up and look in the mirror and think: There she is. She's looking at you.

Then I say to myself: You have to say "she" if it's outside you. If your foot is there, it is there away from you, "her" foot. In the mirror, you see something like your face. It is "her" face.

3.

I am filled that day with vile or evil feelings—ill will toward one I think I should love, ill will toward myself, and discouragement

240

over the work I think I should be doing. I look out the window of my borrowed house, out the narrow window of the smallest room. Suddenly there it is, my own spirit: an old white dog with bowed legs and swaying head staring around the corner of the porch with one mad, cataract-filled eye.

4.

In the brief power outage, I feel my own electricity has been cut off and I will not be able to think. I fear that the power outage may have erased not only the work I have done, but also a part of my own memory.

Later that day, in the rain, I see a crumpled tan thing lying in the middle of the road. I think it is an animal. I feel grief for it and for all the crumpled animals I have seen in the road and by the edge of the road. When I come closer, I find that it is not an animal but a paper bag. My grief is still there. Then I find that I may feel the same grief for a paper bag as for an animal.

5.

I am cleaning the kitchen floor. I am afraid of making the call I have planned to make at nine o'clock. Now it is nine o'clock and I am done cleaning the floor. If I put this bucket away, if I hang up this dustpan, then there will be nothing left between me and that phone call, just as in X.'s dream, he was not afraid of his execution until they came to shave him. He was afraid now because there was nothing between him and his execution.

I begin hesitating at about nine o'clock. When I think it must be nearly nine-thirty, only five minutes have gone by: the length of time I feel passing is really only the enormity of my hesitation.

Now I make the call. The person I am calling answers but says he must call me back, and will call before ten. I am upstairs when the phone rings. Its ring is sharper because I did not expect it for another twenty minutes. I answer; it is someone else, whose voice also sounds sharper.

Now it is ten o'clock. I go out onto the front porch. I think the phone might ring while I am out here. Later I think the phone did ring then.

The phone rings just after I come inside, but again it is someone else. Later still, I will think perhaps it was not that person, but the one who was supposed to call.

6.

I am reading a sentence by a certain poet as I eat my carrot. Then, although I know I have read it, my eyes have passed along it and I have heard its words in my ears, I am sure I haven't really *read* it. I may mean *understood* it. But I may mean *eaten* it: I haven't eaten it because I was already eating the carrot. A carrot is a line too.

7.

I have decided to take a certain book with me when I go. I am tired and can't think how I will carry it, though it is a small book. I am reading it before I go, and I read: "The antique bracelet she gave me with dozens of flowers etched into the tarnished brass." At this point it seems to me that when I go out, I will be able to wear the book around my wrist.

8.

I pass the windows of the little shop that is called a doll hospital and see inside not only the dolls sitting and hanging naked and clothed in the windows and around the walls of the room, but also the old proprietor of the place sitting motionless in an armchair, her legs spread and her arms on the armrests, staring out of the shop with an expression of anger and gloom. I pass again in the other direction a few hours later and she and the dolls are in the same position, and the next day too, when I pass again, she and the dolls are in the same position, and a few days later, the same again. I can't decide whether some deep stillness in her brought her to spend so much time in the company of the dolls or whether the company of the dolls has taught her this deep stillness.

9.

As I sit waiting at a restaurant table I see out of the corner of my eye again and again a child come up onto the white marble doorstep of the restaurant entryway and then every time I look over, it is not a child I see but the shadows cast by the streetlamp, of a branch of large mid-summer leaves moving in the wind from the river.

10.

One night as I lie in the dark before sleeping, on a night when sleep will come easily because I am very tired, I conjure up his image, for pleasure and for company, as I often do, even though he is not with me anymore. This time, I am so tired that I can only imagine him standing in a well-lit place, against the wall of a room. I have him there before me, but almost immediately begin to fall asleep. Now, as I fall asleep, of his own accord he turns and walks away, out of my sight, and I am so surprised that I wake up. I have been too weak to hold him. This time, he was here against his will, and wanted to leave, and was waiting to leave until the moment when I would be too weak to hold him, and when that happened he moved from the well-lit place and walked out of my sight.

11.

Here, the ceiling is so high the light fades up under the peak of the roof. It takes a long time to walk through. Dust is everywhere, an even coating of blond dust. Around every corner, there is a rolling table with a drawing board on it, and a drawing on paper pinned to the board, and dusty boxes of charcoal next to it. Around another corner, and then another, a painting on a wall, half finished, and next to it on the floor, cans of paint, brushes across the cans, and pails of soapy water colored red or blue. Not all the cans of paint are dusty. Not all parts of the floor are dusty.

At first it seems clear that this place is not part of a dream, but a place one moves through in waking life. But rounding the last corner into the most remote part, where the dust lies most thickly over the boxes of charcoal sticks from Paris, and a yellowed sheet of muslin over the window is torn symmetrically in two spots showing a white sky through two small panes of dusty glass, a part of this place that seems to have been forgotten or abandoned, or at least to have lain undisturbed longer than the rest, it does not seem clear that this place is not a place in a dream, though whether it lies entirely in that dream or not is hard to say, and if only partly, how it lies at once in that dream and in this waking is hard to say— whether one stands in this waking and looks through a doorway into that more dusty part, into that dream, or whether one walks from this waking around a corner into the part more thickly covered with dust, into the more filtered light of the dream, the light that comes in through the yellowed sheet.

12.

There is his right leg over my right leg, my left leg over his right leg, his left arm under my back, my right arm around his head, his right arm across my chest, my left arm across his right arm, and my right hand stroking his right temple. Now it becomes difficult to tell what part of what body is actually mine and what part is his, and I find I am kissing my own arm when I expected to be kissing some part of him, whatever part might come up under my mouth.

I rub his head as it lies pressed against mine, and I hear the grains of his hair chafing against his skull as though it is my own hair chafing against my own skull, as though he and I have now become a single being, so that I hear with his ears, and hear from within his head.

244

13.

Out the window of the coffee shop I watch for a friend to appear. She is late. I am afraid she will not find this place. Now if the many people passing by in the street are quite unlike my friend, I feel she is still far away, or truly lost, but if a woman passes who is like her, I think she is close and will appear at any moment, and the more women passing who resemble her, or the more they resemble her, the closer I think she is and the more likely to appear.

14.

I nearly missed the bus: I may not be on it now.

I had trouble finding this place: it may be that I did not find it. And though I am talking to this person I came to meet, maybe he is alone here, waiting for me, because I did not actually find this place.

That was a peculiar thing to say to me. Maybe it was not said to me.

Or I, this person to whom no one is talking at this reception, was an unlikely person to invite: perhaps the invitation was for someone else.

15.

Late in the evening, I am confusd by drink and by all the turns in the streets he has led me through, and now he has his arm around me and asks me if I know where I am, in the city. I do not know exactly. He takes me up a few flights of stairs and into a small apartment. It looks familiar to me. Any room can seem like a room in a dream, as can any window seem like a window in a dream, as can any wall, any bare floor, and any doorway into a second room, but as I look at it longer, I know I have been here before. It was another month, another year, when this was an apartment belonging to someone I did not know.

16

I thought I contemplated a world that was there. I mean it seemed clear to me that I saw the world that was there, or a part of it, and thought about it as I saw it. The world as I thought about it would appear to be different from the same world as someone else thought about it because I would see it differently. All this seemed perfectly clear to me. Then, late one night when I was walking in a dark street, I saw that what I thought was the same world was not the same, that night, as it had been the day before, that it was not the same to me, that it had changed because I had been thinking about it, just as it had not been the same on other occasions, after I had been thinking about it, and I thought that it was not the world that remained the same and I who thought about it as I saw it, but the world that changed before my eyes, if only I had been thinking about it, changed from what it would have been if I hadn't been thinking about it, or changed as I saw it, after thinking about it, or that I thought about it, saw it again, and it was changed. And yet as soon as that seemed clear to me, I had to say that surely the world hadn't really changed, but only my way of seeing it—just as I had thought before.

Nominated by Barbara Einzig and Francine Prose

ONLY ONE SKY

by SAM HAMILL

from AMERICAN POETRY REVIEW

OUTSIDE MY OFFICE window, three young deer graze peacefully on a meal of newly-fallen apples. The first light October frost is just turning the apples red—without frost, apples remain green—and the deer seem to prefer them that way. The buck, a small two-pointer, looks up now and then to keep an eye on the half-dozen human spectators eating their own lunches on a small patch of lawn some sixty yards away. Two kinds of animals each eating lunch and enjoying same, each interested in the other.

The folks eating on the lawn are from Los Angeles. They are here with Robert Altman's crew to film a remake of Stanley Kramer's classic *The Caine Mutiny*, in what I've known for fifteen years as a musty old gymnasium at Fort Worden on Washington State's Olympic Peninsula. When I asked a member of the crew how anyone could hope to improve on such a classic, he said, "When you translate a novel into film, you've got an almost endless number of options. He won't 'remake' the old classic. He'll address other options."

The lunch-hour picnickers are from the crew. I know they are from L.A. because no one around here pays much attention to deer. But even from here, I can hear our visitors calling to the deer. They talk baby-talk at them: "Here, baby! C'mon, honey!"

Watching this little scenario unfold, I remember a review many years ago in *The New York Times*. The reviewer declared, "Gary Snyder's poems are full of trees!" Poems full of deer or trees or wildlife must sometimes seem odd things indeed in Manhattan or Hollywood. Those for whom relationships with animals have involved only the domesticated varieties or those that are caged cannot understand the subtleties, the implications, the "meaning," in writers like Barry Lopez, Gary Snyder, or Robinson Jeffers. Just as I, in turn, am often baffled by the critical attention given to a Merrill or an Ashbery. There is a whole vocabulary of city life known to me only through literature and jazz.

In a country as wide and as various in its possibilities of experience as the United States, there is often, even within the language most of us put to daily use—American English, there is often the need to translate. And for a poet, every poem is a translation into the original: every poem, like every poem in translation, is provisional. And every conclusion is at best marginal as well as excruciatingly temporal. Octavio Paz tells us this: "The history of the different civilizations is the history of their translations."

One cannot help but wonder just how different all our lives might be today had we not, deliberately and with calculated effect, obliterated two hundred languages in the last century—two hundred different ways of knowing that are now lost to North America and the world forever.

The deer continue munching fallen apples, keeping a wary eye on the tourists. Human baby-talk is just so much animal noise to them. And I remember that composing hymns to Krishna, East Indian cultures worked with an octave which was itself built entirely on the sounds of birds and animals, the first note being that of the peacock, the fifth note that of the cuckoo, etc. It follows therefore that in studying, say, the fourteenth-century Bengali poet Vidyāpati—who wrote in a regional language, Maithili, one would want to be aware of the tonalities and repetition of certain sounds because, after all, the peacock's cry carries an entirely different emotional consequence than that of the cuckoo. But one also realizes that by the fourteenth century, much of the original octave has faded from consciousness; the music and the language have continued to evolve, just as classical Greek and Latin have informed, have improved, the linguistic gene pool, but are themselves "dead" languages.

Octavio Paz notes, "With a certain regularity, languages suffer from epidemics that for years infect their vocabulary, prosody, syntax, and even their logic." Roland Barthes, Antonio Alatorre, Julien Gracq, Rexroth—so many critics have warned us away from those who in the service of structuralism would deny the erotic passion of the text. Paz says that passion "rapidly dispels the pretentious notion that we can construct a 'science of literature,' for the foundations of this would be the quicksands of desire."

Romanticism wreaked havoc in nineteenth-century English verse. Once Byron, Keats, and Shelley had been appointed a triumverate by the "scholars" who explained them, once their "means" could be reduced to demonstrable theory, their sincere admirers produced what Pound called "emotional slither." Paz calls for a practice of verbal hygiene.

American English is one of the most beautiful and flexible languages in the world. It is capable of both extreme hardness and sweet communion, often—in the hands of a poet—simultaneously. But before the poet can practice verbal hygiene, he or she must establish a practice of emotional hygiene. By clarifying the emotions, one clarifies one's language. Poetry, the preface to the *Kokinshu* says, begins in the heart. Every poem has a *kokoro* or heart.

And yet so very much recent North American poetry has been the articulation of cultured melancholy, of the elegant ennui and unnamable sadness of the middle class. Most often, we blame the Writing Program or television or the insane policies of corporate publishing. But even that is cowardice. Kay Boyle says this: "Why, after all, should this inability to speak with the heart as well as with the lips be blamed on 'restrictive teaching'? Is it not more of a case of restrictive thinking (induced by restrictive living) causing the muteness, which perhaps no teacher can cure? . . . One cannot be sure the students will dare to understand the words another has said. It takes courage to say things differently: Caution and cowardice dictate the use of the cliché."

Ben Belitt, who has taken his lumps as a translator of Neruda, makes a beautifully apropos metaphor when he tells Edwin Honig (in *The Poet's Other Voice*, University of Massachusetts Press, 1985), "I take my lumps as a translator, hoping as I go that nothing has really been violated and that the proportions of the original have been maintained even though my own dynamics have merged with the poet's. I wear my conscience where it belongs: at the tip of my pen, and not on my sleeve like a medieval garter." Our poetry has been grandly ennobled by translated poetries from throughout the world. It has also suffered a plague of "politically correct" poets wearing their public consciences like medieval garters, poets who devour social platitudes like so many apples in the Garden. The zendos are full of well-intentioned people wearing metaphysical garters and reciting words they do not dare to understand, all in the name of seeking enlightenment.

It is stupid and unthinking to repeat Frost's stupid, unthinking remark, "Poetry is what gets lost in translation." In plain fact, who among us has not been introduced to the world's great literature through translation?

As a child, I was given a "children's" Homer, *The Aeneid*, and *The Arabian Nights*. More than mere introductions to great literature, these books brought me something of the character of their original authors. Nearly forty years after that children's Homer, I hear Matthew Arnold say, "The translator of Homer should above all be penetrated by a sense of four qualities of his author:—that he is eminently rapid; that he is eminently plain and direct both in the evolution of his thought and in the expression of it . . . ; and, finally, that he is eminently noble." Rapid, plain, direct, noble: yes, these are the properties of a readable Homer in English, as any reader of Robert Fitzgerald's Homer will testify. The great challenge is that of capturing the spirit of the thing, the soul of the text, rather than wrestling only with its "form and meaning." In the original, what we find is a form *of* meaning.

What one gets in poetry translation is what Pound called "gists and piths," and, on occasion, poetry. An excellent case could be made for naming Pound's own versions of Li T'ai-po (*Cathay*) the most influential book of this century in English verse, despite the fact that his "errors" have been widely and repeatedly documented. While most of us parrot the charges against Pound, few of us ever take time to look closely at his milieu or pay any attention whatever to what passed as translation both before and after *Cathay*. Here is the E. Powys Mathers translation of Li T'ai-po's most famous poem (from *Lotus and Chrysanthemum*, Liveright, 1927):

THE JADE STAIRCASE

The jade staircase is bright with dew.

Slowly, this long night, the queen climbs,
Letting her gauze stockings and elaborate robe
Drag in the shining water.

Dazed with the light,
She lowers the crystal blind
Before the door of the pavilion.

It leaps down like a waterfall in sunlight.

While the tiny clashing dies down,
Sad and long dreaming,
She watches between the fragments of jade light
The shining of the Autumn moon.

The first line and the last line are tolerably accurate. Everything between seems to have come from the Chinese cliché shop, little pseudo-poetic trinkets and literary bric-a-brac and emotional slither. Mr. Mathers, along with L. Cranmer-Byng, whose work infects the same anthology, has the distinction of publishing the worst translations ever to see print.

Most of what falls short in translation may be laid at the feet of theory. It's easy to settle for the ambiguous line or for mere irony. One should remember that in its original Greek, "irony" meant only "dissimulation," a trait Plato characterized as "a glib, under-handed way of taking people in." Socratic irony comes from pretended ignorance. In the Latin, *ironia* denoted a discourse in which meaning was contrary to words stated. Ambiguity can be, like the use of cliché, a cowardly and/or lazy solution to the problems of seeking the soul of the text. Plurisignation is never easily achieved. Our sense of ambiguity comes largely from William Empson's notion that words *connote* at least as much as they *denote*. One workable solution is to combine the poet's feel for that living soul with a scholar's working knowledge of the text.

W. S. Merwin and Sōiku Shigematsu have combined to produce one of the most beautiful books in recent years, *Sun at Midnight*. One of these Zen poems ought to be memorized by every translator:

NO GAIN

Virtue and compassion
together make up
each one's integrity

251

Nothing that comes through the gate
    from outside
        can be the family treasure
Throwing away
    the whole pile
        in your heart
with empty hands
    you come
        bringing salvation

Translation is an act of love, it is a making *of* love, and is its own greatest reward. The self is subsumed, and the poet rises into a state of service in order to honor the original. Muso's poem in English turns the reader's attention inward, toward "reality." Pound may not have known zip about classical Chinese syntax, but he got the gist of the stuff all right.

Poetry in translation is most often a first step; it is not a substitute for anything. Its necessity is largely informed by the strictures of time. Kenneth Rexroth told me once, "The greatest tragedy of your age is that it is no longer possible to know the entire poetry of the world in the original." It wasn't possible in his age, either, but it is certainly a tragedy.

The translated poem begins an expanding process that sometimes leads into new languages, new cultures, whole new systems of awareness. Chuang Tzu tells us words exist only to give us a grasp on meaning; once meaning has been grasped, he says, we may get rid of words.

Jonathan Chaves gives us this poem by Yang Wan-li, who wrote some fourteen centuries after Chuang:

Now, what is poetry?
If you say it is simply a matter of words,
I will say a good poet gets rid of words.
If you say it is simply a matter of meaning,
I will say a good poet gets rid of meaning.
"But," you ask, "without words and without meaning,
                where is the poetry?"
To this I reply: "Get rid of words and get rid of meaning,
                and there is still poetry."

A translator only begins with the words and their meanings. Beyond that, or through that, the poetry reveals itself. Writing in the third century, Lu Chi says, "The art of letters has saved governments from certain ruin and propagates proper morals./Through letters there is no road too distant to travel, no idea too confusing to be ordered./It comes like rain from clouds; it renews the vital spirit." Lu's first line is lifted directly from the conversations of Kung-fu Tse (Confucius). Each of the following two lines follows the structure of the first, amplifying its meaning by means of repeated patterns of sound as well as by explication and example. It is useful to footnote that last line quoted: "cloud-rain" became a euphemism for sexual congress, the character written differently, but from the same etymological origin.

Beyond the words, understood at some level only as meaning-in-sound, the spirit or heart, the *kokoro*, of the poem continues to establish the rhythm of its experience—"meaning" also "means" the experience of tone and pitch and rhythm. The translator must also "translate" the music in order to have a poem at all. Otherwise, anyone with a dictionary could perform the task.

In Sōiku Shigematsu's brilliant translation of the classic *Zenrin Kushu, A Zen Forest* (Weatherhill, 1981), we can learn these perfect little Zen poems in English:

#190

When cold
    say cold;
When hot
    say hot.

#200

Sand in the eyes,
    clay in the ears.

#462

Three hundred poems
    come to one thing:

"Think
    no evil!"

#653

Blue made
    out of indigo
        is bluer than indigo;

Ice
    from water,
     colder than water.

We see imitations of this sort of thing all the time. It's a literary equivalent of instant Zen, the way a convict, to impress the parole board, will get "born again." But in order to "grasp the meaning" of each tiny poem, one must hold that poem inside oneself, as with kōan study when one learns to sit zazen. With so few syllables, each counts heavily, each should be sounded fully, just as each caesura, each silence of the poem demands its due measure.

During an evening of parlor poetry games one evening, we were writing invective, much of it imitation Catullus. Someone would pick a title, and each of us would be given five minutes to write a rhymed quatrain or whatever under that title. One title (now altered slightly to protect the identity of the one for whom the poem was written, but retaining the rhyme) prompted the following four-syllable couplet:

TO ONE WHO BEHAVES DESPICABLY

Fuck you.
Bless me.

Some will say it is neither a good poem nor a translation. The parlor game I learned from studying classical Chinese—the game itself is a translation. The invective is stolen (read: translated) from the Latin of Catullus who invented the word *defututa*, meaning fucked-out. But it is not entirely incompatible with the apparently

254

superficial self-indulgences one finds in Chinese and Japanese love poems and drinking songs such as J. P. Seaton's *The Wine of Endless Life*, translated from the Chinese of the Yuan Dynasty. The Chinese poet composes verses celebrating drinking, even drunkenness, but no respectable poet would ever appear drunk at a social function, including the famous wine-and-poetry gatherings. Most of these songs were intended to be slightly shocking.

I like the poem because it shows, on the one hand, good-humored invective. The four notes of the text clang large, then small; large, then small. It's here and gone in four quick gongs of a bell. It reminds me of Ikkyu, who was head master at Daitoku-ji, a huge Zen temple in Kyoto, for nine days. Upon leaving, he composed a poem expressing his disgust with the shallowness of life at the temple and saying that he could be found thereafter in the sake shops and the prostitution quarters. Thumbing one's nose, like raising one's middle finger, is sometimes an appropriate gesture even in a poem. One of the major maladies afflicting contemporary verse is the almost complete absence of humorous invective.

The poem above is coupled with another.

SAID THE WISE ONE TO THE FOOL

Fuck me.
Bless you.

As a two-sided poem, it cuts both ways: the initial line of the couplet is high invective; the second is a self-deprecating admonition that is a consequence of indulging in the first. Poetic humor is most often a double-edged sword. When Master Kung tells us, "Governments come and governments go; only the family is forever," his remark is tragic, comic, and pedagogical. Our poetry, so richly informed by various translators' excursions into and importations of other cultures, has begun to sound like it is written in "translator-ese," that bland, indefinite verbiage which is the result of academic minds studying the syntax (the structure) of the original without bothering to learn anything about what poetry is or may be in our native culture.

It is commonplace to find poetry translated from the classical Chinese in a kind of word-for-word way that is true to the syntax and the meaning-in-words, but which fails, either partly or completely,

255

to make tolerable poetry in American English. Greg Whincup recently published a selection of fifty-seven Chinese poems, *The Heart of Chinese Poetry* (Doubleday, 1987) that includes a poem by Tu Fu almost as well-known as Li T'ai-po's "Jewel Stairs' Grievance," a poem usually titled "Night Thoughts While Traveling":

Slender grasses,
A breeze on the riverbank,
The tall mast
Of my boat alone in the night.

Stars hang
All across a vast plain.
The moon leaps
In the Great River's flow.

My writing
Has not made a name for me,
And now, due to age and illness,
I must quit my official post.

Floating on the wind,
What do I resemble?
A solitary gull
Between the heavens and the earth.

Whincup makes a quatrain of each couplet. He is true to the meaning of the words in the original. In his notes on the poem, Whincup tells us that "heaven and earth" mean "the world." Why, then, did he separate the two and place the solitary sand gull between them? Because Tu Fu felt his was neither on earth nor assured a place in heaven. In the first line of the closing couplet, Whincup ignores the repetition of the character "floating" or "drifting," but only at great expense both to the meaning and to the feeling of the line. Whincup gets the words right, but completely misses the powerful emotional meaning of the poem.

In a wonderful scholarly translation of Tu Fu and Li Po together (*Bright Moon, Perching Bird* by J. P. Seaton and James Cryer, Wesleyan University Press, 1987), the aforementioned Seaton gives another version:

256

Slender grass, light breeze on the banks.
Tall mast, a solitary night on board.
A falling star, and the vast plain broader.
Surging moon, on the Great River flows.
Can fame grow from the written word alone?
This officer, both old and sick, must let that be
Afloat, afloat, just so . . .
Heaven, and Earth, and one black gull.

While the inversion of the fourth line rings a hollow note, Seaton comes much closer to the poet's feeling of frustration, especially in the closing couplet. The sixth line says in the original: "office must old sick quit" or "The old and sick should leave office." Both Whincup and, to a lesser degree, Seaton, by inserting Tu Fu himself into the line, create a misappropriate tone—almost as though the poet were whining—that misses the poet's feeling of uncertainty. The occasion of the poem was the death of Tu's patron. The poet, then in his mid fifties, suddenly had to pack up and leave. The fifth line expresses his feeling of the fleeting qualities of literary success, something the poet himself never knew.

In a brilliant little study of a very famous quatrain frequently mistranslated from the Chinese, *Nineteen Ways of Looking at Wang Wei* (Moyer Bell, 1987), Eliot Weinberger begins by saying, "Poetry is that which is worth translating."

Without giving away the many excellent points Weinberger scores, it is worthwhile to point out that sometimes even the most obvious line of a poem creates problems that get passed on from translator to translator. The last line of Wang Wei's "Deer Park" reads in literal:

Again   shine   green   moss   above

The poet is describing rays of sunlight falling in the deep forest. James J. Y. Liu, who has written invaluable books on Chinese poetics, translates the line, "And falls again upon the mossy ground." Rexroth simply ignores the "above" character. Burton Watson has the light "shining over" the moss. Octavio Paz ignores it. In fact, there are a good many more than nineteen versions of this poem to compare, but the only translator I know who approaches the last line with much success is Gary Snyder: "Again shining/on the green moss, above." In his comments to Weinberger, Snyder directs the reader's attention to the most obvious of facts: moss grows in the trees. Had the other translators bothered to look closely at the real and living landscape as the poet had, the line comes almost literally. But it's difficult to see a forest clearly, to understand its most telling details, from the third floor office in the Literature Department.

A hundred years ago, Pinkerton sang in *Madame Butterfly,* "His life is not satisfied unless he makes the flowers of any nation his own treasure." It has been proven to be a prophetic voice. Puccini's libretto is based upon a play by David Belasco initially staged in 1900 at New York's Square Theater.

In his extraordinary study *American Poetry and Japanese Culture* (Archon, 1984), Sanehide Kodama explores the steady growth of a primary literary relationship that begins, really, in English letters with publication of *Gulliver's Travels,* when Swift sends his hero to "Yedo" and "Nangasac" in 1726. Kodama examines several obvious figures: Ezra Pound, Amy Lowell, Kenneth Rexroth, Gary Snyder, and Allen Ginsberg. He also includes lucid observations on the haiku of Richard Wright, and on a poem by Richard Wilbur, "Thyme Flowering among Rocks," composed in seventeen-syllable stanzas of three lines each, counting 5–7–5, the syllabic measure of haiku. *American Poetry and Japanese Culture* ought to be in every poet's personal library. He reminds us of a forgotten poet in his examination of Richard Wright; he presents an accounting of the Pound/ Fenollosa notebooks and their consequences that is *nonpareil;* and his exegesis of Kenneth Rexroth's poetry is a great service to a neglected master and a pleasure to read as we uncover poem after poem brought into English from Japanese classics, but settling into Rexroth's own longer poems of philosophical meditation—they become an integral part of Rexroth's own being.

The real work of the translator/poet transcends even the most honorable of intentions—the bringing into our own language and thus our collective consciousness the classics of other cultures. Poetry demands a wider, fuller, and much more intense response to life. The formalities and idiosyncrasies of Japanese and Chinese poetry, for instance, are relatively unimportant. No one writing in American English is likely to do very much with the rhymed five-syllable quatrain that is the whole foundation of Asian poetry. We North Americans have contributed very little through our haiku-writing. The briefer the form, the more difficult to translate. Our haiku imitators are not much better nor worse than our imitation Romantics. Yet we have a handful of certifiably great haiku from recent years, just as we have a few great Romances.

Jorie Graham told me once about requiring her students to write one hundred haiku each. I don't recall whether she was strict in her definition or whether she allowed "approximate" haiku. It doesn't really matter. Afterward, after much struggle and frustration, she asked them what they had learned from their undertaking. The most common response, she said, was simply, "Humility."

By studying Burton Watson's fairly literal translations of early Chinese poetry (*The Columbia Book of Chinese Poetry*), we begin to understand the deeply humanistic traditions and the clear perspective on our relationship with Nature afforded by poets like Wang Wei or Su Tung-p'o. And we also see that even a thousand, two thousand years ago the poet often suffered hardship and exile by insisting upon the necessity of telling people what they already know but do not wish to hear.

In a more civilized culture, Burton Watson would receive the monument he so richly deserves. His translations, while rarely rising into pure poetry themselves, are accurate, readable, and utterly invaluable. As a scholar/translator, Watson is a national treasure. He has presented us with reliable texts for Chuang Tzu, Han Fei Tzu, Mo Tzu, Hsun Tzu, and the historian Ssu-ma Ch'ien—foundations in Chinese philosophy; he has given us brilliant translations of Su Tung-p'o and Gensei, Han Shan and Lu Yu; he has brought us two large volumes of Japanese literature written in Chinese; and his collaboration with Hiroaki Sato, *Country of Eight Islands*, is a masterwork anthology of Japanese poetry.

A second volume, *The Columbia Book of Later Chinese Poetry* (translated and edited by Jonathan Chaves), has just been published. Chaves, like Watson, is not a poet. But like the former, he presents us with excellent, readable texts beginning in the thirteenth century, where Watson leaves off. Chaves's translations of Yang Wan-li (*Heaven My Blanket, Earth My Pillow*) and Yuan Hung-tao (*Pilgrim of the Clouds*), both published by Weatherhill, are superb, as is his study *Mei Yao-ch'en and the Development of Early Sung Poetry* (Columbia, 1976). This two-volume set is absolutely essential for anyone incapable of deciphering Chinese. While many of our poets satisfy themselves with imitating what they perceive to be the prose descriptive passages of a Chinese or Japanese poem, they generally fail to understand the necessity for those "objectivist" passages. Watson and Chaves, like all great translators, present us with the descriptive passages, but conclude, as all great poetry does, with the essential humane wisdom of the culture.

It's hard to imagine what Gary Snyder's poetry might look like had he not undertaken the intense, lifelong self-discipline which his poems, like all good Chinese poems, reveal. His self-discipline is Ch'an or Zen both in its evidence—the poem—and in its practice. His little poem, "The Uses of Light," from his Pulitzer Prize-winning *Turtle Island*, concludes with a stanza lifted almost literally from the T'ang poet Wang Chih-huan's "View from Heron Lodge."

In another way, we may look at James Wright's great poem, "As I Step Over a Puddle at the End of Winter, I Think of an Ancient Chinese Governor," with its mock-Chinese title, and glimpse a deep personal and humane response to a poem by Po Chu-i written eleven hundred years earlier. Wright's poem would please Po Chu-i. Wright, by embracing the translation of Po's poem, enters into the intense personal experience of the old poet. Out of his experience with a reflection of the original, he molds his poem. The music of the Chinese is not his *métier;* his music is the music of carefully considered American speech. But the emotions and the fierce intelligence of the poem cannot be entirely detached from the classical Chinese.

Thirty years ago, Kenneth Rexroth observed that what we might learn from Asian poetry in translation is that it "accomplishes in one blow the various programs of the twentieth-century revolutions in poetry—and the manifestoes of the imagists and objectivists and so forth have to be fulfilled if you are going to write decent translations of Chinese verse." To which I would add such studies as composition by breath, composition by field, cadenced and open measure along with metrical structure.

In Denise Levertov's "The Poet Li Po Admiring a Waterfall," we find a lovely and sophisticated response not to a particular poem, but to a very generalized yet particular sensibility:

And listening to its
Japanese blues, the bass
of its steady plunging
tones of dark,
and within their roaring:

260

strands of thin
foamwhite, airbright
light inwoven!—all
falling
so far
so deep,
his two
acorn-hatted infant
acolytes fear
he will long to
fly like spray
and fall too, off
the sloping, pale
edge of the world,
entranced!

Most often, the imitation Chinese poem, through the laziness and superficiality of the poet, turns into mawkish sentimentality. James Joyce reminds us, "The sentimentalist is he who would enjoy without incurring a tremendous debt for the thing done." Levertov's poem is full of sentiment and full of acknowledged debt. It doesn't matter that Li Po, T'ang dynasty poet, never heard Japanese music. The poem is American; the experience of the poem is American, the music of that almost breathless experience is American. A conscientious reader is doubly rewarded by an etymology on the final word.

Levertov is not composing an imitation Chinese poem. Rather, she is simply being receptive to that which has been learned from Chinese poetics, adapting or translating the rhythms of perception into a basic line-by-breath that culminates in a four-syllable line from "acolytes fear" on, until the final two-syllable closure. While she makes no particular use of the structure of a Chinese poem, Levertov follows certain of its rhythms of perception and arrives with a poem which is the result of the deep influence of translation rather than the more usual superficial one.

In Robert Bly's best poetry, *Silence in the Snowy Fields* and *Loving a Woman in Two Worlds*, his poems assume their great moral authority in part by embracing classical Chinese and Japanese methods of procedure. Bly, whether consciously or otherwise, has always had a great feel for combining image with statement and grounding the two in metaphor. It is a tactic one encounters again and again in Tu Fu and Li T'ai-po, in tanka and renga, in love poems and in drinking songs. Even as early as "Taking the Hands" in his first book, he writes a poem which could easily pass as a good translation:

Taking the hands of someone you love,
You see they are delicate cages . . .
Tiny birds are singing
In the secluded prairies
And in the deep valleys of the hand.

His "Winter Poem," from *Loving a Woman*, is composed in four quatrains, the middle quatrains almost forming a parallel.

WINTER POEM

The quivering wings of the winter ant
wait for lean winter to end.
I love you in slow, dim-witted ways,
hardly speaking, one or two words only.

What caused us each to live hidden?
A wound, the wind, a word, a parent.
Sometimes we wait in a helpless way,
awkwardly, not whole and not healed.

When we hid the wound, we fell back
from a human to a shelled life.
Now we feel the ant's hard chest,
the carapace, the silent tongue.

This must be the way of the ant,
the winter ant, the way of those
who are wounded and want to live:
to breathe, to sense another, and to wait.

The structure of "Winter Poem" parallels that of a classical Chinese poem in several ways. In Chinese, the poet would use only eight lines composed in four couplets. The middle two couplets would form a double parallelism. Bly's language is far more relaxed, and requires extra syllables, extra lines, extra parts of speech. The Chinese would probably supply no articles, no prepositions, no conjunctions, and the first- and second-person pronouns would be mostly left to the reader to supply. A Chinese poet would admire especially the humility of the first stanza and the intelligence of the final.

In poems such as "Snow Geese" and "Night of First Snow," Bly achieves a moral presence by diminishing his own role in the poem. In the case of the latter, the poem might be even better without the first person pronoun. Bly finds his responsibilities revealed through the power of simple accurate description—snow geese, a drunken father and a little boy, a woman and a basket. And by meditations provoked by a winter ant.

A winter ant, a few deer munching October's apples, a weather pattern—almost anything can propel one into the drive to connect. Both the original poem and the "translation" entertain the possibility of becoming true poetry, *traduttore traditore* notwithstanding. Just as now, the deer gone back up the hill, the lunch crowd gone back into the old gymnasium, and John Coltrane is playing "Ole" on tape. The music, now thirty years old, is as fresh and exciting as Bach's concertos. Listening closely, one hears echoes and adaptations of the basic twelve-beat flamenco rhythm which has its roots in the *cante gitano* of the Spanish gypsies; and, behind that, echoes Greek music, of bouzouki and of that great Greek soul music, *rebetika;* and behind that, the sounds and rhythms of early East India flute, tamboura, and clay tabla. All of it is in one way or another translation. Coltrane, making his music from inside the heart, explores remnants of older cultures from the world over, then creates an utterly original music that is distinctly Coltrane and entirely American.

Another of Muso's verses from the Merwin/Shigematsu collaboration reminds us:

FOR KO WHO HAS COME BACK FROM CHINA

A brief meeting today
  but it seems to gather up
  a hundred years

We have exchanged
  the compliments of the season—
    that's word-of-mouth Zen

Don't say
  that wisdom and ignorance
    belong to opposing worlds
Look: China and Japan
  but there are not
    two skies

Nominated by Naomi Clark, Jane Hirshfield, and Laura Jensen

NICE MOUNTAIN

by GERALD STERN

from POETRY EAST

Great little berries in the dogwood,
great little *buds*, like purple lights
scattered through the branches, perfect wood
for burning, three great candelabra
with dozens of candles, great open space
for sun and wind, great view, the mountain
making a shadow, the river racing
behind the weeds, great willow, great shoots,
great burning heart of the fields, nice leaves
from last year's crop, nice veins and threads,
nice twigs, mostly red, some green and silky,
nice sky, nice clouds, nice bluish void.

I light my candles, I travel quickly
from twig to twig, I touch the buttons
before I light them—it is my birthday,
two hundred years—I count the buds,
they come in clusters of four and seven,
some are above me, I gather a bunch
and hold it against my neck; that is
the burning bush to my left, I pick
some flaming berries, I hang them over
my tree, nice God, nice God, the silence
is broken by the flames, the voice
is a kind of tenor—there is a note
of hysteria—I came there first,

I lit the tree myself, I made
a roaring sound, for two or three minutes
I had a hidden voice—I try
to blow the candles out, nice breath,
nice wagon wheel, great maple, great chimes,
great woodpile, great ladder, great mound of tires,
nice crimson berries, nice desert, nice mountain.

Nominated by Jim Simmerman

HOUSEWORK

fiction by KRISTINA McGRATH

from THE AMERICAN VOICE

THE WORLD would come to an end, she thought, and she'd be here handwashing his linen handkerchiefs. She loved the dangerous rush of water, the small white sink near brimful. There were at least ten things left to do before he got home but she stood at the sink and listened, scrubbing the linen thin, taking pleasure in the way light fell through the cloth when she held each handkerchief to the fluorescent. She loved fluorescent light. Fluorescent never lies, she thought, and scrubbed the linen thin.

She loved to feed him. She honestly loved to clean his clothes. And when she picked up what he let fall to the floor, mended his underwear or just plain splurged and bought him new ones, she felt that she healed him, partook in him, and life also. What she touched, he ate, he wore, and was where he sat or crossed space. The peeled peach (he insisted) was so ripe, so intimate, had been touched nearly everywhere, had changed shape even, that it almost embarrassed her to see him eating it with absolute faith. She pictured him, and he sat there, spotless, eating a peach. It was 1948. She was the secret of his magnificence, and the handkerchiefs rose higher with the water.

Not that she ever thought of it that way. It just made her feel good to have everything done for him. He was somebody. And, he could be so appreciative. Not that that was everything, or anything really. The doing was everything and the thanks was just a little something extra. Well, yes, she decided almost guiltily, she like to be thanked, it made it nice. She loved it when he knew exactly who he had married. Three years ago, come June.

You're so good for me, we'll give it a whirl, he said, get married and she nearly keeled right over. As if God himself had come down from heaven just to tell her: What you are doing for me is fine. She had said no to marriage more than once or twice. His was her fifth proposal. It seemed that every man and his brother from the North Side of Pittsburgh, who was just a little too nice or too shy or too something, had wanted to marry her; but he was somebody. He did drink just a little too much. But she would make him a life so good, there would be no reason for running from things as they are. The regatta of his handkerchiefs floated in the sink.

Life is either pleasant or my responsibility to make it so, she thought. Another clean Monday. She shut the taps and slapped the sink. 100% linen, she said. He would be home soon.

With the car door slam, the songs began. He loved to make up little stories about his day at The Radiant Oven Company by stringing together various song titles and phrases. After roaring up to the curb, skidding on the cobblestone of Franklin Way, shutting off the motor and the radio songs, he boomed. Right then and there in front of the neighbors. Waving from their porches, they seemed to appreciate it, so she didn't mind enjoying it herself. He climbed the twenty stairs of the rented house at 432 Franklin Way, a narrow alleyway cut from the backs of East End streets near Trenton Avenue and the trolley line. The high house suited him. He waved back at the neighbors from the landing, and the door swung open.

Finding her there with everything dropped perfectly into place, including herself at the door, he'd widen his eyes and grin but keep on singing, and without the loss of one beat, hurl himself onto the sofa in time to The Gal (he sat) From Kalamazoo (he crossed his legs with a flourish). She knew that that was Miss Glenny Hayes, Shoo Shoo Baby, who had been fired, My Darlin, My Darlin, In Tulip Time (it was spring). Then suddenly remembering her, he'd say, Whoops well so how are you? and then they'd laugh. He was the first person in the world who had ever really spoken to her in full sentences.

And so, with an old bent butter knife, she crawled to some far off corner (he would be home soon) and began scraping the floorboards, unimportant, invisible really because of the monstrous furniture, except to her, she knew it was there. Dirt should be taken care of like the first small sign of sadness or flu. Otherwise, catching his eye, it would spread under the feet of their company, gad about like sugar, unfurl into the yards of lazy neighbors, the whole city a shambles before you knew it, if each one in it did not take it on under their own roof. Besides, he noticed everything.

It made him happy to see her doing things and she was happy to be of use while listening to the radio news. The world interested her, but there was that problem with the newspaper a year or yes it was two ago (it was his, he said, snatching it back), so she never touched it again. She's Funny That Way, he sang.

Things made such an impression, she thought, as she scraped behind the china closet, remembering that time as a schoolgirl in that convent she loved so much in the best of times. She had accidentally stepped on a white chrysanthemum in the convent yard. It had fallen from some poor excuse for a bush which Sister What-was-her-name-anyway cared for, every day of her life it seemed she was out there, digging. She like talking to nuns. Well not really talking, just listening to them pass in the halls, mouse mouse mouse and holy holy holy (she counted them), was enough. She was one of the chosen, sent regularly on errands, who got to see nuns actually do things like stir soup or crouch digging by a bush. She felt it under her foot. The old nun scowled and lifted, with thumb and forefinger, as if it were a repulsive thing, the farthest tip of her old brown shoe that was always dancing in a place beyond itself. That, child, the old nun snarled, could have been the heart of Jesus. Even now, eleven years later, she felt mortified. It could have been the old nun's heart itself, with all it had to live for other than that old bush. It could have been her own, or his. She promised to be more careful.

On those quick bird feet on her small feet she tiptoed on a Wednesday through the house when no one was there but her and her girl. She knew she was tiptoeing when the girl started it too. She stopped on the cellar stairs, on her way to the kitchen, and set down her heels. Perhaps she had made a mistake, she thought, he was not the marrying kind. There was one child already; he loved her like the dickens, capable of it. But what were these sudden outbursts, what had she done? Perhaps it was the eggs this morning that made him a stranger. She went to an empty room, shut the door, and gave him time. She had broken the yolks. She had done something. She would sit there at the edge of the bed and find it out.

With a confident dash of salt, she seasoned a pot of water. She had the cookbooks memorized like a Shakespeare play. It was a common form of magic, pulling suppers from midair and boiling water on a low budget. Rattling something silver, at her business of which she was fond, of feeding who was hers and scooting them into a design around the table, she built with pots and pans the idyll of her mind and this was daily life: around it with a rag, picking up after it, rowing with the oar of it to the Mother of God, placing it next to itself where it huddled warm and clean in a bunch.

So this was life and this was life. The days were like rows of her bargain shoes that shone in the closet next to his. And here was the sound of the 19th century in a long dress brushing against the cold plaster as she pushed through the closet. And there was the cat on the stairs, climbing toward some higher realm where things would work out. Things would work out because she was in love with the everlasting furniture, with the restfulness of plates stacked in painted cupboards, with the raising of husbands and children all the way down the alley, because she knew she was a part: of something that keeps so many alive. She can please you, knowing the pleasure of safe mason jars and the calm of wooden spoons, the thud of good wood (her mother would have made that sound had she lived). Something sure as a cake could be done, and all of this was great and kind, small hellos to God. She would take care of hers, her corner of it would be a place to live. Cut carrots ran through the water rolling in the pot. The silverware lay ordered in blue shoeboxes with cardboard partitions in the deep drawers with which they were blessed. He had painted flowers and she had painted leaves on the face of the drawers and the cupboards, the two of them conspiring in some small but complicated plot against the larger tides of tornados and gunshots, of derelicts, senators and failed lovers, to be here, to be counted, she said, in this strange world.

Good people, she reminded herself, are recorded in books. Everyone had at least one thing to be recorded. Any sadness you might have is often recorded as a good work. This is the way it is, she said to herself, in love with the beautiful ordeal of packing in the sheets in the small upstairs cupboard, and with the arabesques he sawed into tables and shelves. A good house, she thought, and slapped the sheets. Love, she said, this would sustain, and the feeling went with her into the supermarkets, into the streets, God bless us all. The feeling could go as far as The Radiant Oven Company, into the world, he would carry it there to Penn Avenue. And so she went on with it, this knowledge of where everything absolutely is, all the designs of which she was capable, as she built, to the last detail, the house from the inside.

And he had helped. His heart was to the wheel. He had given her a floor to match her Sunday dress. He painted it yellow with black polka dots, each dot a monument to something they could not understand. He loved doing and doing, yet how he sweat when he did it, sprawled there like a little boy or folded all upon himself, bug-eyed in the corner, goggling his own perfection for days afterward, visiting it like a relative, and they said it couldn't be done. But everything was possible, she thought, what a talent. And told him so. You are a talented man. Everything he did, floor arabesque or drawer, he ran to have her see, and she would say, how lovely, you are a talented man. Tasks like this made him kind, and when he wasn't, well she had enough love to change ten people let alone just one. He showed promise, able to love like that a floor. She had the power. She was in the house.

She had joined history. She was in the house. I love how you touch things, he told her, I know where to find them afterward. He took it personally when she reordered the drawers or dusted the wooden hands of the sofa where he burrowed or sprawled, depending on his mood. It seemed to calm him. But everything needed so much like the banisters. He slid down them just to rile her. Sometimes it seemed he was beyond her like the congressmen and the senators, only a little nearer, when he screamed like that, questioning where she'd been, who had she been with. Everything was converging in their own bedroom, as if they were in an auto accident with history. My husband, right or wrong, she said, wishing there was someone to talk to about birth, about Hollywood and the Attorney General, about Hoover, about hiccups. The child still preferred crying over any other form of human expression. She was expecting again and the house seemed to run under her feet. Mouse mouse mouse, she sang to the child. She would take care of everything. She knew how.

Housework made her dizzy sometimes the way the seasons did when she thought of them too much, how they kept reoccurring like stacks of dirty dishes. She stood at the sink, washing the dishes, feeling at peace with the whiteness of the appliances. Eventually it was her youngest daughter, their last and not yet born, who would replace the seasons and the dishes as an image of time where she saw herself lost, important, found, small, and going on from there in a spin, but now it was the dishes that made her feel eager, indebted, and a part of some great wheel.

Why some of the best things in the world, she thought, happen like housework in circles. Birth and death, for example, not that you could call that best. Funny, but it wasn't anything really, just everything, whole kit and caboodle, one of the few facts (people get born and they die) that was neither good nor bad, though secretly she was convinced: birth was good, death was bad; and she was here and so she swept, on the fifth day, the floor for the fifth time that week. (They hated sugar under their shoes and he was always leaving it there.) And so she swept (the broom was new and bristly) as she said her secret prayer for her father never to die.

Her actions, she felt for a moment, were like those of God. He repeated himself too, heaping snow and flowers, tornados and children down onto earth, taking them away, then heaping it all back down again. God was like one huge housewife, she thought, then blessed herself for the blasphemy. And please, she whispered into the towels, let it be a son.

Anyways, she thought, God was one huge housewife and everything big was patterned after something small, even though they told her it was the other way around. She stuffed the towels into the washer, considering the idea. Neighborhood pride, for example. Why all he had to do was put in one new step, let alone the whole set that he did, and there were new steps all the way down the block, a whole way of life born from a single pair of steps. Enough good alleys like this and you'd have a city. I bring you, she said, this handkerchief, this man; this birdsong, symphony; this washed down wall, this whole shebang. She was brimful with the idea of babies. This woman, she thought, and stopped.

This was silliness and, Skittery, she said, liking the word better than what it meant. The insides of the washing machine twisted back and forth like the shoulders of someone at the scene of an accident. Her daughter made a sound, and suddenly she remembered the head of that lovely African insect she saw in *Life* last night. It resembled the monkey, and the monkey, man; though little girls, she thought, wiping her daughter's chin, resembled nothing and nobody but maybe other women. Your Mummy's a real rumdum, a real odd bird, she said to her girl, making her laugh.

She was afraid to be such an odd brown bird. This was how she thought of herself when she thought too much. When she was in company, some party he was always dragging her to and then he never wanted to leave, she sat in a corner, seeking out other people (usually other women, and only with her eyes, she didn't want to start up anything like a conversation) who could possibly be odd brown birds. Actually, it wasn't odd at all. Brown birds are very common, she thought, except when you felt like one.

Just last night her husband screamed that there was something wrong with her. She felt (whenever he swore like that) picked up and thrown into herself. It just took a while to get back out again, that's all. Anyways, Tip tip, she said to her girl, taking her hand and climbing from the bottoms of the house and thinking (that's what her daughter called it, the bottoms) there was probably some truth to what he said because she did think too much.

She knew she thought too much when she found herself disagreeing with the Bible. Suddenly she believed in evolution and hoped no one would ever find out. Who was she to disagree? Well, she must be somebody (she laughed and snapped the cellar light) because she did disagree, even with Darwin just a little, even if it was as a little joke. Man, she agreed, descended from the monkey—already her son, not yet born or of any shape much beyond light inside her, scrambled like one and tasted sweet as mud, while her daughter, born, sat there like an unborn, like a piece of silk—and women (she went on) descended from space itself (outer space), resembling more a swirl of air than anything with a nose on it.

She meant no disrespect. Women were strangers, unfamiliar in their babushkas, their get-ups, odd and poking in their heads with apology, waiting on their pins and needles to say hello. They apologized for a lack of salt in things they brought, for unrisen cakes, the rain, a husband's lack of social grace. They apologized for being happy (they were never happy, just a little flushed), sad (they were never sad, only slightly under the weather or a little lightheaded), or there at all. Chafing at the bit, skirting the furniture, or wringing their hands in front of movie houses they waited to be invited in and seated. Even in their own houses they were visitors, choosing wooden chairs. And when something buzzed, thudded, was still, they sprang into place which was nowhere. Wherever they were, it was only temporary (they sat on window ledges, they stood on ladders). And finally, they weren't even sure about being a pedestrian in a public space. She watched from the window their feet brimming over curbs or onto them (they raced on their toes), letting automobiles or businessmen pass. They looked funny through the glass, distorted somehow (and pity-full, she said) like large girls.

Men were such a relief. And she was here, surefooted, taking care of one. She enjoyed it. Being inside the house was a comfort. She felt sorry he couldn't get to be a woman too sometimes. Large spaces made her anxious lately, especially when she thought of how she used to cross them, on horseback no less, at a gallop. Even now it made her giddy. Silenced at the moment of the jump, she soared (or rather the old moment did) inside her body, and from this great height she looked down on it (her body), a stranger with whom she no longer liked to dance. Lately she never got far into conversation or Lake Erie, except a toe. The shell was water enough for her and she'd let him do the talking. She rocked her girl.

He was on this talking jag. All a lot of me me me or about people's rumps, everything flowered with parts of the body. You may as well listen to nothing as to that. He was drinking too much, flirting with anything in a skirt, and what was worse, he spit on people's porches. (Like some large space that would outlive her, he was getting out of hand; then he bought her flowers.) It was just another of his many jokes as they stood there marooned on the porch. Thank God, the nice people (relatives) hadn't answered the door yet. Giving him one of her famous looks (at his feet), she bent down and with her new white handkerchief (the one with her initial stitched on it, she loved her own name) wiped at the bleached porch boards, and with the opening door, rose up and smiled.

Housework, she thought, was an act of forgiveness for what you read in the newspapers. (He no longer minded that she read it; he was always off somewhere she didn't name.) By having supper always on time, whether he showed up or not, she felt she forgave some great evil, or death itself, by the fact she went on with it.

The girl in her lap was laughing now and talking of ponies, ready to play alone again. She always invited her everywhere through the house if she cared to come though lately she did not. The child shook her head to the outstretched hand, preferred not to go into the kitchen (she dropped greens into water, flooded a pot in a rush of metal at the sink), into the cellar (she swept with a sawed off broom the last of black water into the bubbling holes of the floor drain), into the upstairs room (she set out his evening clothes, he

274

appreciated it). The girl was forever plopping herself down and having to jump back up again this time of day, late late afternoon (her mother tempted her along with songs) until she gave it up and sat. Little white ponies, baby ones, she said to her girl, and racing by, tickled her on the stomach with her mouth, then was off again on her toes in the staccato of last minute tasks.

What was mean or ugly was not going to stop her, she swore it, from finding something to look forward to. Her son was born. She could hardly bear to look at him she loved him so much. Real corn, she thought, but that's the way I am. She felt accomplished as she climbed down the cellar stairs with her son in a basket. It was 1949.

She felt so clear and sad about the world when she did laundry. She liked this feeling of melancholy. It made her feel like she was telling the truth. It made her feel large, and above her head (she saw it), her soul seemed to drift like a paper boat out the cellar window into the gray sea of all Pittsburgh.

Cellar light was like a trapped thing and the same in every house. She studied it on walks. Windows half above, half below ground interested her, and the tops of ladies' heads bobbing in an element like water at twilight. It was always twilight in cellars, even in summer, even at noon. Down there the day was always ending like someone good who was dying. It made her want to stop and talk on her walks to the store. She imagined herself kneeling at cellar windows, Hey, and tapping on the glass, Hello, all the way down the block. The ladies would be shocked. What a novelty. Seeing some one there full in the face. Not the usual detachments: sawed off ankles and shoes, the eerie crawl of living hoses and grass overhead, all things plain misunderstood into wonderment or fear, or found there as they truly were, a wonderment, a fear: the earth was there, it was watered, it was soft, though sliced, suspended over your head, a lid; the living ones walked there in their shoes, their feet ran to meet each other. But here, a sudden human face, flesh, eyes. From sheer surprise, the ladies' heads would rise like balloons into daylight, followed shortly after by their bodies, one by one, ascending into Wilkensburg (their skin and dresses would be damp, smelling of soap, storage and earth, the twilight smell of warm leftover water, of green things kept out of light, also the sweetness of their tied back hair) and, bursting into view, bumping into one another, all twenty-three of them at once, they would chat, the women of Franklin Way, East End of Pittsburgh.

Dazzling, she thought. And in a rare backward look: I would have been a poet were it not for Sister What-was-her-name. She kissed six of her son's ten perfect fingers in time to the beat of Sister What-was-her-name, six kisses springing from the invisible rhythms of her invisible thought. She should have been a poet, she thought, because she felt aware of things that other people forgot. Not many took pride in what they did. But what she did made her sing, high and slow, this melancholy (as long as it didn't go on about itself more than it had to, she hated anybody brooding) made her feel like she loved her own heart. Always she had this slightest inkling she was somebody.

She held his head for hours and listened. He was so easily upset. Last night President Truman had finally told her that the Russians had set off an atomic explosion and she wished he wouldn't find out. And not about this morning sickness either. He was still upset about that Alger Hiss and his communist spy ring, so they said. Gospel truth, sons a bitches, he said, we'll be on their plates in the end. He sat on the sofa, his legs crossed, flipping his ankle.

Helen Keller was on the radio last night, she said, ironing. He burrowed down into the sofa as if into her voice where he could disappear. Helen Keller listens to the radio, donya know. So how does she do it? Well, it seems she can just feel it. Sound has vibrations, you know, and all she has to do is touch the radio and there it is, the song.

It would be such a joy, she thought, gliding the iron across the deep green of his workshirt, to see Helen Keller actually listening to music. A true and happy Christian, Helen sways lightly by the radio. It was an act of grace to find something lovely. Helen waves a hand to the rhythms of Tuxedo Junction, and with the other listens. In Helen's house, everything has to be just so they said, otherwise, walking across the room would be a terrible danger, from the stairs to her study, a terrible risk. It's like you're in the right church, but which pew do you go into? Was it like stepping through her own mind? she wondered. "Miss Keller rises early and answers all of her own letters." The announcer's voice sounded almost merry.

No one was ungrateful for Helen's sorrow. Everyone seemed to believe in it so, as if Jesus himself lay across her eyes and ears. After all, exactly who would Helen be without her sorrow? To what do you attribute the reasons for your success? asked no one. Our little agonies, your gifts, she answered the same no one and stared at his body, slumped and snoring.

Any day now she would have to tell him about the morning sickness. She was pregnant with their third child. The doctor told her she was in no condition to have two children in two years, what with the miscarriages she had had so far. Her head reeled but the child pulled her to earth with its own slight gravity. She had told her sister months ago. You're thin as a rail, sick as a dog, her sister said, and hit the roof. We will all come out of this better people, she thought, it was a sin to be unhappy.

It was that old public high school feeling. It was a standing joke there, Doncha get it she's Catholic, and the iron shimmied in small tight strokes on the collar of his Richmond Brothers shirt. She stood off in the distance again, it was 1941 in the public schoolyard by a wire fence. She shuffled her feet, burrowing into the dirt her own slight place. She watched the others run shouting across the yard, their sound lost now, but their bodies still twisting with laughter nine years later as if poked with invisible sticks. She stared at the crowd of young men and women. They could all be sent off to war or marriage, packed into houses or trenches, with bad grammar and (she gave them the benefit of the doubt) the tenderness of their pin-cushion hearts. She wished they would all stop having such a good time. It was 1941 by a wire fence in America and she wanted a cookie and rubbed her eye. You're nothing, she thought, without your sorrow. But still it was a sin to be unhappy. For lack of money she had to be sent here and there went peace and quiet, the convent, the singing lessons. (Not that she ever wanted to be a nun, she didn't, she loved horses, children, tennis, men.) That was the only thing she ever pleaded for, those singing lessons, and now, without them, she saw all the little O mouths of the people, empty and soundless, and his, opening and closing. Without your little sorrows, she knew it, you saw nothing beyond your own nose. She made an O in the dirt with the tip of her black shoe. She looked at it and it made her like everyone a little more.

Housework had a rhythm like prayer. During a Hail Mary, God help him, the iron wobbled over the difficult cloth in his work pants, burnishing and polishing at the slightest touch. He hated that. God help him to be happy and nice. Her stomach felt wooden but it made her real. Her legs felt flimsy, as if they were scribbled there in chalk beneath her, somewhere over the flowered carpet. Imagine, she thought, something nice. Imagine a tree in full blossom, she thought, a sunrise, a saint at your front door, the begonias on the sill outside your window and you refused to look. You missed out on something brief that would boost you and your husband and your children up forever. The sunrise, to her way of thinking, was a saint. She would have made a good pagan. There would be so many things to adore. I should have been a pagan, she said to herself, a few years later, and began a rosary then for Senator McCarthy to remain silent, to please shut his trap, as she caught her hand in the wringer and screamed.

Nominated by Barbara Bedway and The American Voice

SONG

by ROBERT CREELEY

from THE COMPANY (Burning Deck)

What's in the body you've forgotten
and that you've left alone
and that you don't want—

or what's in the body that you want
and would die for—
and think it's all of it—

if life's a form to be forgotten
once you've gone and no regrets,
no one left in what you were—

That empty place is all there is,
and/if the face's remembered,
or dog barks, cat's to be fed.

Nominated by Jennifer Atkinson

MUTATIS MUTANDIS

fiction by SHEILA SCHWARTZ

from CRAZYHORSE

(LOVE)

There was evening and there was morning the sixth day, and for what? So that she, Miriam, could walk alone to her bunk every night while the others groped and rustled in the dark, so that her only friend, Renee, could ditch her just like that for a creep named Harvey Haas, so that Chaim Picker could torment her ceaselessly, interminably, with his obscure, a priori liking?

Everyone else that summer got smoke in his eyes, got satisfaction, got do-wa-diddy-diddy-dum-diddy-do. Not her. Not mutatis (though not yet mutandis) Miriam. All she got was, "Nu, Miriam?" All she got was the correct answer every time she raised her hand. All she got was taller and taller. (Five feet ten and who knew when it would stop? Tall like a *model*, her mother always said. An attractive girl. Only thirteen years old and so shapely. Wait!)

But there was no end in sight. Too big, too smart, and on top of all this—the teacher's pet (a real *drip* in other words). It was a simple concept with a simple proof: Chaim Picker was a real drip. Chaim Picker liked her. Ergo, *she* was a real drip.

And so the proofs of *his* drippiness, clear and manifold.

For one thing, he spoke way too many languages all of which were queer. According to the others, his Hebrew was queer, his Yiddish was queer, his English was *totally* queer. (What was all that "Omnipresence" stuff, anyway?) To make things even worse, he wore the exact same thing every single day—a creepy black suit, black shoes, black yarmulkah, and tsitsit (the *epitome* of queerness). When he lectured the tsitsit swayed with him, back and forth, back and forth, Baruch HaShem Amen V'Amen! As far as anyone knew, these fringes were the only things he had ever kissed, in the morning when he put them on, and in the evening when he lay himself down to sleep.

Miriam saw him differently. He wasn't really a drip, just an "anachronism" (as she had discovered in one of her recent forays through the dictionary). For Chaim, it was clear, reminders of God and his commandments were everywhere, not only in the ceremonial fringes he wore, but in the whoosh of pine trees, in the birds flying overhead, even in his tea glass, spoon handle pointing upward like the metal finger of God, admonishing.

A bachelor, born circa 1930, he had a propensity for closed spaces and esoteric questions. Witness the inordinate amount of time spent in his tiny cabin. Witness the thick curtains on his windows, the hours spent in the library studying. Witness (they had no choice) his probing technique in class.

They groaned. Good Lord, more questions! He was going to kill them with all his questions. At every damned word he had to stop and wonder: who what where when and why, and sometimes why again. WHY does it say "in the beginning"? Hasn't everything always been here forever and eternally? So where did this "beginning" come from? And how could God precede it?

And furthermore. What is meant by "the face of the deep"? Wasn't this "face" covered by darkness? And wasn't it also empty and formless, but still visible in the "darkness"? (If it was *truly* darkness.) And how could this "darkness" *and* the spirit of God move upon the waters or whatever they were at the same time and in the same place and did this imply identity? And if so then what is meant by "in the beginning"? Miriam? Good, Miriam. *Correct.* For him, nothing in the stupid book was just simply what it was. Nothing in the whole damned world.

It was true, Miriam thought. Everything had its layers, its surfaces, its unexpected depths, even the riddle he asked them every day at the start of class: "Nu, children. What is the meaning of 'peel'?" Even the answer Barry Sternberg gave for the twenty-fifth straight day, "Miriam" instead of the true meaning "elephant." (Though it might seem otherwise, Chaim explained to her one day after class, Barry really was a good boy, he meant no harm by his remarks. "He's a sick boy," Chaim had said, "a boy with many problems. He needs people to pay attention, and not just *you*. Whom do you think has been scribbling on the walls all summer long? And other pranks I am not at liberty to mention. Just try to ignore him, Mireleh. The more any of us pays attention, the more he'll keep on doing it.")

Barry popped up and took a bow.

"Sternberg," Chaim said.

"What?"

Chaim pointed to the bench.

"Who *me*?" Barry pretended to be astonished. He spread his arms wide to capture his amazement. "What did I do? What in the 'H' did I do?" he asked the class.

"Please sit down."

"Why?"

"Sternberg. You may leave or you may sit down. *Choose*." Chaim placed both palms flat on the table.

Barry pointed. "The right one," he said.

"Sternberg!"

"The left?"

"OK OK OK," Chaim told him. "That was an interesting exercise. You have made for us a good variation on the state of innocence and on the meaning of will. But now, *we* will go on." He clasped his hands behind his back. "Nu, children?" He turned toward the class. "And vus is 'peel'?" His smile was hopeful. He waited.

"Oy!" Barry flopped back onto the bench. "Oy oy oy!" He shook his head. "These Jews. These Jews! They are *just never* SATIS-FIED." Then he went into his act. He made his eyes blink, made his jaws click-clack together. "Nu, Meereyum." His voice came out slow and underwater. "Why don't youuuuu tell us vussss." As though drowning in precision, he sank to another octave. "Cumpute it for him, Meeeeer-ee-yummmmm."

They burst out laughing.

"Sternberg, *leave*."

"Shtarenbeerg, *liv!*" Barry flapped his hands. Shoo! His grin implied a cheering crowd. He made no move to leave.

"OK OK. My accent is very funny; it's very funny indeed, I agree. There's truth in everything," Chaim said. "So, therefore, one more chance, Sternberg. This is Erev Shabbat and I'm giving you the benefit. Now what is 'peel-pool'?" He bent forward and nodded as if nudging him the correct answer.

Which gathered on Barry's face into a big, knowing grin. "An elephant pool—where Miriam swims." He sprang up from the table. "Shtarenbeerg—*LIV!*"

They laughed.

Miriam tried to ignore them, she tried to ignore Barry as Chaim had asked her to. After class he had repeated what he'd said before, "No matter how disturbing these events seem, we must pretend we don't notice. He's a child crying just to hear the sound of his own voice, a sad boy, a very very unhappy human being." And when she hadn't been convinced ("But why does he always pick on *me*?") he had added, "Listen, Mireleh. You are my best student. It's a shame that he spoils your concentration so I'll tell you a secret—for your ears alone, fashtays-tu?" When she'd nodded, he took hold of her hand, as if to prevent her from running in horror when she heard the truth. "Barry is an orphan," he whispered. "*Both* his parents at once—a terrible misfortune. He lives with his aunt. She's been very generous, but he has never gotten used to his fate. For this reason he sees a psychiatrist. A *psychiatrist*," he repeated. "You understand what this means? It's crucial for us to set a good example."

She tried, but it was difficult. Every day Barry sat down next to her. "Sha-loom, Meercyum." Winking to the class, he sprawled himself out until he was so close she could feel his tanned arms and legs glistening against her own pale ones, rubbing sweat. Everytime she moved, he moved over too until there was no place on the bench to sit. She tried to ignore him. She remembered what Chaim had said: "It is better to be persecuted than to persecute others." She tried to believe him. She stared at her hands, and at the trees, and at the big heart carved into the wooden table.

RANDY & JOSH IN '63.

That was the way the summer went; this was the pattern of love. Someone looked at you in services, in class, at dinner. Three times (a holy number). His friends noticed. They kidded him and giggled. *Your* friends heard about it and they told *you*. You blushed and shrugged your shoulders, not yes, not no. Sometime later (after a movie, or lunch, or Friday night dancing on the tennis courts) you heard footsteps on the path behind you, a voice which leapt to life in your ear, "Wanna take a walk?" Sometime later, the ID bracelet, a binding silver promise on your wrist. (Or was it the ID first and *then* the walk?)

That was the way it went and it happened to these people: David Stein and Leslie Gold. Yitzi Feinberg and Shira Oster. Josh Blum and Karen Bregman. Bennet Twersky and Susan Gould. The boys from Bunk 3 and the girls from Bunk 19. The kitchen help and Gladys Ticknor. Stacy Plisky and everyone. Once it almost happened to her, but it was only Norman Levine, the boy with the slide rule.

Still, even love with a slide rule was permissible in certain cases. According to the Talmud there were many faces to love—some smiling, some weeping. Love could be a wind, a deep well; it could be a tiger waiting to spring.

That was all well and good, but *this* was nothing of the kind. According to Leo Goelman, the camp director, love was one thing, *neetzool* was another. He gave them a long lecture about it the morning this sign was discovered painted on the library wall:

SUZY CREAMCHEESE—WHAT'S GOT INTO YOU?

Whoever had done this, Leo Goelman shouted, had no idea what love meant, not a clue. Real love was sacred. It was not something to joke about. What this prankster had in mind was something else—"neetzool" he reiterated. "Neetzool" meant *exploitation*, a lack of respect, a lack of individuality. "Neetzool" was what you felt like doing with anyone at all.

His interpretation discouraged no one.

Every night there was the same rush for the woods, the same giggling in the bathrooms afterwards. Every night Miriam listened to Shira and Renee whispering about what they had done (always, just loud enough for her to hear, just soft enough to make her feel that she was eavesdropping).

"We went to second. What did you guys do?"

"Only first."

Everything was euphemism. First base. Second base. Making out. Popping flies. Once Shira looked at her and laughed. "You don't know what we're talking about, do you?"

When they got between the rough, white camp sheets, instead of saying their prayers, they thought of what they had done, of what they might do tomorrow. They dreamed of scratchy bark against their backs, and later, eventually, of their names carved into that bark.

Miriam saw things differently:

They would meet somewhere, in a park, in a cafe, in the rain. He would be wearing a long coat, military style, black, but, not as black as his hair which was blue-black, seething with midnight. He would smoke thin cigars and know everything there was to know about poetry and film. Whatever he stared at, he would stare at intently. "Ah! A reader," he would say. "That's good. A woman who thinks." His eyes would linger on her face.

She would hand him her copy of *Steppenwolf* and he would turn the pages slowly, his unnaturally delicate fingers slipping beneath the paper. He would pause to read some comment in the margin. "Coffee somewhere?" he would murmur.

Rain would fall. Time would pass slowly. They would go on and on.

Or it might happen like this:

They'd have something in common (a love of nature or justice). Both of them, hard workers, diligent believers in a cause. People with principles! (Civil rights, maybe? disarmament?) Whatever their protest, they would run from the tear gas together, find shelter in a burned-out basement, wrap their wounds, never come out.

Or it might be like this: Before she even spoke, he would love her.

Other girls got letters from their boyfriends back home: "Are you still stuck in that dopey Bible camp? When are you coming home? I have a great tan from hanging around the club. The women adore me. Ha. Ha."

And they wrote back, a big pink kiss on the outside flap: SWAK.

Miriam got letters from her mother every day. "My darling, Miriam," or "Dearest Miriam," or "My darling, little Miriam," they began. She hoped that Miriam was having a profitable summer, that the other girls were nice, that Miriam was wearing all her nice, new outfits.

And as if that weren't enough. "P.S." she said. "You're a wonderful girl. I miss you."

Another week passed and they were still crawling through Genesis. God had made light and plenty of it shining down on every corner of the field, making the air hum, making the horizon, through the waves of heat seem to curl up into the sky. The grove where they had dragged their benches and table was no better. It was too hot to think. It was too hot to answer. Only Chaim in his eternal, black wool suit, was moving.

They had been over and over the Garden of Eden. Chaim had delineated it for them in graphic detail, and had made them sweat blood over it. The fragrance! The fruit trees! The making of each creature—how splendid! The perfection of the whole thing. Now they were stuck on Adam's rib (a difficult passage).

Why was it that Eve had been made from Adam's rib and not from dust, as Adam had been? God could do anything, correct? So why then from a rib?

Shelley Katz did not know.

Danny Goldfarb did not know.

Barry Sternberg did not give two hoots.

"*Think*, children."

"To make them fit?" As soon as she'd asked it she blushed. The heat of her mistake began to rise through her, to swell inside of her, to do something, at any rate, totally awful.

"Nothing would fit *you*," Barry said. "Not even *this*." He showed her with his hands.

"I didn't mean—!" But it was too late. They were too hot to answer, but not too hot to laugh. She wondered what the Talmud had to say on the subject of laughter. It could be a wind? A deep well? A tiger waiting to spring?

Chaim bent forward to block their amusement. "Don't be a clown, Sternberg. Do you never learn? Of course Miriam didn't mean this literally," he said. Then he frowned at them. "You meant it *figuratively*, didn't you, Mireleh? A metaphor? Something for something else, wasn't that your intention?"

She nodded faintly. Something else—oh sure. The road was a ribbon of moonlight. My love is a red, red rose. That was what she had meant—some other perfect fit. "I guess so," she said.

"Correct, Mireleh. That's very good." Chaim patted the table in front of him as though it were her hand. "Very good indeed." He held up his Bible, print outward, and pointed to the passage. "You see, we have here, class, a metaphor—a lesson we can read between the lines—"

"Between the what?"

"Between the LINES, Sternberg." He tapped the page. "Beneath what is said literally, children, we have a second, more important—"

"Beneath *who*?"

Chaim sighed, "Beneath what is said *literally*, a second truth, as Miriam has pointed out—what is good is often hidden."

"You can say *that* again!"

Chaim set down the book. "Please, Mireleh. Please tell us simply and QUICKLY and in what manner, *figuratively*, these two fit."

"Yeah," Barry whispered. "Give us all the figures!"

The blush crept through her, literally, figuratively, fittingly and other wise. However she had meant it she didn't know and didn't care. All around her they were grinning. Barry was grinning; he was coursing with possibilities (loose? tight? dry? deep?). Barry nudged her with his leg, "Nu, Mireleh so tell us already."

She tried to slide away from him and when she did, her legs lifting from the bench made a slurping sound.

"Correct!" Barry exclaimed.

"That *is* correct," Chaim said as though she had answered. His eyes told her: "Bear with him. Ignore him. Be brave." As if to demonstrate how sufferance like this was achieved, he ignored Barry and the sound and their laughter. He ignored everything he could possibly ignore. He clasped his hands together and squeezed. God made Eve from Adam's rib, he told them as he started to sway, to insure a perfect match, to make a coupling of the right and left halves so that no part should be omitted, no part lacking. It was a union perfect as the Garden, a union fragrant as a citron, alive with light. "We're talking about the crown of creation—*you understand me, class*?"

Sure. They understood.

On Friday nights it was standing room only in the woods. She could hear them in there hugging and kissing, fondling and caressing, zipping and unzipping, rubbing, pushing, their desire shredding fabric. She could hear them giggling and whispering and groaning, an ocean of sound that described each touch, that rose like steam through the woods.

(THE LIBRARY)

No one knew as much about that library as she did, except perhaps the librarian himself, and even *he* didn't know it in the same way.

She knew that the wood smelled in the morning, and the dust, of years of thought—resinous. She knew that the sun lit the letters on the bindings, gold. She knew which books had pictures, which ones had tiny, unreadable print. She knew who came there, at what hour, and for what purpose.

Chaim was there every afternoon from lunchtime until dusk poring over commentaries on the Bible. He didn't lean on one elbow like the others, but held his arms stiffly at his sides and swayed back and forth over the text as though he might dive into it. Sometimes he closed his eyes. She could watch him for hours and he never noticed her. Even when he lifted his head for air, his eyes shone with a blank, unseeing light.

Often, after he'd gone, Miriam would slip into his chair. She would pick up the book which still lay open on the table awaiting his return, and she would try to read what *he* had read that afternoon. There were reams of words, some in Hebrew, some in Aramaic, all without vowels, mysterious, impossible. She could only read the very large print—the phrase, or word, that was the subject of all that commentary: IN THE BEGINNING, DARK AND UNFORMED. She sat with the dictionary and puzzled out words. She wrote down translations, verbatim, awkward, but no matter what she did, she found nothing. The words were just words. Chaim still remained a mystery.

Then, eventually, she discovered that the words didn't matter. Maybe she couldn't understand them, but she didn't have to because it was just as pleasant simply to sit in the dark and pretend, to slide her fingers over the page, (occasionally, to sway a little), to skim the elusive grains of sense, silently, as though reading. She imagined that was what mystics did when they meditated. They chose some words, they shut their eyes, they rocked themselves to sleep. Every day she did this a little longer—a half hour, forty-five minutes, an hour—when she should have been playing basketball, or making lanyards, when she saw Barry coming towards her, over the hill.

As for Chaim—. One evening she hovered over the book he had left behind until it was almost dark. The librarian had gone home to his cabin. Dusk had thickened around her and she had let it, had liked it, the feeling of darkness melting into her, the way the words melted into her fingertips and her fingertips melted into the pages, the way the pages melted back into the darkness, slowly, very slowly, and the darkness melted back into her. She was dreaming that the letters had become figures, tall and thin, in long dark cloaks, broad black hats. They had all joined hands and were dancing in a circle around her making the room quake with joy. Faster and faster they whirled until the walls fell away, the sky became a blur—stars, moon, night thrashed against the galaxy: she couldn't catch her breath.

Wood creaked.

She opened her eyes.

A dark figure was coming towards her. Tall. Twisting. A shadow that bent. Unfolded. Bent again as though searching for a path through the twilight.

"Who's there?"she whispered.

The figure stopped. "Vus?"

Not the spirit of a letter, but Chaim. She had conjured him, complete, in his long black coat, his round black hat. "Vus machst tu, Mirelch?" he inquired.

Still not seeing clearly, she blinked. The hat he wore cast shadows on his face making from his features, shapes—caves and crags. "Ah," he said softly. "You're reading. Please don't let me disturb you," as though this were the most natural thing in the world, to be sitting in the dark with a book. She glanced down. She must have fallen asleep right on top of it. The pages were all crinkled and there were spots of saliva. She thought she smelled oil from her hair. Ashamed, she closed the cover. "I wasn't really reading," she sighed.

But he didn't answer. Instead, a white hand leapt to his beard and began stroking it, thoughtfully, gently, as though this were a demonstration of how to treat the world. Something about this puzzled her. Not the motion, but the whiteness of his hand. Her own hands were obscured by darkness, but his shone pale as though lit up from inside. She thought of miracles that she'd studied—the Hannakuh candle that burned for eight days; the bush in the desert exploding into flames. She thought it might be some strange effect from the Ner Tamid, the Eternal Light, that burned above the Ark against the wall. Or, she might have lapsed back into her dream, lulled by his silence.

"Mireleh?"

He was asking her something. One hand soared to his hat brim where it hovered as though waiting for an answer.

"What?"

"Pirkei Avot. The Ethics of the Fathers, you remember? It says there: 'On three things the world depends—on Torah, on work, and on the performance of good deeds.' Do you believe this?" He gestured. His hand swooped towards her like a dove, plummeting down.

Another magic trick? She pushed the book away. "I guess so." Why had he come back this late? Why hadn't he turned on the light? Did he come here to hide the way she did?

He did not help to make things clearer. Folding himself into the chair across from her, he said, "May I sit down for a minute?" Then the conversation began, a long conversation which made no sense, that seemed like words weaving through the darkness, occasionally surfacing, then dipping, then floating up again making strange ripples through all that had gone before.

"So how are you liking it thus far?"

"Liking what—the class?"

"The class. Anything."

"Not bad," she said.

"Ah, I see," he said sadly. His hat bobbed agreement. "At your age life is merely 'not bad.' I suppose God thinks you should be grateful for this. Well. Let's put Him aside for the moment." There was another long silence much more than just a moment, during which pause she wondered, was this really Chaim sitting across from her saying: *Let's put God aside?* She could feel him staring at her, his gaze like the hour after midnight, a mournful, naked look that made her lose her balance, made her fall slowly towards the center of the earth.

Finally, he sighed. "You know what is my favorite poem in the English language?" He recited it for her: "Sonnet number 73," he announced, as though it were a psalm. "'Bare ruined choirs where late the sweet birds sang'—that's Shakespeare, Isn't it sad?"

"I guess so." She didn't understand at all, really. Shakespeare. The Torah. Sweet birds and ruined choirs. What did he want from her?

He didn't explain. Instead, he wished her a good evening as he stood up, then drifted from the room. "You'd better go too, Mireleh. Your counselor will be worried."

But he came back again, the next night. Again, he settled himself into the chair across from hers and began speaking as though no time at all had intervened. Perhaps it hadn't. Whatever was on his mind was still there, pressing him, tugging at logic, winding good sense up into a ball—that came unravelled as soon as he opened his mouth to speak: "Do you know 'Ode to a Nightingale'?" he asked her. "Do you know this one by Hopkins?" Again he recited to her, his voice trembling as though *he* were the poet falling over the edge of the world into discovery. She knew this must be another secret he was telling her; something else he believed in besides God and good deeds and the Talmud Torah, a secret she must not divulge to anyone. The verses frightened her. In bed, after lights out, she chanted to herself all of the lines she could remember: "All is changed, changed utterly . . ." . . ."Though worlds of wanwood leafmeal lie . . ." . . ."I have been half in love with easeful death . . ." —lines that went against what they prayed for each morning: "Blessed art Thou O Lord, King of the Universe who removest sleep from mine eyes and slumber from mine eyelids, who restorest life to mortal creatures . . ." It was as though she'd seen Chaim wandering through a new landscape—a shadowy glen drenched with mist, moss-covered, hopeless.

By the third night, she was waiting for him, for the conversation that made such confusion, that made her grasp the arms of the chair she sat in, so solid, so wooden. He didn't greet her this time, just picked up the threads of their last talk and began braiding them, rocking back and forth as though praying, as though fevered. He spoke until the dark became as thick as a trance, until she leaned into this, waiting, bending towards him so that their knees brushed under the table, his—rough and woolen, hers—bare and tender, very warm. She wanted him to say something that would break the

291

spell, something ordinary: "That's fine, Mireleh," as he would have done in class, "You're a good girl, my *best* student . . ." But he didn't say a word, and what he didn't say gathered between them.

She tried to think of a question to ask him, a polite question to engage his interest, but the only ones that occurred to her pertained, oddly enough, to his legs. What were they like beneath the fabric of his trousers? Pale? Calloused? Were they as white as his hands? As smooth?

Suddenly, he leaned forward as if he had been speaking to her all this time. "And you know what they say? They say that the Torah was written by men."

"What?" She was still thinking of his legs, white as paper, the black curling hairs.

"By *men*," Chaim repeated. His words rushed through her. He was looking at her earnestly. For a minute she imagined he had heard what she was thinking, that this was the way scholars made passes, by a reference, that he would reach across the table and draw her to him; they would kiss across the table, only the outstretched Talmud between them. Then she realized he wasn't looking at her at all. He was staring the way he did when he was unable to pry himself loose from his holy books and go back into the world. "That's what they think!" he exclaimed. "Can you believe it? By men and not God. That there isn't any absolute and, therefore, no suffering. It's as simple as that." He laughed, incredulous. "There are no *real* laws. Only *human* laws. Is that ridiculous? We should think like the others, they say. The Chinese. The Hindus. They think it's better to meditate, that it's all right to leave the suffering of this world behind, while we Jews, we *real* Jews," he shook his head, "*we* stay and suffer, throwing our souls into the fire and groaning when we are burned. And then we think we know." He slapped the table. "And then we think we have done our part!" His fist came down.

She tried to make sense of it later. For several days, she added up the evidence, subtracted what didn't fit at all, and divided by what was obscure. On the one hand, there was the lateness of the hour each time they talked; there was his prolonged stay, the personal nature of his questions, his lingering over the poems, his knees brushing hers. On the other hand, there was his unexpected leap to the Hindus, his discussion of suffering, and after his fist struck the table, his apology: "Never mind," he had told her. "It's late and I've probably driven you crazy with all this nonsense. I keep forgetting you're only thirteen. Thirteen in America is an easier age."

Than what? she wondered.

She began to dream of him at night, a dream bathed in different lights. Gold. Dark green. Over and over.

In her dream it was a Sabbath afternoon, dry as ashes, like a day held under a magnifying glass to start a fire. Everyone was resting, tired, quiescent, in their cabins, reading newspapers, or poems or love letters: "My darling, my dearest, sweetheart . . ."

Except her.

She had been walking for hours looking for something, her eyes were fixed on the road. Whatever it was she had lost it. A bracelet? An earring? She was looking for a glimmer in the road as the sun beat down against her back pasting her yellow shirt to her skin with sweat. It was hot. It was so very hot. The road was a dusty glare— empty, forlorn, forever.

Suddenly, she looked up. There were woods! From nowhere, green rushed out to welcome her. On both sides of the road, deep green, the trickling of running water, branches waving. Leaves. Meadows of thriving grass—Queen Anne's Lace and Wild Timothy.

Someone touched her arm. A tall figure dissolving into shadows in the woods. She followed though she couldn't see, could only feel the deep cool breath of the forest soothing her. She walked for hours, until the setting sun came through the trees in threads— orange, green, yellow sprays of light that dazzled her.

Against this light, she saw Chaim. In black as always, long coat, velvet yarmulkah, clasping in one hand his Bible, the special one from Israel with its silver cover beaten to the shape of tablets, a turquoise stone inset for each commandment. In his other hand, a bunch of flowers, white, which he handed to her, then kissed her cheek. A warm, moist kiss. "I like big girls," he whispered.

They lay down together.

He began to kiss her. Lips to her mouth, lips to her hair, to the hollow of her neck, to her lips again until she shivered though his lips were warm like cinnamon or cloves, and smooth as the wood of a spice box. Then stinging. Then sweet. Over and over, his lips, until his hands moved over her too, touching her and stroking her, unbuttoning clothes, sliding them over her skin as swift as angels, (she was naked; he was naked), reading her body with his fingertips, skimming her arms, her legs, her breasts, with hands that were lighter than whispers, than blessings, until light poured over both of them, into them; they were inside it. He was rocking her back and forth; she was curling herself around him.

By day what remained of her dream? He was naked; she was naked. Nakedness in all its conjugations. I was naked, she thought. *We* were naked. Had been naked. Would be. Might.

She watched him in class as he bent over his text and she didn't see his black clothes, she saw his skin, white and smooth and glowing. When he said her name, she could hardly answer. When he moved his fingers over the pages, she flinched. And when he started to sway she felt her body swaying with him; she couldn't bear to look.

(HUNGER)

Precedents for such romances: David and Abishag, Abraham and Keturah, Isaac (he was over forty) and Rebecca, Esau and Judith, Joseph and Potiphar's wife (sort of), Pablo Picasso and what was her name? his latest wife, someone slim, exquisite; at any rate—a woman to be proud of.

She imagined how it would feel to look like that, as thin and graceful as a lulav—the wand made of palm fronds and myrtle and willow that the men waved on Sukkot, the harvest festival. She pictured herself that way, and then Chaim, taking her by the hand, introducing her proudly: "This is Miriam. She's not only a great reader, she's also very lovely—don't you think?" He would bow to his own words, dazzled, faithful. In private he would touch her as he had in the dream. "I'll tell you a secret, Miriam—for your ears alone. I'll tell you all of my secrets . . ."

But it wasn't just for Chaim she had decided to do this; there were the others as well. How wonderful, she thought, to leap and twirl and float right past them, to rise above their laughter like a wisp of smoke. How wonderful never to hear Barry say again, "Here she comes—THUMP! THUMP!" She would be thin as a switch, that's what she'd be. She'd lash the world with her beauty, make them all run before her—awed, delighted.

If not, then she'd disappear.

She had already given up lunch and sometimes even dinner; it was nothing to give up the rest. The first day she didn't even feel hungry, and whenever she did she drank a cup of tea.

Strangely enough, she seemed to have more energy, not less. Instead of going to meals and activities, she took long walks around the countryside. She hiked through the woods and trekked across pastures so that she could climb to the tops of hills rough with brambles, boulders. She searched for waterfalls, a far-off rushing sound. She made her way through marshes where only algae grew or the stumps of trees pointing upward for no reason.

Each day she dared herself to go a little further. Once it was a walk to the next camp five miles down the road. The following day she went into town, then another five miles past an abandoned church with a cemetery plot, untended, crooked crosses scattered everywhere as wayward as weeds. On Wednesday it rained and still she hiked all the way to the lake at Equinunk. Because it was pouring no one was there, so she took off her clothes and swam. That was beautiful, floating in the lake, rain washing down through the trees, rattling in the leaves, drenching her face. The sky was iron gray, a ceiling of clouds descending.

But then, everything was more beautiful, she found. No matter what she looked at it seemed clearer, as though it lit up under her gaze and announced itself: I am water. A maple tree. The sky. I am stone.

When she grew tired of just walking she began another kind of journey. She watched Chaim. A man mysterious. A man apart.

His curtains were always drawn, but she found some holes in the planking that allowed her to see different parts of the room, though never very much at once. There was the floorboard view and the closet view. There was the view of the bookcase, the view between the bottles and jars in the medicine cabinet. There was a complete view of the ceiling from underneath the bunk, but this required hardships that made it not worthwhile.

She settled for glimpses.

From various angles at various times, she saw his feet in socks, in slippers. She saw a glass of water placed on a chair next to the bed. She saw a handkerchief dropped, a handkerchief plucked up again.

A bag of laundry set down in a corner. Often, a broom swept balls of lint and hair into a pile. Pantslegs! Coatsleeves! All of a sudden—his face! as he leaned over to collect the dirt into a dustpan, as beatific as though he were gathering manna in the desert.

What she hoped to discover, she couldn't say precisely, but every day she made her pilgrimage. Every day she knelt, hidden behind the walls of his cabin, trying her best to peer in.

Some days were more rewarding than others.

On Friday afternoons, for instance, he always polished his shoes so that they would be bright and new for the Sabbath. First he removed the laces, gingerly, as though they were made of silk. Then he took a whisk broom and brushed off all the loose dirt. With a nail file he scraped mud from the welt of the shoe, then poked a pin into all the perforations. When the shoe was finally ready, he shook the bottle thoroughly, a lurching sound, heavy, like medicine being mixed, then removed the applicator and began painting—first the sides, then the tongues, then the heels. Last, he let them dry for half an hour, then rubbed them with a cloth until they shone.

Another ritual was the preparation of tea which he drank, without fail, at 4:30 in the afternoon. He had a small electric kettle stationed above the bookcase, a silver spoon, a china cup.

At night, instead of turning on the overhead light, he burned candles. Miriam could barely see anything then, but the flicker of shadows was enough to intrigue her, the occasional hiss and snap of flame made her shiver.

She shivered, too, the time she spied his slender hand lift a bar of soap from the shelf in the bathroom. As he removed the wrapper her heart leapt up, for had he not closed the cabinet door just then, she would have seen his robe removed as well, would have seen him stepping into the shower.

She never actually discovered anything she hadn't already observed just by sitting on her bench in class with others. He was meticulous. He was thoughtful. He worshipped the acts of ordinary life the same way he worshipped knowledge. Nothing new.

But here, alone and unguarded in his cabin, he was framed in mystery. From her vantage point, each hint of flesh loomed statuesque. Each gesture swelled with meaning. The smallest act became a revelation.

Her devotion turned boundless. From his morning ablutions to his nighttime prayers, she scrutinized every motion. She was his prophet. In a thick notebook she wrote down all he did, printing the words in straight, careful lines as though they were already gospel:

"At dawn, he wakes . . ."

"Late afternoon: he groans and stirs—too much study in one position? . . ."

"Evening: Walks to the window and stares into the woods . . . He sighs . . . Eventually, he lets the curtain fall . . ."

"Later: Night has come. He waits for sleep . . ."

She studied these notes daily, searching for patterns. She asked herself questions: which had more significance—the order of his actions or the spirit in which they were performed? Could she estimate that spirit? Could she guess the exact nature of the intention that informed each action?

No more than she could understand Barry, who daily grew more bold in his troublemaking. She wasn't his only victim anymore. Perhaps because the end of summer was approaching he began to expand his horizons. From simple pranks like graffiti and pool dunkings, he leapfrogged to more elaborate crimes—putting paint in the windshield washer of the camp bus, hiding all the canoe paddles the night before the big trip down the Delaware, making streamers of the underwear he pirated from the girls' bunks and draping them in the trees. He stole cake from the baker's closet—poppy seed strudel and cream puffs and chocolate eclairs, the spoils of the camp director and the rabbinicial staff always kept locked up against just this kind of invasion. During Saturday morning services he let loose a collection of live crickets that rasped and whirred like a demented congregation. He ordered subscriptions to the library from Crusade for Christ, from the American Nazi Party.

Everyone assumed it was Barry. It had to be him. Who else would have had the nerve? Miriam, herself, saw him one night in the camp junkyard breaking windows with one of the missing canoe paddles. The junkyard was a clearing in the woods at the end of a narrow, rutted road. It was the place where they piled all the ruined furniture—the mildewed mattresses and ravaged sofas, the crippled chairs and tables, as well as things like martyred pianos, mirrors that were cracked, embittered.

Over this ruined kingdom, Barry reigned, forcing homage with beatings, breaking spirits that were already broken. He pounded and whacked and hammered and when he'd shattered every window into a thousand frightened splinters, he began ranting aimlessly, "Take *that* you bastard! Take *that* you bitch!" flailing and thrashing and smiting all of the unfortunate subjects in his path.

If his behavior in class was any measure of his loss of self-control then this was to be expected. Late in the season, he and Chaim had learned a new kind of dance—contorted, ugly. It drove away all peace and quiet, all possibility of reconciliation. By this time, it was just the two of them. As though Miriam were a shade that had been lifted to reveal his true enemy, Barry no longer bothered to tease her. Chaim was the target now, a willing target who bent to receive the arrows.

Each morning Barry strolled in an hour late: "Did I miss anything? Are we still on chapter two? That dumb old stuff? Lord! Will this ever be over?"

Each morning he pushed Chaim a little bit further. Excuse me, dear Teacher, Moreleh, Your Highness, I mean. That just doesn't make any sense to me. Is that really the translation? Are you certain this is the answer?"

"Why do we have to study this boring garbage anyway?"

"Well, that's a silly law if I ever heard one!"

He would goad and bully and impugn and just as Chaim was about to lose his temper, as his face began to redden and his voice began to shake, he would pull back: "Hey. Don't get excited, man. Take it easy, will you? I'm just an ignoramus, a clown, a boy who likes to sow his nasty oats—what do you care? Look. Don't pay any attention to me. I don't mean anything, you know. Not really."

Chaim appeared determined to endure. It was as if by yielding to his anger he would prove himself a liar; he would have to admit that Barry was not a "good boy," someone to "bear with." Setting an example was all that seemed to matter. Ignoring the price, he continued to sidestep these challenges and affronts, to pretend that they were merely bursts of high spirits. Kindling.

She was walking in circles. That's all she knew. She was further than ever from understanding him, from understanding anything.

Further still the night she saw this, something so strange she was not convinced afterwards that she had seen anything at all.

She had been fasting for a week, for two weeks, more. She had been living on tea and water and water and tea. Many times she had seen things that weren't there. Flocks of birds when she bent over, swarms of ants, dark fountains sprouting from the ground. She saw afterimages of what she had just seen on top of what she saw a second later—trees on top of buildings, rocks on top of heads.

At night she couldn't sleep. She closed her eyes and had visions (she couldn't think of another name for what she witnessed). Big dots. Masses of color. Parades of geometric shapes. All the parts of the body, in parts: huge eyes, knees, foreheads, ribs. She saw lines, flashes of lightning; as before—letters from all of the alphabets dancing together without shame.

Still. Even this made a certain kind of sense. What she saw in Chaim's cabin—no sense at all.

First his feet walked over to the bookcase. They walked back to the bed and paused. She heard the sound of sheets of paper being ripped from a book, from many books. This went on for several minutes during which time the feet returned to the bookcase, presumably, to remove more books. Then she saw knees, hands, a pile of paper.

A coat was thrown to the floor, then a shirt. One set of ceremonial fringes. And just when her heart began to pound, thinking she would see him at last, she saw, instead, a pair of hands strike a match, reach forward to the paper; and when it was on fire (blazing in fierce darts of color) he muttered something in Hebrew; the hands came down; she saw him lay himself down, back first, on top of the flames.

What would it have meant provided she had actually seen it? After she awoke from her faint she thought of several possibilities. He had a rare skin disease that was held in check, though not cured, by daily doses of charcoal and extreme heat. He had decided to become a Hindu mystic. He was a magician. A pyromaniac. She was crazy.

She knew she should stop fasting. She told herself that every day. She was becoming very light. Much lighter than anyone else. Invisible. A wraith. It was true. She had found the trick. She could pass right through other people and they didn't even notice her. In turn, the words they spoke passed back through her and on into the night as if through ether. What they meant no longer sank into her flesh and lay there trapped.

But it wasn't only that. It was the strength she had achieved; the concentration. It was feeling that once she gave in, once she gave up just a little bit, she gave it all up; she gave up forever herself. It was feeling that she might see again the flames in Chaim's cabin, and, like a ledge or a bridge, some wide open space between heights where she might fall, it was daring to see those flames again, wanting to see them rise through his back.

(CHAOS)

But that was cool, wasn't it? Barry had asked the morning they finished reading chapter three. Wasn't screwing on the Sabbath a double mitzvah? a double good deed? Wasn't that the law—double your pleasure double your fun? So why did Adam and Eve get the boot? What was wrong with one little screw?

Smoke hissed from the torches. Her insides hissed with hunger. It was the evening of Tisha B'Av, a fast to commemorate the destruction of the Temple, the precedent (as Chaim called it) for all the two thousand years of suffering that came after.

They were sitting on the floor reading "Lamentations." By the waters of Babylon, remembering Zion.

He was standing, a man apart, a man mysterious, in a corner by the door, swaying as though he had been swaying for days and days and couldn't stop. The torch light swayed with him, and the congregation, sitting in the long shadows on the floor, chanted: "From above he hath sent fire into my bones, and it prevaileth against them. He hath spread a net for my feet, he hath turned me back: He hath made me desolate and faint all day . . ."

Barry had disappeared. Three days ago. "Who needs your stupid class?" he had said. "Who needs your fucking Torah?" He had stalked off into the woods and they hadn't seen him since.

At first they thought he was just going in there to sulk, to make a scene. "You were right," they told Chaim. "He was really being a

300

jerk"; and Chaim, still furious, still clutching his Bible, had called after him only faintly: "Sternberg, wait."

He hadn't appeared on the baseball field later that afternoon when they were scheduled to practice, nor had he shown up for dinner; and by the time "lights out" had rolled around, they knew he wasn't fooling. They knew they had to look for him.

But, by then, it was too dark to find anyone. The woods had filled with fog.

They were swaying together and the room was hot. They were packed together on the floor, sitting cross-legged, swaying back and forth, voices rising with the smoke. "I am the man that hath seen affliction by the rod of his wrath. He hath led me and brought me into darkness, but not into light . . ."

"Fool!" At Barry's question, Chaim had banged his book down on the desk. "For *this* you suddenly come alive? For *this* you are suddenly familiar with the text? For *this* you open your foolish mouth?"

Whatever had gotten into Barry had gotten into him as well. He was more than just angry. He was a pillar of smoke, an avenging cloud. "How many times have I asked you, children, and nobody knows? How many times and no one has even bothered to ask me themselves or to look? What's wrong with you? Can't you think? All summer long I ask you questions. All summer long, you sit there like death!"

But this was not the worst. He had slammed his Bible down on the desk—a vast sacrilege; in the old days, a sin almost equal to murder. When he saw what he had done, how he had crushed the pages and broken the binding he cried: "Ah, look! Look! Look what you made me do. This is what comes of 'peel-pool'!"

But he hadn't explained.

Instead, he had picked up the broken book and cradled it in his hands, turning the pages gently, slowly. Then, sighing a cold, deep sigh, as though he had found an irreparable injury, he had hugged it to his chest and started swaying back and forth chanting in Hebrew, "Forgive me, forgive me, forgive me . . ."

It was the evening of Tisha B'Av, the start of a fast to commemorate the destruction, the suffering, the marching in of armies, the marching out of hope. The fast had begun at sundown, would con-

tinue until sundown, twenty-four hours. They would pray tonight and all day tomorrow sitting on the floor and fasting, praying, sighing.

Barry had disappeared. Three days ago. "Who needs your stupid class?" he had said. "Who needs your fucking Torah?" He had stalked off into the woods and they hadn't seen him since.

The next morning they had thought they'd find him crouched behind the door of the bunk waiting for the right moment to spring out at them. "Ha! Ha! Fooled you assholes. You gave me up for dead, didn't you? Well, I'll tell you the truth now. I had a superb night. On the town, of course." (Though his clothing might be crumpled, though bits of leaves might cling to his hair.) He had done this twice before, they said. Each time, they had called his aunt. Each time, they had called his psychiatrist. "It's just a manipulation," the psychiatrist said. "His version of suicide." And the aunt had said, "It's true. He runs away all the time. He hides in some safe place. He makes everyone suffer."

"But thou hast utterly rejected us; Thou art very much wroth against us."

Now they were finished with "Lamentations." They were beginning the long litany of suffering. Leo Goelman stepped to the podium. "Two specialties, we have," he said. "Suffering. Memory. Of these we have made an art."

They were lighting candles—one for each phase of history, one for each hallmark of the art. The First Temple and the Second Temple. The exile in Babylon, and the exile in Persia. The Greek occupation and the Roman. The Inquisition and the Dark Ages. The pogroms and the Cossacks. Treblinka and Auschwitz and Dachau . . .

Barry had disappeared, but he couldn't have gone very far. The evidence was clear. There were signs of him everywhere. Books pulled from their shelves. Benches overturned in the classrooms. Messages on the library wall.

And Chaim had not been in his cabin, had not been there for three days. There had been no shoes on the floor, no fringes, no pale, white hand reaching towards her in the cabinet. She had

waited for him and waited, had hoped he might be sitting there in
the dark, within the curtains, clutching a pile of paper, maybe
singing softly or muttering or clasping his hands together and curling himself up in prayer.

Barry had disappeared, but there were signs of him everywhere.
In the prayer books that were stolen, in the candlesticks that had
fallen down, in the pages torn from books and scattered in the grass,
in the things that were missing—scarves, rings, bracelets (handed
back, lost somewhere). Some even said in the weeping at night in
the cabins (from the upper bunks, from the lower).
*Even here, there were signs. The torches burned brightly. They
swayed. She was hungry.*

She had waited until after dark, herself, curled up amid the pine
needles, the weeds and dry sticks, hungry and thirsty, until finally,
when the first damp fog of evening began to seep into her skin, she
felt she couldn't wait another minute longer. She had crept up the
stairs, had nudged the door open, found a room completely empty.
There had been no clothes in the closet, no books on the shelves,
and, except for an old brown suitcase which stood by the door, there
was only a dustpan propped against one wall, the faint smell of
something burnt.

*Smoke rose. Shadows rose. She could feel herself rising with
them, lighter than air, so faint she felt like vapor.*

Barry had disappeared. Chaim had gone after him. She had gone
after Chaim.
All day long, on the hottest day of summer, she had walked.
Through pine forests, through stands of maple, through shrubs
matted with vines and creepers. There was no path, but she kept on
going, drifting along in a cloud of hunger. Every time she moved,
a trail of sound and light churned inside her, turning to heat and
dust, a dry aching thirst that caked her throat, that made her lean
against a tree and gasp.

But even this was not the worst, that she had walked until late
afternoon, until her thirst was so great that it pushed her through
the underbrush to a stream where she drank and drank and drank.

Even this was not the worst, that when her thirst had stopped, when the roaring had stopped in her ears, she had heard weeping, had looked up and seen a man in black sprawled on the ground weeping and weeping and weeping. Nor even this. She hadn't gone to him and caressed him. She hadn't knelt and kissed him; nor had he, in his turn, kissed her, had not said, "I like big girls," had not held her until the sun came through the trees in threads: orange yellow green sprays of light.

It was this—what he *did* say. "You know what is 'peel-pool,' Mireleh? I'll tell you what it really is. Not just the dictionary definition—*casuistry*, the athletic misinterpretation of words, in a quiet room filled with dusty old books . . ."

He had made her sit down beside him. He had held her hand.

"Listen. It was many years ago, not here, but in a village far away. There was a boy just about your age. It was going to be his Bar Mitzvah. He was coming of age. He was going to know what there was to know—about the world, about himself, and his family was very happy, very excited; or they would have been excited. But this was a bad time. A bad place. There was no Torah then. It was forbidden, strictly forbidden.

"The boy's father was a rabbi, the head of a yeshiva until they closed them down. After that, he was a rabbi in secret. He had hidden the Torahs, every single one of them. The penalty for this was death. For being a Jew. They were burning all the Torahs, burning the yeshivot; they were marching us all away.

"Every day whoever wanted to, whoever was brave enough, whoever was left, would slip out of their houses, go to this secret place to pray."

"And the Bar Mitzvah?" she had asked, though she already knew the answer. "Did he have it?"

He shook his head. "When they found the Torahs they would burn them. In a heap they would pile them in the street along with other holy books, law books, whatever they found that looked sacred. They would pour kerosene on top and set them on fire, let them burn into ashes. There were some Jews who tried to rescue them. There were some who believed in Kiddush HaShem, the commandment of martyrdom for God, for His word, a commandment outweighing all the others, but *never* to be invoked, some said. Others, like my father, threw themselves onto the flames."

304

"But did you—"
"I, Mireleh? Not I. Not then."

And that was not the worst. It was not only that, but this: Barry never knew when to stop. "Sure," he had said as Chaim rocked back and forth with the ruined book. "Sure, man!" He had raised his arms and held out both hands in benediction. "We forgive you— no problem. No fucking problem. Forgiveness, *free and complete*. Don't give it another thought."

Chaim had stopped swaying. He had set the book down on the table carefully, very accurately, had set it down in some precise diagram that only he could see of a Bible set down in anger. Then, as if it were also part of the same diagram, one which told him how to convert thought into motion, rage into sound, he had slapped Barry across the face, had shouted: "*You* forgive *me? You* forgive *me?* To whom do you think you're speaking? To some goniff? To the devil? Get out of here you little bastard!"

And this. Finally there was this: "Bergen Belsen, Madanek, Theresienstadt . . ." They were still listing, matching up the horrors with the lights. Barry still hadn't come back. She was still hungry. In this corner, Chaim was still swaying, back and forth, back and forth, Baruch HaShem, Amen V'Amen.

Behind him, the torches swayed, glowing. And for a moment, as he bent over his text, she didn't see clothes, but flesh, saw the pale skin of his back, on either side of his spine, saw letters (the ten commandments? the ten plagues?); she saw the torches burning behind all of them, saw all of them, like Barry, alone in the woods in the dark.

Nominated by Rosellen Brown and Lynne McFall

STRAND: EVIDENCES OF BOOKS AND BOOKSTORE

by THOMAS MEAGHER

from CHELSEA

early on

Masked against the basement dust the shelvers circle through the stacks. They wind within that A to Z all day. Into the alphabetical order they work the books from the sorting table. Each shelver every few minutes departs the sorting table with now one or two books and now an armload. But of the books arriving at that table for sorting and shelving there is no end, while order given the books on a section of shelf is soon undone into new shortlived order.

* * *

I kept to myself. In the beginning I found I could savor the harrowing futility of the routine and I was without interest in the others. Unmasked they spoke together about rock stars and rock music and mouthed the wang-chung of guitar chords or with store pencils drummed licks on the boxes of books.

Little acne'd Tory with her chi-chi purse. Tory went on about the literary magazine which she claimed to be in the process of founding and which was to be called Private Operative. Tory was supposed to have money. It was said she was a Magnate's relation. Whatever, I anyway had watched her spend what would've been four-fifths of a

306

paycheck on a first edition of Marianne Moore's translation of La Fontaine's *Fables* which she said she'd found upstairs in the rare book room to which she'd been sent from the basement on some go-fer errand. For Tory'd only sought the job in the celebrated bookstore in order to give herself what she called "structure," she said she needed "structure." She kept telling them that sort of thing all day. She kept getting to work later and later the ten or so days she lasted, kept repeating with tears in her eyes that she understood while being fired.

The thick dust smeared black on skin and clothing. There was the pent unhealthy stink of dust and sweat mixed in the heavy and unventilated air and which with the dust itself clogged the nostrils. Above the sorting table on a sheet of store letterhead and printed in sloppy childish capitals with a black marking pen: "Books give off more and nastier dust than any other class of objects yet invented—George Orwell." The day in the windowless basement was an unending nine-fifteen to six-thirty (with forty-five unpaid minutes lunch, and fifteen unpaid minutes break in the morning and again in the afternoon), but as much the hours it was the endless filthiness of work in the dust of books that ground one down.

Most of the time of course there were besides the shelvers customers who stood and read or asked for help or wandered and browsed up and down the narrow aisles of the basement stacks (aisles in which also stood in the way the aluminum stepladders that gave access to the top shelves), and "Nightmare all day of the *squeezing* by, *squeezing* past . . ." was already all I could think to note in the early morning prior to leaving my desk for the fourth day's work on 4 September 198__.

* * *

Ordeal I remember. And Waugh, *The Last Word*. Brodsky, *A Part of Speech*. Picano's "gay" novels, each one with its irritating sensitive watercolor of the sort Beachscape, with Homosexual reproduced on the jacket cover. Cott, *Forever Young*. A biography of Anton Webern that weighed a ton.

* * *

There are a few pages of a kind of diary. But the entries (31 August—the day I began work—to 15 September) are merely ludicrous cryptic notes and pointless admonitions.

"7 September
11:33 p.m.
T!
Wake up, T!
dizzying waste
. . . catch breath . . .
. . . —plunge on, *on*
. . . chutes and ladders . . .
8 September
and hit bottom
The desperate stratagem
. . . of note the thorough failure, through first week steadily"
There are two references to the job as hell and a circle of hell and there's that line about the "squeezing" but otherwise no mention of a man or woman or world outside of me. Each entry reads as though it were what had been heard in passing that day of the babble of a madman talking to himself. I was, I suppose, in short, a variety of head-case: dead set on fending off what I'd learned to call the "contingent world" and mad to keep at arm's length whatever this the life I might by chance be living.

Ordeal was by Linda Marchiano who as Linda Lovelace had performed the extravagant fellatio in *Deep Throat,* as well for instance as the sexual intercourse with dogs and the like in perhaps less widely seen reels. In *Ordeal* Marchiano repudiated her Lovelace past and naturally blamed it all on someone else and his control (drugs, "brainwashing") over Lovelace. I knew there were books on the deathcamps and the Nazis which pandered to sado-masochist tastes while pretending merely to expose the savagery of The Hun, and I assumed *Ordeal* a book in a similar vein and that there'd be as much or more pornography as repentance in it. I was wrong. But when at first I had *Ordeal* in hand to shelve I almost always flipped through it.

Once out on the jam-packed shelves the books did tend to go all to hell. Dustjackets would tear and pages crumple. The dust would settle on and soak into the page edges. The boards would warp and skew and the points bend and chip and fray. The cheap glue bindings would split, the spines break. Eventually (and a title had in fact a two-year shelf-life) a book could indeed appear to have been used to dig a hole.

They were all "review" copies and were sold at half-price as used books. But it seemed unlikely that even one in a hundred of the thousands of "review" books could have been the very copy of a title which some "reviewer" had had in hand and had read or skimmed through prior to publishing somewhere or other a "review." No, it was out of the question, there were simply too many "review" copies for them to have been sold to the store by one after another "reviewer" (though to envision a ragged quarrelsome line of self-important brown-nosers snaking up the basement stairs and right through the store onto Broadway was diverting). Later on and after a sort of promotion I was able to an extent to tell just how few "review" books did arrive at the store via any "reviewer." (Certainly Rat Man, for example, never mentioned such reviews as he might have been writing of the hundreds of copies of assorted titles he brought in each week.) And able furthermore to see how piles of certain best-selling titles came to be more or less stolen to order. And to learn where other bookstores' thieving employees and the publishers' editors and editorial assistants and publicists and the friends of same went during lunch and dumped what they'd pinched. Early on, however, I was ignorant of the colossal slipshoddery which was the publishing and the selling of books. Nor as I recall would I (enraged and unspeaking, winding through the alphabet with one more armload of schlock novels and whatever other clothbound dreck) have cared to be told.

Trash. *Heavy Sand. Captain of the Sands. Souvenirs* ("This unusual novel, which operates on several levels . . .") and *Bygones. The Blazing Air* and *Flight 902 Is Down!* and *Last Rights* (". . . this taut thriller . . ."). *Grady Barr* ("A novel charged with raw, hard-hitting power . . ."). *Soho* (". . . who founder in the dangerous depths beneath the glittering surfaces . . .") and *Congo. Zemindar* (". . . her own mutinous heart . . ."). *Amok. End of the Rainbow* ("She was young and she was successful."). *Fish. Ninja. Hearts. Lessons. Eagles. Saving Grace* ("In scenes that flow with the quicksilver lightness of a Harold Lloyd chase . . ."). *Normandie Triangle* and *The Roman Enigma* and *Manhattan* (". . . where the lives of the beautiful, sexy people; the money, power people . . ."). *Rhine Maidens* and *The Officers' Wives* and *The Old Girl* and *The Flesh and the Devil. A Place like Dairy-Anne* ("A doctor had suggested shock treatment, and Abby consented."). *November 22* and *Evidence* and *False Witness* and *Disappearances* and *Still Missing* ("Rarely has a novel . . . Rarely has a fictional . . . Rarely has a story . . ."). *Obsessions* and *Realities* (". . .his eyes like deep blue magnets in the darkness . . .") and *Between Two Worlds. Everybody's All-American. The Book of Revelations* and *Sixth Sense. The Greek Position* (". . . definitive study of financial guile in our time . . .") and *Private Practices. Office Party* (". . .the longest and most terrifying weekend of their lives . . .") and *No More Monday Mornings. Marriage Voices. Bread and Roses* ("Woven into the story are actual historical characters."). *Hobgoblin* and *The Night Chasers* and *Hunted. Chez Cordelia. Lovelife* ("Set against the sophisticated background of the very special playground that is Martha's Vineyard . . ."). *The Hot and Copper Sky* and *Spring Moon. The Siege of Buckingham Palace* and *Diplomatic Immunity. Lionheart* and *Blackrobe* and *Punk Novel by Bad Al* and *The Last Deal. Appassionata* ("Bruna—lingering pensively in shops and cafés . . .").

"We take pleasure in sending you this review copy of." "This is your review copy of." A dis-spiriting leaffall of review slips: the rectangles knifed the air without a flutter and thunked stupidly head-on into the floor or skidded. "We are pleased to send you this book for review, and would appreciate two copies of any review notice that appears." The books shed "Author" stills as well: earnest frauds in beards slipped from thrillers, tarted-up old battleaxes from the Lust and Money run-throughs. There was briefly early on the small keen pleasure of imprinting onto those faces some of that dust in the shape of the sole of my lousy boot. "This is your review copy of."

and This is your review copy of and This is your review copy of and

I soon could read while down there nothing of any of them at all. Long after and far from the basement I came across the essay of

Orwell's containing the sentence as above and in that essay I also found: "Seen in the mass, five or ten thousand at a time, books were boring and even slightly sickening."

later on

BEHIND THE ROPE

The rope was stretched taut at a little below what would have been for a man of average height the level of the throat. It was a grimy sevenfoot cordon and, secured left and right to shelves, it spanned the sort of cavemouth there. "Behind the rope," the cave itself was an intricate cramped corner of the basement and in that corner behind that rope went on much of the store's acquiring of books—the unboxing each "load," the appraising and initial sorting of the books by one or both of the buyers (Artie and Tomás), the establishing a purchase price for the load, and then the boxing up of the now sorted books and the dispatching of the boxes throughout the store to respective departments or storage areas. Upstairs the owner himself directed what appeared to be essentially similar though less frenetic operations. "Behind the rope," however, seemed to be kept hard at this most of each day. There seemed always to be yet another enormous load awaiting a buyer's "doing." I was beginning to be the one routinely called from shelving to set up these loads. I would as instructed tote the boxes from wherever, then as instructed unpack the books onto the proper tables for the buyers. Artie would be saying as I ducked under the rope shouldering another grubby box, "*God*, Baker, you think I *want* to do another load? I don't *want* to, Baker. But Baker—it's my *job*, isn't it? Isn't that *my* job, Baker?" "Well now wait a minute Artie," and Baker would start in and I'd see him come forward from somewhere deep in the corner grinning maniacally and set to play Artie tirelessly for the stooge. Meanwhile the books were not to be otherwise on the tables than face-up in neat and balanced piles stacked neither too high nor too low and so on, and I began to be another cornered there behind the rope and with Baker, Kester, Boyd, and Floyd having the life supervised out of me now by Artie, now Tomás.

"See this? *You* can't have it" was the operative principle.

Of course it was necessary that there be aisles and shelves off-limits to customers, where for example the monthly shipments of thousands of new books to the store's regular library customers could be prepared. And since these regular customers—all the many public libraries in small midwestern towns especially—had to have sent them a.s.a.p. the same best-seller-list drivel (Ludlum, *Parsifal Mosaic*), "review" copies of most "blockbusters" had first to be hoarded and rationed: this one to X in Iowa, next two to Y in Arkansas. Likewise technical scholarly publications, which would be sent on approval plans to regular university library customers only too happy to obtain at half the outrageous price those strange pagefuls of equations.

But naturally in the course of the day-to-day of the store and on the premises themselves the emphasis could be felt to be placed less on the simple necessity of this arrangement than on its exclusivity. First the physical separation of that roped-off corner (fetid and dingy as any other equivalent number of square feet of basement) from the rest of the basement itself was zealously maintained with a gracelessness and petty rudeness that astounded. Plainly there were to Artie's workdays few if any moments headier than when customers blundered on past the rope and smack into his fiefdom and he could stand there and make a face and repeatedly refuse to answer them until they had slunk back under the rope and on *that* side of it waited to address him.

"Now. What do you need?"

And in fact one morning to Saul Bellow Artie said just that. Bellow had been brought to the store by the charming elderly attorney who visited at the rope periodically to discuss book-collecting and the indignities of age. There wasn't any small talk with the novelist who went browsing in Floyd's aisle where as it happened (and had he been for some unimaginable reason looking for any of it) the lit crit, linguistics, philosophy etcetera was to be found.

"What do you need?"

For thus was it consequently accepted that behind the rope was ever an exclusive supply or stash of such choice stuff as the grovelling punters couldn't merely want but must "need" as they might need other controlled substances. And the power to dispense or to withhold this stuff at whim was flaunted with all the subtlety of discotheque doormen their "right to refuse admission."

Then Bellow was gone having said "I don't *need* anything" so scornfully even I blushed with embarrassment for the loathsome Artie K.

STASH

The bottleneck in me was worsening. Although I could in reading see for instance that "strictly to separate from received and customary Felicities, and to confine unto the rigor of Realities, were to contract the Consolation of our Beings unto too uncomfortable Circumscription" (as I'd copied out in my execrable hand into a Composition Book notebook years before from the Norton paperback *Prose of Sir Thomas Browne*), I yet had at the same time to think myself determined to "confine unto" precisely that "rigor," and strain to put the "Felicities" from me. Books though, I did persist in wanting to have to have. Rarely didn't I find as I combed the shelves upstairs during a break at least one I thought I needed added to the *confine*ment ("Palinurus" [Cyril Connolly], *The Unquiet Grave*, first U.S. edition 1945 Harper & Brothers, brittle torn dust jacket and in fountain pen ink on the front endpaper "Natalie Dodd 215 W. 13th Street"). Into my stash I smuggled the finds.

The stashes were against the rules. Downstairs and over by the "break table" several out-of-the-way shelves constituted an employee bookcase and it was there that all books employees intended buying each week were supposed to be held. Then Thursday evenings after closing one got to buy one's books half off. (By 6:31 the pathetic queue of tired stinking workers would have formed and be awaiting the owner's pleasure. It seemed an unnecessarily unpleasant and even somewhat humiliating ceremony. Thus my first Thursday evening in that queue he stuck at allowing me the full employee discount [waterdamaged New Directions clothbound *Letters of Wyndham Lewis*] and cited, as though it were evidence of my trying to cheat, the "hefty discount already" when demanding of me five bucks extra. But no doubt he had—as I certainly didn't until much later on, if then—a good idea how very many books employees stole from him, and perhaps on Thursday evenings he felt that he got a little of his own back while in person recouping some wages.) Fridays or early Saturdays the shelves were supposed to be cleared and leftovers returned to stock.

I needed different. I'd concluded that through the store at one time or other and in some form or other passed every book I wasn't to do without. There would always be too many books I'd mean to read next (Cioran, *The Trouble with Being Born*) and handsome old editions to own purely and simply to fondle (Burckhardt, *The Civilization of the Renaissance in Italy*, revised second British edition Phaidon Press 1945; impeccably bound small hardcover in sturdy unmarred dustjacket with a hundred page section of sepia-tinted plates and on the front endpaper the inscription "To my beloved husband—to aid in *his* book. Bea 6/30/49"). In short there could be to my mind no end to the books I'd be after. A couple of inches of employee bookcase and only till Thursday wasn't of use.

Once in place behind the rope I was in on the stashes. Here was the answer. I found room and *stashed* (Daumal, *A Night of Serious Drinking;* Kafka, *Letters to Felice;* Hannah, *Geronimo Rex;* Pope, *Poetical Works;* Dickinson, *Complete Poems;* Singer, *Collected Stories;* Calvino, *Italian Folktales;* Pound, *Translations;* Wyndham Lewis, *Time and Western Man;* Shörske, *Fin-de-siècle Vienna;* Mumford, *The City in History;* Handke, *Nonsense and Happiness;* Bernhard, *Correction;* Perelman, *The Last Laugh*).

Artie (as Artie informed at length) looked the other way when it came to stashes—"except, *right* Baker?, when they're *out* of con-*trol*!"

Which I learned Baker's pointedly always either was or was about to be. The others' stashes were their few paperbacks and single hardcover hidden behind shelved books in a very low or very high corner of their workspace. Baker however stashed art books. His remarkable collection of for the most part oversized hardcovers had as it were its central and branch locations. There were scores of volumes out of sight (more or less) all over where we worked. Recent acquisitions Baker left out on our shelves where, whenever Artie went off someplace and Baker himself as a rule stopped work cold, he could instantly refer to them: selections from the familiar Abrams and Skira and Aperture series; exquisite things from Bollingen (unforgettable plates of deathmasks in one); perhaps the fine two-volume boxed set of Thomas Bewick's woodcuts; or the gigantic Disney compilation; or else still another brilliantly illustrated volume on Japanese tea gowns, or on any variety of mask or body painting, or voodoo or witchcraft regalia. For in effect the stash was the measure of Baker's insistence that he was a painter who had for the time being to work in a bookstore, not a bookstore drone who imagined himself a painter. Baker with his stash would get on with his work (in that his unrelenting "image hunt" provided him with the sort of unnerving pictorial refuse which he fashioned into paintings of his own—though nothing at all of his vast knowledge of Art could in any way be detected in the odd stark paintings themselves which he soon had on exhibit alongside "graffiti school" stars in a Mercer Street gallery) as uninterruptedly as could be reconciled with not losing the job behind the rope.

It was impossible not to admire his nerve but I wasn't then in any condition to know what else to make of Baker. After the day's "wage slavery" every other employee went about being some manner of "Artist" too, whether film-maker or musician or writer or dancer or actor or whatever the name for the fey poseur who with a straight face claims that his life is his art. But because I thought I recognized in Baker the eager immersion in everything to do with a craft, and the ferocious and as it were selfless single-mindedness it took to make use of a limited but undoubted talent; because, that is, I thought him like me; and because his interest in what mattered to me and what I knew and what I was up to flattered me, I was set to believe him to be the real thing. I'd have liked for my own self esteem Baker to prove genuine. But there was on the other hand his idiot savant routine, his wild delight in which confused and disheartened me. All those interminable colloquies with Artie!—in re The Career (when and to which critic or gallery owner or owners or other painters would *Artie* show this or that set of slides or send a dozen roses or pay a visit or call and lie to), Women (did *Artie* think that Patty might have thought or that Joanne would think or that Margaret etc., and Artie —a nightmare Mr. Manners—would outline dating etiquette and Psychology of The Female, while goggle-eyed Baker seemed to lap up the puerilities), and Art, and Life. I had to wonder: this gabby kook, this joker? Egg the pompous windbag on, sure. But didn't Baker want to *keep everyone out of it?* Wasn't there more *hiding* to do? The P.R. made no sense to me. Wasn't the *real* work secret as prayer? I couldn't grasp this other approach. For I didn't have it in me then to loose myself from what I pleased to think those "confines."

Tomás I never whole-heartedly detested as I did that moron Artie. In fact I was inclined to like Tomás, thinking him perhaps most notably different from the oaf in having brains not just a mouth. Plus he knew books, and knew firsthand and acquainted me with the shark-infested rare book markets of New York. It was only when the drugs ran away with him that Tomás too was unendurable. He might when overfull of cocaine rip into even friends with stunning viciousness. True, he could be at other times as well quite as savagely nasty, as for instance when working up to firing (and in the interim striving to torment into quitting) some poor slob he couldn't stand but who, it would have been generally agreed, worked conscientiously enough not to deserve the boot. So I wouldn't in any case have said that I thought Tomás exceptionally easy to like. (No reason why he should have been, of course.) But at least when not so exaggeratedly wired Tomás trained that fierce, intense maliciousness on other than those of us behind the rope. It was possible in that corner to get along.

Tomás collected Zukofsky. Thus formulated, the "collecting" an author could be made to sound an avocation on a par with the robbing of graves. Even the detailed histories given us by Tomás of items now in his or in a friend's collection usually petered out with Tomás himself asking with a laugh whether it all didn't sound—this mania for scraps of paper, for books already too fragile (though maybe no more than fifty years old) to allow for their pages to be turned to be read—pretty sick.

"But . . ."

And again under cover of shouts of laughter he'd append inconclusively a remark to the effect that when you had to have what you had to have, . . .

Nonetheless those dealers in modern firsts who paid chatty business calls on Tomás at the rope were an odious bunch. Particularly nauseating was the crude boasting; who, knowing something of a certain poet's or novelist's lifelong hard times, could with patience listen for example to the ex-furniture retailer's triumphant account of flogging to wealthy out-of-town clients high-priced and very profitable bits of that writer's "ephemera"?

Such trafficking in the junk of Letters was easy to think contemptible.

As for owning the stuff or craving to own it—was it anything worse than pointless? It sounded a dim-witted, philistine game— e.g. Tomás's "nailing" Reznikoff's copy of Zukofsky's such-and-such, or Dorn's or Creeley's copy of same, or Oppen's copy of other Zukofsky, or for that matter "Zukey's" own copies of both titles—which needless to say hadn't a thing to do with the poetry. The "scarce" this and the "inscribed" that: nothing to do with the writing at all. Therefore to the extent that the poems (stories, novels) were looked upon as mere occasions for the game, then perhaps to that extent to play was indeed worse than pointless.

Still, I liked being able to monitor reports of that game. I might (because at the time trying to believe "Literature" somehow deserved better) keep my distance from their scuffling to get at all the ragtag and bobble. Yet I relished the opportunity to learn the bibliographic minutiae, the biographic gossip.

And owing to Tomás there was a presence of Zukofsky, whom I was beginning to read each night at home (10 Willow Street, Brooklyn Heights; I'd soon discovered poet and family had lived down the block at 30 Willow, and then in "A wish" I'd found for my morning trudge to the Clark Street subway station: "Looking down at the water / three blocks away at Clark Street / if but once a day, / my valentines, / but day after day, / my mind going to work / with eyes on the water / tries me with a prayer, / my sweet, / that my wish wear our look / well, care for our days: / to long life!"), accustoming my ear to the angular music of *All*, the collected shorter poems.

Not the branches
half in shadow

But the length
of each branch

Half in shadow

As if it had snowed
on each upper half
        —from "All of December Toward New Year's"

Hear her
(Clear mirror)
Care.
His error.
In her care—
Is clear.
     —*from "Songs of Degrees"*

The wakes that boats make
and after they are out of sight
the ways they have made in water:
loops, straight paths,
to do with mirror-like,
tides, the clouds the deep day blue
of the unclouded parts of the sky
[. . .]
and the leaping silver
as of rain-pelted nipples
of the water itself.
     —*from "The Ways"*

The hand a shade of moonlight on the pillow
     —*from "Non Ti Fidar"*

And it began to entertain me to note in conversations behind or at
the rope throughout the day the quirky titles cropping up: *Le Style
Apollinaire* (translation by René Taupin); *A Test of Poetry; Some
Time; Barely and Widely; I's (pronounced* eyes); *After I's;* and
Anew. And *"A"* and *All* and *Bottom; on Shakespeare.* And I taped
to a shelf at my workstation a card on which (to tide me calmly
through the worst) I'd copied the final lines of Zukofsky's translation
of "Catullus II" ("Passer, deliciae meae puellae"—to Lesbia's sparrow): ". . . it is the crest of passion quieted / gives way to this small
solace against sorrow, / could I but lose myself with you as she
does/breathe with a light heart, be rid of these cares!"
     Thus was there a measure of grace and melody to the grim job. By
Valentine's Day (six months after having begun at the store) I'd lost
the Willow Street place and become with my ragged life another
occupant of a single room in the seedy George Washington Hotel.
I labored through the baffling vasts of *"A"* once but read and re-read

318

All, giving myself as it were "airs / from that lute of Zukofsky" (Robert Duncan's words). And on two occasions (one the night Baker and I joined Tomás at a reading by Creeley at N.Y.U.) in the "poem room" of Tomás's Twelfth Street apartment I even looked upon—did not touch—the collection itself. I'd have said that of all the narrow room's shelved treasures it was the fragile copy of *An "Objectivists" Anthology* which he particularly savored taking down and holding (in the box he'd had made to try to preserve it) for me to admire. I was shown the items given Tomás by Zukofsky's wife and son and in the "poem room" among those evidences had for a change to feel the blather about "Zukey" and "Celia" and "Paul" was after all a sort of caring too or even love and finally not out of place, so many of Zukofsky's lyrics being his lovesongs to their threesome for the few friends, few readers.

ON VALENTINE'S DAY
TO
FRIENDS

The hearts I lift out of snow
        So few,
The one, two or three, say fow
        Friends who
Eye a heart, wish well what
        I do,
Befriend its festival
        When to
Persist I sing of Celia and
        Of Paul
To R'lene and Edward, Lorine,
        Or all—
Tags, René—that can with a red heart,
        Valentine,
Brush a white-velvet heart in snow
        falling deep to speak
        Be mine.

Mornings I'm first behind the rope. I sweep the floor back there. For two minutes in the quiet basement I take my time and perform with composure the simple pleasing chore.

Kester did my chart. (I'd given in and told him time and place.)

On the sheet compass points are reversed and the circle of the heavens is divided into twelve segments. Reading counterclockwise, segment 1 corresponds to the segment on a clock between nine and eight, segment 2 to that between eight and seven, and so on round through north and west and south and back to due east at segment 12 and nine o'clock.

I'm bunched up, is the striking thing about my stars. Close-knit indeed. Sun, moon, and seven of the eight (earth of course left out) planets have sardine'd themselves within the 4 (Uranus and the moon), 5 (Pluto, Jupiter, Mars), and 6 (the sun, Venus, Mercury, Neptune) segments, leaving Saturn—stranded commuter—bumped from the car 6 crush out onto platform 7. Consequently I lie in nine of my tenths between the north and west, and am further defined in these tenths according to Kester's note as three parts earth (and that "asc"—ascending?), one water, two air, four fire.

No, he answered me, most aren't anywhere near so cooped.

Other significances of my chart are a closed book to me. The fire I like. And I like the cramp, in that I recognize me: shrunk back pent from three wide-open quarters of the availabilities. Perfect likeness.

I try to do nothing. I try to wait with my coffee or tea and toasted bagel with a smear (from the diner at Twelfth and University Place), doing nothing.

* * *

Afternoons I go on break as late as rules allow. There'll be an hour left when I come back.

And every once in a while having had it with books as with bookstore I find myself with my fifteen minutes to kill seated just after five a block away on the steps of Grace Church.

I imagine myself unspeakably grungy in the eyes of the office workers headed along Broadway home or out for the evening.

("It's seven of us packed cornered together and furiously treading books and which begins with Artie arriving groaning 'I feel *sick*, Baker.' ")

Across the street are no high-rises yet.

The Sheltering Sky. The Hot and Copper Sky. The Changing Sky.
Losing myself in that blue a moment quite beyond me.

Nominated by Ken Gangemi and Robert Phillips

ON THE GÖTA CANAL, 1986

by JOAN SWIFT

from BLUE UNICORN

The Town Hall shines farewell and the canal boat
Juno slips from Stockholm's *Riddarholmen* dock.
We crowd on deck for a blend of waves and air,
for last glimpses. That's where the King of Sweden
walks cobblestones. Descartes died there. Yellow
crosses on blue, flags believe against the wind.

We snap pictures from the bow, catching the wind
in the lens, then drink sherry served in the boat's
salon. During briefing, Eva's yellow
pen traces our journey from one village dock
to another, a bee visiting Sweden's
flowers. First we must bundle for Baltic air,

she says in two languages, then promises air
that's gentler, meadow-hemmed canal a sea wind
never bruises. Meanwhile, northern islands, Sweden's
tawny granite, fog, a red buoy, fishing boats
viewed from the shelter deck. Some of us yellow
in the Baltic's chop. Some of us want a dock.

Mem comes none too soon, sun lolling on the dock
like a slattern who loves canals, humming an air

scored totally in lavender, orange, yellow
that stays past midnight. By now we're way downwind
among cows and farmhouses, our small boat
in the first of sixty-five locks across Sweden.

We know about Chernobyl. Still, we see Sweden
is green. Heifers prance and at *Forsvik's* dock
girls in folk dress sing hymns, toss pansies to the boat's
passengers. We should pray. This is the air
of the second night. Invisible on the wind
is Cesium-137, not yellow

but father of all grays. It hides in yellow
roots, in grass, it taints the milk of Sweden's
children. A man whose tongue is Swedish unwinds
binoculars and there are two deer in dock
and daisies chasing each other as if the air
held nothing secret. Ours is a pleasure boat.

It slides between Sweden and heaven. Yet the air
chooses scents of yellow blooms to mix on wind
with danger. We should pray all boats will dock.

Nominated by Harold Witt

BETTER TOMORROW

fiction by ROBERT MINKOFF

from NEW ENGLAND REVIEW/BREAD LOAF QUARTERLY

MARGARET HAD A good job, an airy apartment with views, and a car that banked and dove neatly, but a crucial disappointment shadowed each hour. Love had long ago become repetitious, an expense of spirit in a waste of time.

"What I need more than anything else," she told her friend Jack over dinner in a downtown restauro one evening, "is a wife. Someone to keep my daily life in order. What ever happened to wives?"

"So now you're looking for a housekeeper," Jack said. He had a thick body and, frequently, a slow sly light in his eyes. "You once wanted a husband in the old sense. Mutual support, love."

Margaret shrugged. "I want different things at different times."

"I know." Jack spooned up the last of his fruitsteak. "It's a problem for me too. Trading resumes, trying to feel fresh after long workdays . . ."

". . . politenesses, unfamiliar apartments in the mornings . . ." Margaret looked vacantly at feathered teens clustered around a feelum. "I can almost understand the Zoomi. And people are watching, paying, to see them cut up the kids. It's so hard to feel anything today anyway."

"You're not serious," Jack told her. "You couldn't watch ritual killings for entertainment. You're not dead enough."

Margaret stared at the fresh paste she had not yet eaten, her lower lip slack. "Oh?" It would be an expensive meal. "I don't know, dead?"

"Listen." Jack leaned into the argument. "For a housekeeper you can just get a robot. For your life—well what's wrong with me?

324

We've known each other for years. We get along. We're both tired of looking . . . You don't have to *laugh*."

Margaret pulled back. Jack asked her to marry him every year or so. "I'm sorry, Jack. I don't feel right about it, I've never felt right about it. It wouldn't work."

"Let's try?" Jack asked softly. Again it was nothing new. "We both tell each other about our so many disappointments . . . can't we at least try with each other?"

"Jack please." Margaret drank the last of her tetra. "There are mistakes I don't want to make." She had slept with Jack for a while, long ago. She smiled. "But I will take your advice on one thing."

"Oh?"

"I'm going to get a robot. A male."

Margaret's Robo was a handsome, competent stiff with an almost self-consciously flat voice. The Robo shopped, cleaned, cooked, even picked up Margaret's clothes as she dropped them on the floor.

Margaret was handsome herself, with short black hair and a compact, alert body she inhabited as a nervous overnight guest. She tingled as she undressed every night in front of the Robo, always aware that the Robo was at least nominally a male. Life with the Robo added spice to those sober confessions usually implicit in undressing and sleeping without a lover. And every night the Robo stood impassive, eyes flickering up and down, left to right, as though Margaret's body were only part of the room to scan.

"From now on, I want you to call me Babe," Margaret told the Robo one night as she turned off the light. "Every third sentence, call me Babe."

"Very well," the Robo said, standing erect at the foot of the bed. In the sudden dark the Robo was a steady shadow, a father.

"Tuck me in," Margaret heard herself say. "Do you know how to do that?" She felt flirty, alone and new.

"It is within our programming." The Robo came to the head of the bed and pulled on one of the gossamers, folding the top lightly over Margaret's bare shoulders. Her skin felt pale in filtered moonlight, her body anxious even when still.

The Robo twitched out a smile and bent still closer. A stiff hand grazed across her scalp.

"What are you doing?" Margaret asked, jerking up to escape the Robo's touch. The sheets rested useless at her waist.

325

The Robo's hand pressed her head back down, down, to the pillow. With slow sad jerks, the Robo bent over and above her, his head threatening hers.

The Robo's lips touched Margaret's forehead with a kiss and stayed there, in some impossible gentle machine jam, for long seconds. "Good night," he said at last, straightening. "Babe." He returned to his place at the foot of her bed.

Margaret waited until her breathing returned to normal. She was unspeakably aroused. "Robo," she purred, hating herself, delighted.

"Yes?"

"Tell me something about yourself."

"There is nothing."

This too was exciting. Margaret tossed the light sheets to the foot of the bed and propped herself up on her elbows. At her feet loomed the Robo's dark fantasy figure. She felt glorious, a nude sunbather watching the sun rise and fall in her lap. "What do you know about women?"

"There is nothing," the Robo repeated. "Babe."

Margaret shivered. "Come here." She sat up, her feet on the floor.

Eyes faintly discernible in automatic flickers, the Robo walked around the bed to face Margaret. "As you wish," the Robo said.

"Don't call me Babe," Margaret said. Her eyes probed his. "Call me Robo, just as I call you. Every sentence. Every time you talk to me."

"Yes, Robo."

The Robo's mild tones stabbed her full with hunger. To her nostrils the room reeked of her excitement.

"Do you know how to make love?" she asked. She marvelled to feel her voice welling up, tearing. "Or please, how to pretend?" She took the Robo's hand, a large dry immense man's hand, and lifted it to her breast.

The Robo twitched another smile. "It is within our programming," he said. "Robo."

A Robo alone: most, their chores done, lapse into a machine trance, a kind of low idle. A step, certain noises, will activate them, push them to a higher activity state. They never play, or pretend. Margaret's Robo, alone, would sit on a kitchen chair, crouch in a corner, lie on or even under the bed. Afternoon or evening shadows would whisper through Margaret's rooms. The Robo would remain still, hands clutching shoulders, ears alert as though listening to distant pipes and timbrels, the coursing of hopes and fears anomalously hard-wired within.

Over the weeks, Margaret felt more complete, ready as a horse to run for miles, chest strong, head stubborn, into legends of girl-book heroism. Yet she also felt smaller, lost to the person she wanted to be.

"Don't tuck me in," she told the Robo one night as he stood at the foot of her bed. "Threaten to kill me."

"I will kill you," the Robo said.

"Physically," Margaret said. "I want you to threaten me physically."

The Robo seemed to hesitate. "It is not within our programming. We are not permitted to hurt humans."

Margaret stood and began pacing, nude and itchy in the shadows. At once she turned and struck the Robo across the face. "Well? Hit me back."

The Robo almost smiled in inhibition. "It is not within our programming."

"Why can't you be human?" Margaret cried. "Why can't we all be human?"

"Why do you wish to be human?" the Robo replied. The Robo raised a hand to stroke her hair. "And so suddenly."

Margaret almost heard irony, or worse still compassion, in the Robo's voice. She saw her new dependencies rise in shafts, towers against her until her apartment, even her bed, grew congested, clotted, with failure.

"You're used to it now?" the therapy voice asked. "And you like it. You don't even want the real thing."

"This is almost better," Margaret told the voice. She lay in a numo tube, airjets massaging and turning her in drifts and dreams of eternal caress. "It's been weeks now, and it's always the same."

"His feelings can't be hurt."

"*My* feelings can't be hurt," Margaret agreed. Each night the Robo played out the same inexorable sequence of kisses, strokes, bites, proddings, leaving room for imagined differences only. Margaret sighed, disappointed. A ripple of air cupped her shoulders, palmed the slight tension. Behind her closed eyes purple surf crashed, whispered. "And he can't hurt me."

"You know that your Robo is clearly a defective. And that it is illegal for women to use a Robo in this way?"

"But it isn't for men!" Margaret protested. At once a gust of air pushed against the back of her neck, smoothed the injustice. "Oh, I know. And now I'm thinking of going to one of those Zoomi rallies. That's worse, isn't it?" She stretched to turn up the voice's volume.

"How do you feel about it?" the voice asked.

"I need something," Margaret said, her voice low but stubborn. "I get much, but I need something else." She made the voice younger, the slick padded slide of the toggle switch giving her a tug toward nausea.

"Your needs," the voice said. It sounded more feminine, sisterly. "What would you gain from watching tortures, murders?"

Margaret jerked her head up and opened her eyes. The inside of the numo chamber was smooth and iridescent, a seashell's secret. She would be sick from so much comfort if she didn't stand soon. "Reality," she said.

"Yes?"

Margaret wrapped her feet under her and switched off the airjets. As the machines hissed in relaxation she sank into a loose crouch, then straightened to flick open the recessed closet a few feet away.

"Look at it all," she said as she began dressing, her stomach muscles tense. "We're so out of touch. What I need from the Zoomi is what I need from anyone. Everything. The Robo, my friends, sessions like this . . . it's so *yielding*. Reality doesn't yield."

"Is the session over, then?"

Margaret put on her watch. She was beginning to breathe more easily. "Yes, thank you." A mirror slid down one side of the chamber. Margaret pressed her lips together and nodded at herself, her hair. She would never be satisfied anyway.

"Your account has been debited," the voice said. A high-pitched whine made Margaret turn in time to see her receipt curling up from the control panel. "Thank you and good luck."

Margaret at work: monitoring shallow screens lit with exercising bodies, aerobes gone awry, corporations sponsoring midshift exer-

328

cise to guarantee high performance levels. Digital displays for liver and kidneys, litmoids for cardiovascs. In video, each face retains a cutting edge, and all skin is sallow. Margaret would spend her days in a chair, marking the lightboard body charts, mapping out paths to improvement, desperate to change the world, to swallow it and then disgorge it through the screens. Press the buttons, and an earpiece tells Number 47 (balding, light hair, large jutting chin), "three more minutes lung blows, plus greens tonight." This world so brimming with scattered, subsidiary desires that all time is swamped, glutted in angry loss.

The Zoomi met that month on top of an insurance company building. Divided according to sex, the audience sat in impromptu plastic bleachers facing each other across the expanse of catwalks erected for the kill. To Margaret's left, two elderly women cried in anticipation. Below Margaret a pack of adolescent girls compared lid pierces, the screamers they chewed wailing into the night with merry desperation.

Her mouth dry, her heart pounding as dangerously as on their first night together, Margaret had told the Robo that she would be out late; he could have the night off. She had wanted the Robo to ask her where she was going; she had wanted one more chance not to go.

"So then I bit him," one of the teenaged girls was saying. She pulled her hand through brightly foiled hair. "And he actually fell out!" Her three friends shrieked with laughter. "Really, I didn't want him to *die!*"

Electronic thunder rolled over the skyscraper roof.

"Oh don't worry about it," one of her friends counselled. "They're starting."

A chunky boy wearing only leather shorts and suspenders walked the narrow, spotlit catwalk from one set of bleachers to another. Beneath him the building's air conditioning fans chopped through water green with coolant.

"Yuh," the boy said, holding up one hand in greeting. From the bleachers on both sides came a chorus of catcalls. The boy smiled and bowed, basking.

"Yuh pays yuh money, yuh takes yuh choice," he said. His voice was high and sweet. "First a hoist."

The hoots turned to cheers. The women near Margaret were on their feet, heads lifted, bodies fierce and open. Margaret stood, feeling slow. Beyond the catwalk, the male bleachers were even uglier. Spotlights lurched to illuminate people in the stands for each other, arms waving to signal bets.

Above the boy the lights caught a nude figure, sex indeterminate in distance, suspended from chains. As the figure swung toward the center, the chunky boy called out a question to the victim. Margaret only heard the end: "So?"

Margaret could see more clearly now: the victim had dark hair and was a boy, his pubic hair short with youth.

"Whatever you want," the youth called. His voice was shrill, strained. "Make it mean."

The fat boy grinned. "It should mean?" he asked the women's bleachers.

"Cut him," the women cried.

"Cut," Margaret cried, a little late.

"Or it should *be* mean?" the boy asked the men's bleachers.

"..uhtt!" came the reply, a full snarl.

Margaret looked at the women's faces, as taut with rage as the men's. "I don't know if I can watch this," she said. Perhaps Jack, perhaps the therapy voice, had been right: she wasn't yet dead enough. Then what would it take?

"Nobody watches, their first time," one of the old women said to Margaret kindly. She scratched at her palms with ragged finger-nails. "Your second time, just wait," she said with satisfaction. "You'll see."

Across, in the men's bleachers, some of the men raised their fists. The chains lowered the victim close to the chunky boy, who licked his lips.

Something glinted. The youth screamed.

"Yah-yah," said the girl in front of her. "It's *happening!*"

A fresh pebble fell from the youth's foot. He seemed to be wear-ing a bright red boot.

"One at a time," the elderly woman said. "Oh, he's good tonight!"

Margaret stood to push her way out of the bleachers, away from the crowd. Again the blade flashed, and a toe flew off toward the building's slow sloshing tanks. Beyond that were the shouting men, some with faces so contorted she could almost recognize them: bank clerks, chief executives, anyone with a disciplined life.

"Stick him!" shouted one of the worst, a square-built man with a face bulging with hunger only humans know. "Dig for—" but his eyes caught Margaret's, and he froze.

The hoist shifted, flipping the victim upside down. The blade swirled, and a bright red dot swelled up in the center of the victim's face as the crowd roared. Margaret saw only that the rabid man had stopped shouting; that the cords of his neck no longer stood out; that the fury behind his eyes had eased. Still a handsome stiff, he was pushing his way down the men's bleachers.

She ran after him, cornered him by a wing and fin vendor.

"Why?" she asked, shouted, to be heard over the crowd.

"I didn't follow you here," he shouted back. "I came because you gave me the evening off."

They were both out of breath, their eyes wild from sharp spectacle.

Margaret grabbed his arm and pulled him past the ticketsellers and into the building's bright stairwell. She shut the door. They could still hear the cheers of the crowd, the bleating of the youth.

"That's not what I meant," she said. "Why have you been pretending to be a Robo?"

He tried to catch his breath. "It was how I felt. Why have you been making love to a Robo?"

"You've been making love to me," she said, advancing on him, taking his face in her hands, her own face hot and urgent. "That wasn't Robo, was it! That wasn't Robo work!" She could see the sweat on his forehead, his upper lip.

His mouth clamped shut on so many possible words. "I don't talk about these things."

"You've been making love to me, and I never knew it," Margaret said softly. "That was you, whoever."

He was breathing in great heaves, gulps. "I thought it would be safe, the repetition, but then . . ."

Margaret looked at his eyes: weak, tentative, ill. In the distance, but only a hundred feet away, the crowd roared at still another stage of dismemberment. "How many of these have you seen?" she asked.

He nodded. "This is my second. My first, after my first I became a Robo. But I couldn't keep pretending, not once we started, every night—" His eyes fell. "I didn't tell you, so I began to want to hurt you. And then you even asked me . . ." The man shook his head and lifted his eyes with guarded intensity. "This seemed safer."

331

"You," Margaret said. "You can rescue me."

"I don't want to go to any more of these. But me, rescue?" He grinned with difficulty. "Don't I need help myself?"

To Margaret, to anyone in her city, this was tantamount to a declaration. She shaded her eyes from the stairwell's yellow cinderblocks. Nothing seemed safer than anything else.

She swallowed hard. "Let's go home."

"Home?" He winced, considering.

They took elevators down from the fiftieth floor. Once grounded, they walked the sidewalks with disbelief but no direction. For it is so difficult remembering what it is, to be human.

Nominated by New England Review/Bread Loaf Quarterly

CELESTIAL MUSIC

by LOUISE GLÜCK

from IRONWOOD

I have a friend who still believes in heaven.
Not a stupid person, yet with all she knows, she literally
        talks to god,
she thinks someone listens in heaven.
On earth, she's unusually competent.
Brave, too, able to face unpleasantness.

We found a caterpillar dying in the dirt, greedy ants crawling
         over it.
I'm always moved by weakness, by disaster, always eager to
        oppose vitality.
But timid, also, quick to shut my eyes.
Whereas my friend was able to watch, to let events play out
according to nature. For my sake, she intervened,
brushing a few ants off the torn thing, and set it down
        across the road.

My friend says I shut my eyes to god, that nothing else explains
my aversion to reality. She says I'm like the child who buries her
        head in the pillow
so as not to see, the child who tells herself
that light causes sadness—
My friend is like the mother. Patient, urging me
to wake up an adult like herself, a courageous person—

In my dreams, my friend reproaches me. We're walking
on the same road, except it's winter now;
she's telling me that when you love the world you hear
                                        celestial music:
look up, she says. When I look up, nothing.
Only clouds, snow, a white business in the trees
like brides leaping to a great height—
Then I'm afraid for her; I see her
caught in a net deliberately cast over the earth—

In reality, we sit by the side of the road, watching the sun set,
from time to time the silence pierced by a birdcall.
It's this moment we're both trying to explain, the fact
that we're at ease with death, with solitude.
My friend draws a circle in the dirt; inside, the caterpillar
                                        doesn't move.
She's always trying to make something whole, something
                                        beautiful, an image
capable of life apart from her.
We're very quiet. It's peaceful sitting here, not speaking,
                                        the composition
fixed, the road turning suddenly dark, the air
going cool, here and there the rocks shining and glittering—
it's this stillness that we both love.
The love of form is a love of endings.

Nominated by Brenda Hillman, Sharon Olds and Michael Ryan

TANGIER 1975

fiction by PAUL BOWLES

from UNWELCOME WORDS (Tombouctou Books)

I FIRST MET HER just after she'd bought the big villa overlooking the valley Saudis have it now they've got most of the good properties I remember she asked Anton and me to tea we hadn't been married very long then she seemed very much interested in him she'd seen him dance years ago in Paris before his accident and they talked about those days it was all very correct she had delicious petits fours strange how that impressed itself on my mind of course at that time you must remember we were frightfully poor living on the cheapest sort of food fortunately Anton was a fantastic cook or we should have starved he knew how to make a meal out of nothing at all I assure you well it wasn't a fortnight later that she invited us to lunch terribly formal a large staff everything perfect and afterward I remember we were having coffee and liqueurs beside the fireplace and she suddenly offered us this little house she had on the property there were several extra cottages hidden around you know guest houses but most of them were up above nearer the big house this one was way down in the woods far from everything except a duck pond I was absolutely stunned it was the last thing I should have expected of her then she took us down to see it very simple but charming tastefully furnished and a rather primitive kitchen and bath but there were heaps of flowers growing outside and lovely views from the windows we were enchanted of course you understand there was nothing to pay we were simply given the use of the house for as long as we wished I admit it was a very kind gesture for her to make although at the time I suspected that she had her eye on Anton I was quite wrong as it happened in any case having the house made an enormous difference to us it was a gift from the gods there was as a matter of fact one drawback for me Anton didn't seem to mind them but there were at least twenty peacocks in an enormous aviary in the woods not far away and some nights they'd scream you know how hair-raising the sound is especially in the middle of the night it took me weeks to get used to it lying there in the dark listening to those insane screams eventually I was able to sleep through it well once we'd moved in our hostess never came near us which was her privilege naturally but it did seem a bit peculiar at least she wasn't after Anton the months went by and we never caught sight of her you see we had a key to the gate at the bottom of the estate so we always used the lower road to come and go it was much easier than climbing up past the big house so of course in order for us to see her she'd have had to come down to our part of the property but she never ventured near us time went on then all at once we began to hear from various directions a strange rumor that whenever she spoke of us she referred to us as her squatters I was all for going up and having it out with her on the spot is that why you invited us here so you could ridicule us wherever you go but Anton said I'd got no proof it could simply be the typical sort of malicious gossip that seems to be everywhere in this place he said to wait until I heard it with my own ears well clearly she wasn't likely to say it in front of me then one morning I went to take a little walk in the woods and what should I see but several freshly painted signs that had been put up along the paths all saying DEFENSE DE TOUCHER AUX FLEURS obviously they'd been put there for us there was no one else isn't it extraordinary the way people's minds work we didn't want her beastly flowers we'd never touched them I don't like cut flowers I much prefer to see them growing Anton said best pay no attention if we have words she'll put us out and he was right of course but it was very hard to take at all events you know she had lovers always natives of course what can one expect that's all right I'm not so narrow-minded I'd begrudge her that dubious pleasure but there are ways and ways of doing things you'd expect a woman of her age and breeding to have a certain amount of discretion that is she'd make everything as unnoticeable as possible but no not at all in the first place she allowed them to live with her quite as if they were man and wife and that gave them command over the servants which is unthinkable but worse she positively flourished those wretched lovers of hers in the face of the entire town never went out without the current incumbent if people didn't include him she didn't accept the invitation she was the sort of woman one couldn't imagine ever having felt embarrassment but she could have managed to live here without alienating half the Europeans you know in those days people felt strongly about such things natives couldn't even enter the restaurants it wasn't that she had lovers or even that her lovers were natives but that she appeared with them in public that was a slap in the face for the European colony and they didn't forgive it but she couldn't be bothered to care what anybody felt what I'm leading up to is the party we never caught a glimpse of her from one month to the next you understand and suddenly one day she came to call on us friendly as you please she said she had a favor to ask of us she was giving this enormous party she'd sent out two hundred invitations that had to be surrendered at the gate she said there were always too many gate-crashers at her parties the tourists would pay the guides to get them in and this time nobody was to get in excepting the ones she'd invited what she wanted us to do was to stand in a booth she'd built just outside the gate it had a little window and a counter Anton was to examine the invitations and give a sign to one of the policemen stationed outside to admit the holder I had a big ledger with all the names alphabetically listed and as Anton passed me the invitation I was to make a red check opposite the name she wanted to be sure later who had come and who hadn't I've got ten servants she said and not one of them can read or write it's discouraging then I thought of you and decided to ask this great favor of you is everything all right in your little house do you enjoy living here so of course we said oh yes everything is lovely we'd be glad to help you what fools we were it won't take long she said two hours at most it's a costume party drinks dinner and dancing by moonlight in the lower garden the musicians begin to play at half past seven after she'd gone I said to Anton two hundred invitations indeed she hasn't got twenty friends in this entire city well the night of the party came and we were up there in our little sentry-box working like coolies the sweat was pouring down my back sometimes a dozen people came all together half of them already drunk and they didn't at all like having to wait and be admitted one at a time they kept arriving on and on I thought they'd never stop coming at midnight we were still there finally I told Anton this is too much I don't care who comes I'm not going to stand here another minute and Anton said you're right and he spoke to the guard and said that's it no more people are coming don't let anybody else in and good night and so on and we went down to where the party was the costumes were very elaborate we stood for a few minutes at the end of the garden watching them dancing suddenly a tall man in robes with a false beard and a big turban came up to us I had no idea who he was but Anton claimed he recognized him at once anyway it was her lover if you please she'd sent him to tell us that if we were going to come to the party would we please go and put on our costumes as if we had any costumes to put on I was staggered after getting us to stand for almost five hours in a suffocating little box she has the infernal gall to ask us to leave yes and not even the common courtesy to come and speak to us herself no she sends her native lover to do it I was starved there was plenty of food on the buffet but it was a hundred feet away from us at the other end of the garden when we got back down to our house I told Anton I hate that woman I know it's wrong but I really hate her to make things worse the next day she came down to see us again not as you might think to thank us far from that on the contrary she'd come to complain that we'd let in people who had no invitations what do you mean I cried look at the cards and look at the book they tally what are you talking about and she said the Duchesse de Saint Somethingorother was missing her evening bag where she'd put her emerald earrings and I said just what has that got to do with us will you please tell me well she said we'd left our post our post she called it as though we were in the army and after we'd gone some other people had arrived and the police let them in Anton asked if they'd presented their invitations well she said she hadn't been able to get hold of that particular policeman so she didn't know but if we'd been there it wouldn't have happened my dear lady I said do you realize we were in that booth for five hours you told us it wouldn't take more than two I hope you're aware of that well it's most unfortunate she said I've had to call in the police that made me laugh eh bien madame I said since according to you it was the police who let the thief in it ought to be very simple I don't see that we have anything to do with it then she raised her voice all I can say is I'm sorry I was foolish enough to count on you I shall know better another time and she went out it was then that I said to Anton look we can't go on living in this woman's house we've got to find somewhere else he was earning a little at that time working in an export-import office

338

practically nothing but enough to pay rent on a small cottage he thought we should hang on there and hope that things would return to normal but I began to go out by myself nearly every day to look for somewhere we could move to this turned out later to have been very useful at least I'd seen a good many houses and knew which ones were possible you see the party was only the prelude to the ghastly thing that happened less than a month afterward one night some teenage hoodlums got into the big house the lover had gone to Marrakech for the weekend so she was alone yes she made the servants sleep in cabins in the upper garden she was alone in the house and you know these people they're always convinced that Europeans must have vast sums of money hidden about the premises so they tortured her all night long trying to make her tell where it was she was beaten and burned and choked and cut and both her arms were broken she must have screamed I should think but maybe they covered her face with pillows at all events no one heard a thing the maids found her in the morning she was alive but she died in hospital that afternoon we knew nothing about it until the police suddenly arrived two days later and said the property was being padlocked and everybody had to leave immediately meaning the servants and gardeners and us so out we went with all our things it was terrible but as Anton said at least we lived for more than a year without paying rent he always insisted on seeing the positive side of things in a way that was helpful later when I heard the details I was frightfully upset because you see the police traced the hooligans through a gold cigarette case and some other things they'd taken the night they tortured her and then it was discovered that they also had the Duchess's evening bag one of the criminals had arrived late the night of the party and slipped in along with a group of Spaniards after Anton and I had left the gate and of course that gave him the opportunity of examining the house and grounds for the break-in later so I felt terribly guilty of course I knew it wasn't my fault but I couldn't keep myself from thinking that if we'd only stayed on a little longer she'd still have been alive I was certain at first that the lover had had some part in it you see he never left her side she wouldn't hear of it and all at once he goes off to Marrakech for a weekend no it seemed too pat it fitted too well but apparently he had nothing to do with it besides he'd had every chance to make off with whatever he wanted and never had touched a thing so he must have been fairly intelligent at least he knew better than to bite the hand that was feeding him except that in the end he got nothing for his good behavior poor wretch I've tried to think back to that night and sometimes it seems to me that in my sleep maybe I did hear screams but I'd heard those blasted peacocks so many times that I paid no attention and now it makes my blood run cold to think that perhaps I actually did hear her calling for help and thought it was the birds except that the big house was so far away she'd have had to be screaming from a window that looked over the valley so I keep telling myself I couldn't possibly have heard her they wouldn't have let her get near a window but it's upsetting all the same

Nominated by Tombouctou Books

INCIDENT AT IMURIS

by ALBERTO RÍOS

from THE LIME ORCHARD WOMAN (Sheep Meadow Press)

Mr. Aplinio Morales has reported this:
They were not after all
Watermelons, it was not the wild
Fruit patch they at first had thought;
In the manner of what moths do,
These were cocoons, as every child has
Picked up and squeezed,
But from in these came and they saw
Thousands of green-winged half moths,
Half moths and not exactly butterflies,
Not exactly puppies—
A name for them did not exist here.
Half this and some of that,
What was familiar and what might be European.
And when the fruit rotted, or seemed to rot—
Almost all of them on the same day—
From out of each husk the beasts flew
Fat, equipped, at ease
So that they were not so much
Hungry as curious.
The watermelons had been generous homes.
These were not begging animals,
Not raccoons, nor rats,
Not second or third class;
These were the kind that if human
They would have worn dinner jackets

And sniffed, not at anything in particular,
Just as general commentary.
Animals who had time for tea.
Easily distracted and obviously educated
In some inexplicable manner,
The beasts of the watermelons left
The same day, after putting their heads
In windows, bored already
From chasing the horses
And drinking too much from the town well.

Nominated by Sheep Meadow Press

GARBAGE

fiction by RON TANNER

from THE IOWA REVIEW

CAPTAIN SAYS we can't dump here because the tide's too strong and will wash everything ashore, which'll catch us hell when we return. So we head out, losing sight of the city, its towers sticking tops through the haze like gray fingertips through dirty rags—like someone drowning in garbage. No one's drowned yet on our run, dangerous as it is, though my mate, Douglas, fell in once when we were dumping and the load dragged him fifty feet down, he said. But he was buoyed up finally by a loose trash bag that had filled with gas somehow. A chemical reaction, Captain said. So we found Douglas grasping black plastic and bobbing barely afloat amid the debris, gulls swooping and shrieking excitement, and the sharks starting to stir in the distance, their fins cutting closer through the flotsam. It seems to bring everything to life, the dumping, contrary to what the critics say—we're feeding the seas. You never seen so many fish surface, wallowing in the burbling sinkage, mouths gaping as if they'd swallow the bricks of crushed vegetable and rag waste whole. Gulls clamor and clap, delighted it seems, lighting on the barge decks to watch what comes rolling up—squared-off packs of compressed stuff the size of compact cars, which bob in the foam for a while as hundreds of gulls begin pecking, leaving each garbage block oozy and brilliant white with droppings, before the packs sink finally, carried off the continental shelf by outbound currents and to the sea floor some two thousand feet down, where they will sit for a million years, Captain says, until they are nothing but sand-covered slime.

We don't usually unload until we're three miles out, on the international sea, but sometimes Captain gets tired and lets it go early. He's got no patience with the tender-hearts who are making things hard nowadays, trying to ban sea dumps. Just like the people who eat steak, he says, but can't stand the thought of butchering and want their meat well done so they won't have to look at the blood. You got to take the heat if you're going to cook with fire, he says. They should be out here to feel what it's like. Tell us where to put a 30,000 ton load. It's five barges long and Captain can barely pull it. We're four knots into the chop, the barges rolling on the wake like a flag in a breeze, the wash spilling up and over, our pumps working full-throttle, and a dark cloud of gulls a mile long spiraled behind like an airborne waterspout. Captain says we might go over night if the chop won't let up.

A night dump's something to see because some of this stuff glows. More chemical reaction, says Captain. Some of the fish glow too. Captain can't explain that, but says it's just the way things are—you see all kinds of things people ashore can't figure. I was looking once to make sure the dump's going clear and suddenly a silver flash as big as a baseball diamond came up at me in the black water like a constellation falling from the sky. I toppled back and was nearly mauled by one of the lifters as it slammed into place. Just a school of fish, Captain told us, don't be scared, tender-hearts. He teases like that. But we do get scared sometimes. And Captain says smart people ought to. It's the only way to stay alive.

Here's trouble: the Canadian Coast Guard telling us over loud speakers to back off, their huge red maple leaf flapping overhead as they arc around our bow, their uniformed young men at attention, squinting at us from one side. They wear little caps that look like artist berets, every man clean-shaven and frowning at our smell, which the sun makes bigger than usual. You get used to it, Tender-hearts! I shout at them, but they can't hear. Douglas turns to smile at me. It's a baby-like smile because he's got no teeth. Captain is cursing in the cabin. He blows the horn, then starts talking to the Canadians over the radio, the static crackling like burning wood. If we let go here, they tell us, the stuff will find its way back to Newfoundland—they've got the currents figured out and there's no arguing with them because they've got guns and speed. Captain carries a rifle, shotgun, and two revolvers, enough for each of us, though we've never had reason to use them; but I can't say we won't ever, things are getting so rough out here.

South we go, says Captain, steering that way. First Mate winches me and Douglas to the barges to make sure nothing comes loose as we make the course change. First Mate reminds us to wear our life vests, something we didn't start doing till Douglas went over that time. It does good to be unhampered by clothes back here, there's so much that gets in the way. So when it's real hot, life vests are all we wear, me and Douglas running along the rusted barge sides like Adam and Eve their first day, Paradise piled in steamy stacks before us and Nature clamoring all around. Douglas is what they call "dumb," unable to speak anything but a grunt, so he's got a whistle around his neck he uses to signal me. Nobody can read him as well as I can, so Captain counts on my abilities when we need Douglas bad because Douglas is the one who does the dangerous stuff, dropping between two barges, say, to secure a chain when the chop could crush him like a cracker; or climbing up the barge tower in a thunder storm to fix the antenna so we can call for help. Don't know where Captain got Douglas, but when I came on, his mate had just fallen dead from heart failure—an old man who'd been like a father to him—so Captain was looking for someone to bunk with Douglas and take the old man's place. I'm not that old but I was willing to hold a head now and then and say, There, now, it's not so bad, as Douglas bawled silently, his eyes awash but without a break of sound. I'd never seen anything like it.

Douglas enjoys running through the clouds of flies that hover always over the stacks. The birds give him a hard time because they think it's their territory—they swoop at him and even rain droppings. But Douglas doesn't mind. It's like he's one of them. He whistles to let me know the pump on number three is out. He's standing on a stack, gulls circling over him, a cloud of flies like a black halo around his bald head. He has no body hair to speak of. Mutation, Captain calls it. Which means things didn't go right when his father and mother made him. But he's OK in the head. No one finds as many things wrong as he does—he can spot it immediately when a pump's out or a stack's giving way. I wave back to him to say I got the message, which I shout back to First Mate, who just shakes his head in disgust because he can't stand to see things go wrong the way things are starting to go today. First Mate's a young man who wanted to be in the US Coast Guard but failed for some reason. Maybe because he couldn't stand to see things go wrong. It gets him twitchy, his right leg jittering like he's having spasms.

Douglas and me take off our clothes, it gets so hot, the barge mounds blasting furnace waves of odor, decomposing fast. We eat lunch under the barge tower on number five. Great thing about eating back here is that the flies and birds leave you alone, they have so much other stuff to pick at. Wave wash reaches where we sit, cooling the iron and making foam steam along the barge edge. Sitting out here's made us so dark we don't get blistered any more. We got cans of chili and two handfuls of hard water biscuits for eats. Douglas tips his can to his mouth like drinking soda, the beans clinging to his upper lip and chin. When he's done he just tosses it overboard and I wag a finger at him: Tender-hearts are going to sue you for that, Douglas. He grins and gives me the finger.

A chopper overhead startles us because it seems to come from nowhere, dropping from the white-sunned sky like a monster bird about to settle on the tug roof and sink it. First Mate is shaking his fist at it. Douglas and I run up to see what's the matter. Turns out the state of Virginia is afraid we're going to let go nearby, which would foul the Chesapeake, so they're warning us off. It's like that all the way down the coast—two weeks and three refuelings later. First Mate says we ought to let go wherever we damn well please because these are international waters. But not international currents, Captain reminds him, smoothing a wrinkled hand over his gray beard. He looks at us like we have ideas. Where are your clothes? he asks. Douglas and I look to the barges and shrug. We forgot about them, we've been so busy, I tell him. Barge three is about to give in, so we've been trading pumps, moving four to three and back again. But it can't go on like that. We're exhausted. The wind's picked up so much the flies are clinging to the heaps like barnacles and the gulls waver overhead, fighting to keep up with us, their wings outstretched like stiff kite sails.

When the Florida Coast Guard speeds towards us First Mate pulls Captain's shotgun from the rack and aims it out the cabin window. Douglas, on the outside, jumps up, putting his face to the gun barrel and blows his whistle, startling First Mate so bad it gives Captain a chance to slam him with a cola bottle. By the time I get there they've got First Mate tied on the floor, Douglas sitting on his chest grinning and naked except for his orange life vest. It all happens so fast the young Coast Guard men don't see it—they're too serious to imagine such a thing, Captain says, every boy with narrow eyes and pinched nose like we were some kind of floating plague. Go south, they tell us. So we do. But Captain's discouraged. Says he's getting too old for this kind of run around. The city commission's going to hear about it. Things are getting too political, he says, glancing down at First Mate, who looks asleep, a welt the size of a hardball at the back of his head.

Douglas and I take turns holding ice on First Mate's head till he feels better. We spoon soup into his mouth but he lets half of it spill out, he's so angry. Let me go, he says, over and over. Douglas shakes his head no, and holds out another spoonful of chicken noodle. Eat, I tell him, or you'll get sick. He tells me to go to hell. We can't run the barges without him, he says, because Captain's too old to do the work of two men. Already pump four's starting to sputter with weakness, it's been moved and worked so much. One of the barges is going down. It's just a matter of time, says First Mate, glancing from me to Douglas and back again. Douglas shakes his head—no—once more. First Mate tells him to go to hell.

I winch Douglas to the barges so he can check the pumps. Captain's looking at charts and shaking his head. We may have to turn back, he says, though it might mean the end of his career. You just don't go out with 30,000 tons and come back with it a month later. It costs a fortune. He's got to dump somewhere. First Mate says Mexico is the best bet. The whole country's a dump, he says. Captain tells me to take the wheel while he goes down for more charts. First Mate smiles up at me and says I'm the only one with brains on the boat. I'm the only one who's ever made sense in his thinking. After all, he says, who can understand Douglas best? And who does the Captain rely on when things get rough? I turn around to look at him. Me? I ask. Look who's at the wheel, he says: you. Let me go, he says, and I promise I'll behave. He speaks so kindly, I do what he says. Then he punches me in the stomach, takes a pistol from Captain's drawer, and tells me to stand. Captain looks about to faint when he comes up and sees what's happened. To Mexico, First Mate says. He makes Captain pilot and he keeps the gun to my head, his right leg jittering. Douglas is whistling that barge three's about to go. But I don't answer. When I glance back I see him standing on a stack and waving with both arms. But no one waves back. He's stuck out there now.

We'll drop in the gulf as soon as we can, First Mate says. The tug's slowing because barge three is filling with water. Douglas keeps whistling and the gulls shriek in response, they're so irritated. We'll all go down if we don't do something about that barge, Captain tells First Mate. Soon as it's dark, First Mate says, we're sinking the barges. All of them. The whole thing will be logged as a catastrophe. That way nobody will be to blame. What about Douglas? I ask. First Mate shrugs. What about him? Suddenly we see an ocean liner, drifting like a white cloud on the horizon, the first ship we've seen since leaving the city, not counting flecks of sail boats in the distance now and then. If we're going to log an accident, Captain says, we'll have to signal distress. First Mate's eyes go wild with panic. He shoots the radio. You shouldn't have done that, says Captain, sounding very tired. Douglas keeps whistling. The gulls cry.

Something jerks the tug and we look back to see barge three going down, garbage blocks beginning to float, birds swooping madly, stirred by the change. Douglas is behind with number four trying to unhook the linkage—he wants to save what he can. Captain groans. Untie! First Mate tells me, Untie! He shoves me to the back of the tug. I'm on my knees staring at the froth churning from the tug-end, chains clanking against the grease-streaked stern, the blue-green water below. Captain cuts the engine. First Mate pushes his pistol into my neck. The cold makes me shiver. My hands grip for algae-covered chain links but they're too slippery and too heavy. It takes two! I'm shouting, two people! A jolt knocks First Mate down. Douglas has sent load four over, emptying the barge, but the force of it, dragged with sinking number three, makes the barge line buckle. Now four is sinking and Douglas stands on five, whistling for help. We're going down. I'm about to leap on First Mate when Captain starts shooting, aiming for First Mate, but missing, the bullets pinging off the deck. First Mate dives. Then we follow.

The suck of sinkage pulls me down like a vacuum, yanking off my life vest and spinning me like a cork screw until I'm so dizzy I don't know which is bottom and which is top, my head and nose so full of stinging water it seems my eyes will pop out. Pain inside and darkness everywhere. Confusion. Then there's light, a blinding glare on the water, so suddenly calm now. I spit up, blinking, reaching for something to save me—a clump of foam. Heaps all around burble as they sink, water bubbling and foaming, flies swirling in angry knots at the surface. I'm kneeing through, almost crawling, the dump load is so thick in the water. Captain dog-paddles towards me, his gray beard dripping, his eyes sad like a spaniel's. Follow me, he says. I'm panting, trying to call out for Douglas, but all I do is cough. The idea is to get as far from the junk as possible before the sharks come. Schools of fish flutter by, flashing in the turquoise below. There will be so much confusion, the sharks'll tear into whatever moves, tails flailing, fish darting frenzied through the dark passages of gnarled waste. Gulls watch us from sinking piles, their black eyes blinking as we paddle close by. They gobble strands of vegetable muck and snap at flies. A ship—the liner—sounds its horn, a distant moan. Does it see us? How could it miss? Captain says.

What looks like a mound of oil-soaked fabric and foam just ahead is Douglas, we discover, dragging First Mate, who nearly drowned. Douglas smiles in greeting. I kiss his forehead. First Mate sputters, flailing in his savior's arms. He's as pale as fish belly. Captain says we should swim slow and easy, conserving our strength because it's a long way to the liner. But we're saved, he says. They'll send a boat to pick us up. Expect an investigation, he tells us, and much controversy. But that will change nothing, I know, because by the time we get back to the city another 30,000 tons will be waiting for us, the people desperate to get rid of it, and so about this time next month we'll be at sea again, pulling another barge line and seeking another place to drop our load, me and Douglas working in the sun all day with the sea lapping our feet like nothing else exists except it, the stacks of garbage, and the endless horizon.

Nominated by Joyce Carol Oates

JAMES JESUS ANGLETON (1917–1987)

by ELIOT WEINBERGER

from SULFUR

O<small>N HIS STRANGE</small> mission to America in 1939 to persuade Roosevelt not to enter the European war, Ezra Pound took time from his meetings with low-level bureaucrats and high-level avant-gardists to travel to New Haven to visit a Yale student named Jim Angleton. Angleton, still an undergraduate, was an energetic *littérateur*. He had visited Pound in Rapallo, and shared his enthusiasm for Mussolini. He was chummy with Cummings, met Marianne Moore, lunched with Thomas Mann, and had brought in the ambiguous William Empson to lecture; he helped James Agee with the manuscript of *Let Us Now Praise Famous Men*. Now, with his roommate Reed Whittemore, he was editing a poetry magazine called *Furioso*. Pound's "Introductory Textbook" had appeared in the first number, and the poet was as eager as ever to tell the young editors whom to publish.

Details of that encounter are not known: the two major Pound biographies grant the incident only one, nearly identical sentence each. After four issues, *Furioso* suspended publication, to be resumed after the war with Whittemore as sole editor. Angleton was published only once, in the *Yale Literary Magazine:* a bad poem with a prophetic title, "The Immaculate Conversion." In the middle of the war, Angleton was converted—"turned," he would say—by his English professor, Norman Holmes Pearson, from poetry to its twin, espionage.

Pearson, a Boston aristocrat and a diminutive cripple, is now remembered for his writings on 19th century American literature, the extraordinary *Poets of the English Language* anthologies he edited with W. H. Auden, and as H. D.'s editor and literary executor. In 1943, despite the fact that he had been a Nazi sympathizer until the invasion of Poland, Pearson was sent to London to become the head of X-2, the counter-intelligence branch of the O.S.S. (Office of Strategic Services). There he learned the British "Double Cross" system of psychologically coercing captured enemy agents into working for one's own side. Pearson's counterpart (and nemesis) at the British M.I.6 was Kim Philby; his code name was Puritan; in espionage literature he is called "the father of American counter-intelligence."

Angleton turned out to be Pearson's greatest find. Their relationship during the war was close: father-son, or master-disciple. After work at the London O.S.S. office, Angleton traveled in the Pearson circle: Eliot, the Sitwells, Benjamin Britten, Graham Greene, E. M. Forster, Ralph Vaughan Williams, Norman Douglas, Elizabeth Bowen, Compton MacKenzie. He was a frequent guest at H. D. and Bryher's flat.

The O.S.S. office itself was no less literary. Angleton had, in turn, recruited two close friends: Edward Weismiller, the Yale Younger Poet of 1936, and Richard Ellmann, the future Joyce scholar. Fellow agents included along with superspook William Casey (Reagan's C.I.A. director)—Donald Gallup, the future Pound bibliographer, and Louis Martz, the Milton scholar who would later edit H. D.'s *Collected Poems.* Angleton's secretary was H. D.'s daughter Perdita. (H. D. seems to have been surrounded by spies. It is curious that Bryher was apparently the only outside person to know Pearson's code name.)

After the war, Pearson returned to Yale, where he continued to recruit students for the newly-formed C.I.A. He served on the board of advisers to Pound's Square Dollar Books, which folded after its publishers, Kasper and Horton, went to jail for instigating segregationist riots. In 1975, on a tour of the Far East, Norman Holmes Pearson fell ill in Seoul and died soon after. Mrs. Pearson believed that he had been poisoned by North Koreans—proof that he was still working for the Company.

Angleton, when he surfaced in public in the late 1970's, was revealed to be the chief of C.I.A. counter-intelligence, the "ultra top secret deep snow" unit. He had files on two million Americans; had directed an operation that infiltrated the U.S. Postal Service and opened and photographed 200,000 personal letters; believed that Lee Harvey Oswald and Henry Kissinger were KGB spies, and that the Black Panthers were a North Korean front operation. He had been Kim Philby's best friend. For twenty years after the defection of Philby's partners Burgess and MacLean, Philby and Angleton were locked in a "deep game" of double and double-double crossing—a "wilderness of mirrors," Angleton called it, quoting Eliot—as Angleton decimated the ranks of the C.I.A. in search of double agents, the "moles." Angleton's boss, Allen Dulles, was kept uninformed, and Mrs. Angleton, after 31 years of marriage, had never known her husband's position.

Angleton, who kept reading poetry all his life, claimed in later years that he had always tried to recruit agents from the Yale English department. He believed that those trained in the New Criticism, with its seven types of ambiguity, were particularly suited to the interpretation of intelligence data.

Consider, after all, the ways a spy's message may be read:

1) It is written by a loyal agent and its information is accurate.

2) It is written by a loyal agent but its information is only partially accurate.

3) It is written by a loyal agent but its information is entirely inaccurate.

4) It is written by a double agent and its information is completely false.

5) It is written by a double agent but its information is partially true so that the false parts will be believed.

6) It is written by a double agent but its information is entirely true so that the allegiance of the agent will not be discovered.

Moreover, the message is written in code, and liable to the vagaries of translation. And it is written in a highly condensed language, whose meanings can offer varying interpretations. Like a poem, the message is only as good as its reader. Roosevelt refused to believe a report on the imminent invasion of Pearl Harbor; the F.B.I. thought that the *Pisan Cantos* were the encoded communications of a spy.

There is a book to be written on poetry and espionage. A spy must know where the best information is, collect it without being discovered, and safely transmit it. In antiquity, the bards and troubadours were perfect for the task: they were free to wander; they had access to the courts; and as poets they relied on their powers of observation to compose and their memories to recite. The first literary spy is the creation of such a bard: Odysseus, who (in Book IV of the Odyssey) disguises himself as a beggar to gather intelligence in a Trojan city.

Chaucer was a spy on the continent for John of Gaunt. Marlowe was recruited by Sir Francis Walsingham—Elizabeth's great spymaster and Sir Phillip Sidney's father-in-law—to inform on English students who were enjoying Catholic hospitality in Rheims. (And later, he was murdered by Walsingham's men because of his involvement with Sir Walter Ralegh, another spy, in a plot to depose the queen—a murder that was neatly staged to look like a barroom brawl.) Wordsworth was a spy in France; Basil Bunting a spy in Persia. Whittaker Chambers started out as an Objectivist poet.

Poetry arose as the voice of sacred power—the formula, the mantra, the oracle, the prayer: rhythmical condensed speech. Because of taboo, it was a voice that spoke in metaphors: the only way to express the inexpressible. Even as it lost its sacred function, the power continued in the poem: poetry, said Dickinson, takes the top of your head off.

That split—between the power of the poem and the powerlessness of the poet in society—has led poets into lives quite similar to the lives of spies. Poets have believed that they are the "unacknowledged legislators" (which, in its way, is another name for the secret police). They have been attracted to secret societies, from the Elizabethan School of Night (whose members included Ralegh, Spenser, Chapman and Marlowe, as well as Thomas Hariot and the alchemist Walter Warner) to Yeats' Golden Dawn. They have preferred to publish anonymously or under pseudonyms. They are—like Milton writing his elegy before he had a suitable corpse—masters at the counterfeiting of emotions. They band together into groups and movements that, like Angleton's C.I.A., become obsessed with betrayals from within. They encode private messages and secret strengths into their poems, like Zukofsky embedding the formula for a conic section into the letters n and r and "A"-9. They believe they are serving great powers: Stalin, Mussolini, the Revolution, the

Church. They walk, like Baudelaire, Lorca, Reznikoff, invisibly through the city, watching and listening.

Writes Mina Loy: "To maintain my incognito the hazard I chose was—poet." In its obituary, *The New York Times* reported that Angleton's favorite poets were Eliot and Cummings.

Nominated by Ken Gangemi

WITNESS

fiction by DEWITT HENRY

from BOULEVARD

OUR HOME MOVIES predate my memory and perplex me with images that have since become confused with memory and with family legend. My earliest, or at least most easily dated memory is my fifth birthday, June 30, 1946, when I was digging in our backyard with a gardening fork and struck downward and into the middle of my right shoe, leaving a neat, square hole right through the shoe, top and sole. I bled, but felt no pain. There was a bad cut between my first and second toes, but I had missed the foot itself, and after washing it, my mother fussing (I'd just wandered into the kitchen, leaving bloody footprints, and said I'd hurt my foot), that, except for a tetanus shot later, was it. The same afternoon we are at the dinner table and my oldest brother, Jack, whose sixteenth birthday is the following week, gives me my first bubblegum ever (an adult privilege); he has been hunting and brought back rabbit, which is supposed to taste "racy," and we eat as an event. Other memories, dimly: I pretend to read *Time* magazine at dinner and my mother pretends that the words I invent are what it really says, and marvels. My Grandpop Henry, a warm and friendly man, whom I love, rides me on his shoe, one leg crossed over the other; he died, I realize now, of a heart attack at his summer home in Ocean City, just nine days after I turned five.

But then we have the movies, which document this time and earlier, all poignantly for me now, since I am older than my parents then, and my own daughter is five and starting memories of her own.

There is Jack as a baby, six months old; then Chuck as a baby (Jack as a toddler), then Judy as a baby; then, finally, at the Bloomingdale Avenue house, my mother pregnant with me and turning from the camera, me as a newborn wriggling in my carriage, which my mother rocks, me as a baby being held by Jack, Chuck and Judy in turn, me being prodded to crawl by Judy, me as a toddler in a snowsuit being pulled on a sled by Judy at age eight, me at Christmas in a sailor suit, and Mom still dark-haired, slender and bright-eyed (she's always resembled Katharine Hepburn, to my mind). Another film, in color, shows Easter at Ithan, my grandparents' big stone house and backyard, surrounded by woods; the time must be 1945, since Aunt Kitty is there with Bunny as a toddler, but without Uncle John, who is still in the Army, and since Grandpop is there, and Peggy, too, with Dale as a baby. The shock for me, viewing shortly before or after I married some ten years ago, was the image of me at four apparently carefree, happy, running towards the camera in shorts and t-shirt; more recently, the shock has been the image of my father (he is missing from most of our films, since he was the one taking them). He is clowning for the camera, lifting me up and swinging me and finally setting me on his shoulders, exactly as I do my daughter now, and with obvious pride and delight—feelings I never thought he felt for me or showed. "He did love his children," my mother comments this time. Years before, when I was home from college and Dad asleep upstairs, we ran the film on the basement wall at St. Davids, and she had said, "I was furious then; that was the bad time."

The troubling thing is that I have no direct memory of my father before I am eight, when we moved from Bloomingdale to the St. Davids house; while otherwise, my memories of Bloomingdale, dating from when I am five, or even earlier, are rich. I search for him, for where he must have been (*some*one is playing Santa Claus and calling to me down the chimney), but nothing is there. My sister claims a similar blank.

* * * *

Our Bloomingdale house, according to an old deed, dated from 1880. There were fifteen rooms—downstairs, the livingroom, onto which the front door opened, side porch, Saturday room, sun porch,

356

diningroom, pantry, stairs, kitchen and back porch; second floor, the boys' room (over the livingroom), my room (over the Saturday room), connecting by a bathroom to the master bedroom (over the diningroom), then another bathroom off the central staircase and landing, then Judy's room in back and the backstairs down to the kitchen; third floor: mattress room (where all our old mattresses were laid out wall to wall for roughhousing), Anna's room and bathroom, and a large L-shaped attic, where among two generations of family paraphernalia, was the handed, treasure-chest-shaped trunk that my great grandfather had brought from Ireland. Also in the third-floor hallway was an old wind-up Victrola, with stacks of wax records in its cabinet (the teenage acquisitions of Aunt Peggy, I realize now), which on rainy days we would play, and which included such songs as "Reefer Man," "Button Up Your Overcoat," and "Red Sails In The Sunset." Then in the basement: coal bins, back under the diningroom, which would be filled down a chute through a basement window; and in the center, the furnace, which the boys must fill, rope-handled coal bucket after coal bucket, down a hopper on top, and which had a metal plate in the front off to one side. This the boys would lift up, reaching with a hooked pike down a concrete ramp underneath and dragging up and out cans of warm ash. One whole wall was filled with shelves of preserved vegetables from the victory garden out back, mostly stewed tomatoes in Mason jars. Out front was a wide plank porch running the house's length and shaded by striped, fringed awnings in the summer; here, between support columns on the Lenoir Avenue end, hung a canvas hammock, in which Judy or the boys would close me, turn me over and over, then let me spin back; here also, during thunderstorms, with rain drumming on the roof and pouring off the awnings, with chill gusts, and with the lights from inside casting from behind us, Mom or Judy would bring me to watch the lightning flash: now count, each second measuring another mile, four, five; until the crack of near, or rumbles of more distant thunder. The yard was one acre. A three-foot-high iron fence with horizontal rods ran along the Bloomingdale Lenoir borders, broken midway out front by a swinging gate where our front walk joined the sidewalk (I would ride the gate open and shut to grinding hinges). On the wooden steps down from the porch, there was a "114" in metal numerals. Tall matching pines stood on either side out front, along with smaller bushes and trees.

On the Lenoir side were two magnolias, which perfumed the air when they bloomed and afterwards littered the ground with leaf-sized fleshy petals that turned brown and spotted with rot. The smaller of these, the red, standing off the sunporch, was the only tree I could climb; the light pink, which stood off the diningroom and kitchen and whose blossoms could be seen from the master bedroom (a view my mother painted in oils), I somehow did climb once, only to get stuck and cry out in panic until Chuck climbed up to rescue me.

Out back, along Lenoir, was the gravel driveway and the carriage barn, with hinged double doors, used by us to house two cars, while upstairs, in the earliest years, there were fifty chickens (a victory effort and Jack's first "business") and the boys would go to collect eggs each day. I was impressed by the porcelain eggs planted to make the chickens lay. Later all the chickens were slaughtered, hung upside down, by Jack's account, killed by a single cut up the beak and into the brain, bled, soaked in a steaming tub and plucked, then sold or eaten—a sheer labor of killing that my mother would refer to even after with revulsion. By war's end, the chicken roost was turned into a playroom, where the boys had parties, where they built a mammoth "0" gauge model train layout, and where an intercom—a little box affair, with a hook on which hung the ear piece, and a button to buzz the other end—was strung to connect them with the house, so Mom could call them to dinner.

Midway along the back property line, which joined Mr. Smith's yard (Mr. Smith taught science at Radnor High), grew a venerable oak, five feet across at the trunk and highest in the yard. A good twenty feet up, level with the top of the barn, the boys had built a treehouse in the central crotch: walls, windows, roof, and a trap-door underneath, through which they disappeared by means of a rope ladder that swung and swayed and I was forbidden, ever, to climb. When I did test its lower rungs, its unanchored twisting and give left me hanging in fright. Later, after one of the neighborhood kids wandered into the yard, climbed without permission, and fell from the ladder and broke his arm, the treehouse was pronounced too dangerous and torn down. I never got to see inside of it. The boys dug an underground clubhouse next. Somewhere between the tree and the garden, they started with a six-foot-long trench for the entrance tunnel (carrying and spreading dirt along the back fence), then a pit for the main room, and covered the whole thing over with boards, tarpaper, dirt and sod, so no one could tell it was there. Even the trapdoor entrance was covered over with grass, and they would be there underground and hear Dad walking overhead (who if he'd known, had forgotten the clubhouse existed) or Louie-the-gardener's lawnmower passing over, and exult. They did let me down once, and offered Judy too, but she refused. First, Jack; then me, then Chuck: down steps into the tunnel, crawl forward over pine needles (laid down to keep clothes clean) into darkness to the main chamber, cavernous, and—careful—helped down a ladder until I could stand upright; then Jack's electric lantern on, which was hooked overhead like a regular light, showing as Chuck backed down to join us a room maybe five feet across, with table, chairs, a bench all around cut out of the wall, niches for comic books, coke bottles with candles, a vent for air. Despite Jack's assurances, Mom, after investigating, at some point, worried that it might cave in, and she and Dad had it torn up and filled in before I was old enough to go down on my own. Dad had Louie do it, and both were shocked to discover the extent and depth of the holes: Louie had to bring in a truckload of topsoil to do the job.

Down Smith's fence to our back corner, where I loved to play in the shade and dirt, ran a long grape arbor, over whose lattice the boys would climb and from which, later, they had hung the chickens for killing. Captain Bones's, the police chief's, yard began at the corner and bordered ours back out to Bloomingdale. In front Bones's yard and house stood level with ours, but his back yard rose steeply to a terrace, where a reservoir from Wayne's earliest days had been filled in. In the back corner, its bank was only three or four feet high, but it grew to as much as six feet farther down. The slope up from our side had been planted by Nana Henry as a rock garden, with boulders I could jump from, one to another, without crushing the flowers between. Up on the terrace, Bones's yard was left wild and overgrown as a woods and to me as exotic, since we were forbidden to climb into it, though the boys sometimes did to retrieve a baseball or to dig BB's out of the rotten tree they used for target practice out their bedroom window. The tree had been struck by lightning and burned and crows, which Captain Bones himself would shoot at from his back porch, would flock to its leafless branches. The first time Jack let me shoot his BB gun, a pump model, he had me sight the tree from their sill.

The victory garden was in that quadrant of our back yard, too, enclosed by a picket fence with an arbor and gate, and with plank walls between the beds of vegetables; because the boys used to lock me in here, teasingly, it was my first thought when I heard "Don't Fence Me In," a popular song then. Between the garden and the back porch stoop with its overhang was Mom's clothesline, strung like telephone wires between poles and propped up with notched clothesprops, which the boys later used for stilts. Where kitchen and pantry wall abutted part of the livingroom and the side of the sunporch, with its door and wide steps, Mom had put in a flagstone patio, perhaps ten or twelve feet square and also enclosed by a picket fence with arbored gate; here, in shade, my sandbox had been kept, and in one movie, I am sitting at age four, sailor-suited and bare-kneed, beside my younger, blond cousin, Priscilla, whom I seldom saw, and who belonged to Uncle Marvin and Aunt Fronca on Mom's side, far off in New York. Off this patio, down from the rock garden and rhododendron bushes and up against Bones's shed, was a weeping willow that had grown from a twig that Grandpop had stuck in the ground twenty years before. A wooden swing hung from one branch, where Judy would push me; also we would tear off willow strands, strip the leaves, and try to snap the strands like whips—stinging, sometimes, at each other. Or I would walk and turn through the fronds, which felt like hair. Patio, willow, and the area off the back stoop formed our favorite family spot, for its privacy and shade. In another film, Nana Henry sits on a bench under the willow, sprinkling us with a hose as we dart around, skinny in our bathingsuits, and jump in and out of a zinc laundry tub. Fat, complacent, bemused, a little devilish: she waters us like animated flowers. Sparky is there too, a wire-haired terrier, whose dog house stands by the garden, and who was later put to sleep for turning and biting me; taking "wire-haired" literally, I had tried to pull his hair out with pliers. Still other films show family picnics in the willow's shade, at a table: Grandpop, Nana, Dad, Kitty. The boys and even Judy cavort around, playing on the name and riding saw "horses" for the camera; Jack marches with a flintlock rifle. Judy sits on the back porch steps, sewing, hair in braids.

* * * *

I have no memory of our customary drive one Sunday, Dad at the wheel, Judy and me in back, Mom in front. "Daddy's sick," I say.

360

"He's a sick man. Anyone can see that. Anyone can see that man is sick." And he keeps driving, stiffened, staring straight ahead, saying nothing.

Or of another time, at night, when I run to Mom: "I heard Daddy—he's not really going to cut you up in pieces and throw you out the window, is he?"

Nothing's there.

* * * *

Jack's and Chuck's experience at Haverford School (where they went not only for family tradition, but because of the poor quality of so-called progressive education in the Radnor schools, which caused a number of their Wayne friends to transfer to Haverford too) augmented their league as brothers. They would talk of Severinghast, the principal, who hit them with a yardstick for demerits, practice for the wrestling, football, baseball, and swimming teams, play jokes on the conductors on the Paoli local, wear school jerseys and caps; and then, come summers, leave together for eight-week sessions of Camp Allegash, in Northern Maine. They were away the summer of 1945 on a canoe trip far into the Maine and Canadian wilderness, so they didn't hear that the war was over until two weeks later, when they came out of the woods. Mom sewed their names on everything from underwear to sleeping bags; each had his own barracks trunk, and we would drive them and their trunks to the 30th Street station in town and put them on the train, and greet and pick them up there at summer's end.

At Allegash they learned to tie their own flies and to fish for pike and trout, whipping their fly rods overhead with the line curling back, snapping forward, and lying gently on the water sixty or seventy feet out, so the fly would touch the water like a falling bug. Whatever the geographical, social and professional divergence of their adult lives, Allegash and their passion for fly fishing would prove a sure key to kinship. Both had known those special woods (unlike any others, by their telling), the canoeing, the rivers, lakes, the rapids, the portages, the camping out, the moose, bear, the Canuck guides. Allegash, too, was where Jack contracted his love of flying, which otherwise had been bred with balsa gliders, then motor-powered models through his early teens. His first year up, having won a ping-pong match, he broke his toe while jumping for joy and so was left behind when Chuck and the others set out on their canoe trips; and for several weeks, cast on his foot, he flew with a fish and game ranger, helping him stock lakes with fishery-bred trout. The plane was a small, single wing over, with pontoons, and perched by the open door, as they swooped suddenly over treetops and down over some small lake, Jack would have a can ready, from a store of cans behind their seats, and empty it, like a shower of silver, as the hundreds of tiny fish rippled the surface and shimmered, and then the plane would climb, engine roaring, bank, and clear the rushing trees, and they'd be off. The same pilot, who could land and take off on bodies of water smaller than a football field, later flew Jack upriver, toe healed and cast off, to find and rejoin the advanced canoe group for his last week of the trip.

* * * *

Judy had longed so much for a sister that from the moment I was born she refused even to look at me for several weeks; but then she took over, little-mothering me as her special charge. In the movies, she is prodding me to crawl, cradling me, making angels with me in the snow, pulling me on the sled. I loved her room in back, with its alcove and windowseat, where she had arranged all her dolls and stuffed animals, and where she would read to me. Her friends were the Hartsorns, down Lenoir, a family of all girls with one St. Bernard, which followed Judy home one day. We were sitting at the dinner table; I was in my highchair (I can remember) and Mom beside me, when Mom called for Viola, the maid, to bring in dinner and in came this monstrous dog instead, tall enough to rest its shaggy head on the table between Mom and me. Viola had been terrified and refused to serve anything until we got that dog out of there. At some point, the boys had learned to stand and walk on their hands across the livingroom, and Judy practiced and practiced, Chuck even helping by holding her feet, until she could do it readily too, but then one wrist collapsed and broke; none of us were allowed to try after that. She lived in the fantasy world of her reading a good deal and would play "secret garden" under the rhododendrons by the rock garden; her drawings were of elves, pixies, fairies and fairy castles, and she encouraged me to draw too, my first crude cartoons. She took dancing lessons, ballet and tap; then music lessons (her practicing on our upright proved maddening to all of us, but especially so to Chuck, who would pile pillows over his head), but quit because her lady piano teacher's breath was so bad. When she was in 5th grade, in Mr. Shock's class (he would be my teacher, too, at Radnor), Mom wanted to transfer her to Baldwin School, the equivalent of Haverford for girls, but the Radnor schools were so poor that Baldwin refused her until she had had a year of catch-up work at Friends Central. But she was attending Baldwin, wearing a blue tunic uniform, kneehigh stockings, and carrying her canvas book bag for our last years at Bloomingdale. I felt jealous then, too, that my cousin, Bunny, a girl, had supplanted me in her attentions; and that Aunt Kitty and Uncle John would invite her to the shore with them to babysit.

* * * *

Grandpop's death in 1946 was remote to me, though I tried to picture him going about his ordinary morning life, in their house, which I had never seen, at the shore, showering and shaving, when suddenly "he just keeled over" (as I'd heard) and Nana found him later. I wasn't allowed to the funeral, but I was taken to visit the graveplot on major holidays, when, often with Nana, we would put on flowers: the graveslab fascinated me because my name was there, chiseled in marble. I had loved Grandpop and felt robbed of his love and attention; death was as if he had moved away, forever; we would never see him again, and that neverness echoed as a new perception in my heart.

* * * *

I am lying in the dark one night, wakened, or falling to sleep, when at one of my two big windows, which open over the front porch roof, and where leaf shadows from the streetlights regularly and familiarly play, there is something terrible, alive, malevolent suddenly, looking in, like a man, but not, with some kind of leering, angry, twisted face. It is there and real, and I scream and scream hysterically, and everyone comes rushing in—Jack and Chuck and Mom, and Dad, too, I think—and they open the window and look outside and Chuck gets out onto the porch to look and prove to me that nothing is there, and let me look.

363

When Mom demanded of the boys, then and later, whether they'd been playing a trick, whether one of them had gotten out their window onto the roof and come around to scare me, they swore and insisted, and have for all these years, no. So the only explanation is a dream, or dream mixed with my seeing some pattern in the swaying shadows. But it wasn't a dream, I told them, knew then, feel now; and it wasn't shadows; and what it was I couldn't describe and can't to this day, but I know it was there, was real, was inexplicable.

* * * *

Mom's big, cumbersome artist's easel (which she'd found abandoned in a garage of their rented house in Illinois, years before I was born), was set up in the sunporch on the Lenoir side, "for the light." The same room, at different times, held our ping-pong table, train layouts, and the matched black- and-polar-bearskin rugs, in whose coarse, deep fur I liked to roll, and whose lifelike and lifeless heads, marble eyes, leather noses, ceramic tongues and gums, and actual fangs menaced each other, face to face (both had been kills of Gail Borden's, and come to us, I've learned, as legacies of Aunt Peggy's divorce; I imagine her toasting him on them, in happier times, brandy snifters clinking in the firelight). Mom would paint for several hours in the morning, wearing a "smock," and holding her messy pallet with its thumbhole. She mixed her colors by squeezing and rolling up the oils from the bottom, like so many tooth-paste tubes, a dab of white, of red; then thinned the paint with turpentine and painted with different, long brushes. I grew jealous of her immersion and would whine and clamor for attention; always, I felt, she painted in spite of me, and I dreaded her remoteness.

Among her pictures from Bloomingdale were the pink and white magnolia blossoms against the sky, covered bridges at Eaglesmere and Valley Forge, and a Maine fishing village seascape (many others, especially still-lifes, from earlier and later, adorned our walls always, and caused visitors to exclaim, "Kay, you mean *you* painted that?" and then they'd want to see everything). I drove with her to and through the covered bridges, where she set up a portable easel at roadside or on a sandbar, with her open paintbox. She was especially challenged by the problems of water, reflections, the play of light, by the textures of trees and clouds, and took trouble, dissatisfied past any reason I could see, touching, retouching, over and over, until the paint dried bumpy. Finished paintings took weeks to dry and then she would shellac them. The seascape, her largest and most ambitious, she based on a photograph in *American Artist*: huts in the foreground, beach, choppy surf, then a towering offshore cliff from a severed peninsula. She worried while painting that it wasn't "convincing" and finally invented and agonized over a fisherman drying his nets over a fence up close; the painting won first prize in a local show and a picture of her with me beside it appeared in *The Suburban*. At sunset, on the sandbar where she was painting a covered bridge and I was playing with pebbles, she once said, "No one would believe a sky like that even if I could paint it; it doesn't matter if it's *true*; no one would believe it." I felt proud of her talent; but with the seascape, she stopped painting until after we'd moved, I was older, and she had a back room to herself. Her decision to stop, I felt, was made in the context of my needing her, and I remember some elation and relief at hearing the announcement, despite its bitter edge, and seeing the easel dismantled and carried away.

* * * *

Anna King was our colored maid. Before her was Viola, and before Viola, Catherine Dougherty, whom I was too young to remember, but who, by family report, would take out her false teeth and click them for me. Anna started with us at age 50, when I was 4, coming in days for a while, then moving in, wearing uniforms, and living over my room on the third floor, with that bathroom to herself. She cooked, cleaned, served meals, and looked after us (me, mainly) when Mom was busy or away. Broad-beamed and plump, she had a moonish face and black hair, pulled back, and smooth-complexioned upper arms as large as thighs. She complained often of aches and pains, and had Mom buy a knee-pad for when she kneeled, scrubbing floors. There was always a faint, burnt-wood fragrance to her and her things, her bedspread, her ironing, even, that I loved; and her manner with me was teasing, scandalized, admiring, and ceaselessly fond. She would marvel at my craving for Velveeta cheese and peanut butter (which I exaggerated for her benefit)—"Oh, no, you can't want to eat all *that!*"—or something I'd say or draw would cause her to exclaim, "Oh, he's just so *smart!*"

One chilly fall day during the war, Mom was down at the Red Cross, Anna and I were alone, and somehow we got locked out of the house. We were on the back porch, where there was a woodbox and an axe. She bewailed and worried what to do, and I kept saying, gallantly, feeling manly and in charge, that I would take the axe and chop down the door, but she wouldn't let me, even though I told her it was my house and all right: "No, you can't do *that*. Put that axe down; don't you pick up that." We waited and waited, achingly, for someone to come, which was her solution; she took off her sweater and insisted I wrap it around me. Another time, while Mom was at the store one afternoon, I was in the bathroom between my room and the masterbedroom, with both doors locked, and hadn't learned to wipe myself yet: this was something Mom always did; and when I called out for Mom, Anna answered, and was right outside the door, pleading with me: "Your Mommy isn't home and I don't know when she's coming; let me in and I'll wipe you!"—"No!"—"It's okay, I've got a little boy too!"—"No!"—"You don't want to sit there all afternoon; unlock the door, now!"— "No!" And so forth, bemused coaxing on her part, total fear or shyness on mine: only Mom could, I would wait; and did, for god knows how long; but then Mom did come back, I unlocked the door, and everybody thought it was funny.

Later, at Bloomingdale, while Mom and Judy were shopping, Anna's room caught on fire. I smelled smoke, yelled, and she came running, charged upstairs, and suffered third degree burns before Jack or the firemen, who came quickly, could pull her out. She'd been trying to get her money out of the burning mattress, which was where, from bad wiring nearby or a forgotten cigarette, the fire had begun.

That Anna had moved up from North Carolina, where she had worked all her life for the Reynolds family, even been given a brick house. That her husband had been an alcoholic, who beat her, and whom she finally divorced. That she had had no children of her own but that her sister in Philadelphia had sent down one child a year for Anna to clothe, feed, and school. That she'd grown attached to one nephew, Billy, and when unionization had changed things "for the worse" at work, she had moved North with him to live at her sister's, in the colored section behind Wayne. That she continued to live there, contributing to their home and never having one of her own.

That as Billy grew up, married, and had children, he proved a pride to her, but a heartache too, since she had tried, at one point, to move in with him, but it hadn't worked out . . .

She would confide all this to Mom, off and on, peeling potatoes, say, while I sat listening. Sometimes, too, she and Mom mentioned "race" or "her people." But I had little sense, ever, of her personal life, or of the world, apart from and foreign to ours, where she would come from and return. I did gather from her talk that at her sister's, at least, this was a world of violence, greed, squalor and want, that she was not loved or appreciated there as we loved her or felt she deserved, and those times we drove her home (mainly from St. Davids, when she no longer boarded with us), I didn't like sending her back—one of us—to what other life waited behind those windows, those walls. But she would snort, smile fondly, and say, "Don't you go thinking that way. This is my house, here. This is my family, understand? Don't worry about me."

She is in none of our family pictures, movies or stills.

* * * *

Mom left us to go alone to Bermuda for six weeks on January 1, 1947. She left on Doctor Truxel's orders, I was told then and for years later, to recuperate from a nervous breakdown. Before leaving, she told me she loved me; she didn't want to leave, but she had to. And she'd be back just as soon as she could.

She'd always said my prayers with me and tucked me in (the "Now I lay me down to sleep,/I pray the Lord my soul to keep . . ." terrified me with its message that I could and might die in my sleep, that my soul was mine only on loan, belonged to "the Lord," and could be taken back at will). We had never been separated before, and, according to Judy (I have no memory of it), for these long days, nights, and weeks, I would cry myself to sleep.

A housekeeper, Mrs. Pinkerton, whom we called "Aunty Pink," was hired; Anna stayed on as live-in maid and cook; Nana Henry visited; and Jack, as man of the house, was responsible for the rest of us. Sixteen, then, he was in his junior year at Haverford; Chuck was in his freshman year; Judy at Friends Central, and me in Kindergarten.

Dad was absent not only to my memory, it turns out, but in fact, having been admitted for alcoholism to the Pennsylvania Hospital

367

Institute in Philadelphia two days after Christmas, where he would board until mid-March. (The dates I know from the monthly hospital bills, which Mom has kept and recently shown me, along with other papers from then.) In reluctant and troubled recollection, and having "thought about it a lot over the years," Jack corroborates the adult facts that Mom has told, at my adult urging and since Dad's death. That Dad's "bad times" were off and on, from 1943 on, but that the worst came after Grandpop's death the fall I started Kindergarten and climaxed on that Christmas Eve, 1946. Before this incident, says Jack, the drinking had been private and secret, even within the family; but this night, downstairs, Dad was drunk and sitting surly during dinner; then after dinner as we trimmed the tree, kids from the neighborhood, Jack's, Chuck's and Judy's friends, came up the front walk, carolling, and Jack was too ashamed to let them in. But Dad jumped up, roaring, and came out on the porch yelling for them to go away. I remember none of this.

According to Mom, Dad had asked her for a divorce the night after his father was buried, July 14, 1946, and she had told him: All right, but not until he'd gotten himself straightened out first; that he was ill; that he needed a doctor. By then his affair with a girl at the factory had been open between them for some time. The girl had started as a clerical helper, and, during the war, would talk to Dad about her dates with sailors. She was a "beautiful young girl," says Mom, "not much older than Jack—she could have been Jack's date, when he was working in there." Before long, she had gotten "under [Dad's] skin"; he wanted Mom to find his fraternity pin and give it back, so he could pin her. He made her his private secretary, even building a private office for her after his father died. She'd call Mom openly at home: "He there?"—at first pretending to be the real estate company, or on some thin pretense of business, but then with no pretense at all. He wanted to marry her, he'd repeat to Mom, and start a new family, since he'd "botched this one so badly"; other times, he was talking and thinking suicide: "I should just go ahead and drive over a cliff. That's the only way I'll ever get over and out of this mess." The girl, meanwhile, just before he finally submitted to treatment, called up to threaten Mom, who had told her flatly she would never grant him a divorce: "Just tell him for me. Tell him I said that he has *compromised* himself, understand?"

All along, with the drinking, once the children were in bed, or supposedly so, Mom and Dad would fight, Dad shouting, threatening, even hitting Mom. From the age of fourteen and younger, Jack would hear them and creep down the hall to listen outside their door (as would Judy, from the back room, without Jack or Mom knowing). Several times, in winter, Dad dragged, shoved and locked Mom out of the house in her nightgown, so that Jack had to help her up the porch and in through the secret window (which was how she'd found out about it). Once Dad actually came at her with a kitchen knife; she knocked it out of his hand and shoved him out the door. He would go into Judy's room and cuddle her drunkenly, so Mom had to pull him out. "He could have burned you," Mom has told me, "chased you with a knife, urinated in an ashtray and up the wall, and next day, he'd have no memory; we'd all go for the Sunday drive, visit his parents . . . " Early on, Jack began to sleep with his squirrel rifle ready under his bed (the gun that Dad had given him), but only once, during one bad fight, did he intervene, aiming the loaded rifle at Dad and telling him to quit, get out, or he'd shoot. "I would have, too," he says now, evenly; "I came that close to being a fourteen-year-old parricide." But Dad, speechless, wide-eyed, had sobered at once, taking in the boy and gun; then turned and left. Otherwise, Mom had handled most of the trouble herself.

But then that fall, 1946, the whole family had caught measles and Mom was run down from lack of sleep. She was taking B-1 shots, sleeping pills, wake up medicines; her teeth, hair, skin, everything had begun to go. She weighed ninety-six pounds. Dr. Truxel sent her to the hospital for a heart test, which showed arhythma. He told her she was "terminal"; she had a bad heart and couldn't live another three months this way. She had to get away, say, to Bermuda. She couldn't take care of four children, and she'd "be away permanently" if she didn't take care of herself. He asked her what was doing this to her, and then had guessed; so she had told him about Dad. At first he told her to get out of the marriage, but when she wouldn't, put her in touch with his friend, Kenneth E. Apple, a psychiatrist connected with the Pennsylvania Hospital. Apple refused to treat Dad while he was still drinking, and called in a Mr. Chambers, who wasn't a doctor, but was with A.A. Chambers talked and met with Dad; and Chambers was the one they called for help on Christmas Day and who took Dad into the Institute, where after drying out, he would spend nights, while continuing to work at the factory. Here, also, he would admit to alcoholism, see Chambers regularly, meet other alcoholics, and read such books as "Alcohol: One Man's Meat" (for which he was billed January 7) and "It's How You Take It" (February 18).

Mom, meanwhile, went ahead with her Bermuda trip as planned. She had made it clear, even before the Christmas trouble, that Dad could not stay with us while he was drinking. She had hired a housekeeper. He could go for treatment or he could stay at a hotel. Her plane left on December 29, and influential friends of her father's sent letters of introduction to influential Bermudians ("Mrs. Henry is the daughter of Mr. Jerome Thralls, a long-time friend of mine who holds a very responsible position in one of our important Government agencies—the RFC. If Mrs. Henry is in need of any guidance during her visit I can think of no one who could be of more help to her than you"), though her father himself, guessing nothing about Dad, assumed that she was leaving the marriage for another man, and sent a Pinkerton detective after her; years later, as executrix of her father's estate, she would be shocked to learn this, coming upon the detective's report in his files.

Aunty Pink I recall resenting as an interloper, who slept in Mom and Dad's room and who consumed all the chocolates that Jack could bring from the factory. We called her our "mickey-mickey" after a demon in a children's book, who sneaked any candy in sight. Besides that, she was self-important, strict and humorless, so we banded together—Anna, as well—to tease and manipulate her, at least in little things. Says Jack, she learned not to tell us to go to bed, but to ask.

I got an ear infection, then, which confined me to bed and grew serious enough that they wired Mom to come home. (The family legend has it that I got sick to make her come back.) Dr. Truxel came and went. He told Jack and Chuck to punch a hole in the end of a grapefruit can and mount a 60 watt lightbulb inside; I was then to hold this can, with the bulb on, constantly to my ear, to keep it hot, which solemnly and scrupulously, I did. If this didn't work, I overheard him tell Jack, I would need an operation. My wallpaper, day after day, became oppressive—a repeating pattern of appletrees, ladders, men picking, and overflowing baskets, which I myself had chosen (come repapering time, I'd also been allowed to scribble and draw with abandon on my walls before the new paper was put on). Anna or Judy would bring me food on trays; Judy would sit with me, read to me, draw; Jack and Chuck would stop in reg-

ularly to cheer me. At the worst of my fever, they had brought me
Mom's special picture, in color—a tiny oval, mounted in gold, covered with glass, and hooked in a wooden case that opened and had
red velvet inside. I would take out the medallion, which felt smooth
and cool, gaze at my beautiful mother with the brown hair, the dark
eyes, then kiss and close it in my hand.

Mom, then, foreign in her suit, and tan, and groomed for the
outside world, was suddenly, actually filling my door, coming in,
taking me up in the bed and holding me—all in one delirious rush.

*   *   *   *

The trip took five or six hours, which seemed all day. Out Lancaster Pike, Route 30 (before there were turnpikes anywhere)
through gentle, rolling Amish country, and cities and towns all the
way, to Harrisburg. Then we'd turn north up two-lane roads, no
towns hardly at all now, only fields, and passing somewhere one long
graveyard, miles long, too long for me to hold my breath at one gulp,
and I would cheat, quietly breathing in or letting out breath without
showing. We carried a milk bottle for me to pee in. We'd watch out
for Burma Shave signs with their staggered messages. And I'd get
cranky and restless, the seat hard; and they'd keep promising, I'd
see the mountains soon. And then we'd come to a place called Lu
Porte, where wooded banks rose from the road, and I'd crane to
look out for the tops; and these were "mountains." They told me to
yawn, so my ears would pop; and Judy, who always got carsick
travelling, would start chewing gum, though the highest Pennsylvania mountain is 3000 feet, if that. But we'd be going up, the road
narrowing, winding and climbing until we came out someplace
where you could look out over the mountains and see the lake itself;
and then, still longer, and we'd arrive at the far end of the lake and
pass a motel called "Snow White and the Seven Dwarfs," where
each cottage was named after a dwarf, then cross a bridge over an
inlet choked with lily pads; then back into trees, so we couldn't see
the water, around, and finally we'd come to downtown Eaglesmere,
with its General Store, Sweetshop, movie theater and board sidewalks, like in cowboy movies, and turn right gently up hill on a
potted macadam road, and to our right would be the lake and
waterfront, beach, rafts, boatdock, changing huts, and a wide expanse of tree-shadowed lawn, like a park, and farther back in the

trees, the little theater building, and up from that, the bowling alley, and then dominating, at the end of the lawn, the long hotel, with its open, awninged porch, where guests sat in deck chairs, gliders, or slatted rocking chairs, looking out over the lake. To our left would be the cottages and yards and dirt side streets, and that was where our cottage was, down one block, right, and up a short way, on its own corner. A shingle over the door read "Buzz Fuzz" in rustic lettering. A parlor, diningroom, and kitchen were downstairs. Upstairs, I had a room to myself, next to Judy's, and we would signal and talk through the wall; Jack and Chuck were across the hall and Mom at the end, past Judy's door. Again, though Dad came up on weekends, I am told, I recall no joy of greeting, nothing we did together, no scene in which he figures.

Occasionally Mom cooked on the cast iron stove, which we'd fuel from a box of chopped logs and kindling out back, where there was also a trash box (bears, raccoons and skunks were said to forage there at night). But usually we took our meals in the big formal diningroom at the hotel, where we had our table assigned, and Jack and Chuck tried to teach me to wet my finger and rub it around the rim of my waterglass, making a high-pitched ringing sound; Chuck was best, as always. For the various courses we had a complex array of knives, forks, and spoons, and I was told to use the outside ones first and work in. For breakfast, I'd get tomato juice, set in the same silver bowl-like things that Mom's or Chuck's grapefruit came in; then eggs and bacon or pancakes, either of which would arrive covered by a silver dome, which you'd lift up and they'd be steaming. For lunch would be salads, fruits, and sandwiches, with soup. We'd have to dress for dinner, and the tables throughout the room would be busier and fuller than for any other meal. Our waiter, one of Chuck's friends, who was interested in Judy, would take our order and disappear through the swinging doors, then emerge with someone else's round tray on high, and we would stare enviously as their plates were uncovered and set out; at last, then, came ours: roast beef au jus, mashed potatoes, and different vegetables; then ice cream for dessert, vanilla for Chuck, chocolate for the rest of us. There may have been finger bowls. Excused, we'd gather dinner mints at the door and head into the lobby, where groups of sofas and easy chairs were arranged like islands, and where, for evening entertainment, in the far corner would be the violin, piano and viola concert—three white-haired musicians playing music that was whiny and interminable—and then, two or three nights each week, the hotel would run a BINGO game.

Behind the hotel, alongside tenniscourts and a deserted sawmill, were the riding stables, where Chuck took me for my first horseback ride. Wearing my Roy Rogers chaps, vest, bandana, hat with chin cord, and capgun, I was granted a Western saddle (they only had two or three; the rest were English), which the stablemaster slung over the back of a "gentle" paint. He boosted me up, adjusted the sheathed stirrups, and told me that only greenhorns grasped the saddlehorn. Chuck, meanwhile, boasting that he was as good a rider as Jack (who had worked in the stable), asked for Flash, a palomino, and the fastest and most spirited of the string, which only the stablemaster himself and a few others could take out. As soon as Chuck was up, the horse pranced, ducked and wheeled. "Sure, sure, I can handle him," Chuck insisted, hauling on the reins. "Yeah, well, go easy," the stablemaster warned. "Don't get him worked up, okay?" Then Chuck took my reins and led me out at a walk, just us two, to the dirt and hoof-mulched trails through the woods and around the lake and back. I was shocked by the casual way his horse lifted its tail and dropped a stream of fresh, round turds, but otherwise, I was intoxicated by the realness of riding, the creaking leather, the sway and plod of living flesh, the shake of head, blow, twitch of hide and ears. I turned and propped myself, arm stiff, hand on the horse's rump, which was as broad and solid as a table. Then, half way around the lake, Chuck handed me my reins and told me to wait; he was going to find out just how much his horse could do. With that he took off down the trail, crouched, kicking with his heels and slashing with the reins and disappeared around a bend; a minute, two, then they were coming back, breakneck, both horse and rider set, intense; then Chuck pulled back, and, standing in his stirrups, posted past me, the horse panting and shiny with sweat. "Jesus, he can run," Chuck announced, sweaty himself and red-faced, as he came up to take my reins. When we got back to the stable, the stablemaster was furious. "What've you been doing with him? Look at him! He's all lathered up!" Unsaddling Flash, he threw a blanket over him; later he would have to curry him down. He swore at Chuck, over Chuck's protests that he hadn't galloped much. "I told you not to gallop. Wise-ass little rich kids. Listen, don't you come round again; you're not riding here again! You want to give him pneumonia?"

The bowling casino, adjoining the hotel, was primarily a teenage hangout, as were the Sweetshop in town and the barn-like movie theater. "Nature Boy" and "The Woody Woodpecker Song," that summer's favorites, played constantly on the jukebox, and there was a deep ice cooler, into which you plunged your arm to fish out *Hi-C* or some other soda. The six alleys gleamed, echoing with the rumble of balls and crash of pins; and the bowlers would grimace, leap and posture as their turns came to perform. Lane 3 was best according to Chuck. Games cost 50 cents, you rented shoes, chose a ball to fit your fingers (we each had numbered favorites, which we sought) and hired or supplied a pin-boy, whom you tipped. Occasionally Chuck worked as a pin-boy, and once or twice, later, I tried, while he, Jack, Mom and Judy bowled. It was hard work. The balls were heavy; you had to clear the fallen pins and stick them into the overhead rack, then lift and send the ball down the return track with enough force to carry it up the alley and make it climb into the bowlers' rack, clunk against the other balls (when I failed to give enough push, the ball stopped halfway, so, embarrassingly, someone had to come get it). Then you scrambled up the padded pit back, out of the way. Chuck's dream was to bowl a perfect 300, and one afternoon he claimed a 290. He would swing the ball back high in the air, until his arm went straight up, then come looping down with his approach steps, a powerful swoop, glide and release, and the ball would hook or slice as he wished and smash into the pins, sometimes for explosive strikes, sometimes for splits, sometimes sending pins leaping and spinning into adjacent alleys. He and Jack always scored over 200, while I rarely made 100 and was usually beaten by Judy and Mom.

Most sunny days, we went swimming or boating, or both. The beach was small, but sandy, with the swimming area divided from the boating by a floating walkway, which joined a diving dock twenty-five yards out, with high and low diving boards and a lifeguard stand. To the left were the boat sheds and docks, where Jack worked, connected to a series of changing rooms, like a triple row of outhouses, each with a bench, coathooks, and a mirror inside the door. We'd take turns changing, Mom and Judy emerging in their bathing suits and caps, and each door locked with a padlock, to which you kept the key. We were a family of good swimmers, rep-

374

utably; and at that summer's waterfront festival, Chuck won the men's butterfly, Judy the junior freestyle, and I came in third in the smallfry race. Jack and Chuck took part in the canoe jousts too, with Chuck jabbing a padded pole at the rival canoes, while Jack maneuvered with his paddle; but soon they were overturned.

With tackle-boxes full of special lures, Jack and Chuck would row out to fish the lake for bass and pike; one memory of my going with them is of being offered one oar, which, when it dug into water, seemed to be pulling through sand; another is of growing restless, as we drifted and they fished; of being warned to sit still or my lightest movement would scare away the fish. More often, I went canoeing with Mom. The boatman (Jack, usually) would slide out a canoe, swing it off the dock into the water, put in paddles and a back rest, then help us in, as the canoe gave and rocked. If Judy came, she'd paddle on one side in front, I'd ride in the middle, and Mom would paddle and steer on the other side in back. With Mom alone, I would ride in the bow, trailing my hand, as she paddled first one side, then the other, and we glided away from the beachfront, out into the deep center of the lake, where there'd be just us, the water lapping, sky, breeze, distance, and the sun, and now and then the hotel launch might pass, leaving us rocking in its wash, or far off we'd see another canoe or sailboat passing. When the day grew hot, we'd head for a "cove" (another new word for me) along the shore, where pine boughs dipped over the water. The rocky bottom would grow visible, then shallows, Mom would ship her paddle, and, holding or parting the branches, we'd slip underneath, to eat our lunch, stretch out in the canoe and nap, eyes closed, canoe gently bobbing, swaying, and overhead the branches closing us from view.

Torrential rain kept us all in Buzz Fuzz one full day, reading, fly-tying, playing card games, listening to the radio, or working on jigsaw puzzles. I'd heard the boys and Judy talk about other storms, other summers, when they had seen lightning "run down the street," something I could neither believe nor imagine, so as thunderclaps intensified and came instantaneously with lightning flashes, I kept my face to the window, holding aside a tasseled, crocheted curtain, and staring out into rain-slashed air, gutters pouring, hail pellets bouncing, when there came a flash and crash and I saw: the incandescent, dancing, jagged branch, like a neon scribble down the water-filled ruts out front; an instant, gone, leaving my eyes ringing from the flash as much as my ears and body from the noise.

That same afternoon, or one like it, perhaps after she had argued with Mom, Judy sat curled on a chaise in the parlor, beneath a reading lamp, and, staring off moodily, insisted that she had been an adopted child; she could never have been born into this family; but that I didn't have to worry, I wasn't adopted.

*　*　*　*

We crashed in heavy rain on the trip home, somewhere between La Porte and Harrisburg. The boys were an hour ahead in the Model A. I was riding in front and Judy in back, painting her nails, when Mom lost control on a curve, the car ran up an embankment into rose bushes, rolled over, and landed back on its wheels, facing forward. I remember the jolt, noise, and tumbling, then finding myself under the dashboard; a choir was singing (we joked later about thinking it was angels, before realizing that the radio had come on) and rain was drumming on the roof. Shaken and dazed herself, Mom demanded how we were, feeling us all over. She had hit her head and cut her arm, and Judy had sprained her wrist against the roof, but I was unhurt. Then Mom got out in the rain, climbed the embankment and disappeared to telephone from a nearby house. We were towed to a crossroads gas station, where after Mom called Dad and Dad had spoken to the mechanic, we waited all afternoon while they worked and banged on the car, up on a lift; we were back underway by nightfall. Jack and Chuck told us that they had skidded on the same curve, which was called "dead-man's curve": and we agreed, repeating the words of the mechanic and policeman, that we'd been "very lucky."

*　*　*　*

During our time away ("the most enjoyable summer I can re-member," Judy calls it in a Baldwin theme), Dad had his relapse. On into that fall, apparently, he was drinking again, involved with the girl still, and asking Mom for a second time for a divorce, which she refused, all of which peaked by Thanksgiving. By then Jack had "flunked out" of Cornell too, and come back home, worried about Mom and the family. Dad told Mom that he was through with her, with Dr. Apple, everything; he was leaving, and had Jack drive him in town to the Warwick; then a few hours later called home and simply said, "Come get me."

The hospital bills show a second stay from Thanksgiving, 1948, through January, 1949, when Mom left for her second Bermuda trip. From Bermuda Mom wrote to Judy, "this time you must feel better having no Aunty Pink and Dad back in his own room again." Dried out, reconciled, he was staying with us, which I myself cannot remember. There is also a letter from Dad to Mom—"The one and only time he ever apologized to me," she said. It is on Judy's blue stationery with the Bloomingdale address. He writes:

Dearest:

I am sitting on the edge of Judy's bed and it is 5 a.m. I haven't been asleep. I don't know where you will be when this letter is handed to you. Maybe I will hand it to you myself, because I will be in Bermuda—where you are. I hope you will forgive my barging in on you like this, but I couldn't wait until you returned to Wayne.

Kay, it has been a long, long detour, and I have been badly lost on the way, but I now feel that I have both feet on the main road for the rest of my life. I believe that I am finally the man you expected when you married me.

I hope I am not too late, because I love you with all of my heart, soul, and body. I want the chance to prove it to you "until death do us part."

John

P.S. I think maybe it was meant to happen this way—to make a man out of me.

He had been in full analysis with Apple and shaken by an EKG which showed brain damage. Despite his initial doubts, Apple is quite satisfied with Dad's progress and wires Mom in Bermuda on January 27: "Things fine. Very pleased last visit and trip. Don't discuss past considerations. Best wishes."

They bought the St. Davids house a few months later, as if to dramatize the new beginning and cut ties to the Bloomingdale past. Dad's cousin, Mahlin Rossiter, the carpenter, was working on the house by April and Alfred Reahm, the decorator, papering, painting and sanding floors in May. We moved in the fall, 1949, when I also started third grade, moving from the Primary to the Grammar school building, and riding my bike the mile to school, each way, or walking, since we still lived too close for me to qualify for the schoolbus.

I am eight.

At this point my memories of my father begin.

* * * *

Nominated by Elizabeth Inness-Brown and Lloyd Schwartz

INTERPRETATION OF A POEM BY FROST

by THYLIAS MOSS

from EPOCH

A young black girl stopped by the woods,
so young she knew only one man: Jim Crow
but she wasn't allowed to call him Mister.
The woods were his and she respected his boundaries
even in the absence of fence.
Of course she delighted in the filling up
of his woods, she so accustomed to emptiness,
to being taken at face value.
This face, her face eternally the brown
of declining autumn, watches snow inter the grass,
cling to bark making it seem indecisive
about race preference, a fast-to-melt idealism.
With the grass covered, black and white are the only options,
polarity is the only reality; corners aren't neutral
but are on edge.
She shakes off the snow, defiance wasted
on the limited audience of horse.
The snow does not hypnotize her as it wants to,
as the blond sun does in making too many prefer daylight.
She has promises to keep,
the promise that she bear Jim no bastards,
the promise that she ride the horse only as long
as it is willing to accept riders,

the promise that she bear Jim no bastards,
the promise to her face that it not be mistaken as shadow,
and miles to go, more than the distance from Africa to Andover,
more than the distance from black to white
before she sleeps with Jim.

Nominated by Stuart Freibert

PARTY

fiction by JOYCE CAROL OATES

from THE BOSTON REVIEW and THE ASSIGNATION (Ecco Press)

JUDITH LAMBERT WAS dying at last. She had come home from the
Medical Center for the fifth and final time in how many months?—
eighteen?—since her cancer was first diagnosed. But the Institute
party was scheduled for that night, the handwritten invitations sent
out weeks ago, so they were at the party, Judith's many friends and
a number of her colleagues from the Bedminister Choir College,
where Judith had taught voice for fifteen years, how sad they were
saying, how tragic, she is such a young woman,—forty-seven: and
looks ten years younger despite the chemotherapy—gathered about
the long candlelit table where plates of hors d'oeuvres were set
amidst coolly fragrant spring flowers, daffodils, jonquils, hyacinth,
taking up Swedish meatballs on toothpicks, jumbo shrimp dipped in
Mexicali hot sauce (Take care, the director's wife warns,—that sauce
is hot), how lovely everything looks tonight, and this wine, this is
superb wine, German, is it? and how delicious the stuffed mush-
rooms, did you make these yourself, Isabel? Judith Lambert's spring
concert last year was a great success everyone said, I wasn't able to
get to it myself because I had to be out of town, yes you missed a
lovely concert Judith sang songs by Schumann, Schubert, Fauré, I
think, miniatures, most of them, such a fine clear beautiful voice
she had, something plaintive about it, not strong of course, not
powerful, once I heard her sing that Mozart aria "Bella mia fiamma"
and you could tell she'd reached her limit but she had a haunting
voice, it's all such a pity. Judith's daughter was saying, Mother?—
please, Mother?—are you awake, Mother? The bedroom was papered in a floral design, fine-patterned, French silk, lavender, soft

381

green, ivory, matching bedspread and a thick ivory carpet. Ginny Mullin had visited her the week before, it's so sad she said, tears welling in her eyes, yes she has changed a good deal now, she looks so frail, so thin, thank God her daughter is with her, and thank God for morphine. A new couple had just entered the hall, shaking hands with the Institute director Dr. Max and his wife Isabel, tall flaxen-haired sharp-eyed Isabel, if you decline one of her invitations she will never invite you back. That dinner party Judith gave at Christmas,—there must have been twenty of us and she tried to do it all herself, not even a student to help in the kitchen, of course it was a buffet, and not so much trouble: but still. And do you know I never got around to inviting her back, this season has been sheer madness, we were in Minneapolis, and we were in Atlanta, and where else, Los Angeles of course. I am reminded of a line from a play, or is it a poem, *Shall I ever have time to die?* the heroine asks. Her doctor said she'd have a year to live with the treatments, I think that was terribly blunt, and cruel, don't you,—and wrong by about six months too. She has been taking chemotherapy off and on all this time and the wonder of it is, her hair, her lovely hair, didn't fall out: can you imagine Judith without her lovely red hair? So brave, such a model of courage, endurance, such a vital attitude toward the future,—this cheese is exquisite, is it some kind of Italian cheese— *this* is goat cheese, Mark you must try it—her attitude was so positive it was daunting sometimes, the way she spoke of the future, plans for next year's concert series at Bedminister, and the year *after*, Mark says it was a necessary blindness, a kind of denial, where did you get this pate, Isabel?—it's duck isn't it?—That little store on Charity Street, off South Street, do you know the one I mean? Yes I've seen it but I haven't gone inside. I feel so bad about Judith, that lovely party she gave and I never invited her back, it's so awkward with a single woman at a sit-down dinner don't you think. Did I tell you, Mark is flying to Johannesburg on Monday, some sort of confidential government business, I'm concerned there will be a civil war while he's there and he won't be able to get out. Judith looked so lovely at the Christmas concert, directing the women's choir, that white dress she wore that looked like an antique dress,—full-skirted, flounced, with ruffles at her throat, long sleeves, lacy cuffs—I think it was to disguise the fact she'd lost so much weight. Oh just the *Messiah* I think—the usual. Yes it was a shame about Rod leaving her but it seems to have worked out for the best, Judith was the happiest I've ever seen her after the divorce came through, there's no bitterness between them that anyone ever noticed, though there must have been some emotion involved, you can't be married for twenty years without some emotion being involved, yes but the daughter is grown up, all our children are grown up. Have you noticed, it has happened so quickly: all our children are grown up, and most of them are moved away. A faint sickle moon was shining through the tall leaded windows of the Institute's main hall, where one hundred guests were gathered, and a string quartet played in a corner, on a raised platform edged with flowers. In the din of voices no one could hear the music but the musicians, good sports from the Bedminister school, played briskly on: something by Beethoven, it sounded like. Is that the moon? Where? In the trees. There. The moon?—I don't think so, it looks like one of the lights in the parking lot. Mother, said Judith's daughter,—can you hear me? Are you awake? Mother I love you, Judith's daughter said, but it wasn't clear that Judith heard. The skin around her eyes looked stitched, bruised pouches beneath the eyes, it must be the mask of death since Judith is dying but her daughter stands transfixed unable to judge. I remember Roslyn Lambert when she was a little girl passing plates of hors d'oeuvres at one of their parties, a lawn party it was, Rod and Judith certainly gave the impression of being happily married then, such an attractive couple, Judith looked like one of those pre-Raphaelite women, you know the ones I mean, didn't that artist who lived in the Hawleys' coach house paint her?— and what came of the portrait, I wonder? His new wife is very sweet they say though I've never met her, one of his graduate students evidently. Doesn't time pass swiftly now! And incessantly! They were talking of the new women's choir director, the blond young woman from Juilliard whose husband is assistant dean at the Seminary. An attractive young couple but there are so many attractive young couples these days. Thank you so *much* Isabel for inviting us. Thank *you* for coming but isn't it a little early to be leaving? I called Judith last week but Roslyn said she was sleeping and couldn't be disturbed, she spoke rather sharply to me, I thought, I *was* a bit hurt, after all I've been a friend of Judith's for so long and was one of the first people Judith told. Max said he'd bought a case of this by way of that dealer in Pennsfield, Bernkasteler Doktor Auslese 1982, not what you'd call cheap but it was a bargain. The funeral will be next week probably, and the memorial service has to be planned, not until May I suppose. Did you go to Dr. Emory's memorial?—it was fairly well attended but I was surprised at the people missing you'd have expected to see there. He was so well loved, his students adored him. That's usually the case, this time of year. It's madness this time of year. I'm committed to a conference in Geneva next week I wish I could get out of, a week-long session in Tokyo next month, loans and financing for the Third World, more of the same thing, the situation is hopeless and getting worse but don't quote me. Is Judith's daughter with her? No? I thought someone said she was. She *is?* I heard they'd hired a private nurse, I guess you have to, in cases like this, dying at home, poor Judith, but at least she's in comfortable surroundings, and where is Rod?—He won't dare miss the funeral but he hasn't visited her in a year. He's very big, they say, at La Jolla: found his niche at last. Did Florence tell you, they're having a reception for the French ambassador next week, I hope there isn't going to be an awkward conflict with the funeral. Judith closed her skeletal fingers around her daughter's wrist and seemed about to smile as she so frequently did though her eyes flashed with panic but this time she did not smile, she whispered, Help me, and her daughter said, I'm right here, Mother, I'm not going to go away. A faint moon through the window, in the trees beyond the house, hazy like the lamplight in the room, the only light burning, filtered through the fluted flesh-colored shade. Our new astrophysicist is being wooed by the California Institute of Technology already, did you hear?—it's outrageous. Everyone bids on the stars and no one much wants the others. I hope I won't be out of town for the party, this time of year is such madness. Are those dogwood sprays? Apple blossom? So lovely. Shall I ever have time to die, she wondered. She was staring into a corner of the room where friends with the look of strangers were talking and laughing loudly. Someday yes. Judith's daughter dialed the number she knew by heart and said into the receiver, calm as words said many times, I think she has died. Yes. A few minutes ago. The funeral will be this week, the memorial service in early May, we'll have to get together with those boring Bedminister people to plan it. At the door Ginny Mullin squeezed my hand and whispered in my ear, the invitations should be in the mail by next Friday but remember: keep the night of May 11 open. For us.

Nominated by Philip Booth

EXPLANATIONS

By JUDSON MITCHAM

from THE GETTYSBURG REVIEW

A boy holds a blown glass sparrow in his hand
and can't resist testing one finger against
a clear, fragile wing. When it gives,
the child looks up at his mother. As if
to revise what has happened, he explains:
he didn't press hard enough to snap it. The crippled
figure is to blame.

               And when Nietzsche went insane,
when he buried his bushy face deep in the neck
of a horse whipped hard in the street, of course
there was someone to haul out the photograph
of Nietzsche himself hitched up to a cart
driven by the woman he had loved, the young
Salome wielding a whip.

                    I remember
Jesus' explanation to his puzzled disciples
of his speaking in parables. Otherwise, he said,
the heathen would understand too, and they
would also be saved. I have always believed
Jesus had a zany sense of humor.

                  Consider
the way we are taught and defeated, at once,
when a thought angles back on itself,
as when Plato alleges that Socrates lies
with every single word from his mouth, and then
Socrates owns up, holding, with a smile,

that Plato has spoken the truth.
                              I recall
my son and his best friend, each one lost
in his own loud monologue, rolling their battered
matchbox cars down the driveway.
My son said, "History can start any time."
And his friend fell silent, appearing to ponder
how history is born,

then shook his head yes, as if something were settled,
as though he had understood fires, freak wrecks,
leukemia and early, slow death well enough
to start off walking down the hill, not saying
just anything he happened to think of.

Nominated by Mark Jarman

COUPON FOR BLOOD

fiction by SANDY HUSS

from TRIQUARTERLY

For a brain, Phin had to cope with hard baked clay. This he owed to his maker, who—though he had blown Phin up tight as a rubber raft, inspiring every chamber of his body with pure and lucid air— hadn't thought to give Phin much of anything else. In the beginning, moist and infused with oxygen, the lush gritty clay of his cerebrum had been good enough to eat, rich in salubrious minerals— food, indeed for thought. But from the time Phin turned thirteen he had tried to jazz it up, had bled out the air, had baked and fired, with the result that now his head rattled with potsherds and jagged bits of roofing tile. Occasionally his inner eye, working like the mirrors of a kaleidoscope, trained itself upon this chaos, reflecting some seeming order out of this substance for thinking that could no longer support a thought. But the mirrors too had been damaged over the years, their silver scratched and charred, so that the images they presented were crazed and dim, and what passed in this brain for memories, information or ideas were often chimerical—and sometimes alien even to Phin who had given them birth.

But he had no doubts about what he saw just then. Even from the box canyon of the bus's back seats, Phin could tell that a coupon for blood waited to board. While the driver (out on the street, babysitting her children over the phone) held the pay-phone's metal cord to her heart, the coupon for blood kept its tail to the wind. While the passengers already aboard the idling bus clucked to each other about company time, the coupon for blood stamped its feet and pressed its great hooked fingers to its lips. Phin, temporarily out of the late

387

November cold and agog that a coupon for blood was headed his way, hugged himself and clapped the soles of his sneakered feet.

Everyone waited while the driver changed a diaper over the phone. She wiped her fingers over and over through the hair at her temple, explaining to her daughter how to charge the safety pin with static, so that the pin—filmed with deposits of urea or not— would glide. Phin didn't mind the delay: as long as a nine-year-old struggled to pierce layered folds of diaper without stabbing her infant sister, as long as she fumbled against the tension of the gaping pin, Phin could picture himself stretched out on a narrow table, tethered only by dreams of what his pint of blood (worth two bucks more than usual, once he got his hands on the coupon) would buy.

Next to lying on the table itself, nothing made Phin more light-hearted than imagining himself there, his blood draining through a rubber tube that lay in a loop across his forearm like an out-of-body vein, the loop counter-balancing the drag of gravity that sucked his red and white cells into a little plastic pouch. At the same time that the loop's weight kept the end of the hollow needle buried in his skin, its precise curve prevented the tube from kinking and imped- ing the flow. Every technician at every blood bank made the same loop, as regular as a coil in a handwriting exercise, as practiced and legible (even to Phin for whom sentences had become a chore) as an *l* or *e*, rising and backtracking across his forearm, one after another, for as many months and years as his marrow could crank the he- moglobin out. Phin reveled in the regeneration of his blood. It was a wonderful world, he thought, that would give him money for something he couldn't hold in his hand.

When Phin slapped his feet together, Deedee, catty-corner across the aisle, had been startled and relieved. Until then she had read in his face prostitution and unrelenting pain. Phin was ravish- ingly poor: his skin, the color of a tarnished penny, clung to his cheekbones, and his sparse curly lashes tossed diaphanous veils before his eyes. His cheap tight pants bound his thighs and genitals, and his skimpy T-shirt, its pieces stamped out haphazardly along the bias by machine, hung in a skewed line that barely covered him. He was nineteen, Deedee's age, and his remaining beauty had the fragility of a pear ripe too long by a day, a pear whose skin is still thin and promising, still so primed to yield that the gentlest thumb- smear can skim it away, but whose flesh beneath is pocked with

rotting translucence so that it no longer tempts the tongue, so that
its only use is a matrix for seed. Sitting modestly upright, his tapered fingers caging his knees, Phin had seemed to Deedee to be
awaiting absolution, to be dogged by regret for having loosed all evil
upon the world. Deedee (white, enrolled in one of the better state
universities, and hungry for her lunch) had been glum, having recently been taught how she caused Phin's poverty, how it profited
her. She took heart at his little leap.

She was so relieved that she unzipped the knapsack propped
between her feet and felt through it until something crackled in her
hand. With both hands buried in the knapsack she forced apart
stubborn cellophane welds. Casually she lifted a barbecued chip to
her lips. Even as she broke its back with her teeth she knew she was
rude, but now that Phin wasn't starving there was only one other
person near enough for Deedee to offend—a woman of fifty, straight
across the aisle—who probably already thought of Deedee as a slob:
the older woman was magnificent. Black as basalt with a cast of blue,
her skin seemed to have just lately cooled, and the light in her eyes
suggested that she yet smoldered within. Katy (for that was her
name) had anchored herself in her seat with her severe Etta Jenicks,
with her own sense of worth.

Even when a bus is idling, its backmost passengers brace themselves. In the bench seats above the wheels, they, like Deedee and
Katy, like Deedee and Phin, face each other—usually there are
mothers with strings of children (and strollers that won't collapse),
indigents and evangelists, high-school kids with graffitied notebooks, sometimes a bold unattended child—and they brace themselves against their own sidelong hurtling, unrestrained by each
other's arms (even if arms were offered, there'd be too much open
space in which to fall). They brace themselves against their roll to
the front like so many thudding cabbages, where they would lie in
a heap beneath a box of shifting coins.

This bus made its last stop within two blocks of the Greyhound
station, and Katy—like Deedee—was headed there: beneath her
seat a gray cardboard suitcase lay, ancient and ungainly, like something beached and stoically smothering beneath its own weight.
Deedee, untucked and overslept, her student pallor unvaried by
any blush of health, her own luggage a collection of knapsacks and
canvas bags splotched with coffee and ballpoint ink—felt she must

seem a flibbertigibbet in Katy's eyes. The woman was a monolith. How had she made that of herself? Deedee wanted her approval, but saw no chance of it, so pulled the little cellophane bag out into the open and munched away. The chips were stale, but Deedee accepted their staleness as a punishment: they were half gone by the time the driver and the coupon for blood climbed aboard.

Deedee, not in the market herself, naturally didn't realize that a coupon for blood was about to enter her life. She saw only middle-aged Harper in his green all-weather coat, clamping the *Post-Dispatch* under his arm. He must habitually have carried a paper there: a smeary stain had swallowed his armpit and spread halfway down his side. Deedee had the meanness of spirit to be ashamed of him, being guilty of such carelessness herself: she often left a thumbprint of chocolate or cheese dust on a library page. She sometimes felt that at any moment she too could become a walking stain.

For the length of the aisle Harper ducked his head, one hand lifting his green plaid hat by the crown—in obeisance to the ladies, it seemed. Yet he swaggered at the same time, trilled unselfconsciously, and flapped his hand in the pocket of his coat so violently that the hem knocked away Deedee's little cellophane bag. She said, "Hey!"— but as she spoke, Harper heedlessly punted the chips all the way to the back of the bus, and as Deedee said, "Hey!" again, Harper stepped on the bag, pivoting as he sat down on the bench that faced the front. Barbecued crumbs spilled from the bag's mouth beneath his shoe.

Deedee rolled her eyes and gave out an exaggerated sigh. She saw Katy turn her face toward the back of the driver's head. At least they were finally on their way.

Harper dropped his paper next to himself on the seat within reach of Phin, who—oblivious to Deedee's little disaster—bent toward the newsprint dotingly. He'd been prepared to change his seat if necessary, but the coupon had come straight at him.

"So sorry." Harper lifted his hat to Deedee, higher than before, revealing an oily baldness marked by parallel tracks of surgical scar. They ran from his eyebrows across his crown toward his nape as if he were a waxwork whose pate had served as a toy truck's proving ground. His hat back on, he bent over and with fastidious fingers swept the broken chips, a cigarette filter and a scrap of religious tract into the bag. Meanwhile, Phin's hand hovered above the neglected paper, but he did not touch.

Harper held the little bag out to Deedee, who took it, though she pinched it by a corner, dangling it away from herself like someone else's trash. She looked over at Katy. Katy looked down.

"Shit." Deedee glowered at the floor.

Harper raised a disciplinary finger in the air. "No smoking, food or drink," he said, ticking his finger toward the posted rule. Ignoring the covetous Phin, Harper selected a section of his paper and snapped it open with a sharp crack, sealing himself away behind it as if the bus were his own living room. Poor Phin, the drudge wife, inclined toward the newsprint, his eyes bashful and full of need, one hand with its long fingers just barely raised.

Behind that paper Harper's flesh was pulpy, his skin squamous, and his chemical sweat might have come straight from the embalmer's gun, but he thought of himself as oozing vitality. Living either on the street or in the bin, he rarely saw himself in anything besides window glass or bumper chrome, but even if Harper's world had been filled with highly polished mirrors, his clamminess would have registered with himself as a glow. Harper had been repeatedly doctored: he almost always felt good.

Now that he had taught that girl a lesson he felt wonderful, and his face flushed with righteous blood—some of which (as you might expect) had once streamed (though with different perceptions) through poor Phin's arteries and veins. Last summer Harper had lectured a less docile mark than Deedee: a hospital attendant bearing Harper's dinner on a tray. The young man had taken offense at the word *Jigaboo*, and couldn't be persuaded to approve it even after Harper explained that he had been set down on the planet expressly to assign the lower animals their names. The attendant likewise could not credit *Shine*, *Smoke*, *Junglebunny* or *Coon*, and didn't give a rat's ass what Harper had been taught in Sunday School. By the time the other workers separated the attendant from his heavy tray, Harper had lain in a coma and a slick of gore.

Harper remembered none of this, had even momentarily forgotten his mission to name (which he usually forgot when he took his Mellaril instead of trading it for sex or food), but that was how it had come to be that Harper had been transfused, that it was in part Phin's blood that Harper's heart now pumped, first to his lungs, then to his spackled brain, giving him a magnanimous idea.

"Here's the sports page, buddy," he said to Phin. "You can keep it, I'll just throw it away." He went back behind the business section, which he pretended to read.

Phin held the paper up in front of himself at arm's length as if it were sheet music and he would momentarily begin to sing. But he spoke, instead, in a voice that was soft and musical. "Does this have here a coupon for blood?"

Harper feigned absorption in the world of commerce for a moment, but then folded down the paper, "Well, I don't know . . . a coupon for blood?"

"Yeah. For two dollars."

"What do you want to buy blood for?"

Katy and Deedee looked for a heartless instant at each other, then away.

"Not buy. Sell."

"With a coupon they give you two dollars?"

"They give you eight dollars, but with a coupon they give you two more."

"Ten dollars?"

Phin poked around his broken brain, looking first at eight dollars, then at two. He couldn't bring them together in any way, but he didn't want to disagree. He smiled slowly, keeping his lids down for a moment, then raising them languidly. Phin had sold sex as well as plasma, and could say yes wordlessly.

Harper didn't smile in return. "Well, you can look." He withdrew behind his paper and sat very still.

Phin peeled open his allotted section, still holding it at arm's length, still sitting expectantly straight. As he paged through, the bell rang, and an old woman in the middle of the bus who had been facing the front stood up, walked toward the back, and waited in the stairwell near the back door. She held a sack of groceries against her hip, and took a long look at the two raised walls of newsprint that were Harper and Phin. "Huh," she said, and got off.

Just as she closed the door behind the woman, the driver perceived a presence in her womb. From the time she'd been an adolescent she had set her inner ear to listen for change, so that even sleeping her body had always known when to wake itself with the news that she was about to bleed. And now she heard a familiar burgeoning, the forbidding sound of the division that is multiplication, and she knew what she had known for several days. For a long while this sound would only get louder, its frequency higher, until the train of transformations that would bring her new baby to her had passed. For a moment she allowed tears to gather, but by the time she had pulled back out into traffic and begun to inventory the cupboards at home (planning what her eldest could fix for lunch), her eyes were dry.

Phin had some ideas about the coupon: a shape, some dotted lines, its location on the page: someone, he was sure, had recently shown him one. There would be a cross in each corner of a rectangle, he thought. Crosses hung before his mind's eye as if he had just sped past a family plot on the open road, could still see tracers of gold and blue.

He studied every page. The fine print of the box scores snaked before his bloodshot eyes. He squinted for some time at a photograph wherein a man holding a soccer ball seemed to be sitting on another man's head, a flagpole growing out of his own. Phin forgot for a horrible moment what he was looking for, but then he remembered, and felt a glow of good fortune returning to surround him like a divine cloud that would protect him and show him the way. A clip-and-save box in the classifieds gave his heart a little thrill, but there were no crosses, and the bold *WORD PROCESSING* meant, Phin was positive, that the coupon had nothing to do with him. There were pages of cars for sale, and Phin's eyes sucked the names of some of them into his crumbling brain: Phoenix, Aries, Delta 88. Electra . . . Electra . . . Phin had ridden once in a midnight-blue Electra—or had he just leaned on it in a blue and midnight street?

The coupon wasn't here. Phin took his bearings by looking through a film of pomade on the window: they hadn't yet reached the numbered streets. He had seen Harper somewhere before, he was sure, maybe on this very bus. He bet that Harper would ride with him to the end of the line. There was plenty of paper still to check, and he had five— maybe six—more miles. Phin trued up the corners of the sports section, folded it precisely and balanced it on his knees, waiting for Harper to notice him.

And Harper lowered his paper as if he had not been reading at all.

With Harper's eye on him, Phin spoke again, a music box in Harper's hands. This was as clear to Harper as it was to Deedee and Katy, more clear perhaps, because polluted by chemicals he was free to see the delicate porcelain ballerina twirling in Phin's throat. It gave him great pleasure to arouse such attentiveness and modesty

in Phin, as if he were, by tiny increments, leading him from bar-
barism to light. Phin sounded more and more angelic to Harper's
ear: "Would you mind if I just checked those?"

Phin pointed to the stack of paper on the seat, but Harper knew
better than to relinquish anything. "I'll see if it's in here," he said,
and flipped through the business section so fast that the back of the
bus filled with the flapping of gigantic wings. "There's no coupon for
blood in here, buddy. There's nothing in here but the Dow Jones."
Harper shrugged his shoulders with a crackling of paper and withdrew again.

Phin brought the pads of his fingers together in imitation of the
Praying Hands. Very slowly he turned his head away from Harper to
look outside. Twenty-first street. When he checked back, Harper
was watching him. "What about those?"

Harper, affected by Phin's pretty smile—a smile that Harper
would like to keep on Phin's face if he could—graciously picked
through the paper at his side and handed one more section over. "I
guess you can have this, buddy. I'll just throw this away."

Deedee opened her mouth with a click of her tongue and a quick
intake of breath, but closed it again and turned red.

Katy covertly kept an eye on her. Deedee had a pointed chin and
two dark moles—one above each corner of her mouth—that gave her
face a catlike triangularity. Her slit-eyed twitching heightened the
effect: she seemed as tortured as a house cat spying on a pair of
warring toms from the wrong side of a screen—the stink of hot fur,
the sight of backs bristling and humped cause her heart to pound,
oxygen to crowd her cells, and blood to stream, messianic, through
her veins. But she sits, contained, on a windowsill, slapping at
it with her tail, raising nothing but backlit, floating motes. Once
the fight moves down the block she'll throw herself down from the
window and charge—dishing throw rugs one after another out of
her way—as far in one direction as the walls of her house will
permit, then wheel and take another tack, crash behind the couch
and end tables, bruise herself against the furniture.

Deedee for now was still at the window, and the poor stymied
thing kept sneaking looks at Katy, wanting Katy to nanny her, wanting Katy to nanny the whole bus. But Katy intended to let those
nasty boys run *each other* ragged—she had problems of her own.

Phin began to page through a thick sheaf of department-store ads
as daintily as he had waded through the sports, and Deedee's heart

went out to him. Someone who could read ought to step in. Phin, scrawny as he was, probably shouldn't be peddling drop one, but Deedee wanted him to do—to have—whatever he desired, for reasons even she was suspicious of: his blackness, his wasted beauty, that bastard Harper's lunacy. Deedee still clutched her trashed bag of chips out of a horror of littering. Yes, she wanted that smug son-of-a-bitch—crazy or not—to do the generous thing. She imagined herself commandeering the paper, finding—or not finding, definitively—the damn coupon. But every reaction she anticipated from Harper was withering. She couldn't bear to give him an opening.

If Deedee's mother had still been alive, Deedee would have had more to offer than the heroics of a busybody. If Deedee's mother had still been alive, Deedee wouldn't have been headed back to school the day after Thanksgiving with nothing in her luggage but half a round-trip bus ticket and a desiccated, bloodless meal: she had rice cakes and peanut butter left, stuff suited to the fitful stomach of chemotherapy. (The barbecued chips, Deedee figured, must have been a whim, mentioned by her mother wistfully, fetched by husband or son in a hell-bent car, then rejected from a pit of nausea.)

If Deedee's mother had still been alive, Deedee would have had a couple pounds of turkey in tow, half an apple-cake and a fistful of cold hard cash—the price of her bus ticket and then some. But though Deedee had cooked the holiday meal, she had left it all behind, sure that control over the family larder didn't transfer to the temporary help. Taking the leavings of her mother's restricted diet couldn't possibly offend—no one still living in her father's house considered it food.

If Deedee had asked her father for groceries, for cash, he doubtless would have given her enough to tide her over until her check for workstudy came in Monday's mail. But unless she asked, her father seemed to assume that she could chow down on the intellectual breeze. Her mother had been dead now for months, it was not as if her father were still hazy with grief. Deedee was simply out of sight—even when *in* sight—out of mind. She felt too insubstantial to ask for a loan. Deedee had expected to miss her mother when she died, but she hadn't expected that her mother's death would give birth to her own poverty.

Musing in this vein, Deedee hid from herself the fact that she had what Phin was looking for: in the shape of a two-dollar bill, a bill so new and crisp it could have held knife pleats. She kept it folded within a concealed compartment in her wallet, safe from even her own emergency. As far as Deedee was concerned it was a relic that wouldn't spend.

By the time her mother died, the sick woman's purse had long been out of her control, her cash spent on grieving people's groceries, her lists of things to do ticked off by grieving people's hands. Deedee had often carried the purse itself from house to hospital to market; her brothers had taken out their mother's wallet and crammed it into their jacket pockets; everyone in the family had had occasion to dig through the linen and leather bag: tallying check stubs, tracking down rolls of film and dry-cleaning or reading off strings of numbers from insurance cards. Her mother's purse had been an open book. So when Deedee, boxing things for the Goodwill, had discovered a stash of two- dollar bills wedged in the wallet's plastic album between a list of clinic phone numbers and an organ donor card, she had been annoyed with herself that she hadn't noticed it before. The little lump of cash wasn't so little that it shouldn't have been obvious all along.

With the lump unfolded and four two-dollar bills laid out on the floor, Deedee had felt contempt for her mother as she had suddenly felt contempt for all people who refuse to honor a certain kind of currency—then end up holding it all. People with caches of fifty-cent pieces and Susan B. Anthony coins, people whose imagination limited money to denominations for which there were slots in cash registers and vending machines. But at the same time she had felt a loopy joy that her mother had left this weird legacy. Like the marvelous irrelevancy of the donor card, the money seemed a symbol to Deedee that her mother had intended to save her own life— but Deedee blushed at the thought of saying as much to her father or to his sons. So she kept a single bill for herself and stuffed the rest inside the stand for her mother's best wig, which she hid in an attic trunk.

Everyone on that bus but Phin had at least two dollars, but everyone's money was already spent. The driver's roll of quarters was destined for pay-phones, and the woman wearing a sweatsuit would need the four ones in her pocket for a box of tampons—soon. The woman with blue hair, who had just gotten on, and who was painstakingly threading her gauzy headscarf through the top buttonhole of her coat, had only her weekly allowance from her sister for Bingo cards. The guy carrying a new fire extinguisher was saving to straighten his kid's teeth, and the couple reading the Bible together wanted someday to have furniture in their living room. Even Harper's three dollars from selling his Elavil (which was supposed to counteract his Mellaril) had been budgeted for lunch at Burger King. Phin may have had no cash, but then he had only a few needs that he could remember, and he took solace in what Deedee found appalling: he was a walking factory of sex and blood. He was always on line. And he knew he would get the coupon, it was meant to be.

Katy had more money on her than the rest of the riders combined—and it never occurred to her to share it with Phin. She needed it to put up her daughter's bail. Their phone conversation had been unsatisfactory because they'd been whispering on both ends of the line—her daughter to thwart her guard, Katy to let her husband sleep—but Katy knew for sure that her daughter had been picked up driving a stolen car, a car she had thought belonged to her new boyfriend. Her daughter had known he was AWOL—had even, she admitted, mostly approved—but she had never once doubted that the car was his. That much she had promised Katy, in an insistent whisper Katy had to believe.

Even from two states away, her daughter could fill Katy with disappointment and self-reproach, from two states away she could make Katy's wallet gurgle like an open drain. In the past year Katy had bought eyeglasses when her daughter's prescription changed, neutered her adopted cats, kept up the insurance on her car. Now this.

Her daughter seemed to have been spun out of her, but never to have detached from her, seemed in fact to contain *her* now, like a cocoon. As her daughter grew older, it was Katy who changed, who was forced to embrace her daughter's chaos if she were to embrace her daughter at all. Katy supposed it was inevitable that her daughter would lead a fitful and struggling life, having spent her childhood in Katy's steady shade. For her daughter Katy could leave her husband this once. He would survive: he loved the pork-chop sandwiches they made at the neighborhood bar.

Phin's progress through the paper went more and more slowly; he had to look repeatedly over his shoulder out the window—they were nearing the end of the line. The more the fragments of crockery in

Phin's head tried to piece together a vessel that could contain Harper, the more Phin remembered Harper saying he loved him, saying that Phin was a beautiful bitch. Phin remembered Harper's pulse quickening, Harper's fingers at Phin's nape kneading Phin's hair. Harper had never *had* such raunchy sex before, he had said, that had been the *most lewd* experience of his entire life, Phin was a Grade A, floor-licking, cock-sucking whore.

Even if Harper hadn't tipped Phin while he still knelt at Harper's feet (without Phin having to dogtrot after him, flirting and begging just a bit), Phin would have remembered Harper fondly, would have preened himself over being called Grade A. It was what he had always thought about himself, when he could still think—that he was choice.

And here again was that smitten man.

That it might have been someone other than Harper who had been so good to him, Phin had no reason to believe. It seemed likely enough, as likely as the coupon itself, as likely as its ultimate transfer to his own hands. Phin had the optimism of bad memory. He shifted his seat next to Harper and looked up into his face. Harper had loved him once, he was sure. "Look," Phin said, thumping a health-club ad, "it looks something like this here."

Harper let the business section crumple in his lap as if his weary arms couldn't support it any more. "Buddy," he said, "it ain't in here, I looked."

Harper felt the high drama of his beleaguerment, of his duty to be magnanimous and kind. He looked around for an audience. The girl and the nigger woman both looked at their hands, but the bus driver had an eyebrow cocked at him in the rearview mirror. Harper panicked: they were at the end of the line. Harper hated to give the driver a reason to cast her evil eye his way. "Sorry, buddy," he said, and scooped together his paper, including the sections he'd given to Phin. He lurched out the back door, holding onto his hat as he stepped into the wind. He heard Phin's footsteps behind him, rubber soles as hard as old erasers clunking on the stairs, but Harper didn't look back.

With the men's departure, Deedee roused herself, folded the chip bag over and over at one end, and stuffed it into the pocket of her parka where it slowly opened, making tiny rustles and pops as she gathered her book bags. With the men's departure, she had a little trouble believing what she'd just heard and seen. If she'd only done something, she'd know how it all turned out. When she got to the stairwell, she saw that in her bending and leaning she'd been hogging the aisle, making Katy wait to draw her suitcase from beneath her seat. Deedee might not be able to help anyone, but at least she shouldn't be getting in their way. She sighed and shrugged piteously, but refused to let herself wait for any look of tolerance—let alone forgiveness—in Katy's eyes.

She started down the stairs, and there was Phin in the street, bouncing up and down, a parade-struck child, one moment craning his head to watch Harper zigzag down the street like a pigeon, the next moment eyeing the door of the bus. He was waiting, it turned out, for her.

He looked up at her and showed his teeth, but his eyes were flat and expressionless, their color that of raw liver, of clotted menstrual blood. "Help me, baby," he said.

Deedee couldn't understand what Phin wanted from her, it was too late, she had nothing, she was no match for Harper after all. But as she stood in the stairwell struggling with an answer for him, she became transfixed by the sudden knowledge of the two-dollar bill in her wallet, by the sound of her mother's hands folding it, by the image of the full white moons rising on the horizons of her mother's fingernails. Deedee felt that she could never step off the bus into the stream of trouble that was Phin: he was a sluice of one way values. She would pool forever in the loggy legs of the universe if she gave him anything.

But how could she refuse? Phin waited with the confidence of someone people loved.

All Deedee's life she would remain uncertain whether it was Katy's hand or the curved edge of Katy's suitcase in the small of Deedee's back that pushed Deedee from the bus and kept on pushing until she was well past Phin. She felt she deserved only the suitcase, the suitcase accidentally, at that, but she hoped for Katy's hand. When the pushing stopped, Deedee looked lovingly at the side of Katy's face, but the older woman surged by, her eyes on the sign that read *BUS*, one shoulder dipped to balance the suitcase in the opposite hand.

The bus's door closed, and in the driver's womb a blastula of cells implanted itself. The driver could give it only divided attention, being—always—otherwise occupied. She closed her doors, checked her mirrors, and began her shuttle back to the other end of the line.

Deedee, her lumpy luggage banging around her knees, followed a respectful distance behind Katy, and slipped forever through the dross of Phin's brain. He fixed his eyes on something at the end of a long city block: that hat and that dirty coat, that pale bald neck would be easy to track. Phin ambled along in his sneakers, waiting for Harper to throw the coupon away.

Nominated by TriQuarterly

LEARNING TO EAT SOUP

by EDWARD HOAGLAND

from ANTAEUS

Learning to eat soup: Like little boats that go out to sea
  I push my spoon away from me.

At my parents' wedding in Michigan, one of Mother's uncles leaned over before the cake-cutting and whispered to her, "Feed the brute and flatter the ass." The uncles threw rice at them as they jumped into their car, and Dad, after going a mile down the road, stopped and silently swept it out. That night, before deflowering each other (both over thirty), they knelt by the bed and prayed to consecrate the experience.

To strike a balance is everything. If a person sings quietly to himself on the street people smile with approval; but if he talks it's not alright; they think he's crazy. The singer is presumed to be happy and the talker unhappy, which counts heavily against him. . . . To strike a balance: If, for example, walking in the woods, we flake off a bit of hangnail skin and an ant drags this bonanza away we might say that the ants were feasting on human flesh; but probably wouldn't. On the other hand, if a man suffers a heart attack there and festers undiscovered, then we would.

Baby inside M.'s stomach feels like the popping and simmering of oatmeal cooking, as I lay my hand across. Pain, "a revelation to me like fireworks, those comets that whirl," she says in labor room. She lies like a boy-under-stress in the canoe-shaped cot, the nurses gathering gravely, listening to the baby's heartbeat through the stethoscope between contractions—heart like a drumbeat sounded a block away. Baby, with bent monkey feet, is born still in its sack. Doctor is unlocatable. The interns gather. A nurse picks up both phones simultaneously and calls him with urgency. The crowd, the rooting and cheering in the delivery room—as if the whole world were gathered there—after the solitary labor room.

Very old people age somewhat as bananas do.

Two Vietcong prisoners: an American drew crosses on their foreheads, one guy's cross red, other guy's green, to distinguish which was the target and which the decoy to be thrown out of the helicopter to make the target talk.

Winter travel: snowbanks on river ice means thin ice because snow layers shield the ice from the cold. And water is always wearing it away from underneath; therefore keep on the *inside* curves and away from all cutbanks, where the current is fast. Travel on barest ice and avoid obstacles like rocks and driftpiles sticking through which also result in a thinning of the cover. Gravel bars may dam the river, causing overflows, which "smoke" in cold weather like a fire, giving some warning before you sink through the slush on top and into the overflow itself. Overflows also can occur in slow sections of the river where the ice is thick and grinds against itself. A special danger area is the junction of incoming creeks whose whirlpools have kept the water open under a concealment of snow. If the water level falls abruptly, sometimes you can walk on the dry edges of the riverbed under solid ice which remains on top as though you were in a tunnel, but that can be dangerous because bears enjoy following such a route too.

You butter a cat's paws when moving it to a new home, so it can find its way back after going out exploring the first time.

My friend Danny Chapman, the Ringling Bros. clown, had a sliding, circus sort of face, like the eternal survivor, marked by the sun, wind, pain, bad luck, and bad dealings, the standard lusts and equivocations, like a stone that the water has slid over for sixty years. Face was much squarer when not in august-clown blackface; it

402

seemed smudged by reacting to all he'd seen, and holding so many expressions in readiness that none could be recognized as "characteristic" of him.

Success in writing, versus painting, means that your work becomes *cheaper*, purchasable by anybody.

The *New York Times* is a vast democratic *souk* in which every essayist can find a place to publish his or her voice. But otherwise, for a native New Yorker with proud and lengthy ties to the city, it's not so easy. The *New York Review of Books* is published by a group of sensibilities that give the impression of having been born in this metropolis, but of wishing they were Londoners instead. And *The New Yorker* traditionally has been the home of writers and editors born in Columbus, Ohio—who yearned so much to seem like real New Yorkers that their city personalities in print had an artificial, overeager sophistication and snobbery.

I ride my stutter, posting over its jolts, swerving with it, guiding it, if never "mastering" it.

At the annual sports show at NYC Colosseum, "Stay straight with sports," says a poster, a picture of a girl wearing a tee-shirt with that slogan over her breasts An exhibitor tells me he just saw two men fondling each other in the men's room—"It just turns your stomach." A woman wearing a huge odd-looking hat made of dried pheasants' heads is cooing affectionately at a cageful of pheasants. A skinning contest is held in which three taxidermists go to work on the carcasses of three Russian boars.

If two people are in love they can sleep on the blade of a knife.

Karl Wheeler used a baby bottle until he was five years old, whereupon his mother said to him, "That's your last bottle, Karl. When you break that one you'll never get another one!" and he began to toss it idly in the air to catch it, but he missed.

First white men in British Columbia sold some of the Indians their names: $10 for a fine name like O'Shaughnessy, $5 for the more modest Harris.

At 6:00 A.M. I shoot a porcupine in the garage (knew about it from seeing Bimbo vomit from a fear reaction after his many tangles with porcupines). It goes under the building to die but not too far for a rake to reach. I take it to Paul Brooks' house. In his freezer he has woodchucks, beaver, bear, deer, bobcat, and porcupine meat (he is a man living only on social security), and he cleans it for me. We see it's a mamma with milk in her breasts. His mouth fills with saliva as he works; he's also preparing a venison roast for lunch with garlic salt, Worchestershire sauce, pepper, onions, etc. Says this time of year, first of June, the woodchucks are light as your hat, the winter has been so long for them; you can feel their thin legs. Porcupine liver is a delicacy, the rest not so much. The porcupine had been chewing at my garage; I eat the porcupine, therefore I'm eating my garage—dark drumsticks that night by kerosene lamp. Game tastes herby even without herbs—best is bobcat and muskrat, in my experience, not counting big meats like moose. One countryman we know had his ashes scattered on his muskrat pond. The porcupine had chattered its teeth and rattled its poor quiver of quills as I had approached with my gun. Was so waddly it could not even limp properly when badly wounded. Lay on its side gurgling, choking, and sighing like man dying.

At the Freifields' one-room cabin with snowshoes hung under the steep roof, I read Larry's father's hectic journal, written in Austro-English, of desperate orphanhood on the Austrian-Russian front in WWI. He, adopted by the rival armies as they overran the town, living in the trenches with them, living off stolen crusts otherwise, surviving the bombardments, dodging the peasants who hated Jews, but cherished by Austrian soldiers, who then were killed—saw one's legs blown off just after he'd changed places with him. That night peed in his pants in the trench and froze himself to the ground.

"Old Bet," the first circus elephant in America, was bought by Hachaliah Bailey from an English ship captain in 1815, but was shot eventually by religious fanatics in Connecticut as resembling the biblical Behemoth of the Book of Job (as indeed she did).

My first overtly sexual memory is of me on my knees in the hallway outside our fifth-grade classroom cleaning the floor, and Lucy Smith in a white blouse and black skirt standing above me, watching me.

My first memory is of being on a train which derailed in a rainstorm in Nebraska one night when I was two—and of hearing, as we rode in a hay wagon toward the distant weak lights of a little station, that a boy my age had just choked to death from breathing mud. But maybe my first real memory emerged when my father was dying. I was thirty-five and I dreamt so incredibly vividly of being dandled and rocked and hugged by him, being only a few months old, giggling helplessly and happily.

Had supper at a local commune where they have a fast turnover and have made life hard. They buy $20 used cars instead of spending $200, use kerosene instead of the electricity they have, and a team of horses to plow. They got 180 gallons of maple syrup out of their trees but they washed 1,400 sugaring pails in the bathtub in cold water, never having put in a hot water heater. Much husky embracing, like wrestlers; and before they eat their supper they have Grace, where twenty-some people clasp hands around the table, meditating and squeezing fingers. Bread bakes on a puffy black wood stove. Rose hips and chili peppers hang on strings, other herbs everywhere and pomegranates and jars of basic grains. The toilet is a car on blocks up the hill. Supper is a soup bowl full of rice and chard and potato pancakes with two sour sauces and apple butter, yogurt for dessert; and we drink from mason jars of water passed around. And the final "course" is dental floss, which everybody solemnly uses. A dulcimer is played with the quill of a feather accompanied by bongo drums. The women ended the public festivities by each announcing where she was going to sleep that night, which bedroom or which hayloft, in case anyone wished to join her. Clothing is heaped in a feed bin near the bottom of the stairs, and everybody is supposed to reach in in the morning and remove the first items that fit them and come to hand, without regard for which particular sex the clothes were originally made for. The saddest moment of the evening for me was when a little girl came around to her mother carrying a hairbrush in her hand and asking to be put to bed. The mother lost her temper. "Why run to me?" she said. "Everybody in this room is your parent. Anybody can brush your hair and tell you a story and put you to bed."

Manhattan, now 14,310 acres, was 9,800.

405

Bernard Malamud speaks of writing as a battle: "go to paper" with a novel. At this age, sixty-one, is trying to "write wise," new aim, and hard. Being between books, I say I'm in a period of withdrawal and inaction like that of a snake that is shedding its skin.

On the crest of Moose Mountain is an old birch growing low and twisty out of the ruins of a still older, bigger bole, surrounded by ferns, and it's there that the deer that feed in my field bed down during the day.

There is a whole literary genre which consists, first, of foolish writing and then later capitalizing upon the foolishness by beating one's breast and crying *mea culpa*. Why *was* I a white black panther, a drug swallower, a jackbooted feminist, a jet-set-climbing novelist, a 1940s Communist? How interesting and archetypal of me to have shared my generation's extremes.

Busybodies are called in Yiddish a *kochleffl*, a "cooking spoon," because they stir people up.

The hollow in the center of the upper lip is where "the angel touched you and told you to forget what you had seen in heaven."

Wife of F.'s uncle, to prevent him from going to work one morning when she preferred he stayed home, set the alarm so that it seemed it was too late for him to make the train when he woke. But he did rush so terribly he got to the station, and there collapsed and died, and she, only twenty-seven, never remarried.

Joyce consulted Jung, who diagnosed his poor daughter as incurably schizophrenic partly on the evidence of her brilliant, obsessive punning. Joyce remarked that he too was a punner. "You are a deep-sea diver," said Jung. "She is drowning."

The cure for stuttering of holding stones in one's mouth works because of the discomfort of them rattling against one's teeth. Stones from a crocodile's stomach were thought to be the best.

Amerigo Vespucci said that Indian women enlarged their lovers' sexual parts by applying venomous insects to them.

After losing her virginity at seventeen, she felt unstoppered on the street, like a hollow tube, as though the wind could blow right through her.

The sea, at the village of Soya on Hokkaido Island in 1792, was so fertile that twelve quarts of dry rice could be bartered for 1,200 herring, 100 salmon, 300 trout, or 3 seal skins.

How Davy Crockett kept warm when lost in the woods one night: climbing thirty feet up a smooth tree trunk and sliding down.

Am drunk from soft-shell crab lunch with Random House's Joe Fox, but stutter so vigorously with William Shawn as to obscure both from him and myself my drunkenness—stutter through it and give myself time to recall names like Numeiry and Assad, necessary to win Shawn's backing for the trip to Africa. He, as reported, is excessively solicitous of my comfort and state of mind; insulated and jittery; heated by electric heater (in August), yet fanned by electric fan; in his shirtsleeves, and immediately suggests I remove my coat. He has an agonized, bulging baby's head with swallowed up eyes, like that of the tormented child in Francis Bacon's painting *The Scream*. Questions me effectively, however, on my knowledge of the Sudan and the prospects for a salable article there. Says okay. Lunch the next day with Alfred Kazin, my old teacher. Kazin as always is a veritable tumult of impressions, like H. S. Commager and other busy intellectuals I have liked, but in Kazin's case it is enormously in earnest and felt. Expresses hurt at Bellow's recent inexplicable anger. Otherwise an outpouring of talk about his new book on the forties, when he published his first book and met the literary figures of the day. Played violin with drunken Alan Tate. Advances the idea that William James, a hero of his, is a better direct heir of Emerson than Thoreau; also the view that students now resent the fact that a professor knows more than they do, want him to learn along with them in class, as in group therapy, and when caught out on home-work facts, get offended instead of trying to fake through, as in the old days. On Ph.D orals, the candidates seem to have no favorite poem, no poem they can quote from, when he asks them for one at the end.

I like easterners more than westerners but western geography more than eastern geography; and I like the country more than the city but I like city people more than country people.

Essays, the most conversational form, have naturally drawn me, who has a hard time speaking in ordinary terms.

Tail end of hurricane rains buckets, flooding Barton River. Then the sky clears with nearly full moon, and I hear the deer whickering and whanging to one another gleefully, the mountain behind them gigantic and white.

Bellow says in Jerusalem journal that "light may be the outer garment of God."

Oil spills seem to attract aquatic birds; the sheen may resemble schooling fish. Also oil slicks calm the surface, look like landing area.

Roth speaks of his debt to both Jean Genet and the Fugs for *Portnoy*.

Roth a man who wears his heart on his sleeve, thus rather vulnerable to insult and injury; part of his exceptional generosity. Tells story of man bleeding in front of God but trying to hide blood from His sight apologetically.

William Gaddis: jockeylike, narrow-boned, fastidious Irishman, clever and civilized, with none of the usual hangdog bitterness of the neglected writer.

Warhol: keen, Pan face with tight manipulated skin that makes it ageless except for his eyes. Bleached hair hanging to his leather collar. Fame based upon being immobile.

Pete Hamill, bursting personality, does columns in half an hour, movie script in three weeks, discipline based upon not drinking till day's stint is through. Fewer bar brawls now, more empathetic, though still lives from a suitcase. "Irish Ben Hecht," he laughs.

Malamud: not at all the "Jewish businessman's face" I'd heard about, but a sensitive, gentle face, often silent or dreamy at Pod-

horetz's, disagreeing with the host and Midge, but holds his tongue
and hugs him at the end with professional gratitude to an editor who
once published him. When he speaks, his voice is young, light and
quick, an enthusiast's, idealist's. Hurt by attacks on him in Jerusalem *Post*, for dovishness. Extremely solicitous of me, as kind in his
way as Bellow, though style of it is modulated lower. Both of us
distressed by Israeli's grinning description of Arab prisoners being
beaten up. William Phillips says he thinks the Palestinians probably
have a point but that he's not interested in hearing what it is.

Grace Paley; short stocky woman who at first sight on the Sarah
Lawrence campus I mistook for the cleaning woman; asked her
where the men's room was. We rode rubbing knees throughout that
semester in the back seat of a car pool. She'd been marching in
protests since high school (Spanish civil war), but her exhilaration at
being arrested in Washington peace march in midterm reminded
me of my own exuberance at completing the hard spells of army
basic training. Yes, we were good enough!

Heard MacLeish at YMHA. Afterward unrecovered yet from defeat
of his play *Scratch* on B'way. Sweetness and bounce of his voice,
however, is unchanged in twenty years; sounds forty, a matinée
tenor, and the old lilt to his rhetoric. Face like a sachem's, too wise,
too heroic, with a public man's nose. Talks of friendships with Joyce
and Hemingway and imitates Sandburg's O very well. Talks of Saturday Club in Boston where Harlow Shapley monthly debated Robert Frost. Reminisces of artillery-lieutenant days in World War I,
"making the world safe for democracy," where his brother was
killed. Five years later he and other non-dead *did* die a bit when
they realized it had been a "commercial" war and they had been lied
to. He is a man of Hector-type heroes. Says Andrew Marvell poem
was written while going home from Persia after his father's death.

Berryman given $5,000 prize at the Guggenheim reading, wearing
a graybeard's beard which hides tieless collar. Reads best "Dream
Songs," plus two sonnets and Rilke, Ralph Hodgson and eighteenth-
century Japanese poet. Emphatically, spoutingly drunk, reads with
frail man's grotesqueries, contortions, and his own memorable con-
coction of earnestness, coyness, staginess, name-dropping, and
absolutely forceful, rock-bottom directness. Becomes louder and

louder at the end of this floodlighted moment after long years of obscurity and hardship. Here was the current Wild Man, people thought, successor to Pound, there being one to a generation, though many others may have been reminded of Dylan Thomas, as he fell into the arms of Robert Lowell, punching him affectionately, when he finished. His whole life was thereupon paraded before him, when old mistresses and chums and students like me came up, expecting recognition, and one of his old wives, presenting him with a son whom obviously he hadn't laid eyes on for a long while. He boomed with love and guilt, with repeated thanks for letters informing him that so and so had had a child or remarried, till one was wearied of watching. One felt guilty too, as though competing for his attention with the neglected son. I felt Berryman had not long to live and I ought to be content with my memories of him and lessons learned and not join in the hounding of him. Nevertheless, I did go next afternoon to Chelsea Hotel, with bronze plaques outside memorializing other tragic figures like Thomas and Brenden Behan. He'd said the son would be there, so I was afraid that I would be taking time away from a son who needed to see him much more. But the son had left—all that remained was a note in Ann B.'s handwriting. Instead a *Life* photographer and reporter were talking with him, plying him with drinks, though he was holding back dignifiedly, talking of fame, of Frost, and his own dog Rufus. Frost was a shit who tried to hurt him, but he quoted the wonderful couplet about God forgiving our little faux pas if we forgive Him His great big joke on us. Is bombastic in his total commitment to words. Legs look very small but chest inflates with importance of uttering snatches of poems, till he collapses in coughs. Rubs beard and hair exhaustedly, recklessly spendthrift with his strength, and begins harder drinking; leads me to bar, where waiter, thinking from his red face and thin clothing that he is a bum, won't serve him till he lays a ten dollar bill on the table. I soon leave, but he was hospitalized within a couple of days. "Twinkle" was his favorite word at this time. He used it for commentary, by itself, and irony, or expostulation, quoting an enemy like Oscar Williams, then merely adding a somber "Twinkle."

Turgenev's brain was the heaviest ever recorded, 4.7 lbs.; 3 is average.

Child's tale about a man who suffered from shortness of breath. Afraid he would run out, he blew up a bunch of balloons as an extra supply for emergencies. Blew up so many that he floated away holding on to them.

Updike comes to U. of Iowa for first workshop session in three years (hasn't really taught for sixteen years), but handles himself in a classy manner nevertheless, and very well prepared with students' manuscripts beforehand, and in the exhilaration of reading his own work in front of 1,000 people in McBride Hall (which we call Mammal Hall because it's part of Nat'l Hist. Museum) freely sheds his private-person role that had made him a bit stiff before, when he'd refused even a newspaper interview. Signs autograph cards for eleven-year-old boys and physics texts for Japanese students and mimeo forms for students with nothing better to offer him. Wife is ample, attractive woman with large intense face, obviously both loving and sexy, a relaxed, close companion—he is wearing a wedding ring and ignoring the ambitious students who show up for his morning class wearing cocktail dresses. We talk of Africa—both finishing Africa books—and classmates and lit. hierarchies. He mentions Cheever's drunkenness, whom once he had to dress after a party like dressing a father. Our mothers are same age. "Poor Johnny," his said, watching a TV program about senility with him recently.

Updike says he quit teaching years ago because he "felt stupid," seeing only one way to write a given story properly, not the endless alternatives students proposed in discussions.

Indians used to scratch small children with mouse teeth fastened to a stick as a punishment for crying in front of white men. (White man, of course, a "skinned" man.)

Short stories tend to be boat-shaped, with a lift at each end, to float.

Yates says art is a result of a quarrel with oneself, not others.

Five toes to a track means it's wild, four toes means cat or dog.

Writers customarily write in the morning, and try to make news, make love, or make friends in the afternoon. But alas, I write all day.

Bellow says he spent the first third of his life absorbing material, the second third trying to make himself famous, and the last third trying to evade fame.

"A woman without a man is like a fish without a bicycle": tee- shirt.

People say they'll take a dip in the sea as if it were like dipping into a book, but I nearly drowned in surf's riptide off Martha's Vineyard's South Beach. Repeatedly changed swimming strokes to rest myself as I struggled in the water, surf too loud to shout over and I'm too nearsighted to see where to shout to. Reaching beach, I sprawled for an hour before moving further. Spent next day in bed, next week aching.

New England is "pot-bound," says Charlton Ogburn; thus super-fertile.

Petrarch, climbing Mount Ventoux in 1336, began the Renaissance by being the first learned man ever to climb a mountain only for the view.

Rahv told Roth, "You can't be both Scott Fitzgerald and Franz Kafka."

People who marry their great loves sometimes wish they'd married their best friends; and vice versa.

Trapeze artists some days complain "there's too much gravity," when a change of the weather or the magnetic field affects their bodies. Elvin Bale bought his heel-hook act from Geraldine Soules, who after a fall started doing a dog act instead. Soules had, in turn, bought it from Vander Barbette, who, walking funny after *his* fall, had become a female impersonator and trainer of circus showgirls.

In old-time Georgia you ate mockingbird eggs for a stutter; boiled an egg for jaundice and went and sat beside a red-ant anthill and ate the white and fed the yolk to the ants. For warts, you bled them, put the blood on grains of corn and fed that to a chicken. Fiddlers liked to put a rattlesnake rattle inside their fiddles.

The fifties are an interim decade of life, like the thirties. In the thirties one still has the energy of one's twenties, combined with the judgment (sometimes) of the forties. In the fifties one still has the energy of one's forties, combined with the composure of the sixties.

The forties are the old age of youth and the fifties the youth of old age.

Adage, "God sends meat, the Devil sends cooks."

Carnival stuntman whom Byron Burford banged the drum for used to swallow live rats and ping-pong balls, upchucking whichever ones the crowd first asked for. Stunned the rats with cigar smoke before he swallowed them.

> The intellect of man is forced to choose
> Perfection of the life, or of the work,
> And if it take the second must refuse
> A heavenly mansion, raging in the dark.
> —Yeats, "Choice"

Lying to my lieutenant as a private at Fort Sam Houston as to whether I'd shaved that morning before Inspection; or only the night before—he reaching out and rubbing his hand down my face.

Glenn Gould liked to practice with the vacuum cleaner on, to hear "the skeleton of the music."

Nature writers, I sometimes think, are second only to cookbook writers in being screwed up.

Deer follow moose in these woods, says Toad. I say maybe they look like father (mother) figures to them.

At Academy-Institute ceremonial, the big scandal is Ellison's lengthy introduction of Malamud for a prize, and Barbara Tuchman's brutal interruption of it. Stegner very youthful, as befits an outdoorsman. Cowley very food-hungry as always, as befits a 1930s survivor. Commager tells my wife that his daughter loved me and so he loved me. Lots of cold-faced ambitious poets cluster around each other and Northrop Frye; Galway seems likably unaffected and truthful next to them. Ditto Raymond Carver. Ellison had tried to speak frankly of blacks and Jews.

Joe Flaherty's line for the Brooklyn Bridge: "the Irish gangplank."

Whale mother's milk would stain the sea after she was harpooned and the calf would circle the ship forlornly. "I do not say that John or Jonathan will realize all this," said Thoreau, in finishing *Walden*; and that's the central and tragic dilemma as the environmentalist movement fights its rearguard battles.

In starving midwinter, foxes catch cats by rolling on their backs like a kitten ready to play.

Warblers average eight or 10,000 songs a day in spring; vireo 20,000. Woodchucks wag their tails like a dog. Blue jays like to scare other birds by imitating a red-shouldered hawk.

My bifocals are like a horse's halter, binding the lower half of my eyes to the day's work.

At my frog pond a blue heron circles low overhead while a brown-muzzled black bear clasps chokecherry bushes and eats off them thirty yards away from me.

Only six hours old, a red calf stumbles toward the barn as mother is herded in by Hugh Stevens on ATV vehicle, and is eventually tied to its mother's stanchion with hay twine, while a six-inch red tab of its previous cord still hangs from its belly. It's as shiny as a new pair of shoes, its deerlike hooves perfectly formed, including the dew claws. Mother and calf had had a brief wild idyll under the summer sky before they were discovered by Hugh—the last sky this vealer will ever see.

Old people seem wise because they have grown resigned and because they remember the axioms even if they've forgotten the data.

"When you come to the end of your life, make sure you're used up."

414

I trust love more than friendship, which is why I trust women more than men.

"All hat and no cows": Texas saying.

"Eat with the rich, laugh with the poor."

Buying a new car after thirteen years, I discover why country people like to keep the old one about the yard. First, it makes the house look occupied. Second, it's a nesting site for ducks and geese and a shelter for chickens during the day. Third, it reminds you of *you.*

Nominated by Rick Bass and Barbara Thompson

BILL'S STORY

by MARK DOTY

from GREEN MOUNTAINS REVIEW

When my sister came back from Africa,
we didn't know at first how everything
had changed. After a while Anne
bought men's and boy's clothes in all sizes,
and filled her closets with little
or huge things she could never wear.

Then she took to buying out
theatrical shops, rental places on the skids,
sweeping in and saying, *I'll take everything.*
Dementia was the first sign of something
we didn't even have a name for,
in 1978. She was just becoming stranger,

all those clothes, the way she'd dress me up
when I came to visit. It was like we could go back
to playing together again and get it right.
She was a performance artist, and she did
her best work then, taking the clothes to clubs,
talking, putting them all on, talking.

It was years before she was in the hospital,
and my mother needed something
to hold onto, some way to be helpful,

so she read a book called *Deathing*
(a cheap, ugly verb if ever I heard one)
and took its advice to heart;

she'd sit by the bed and say, *Annie,*
look for the light, look for the light.
It was plain that Anne did not wish
to be distracted by these instructions;
she came to, though she was nearly gone then,
and looked at our mother with what was almost certainly

annoyance. *It's a white light,*
Mom said, and this struck me
as incredibly presumptuous, as if the light
we'd all go into would be just the same.
Maybe she wanted to give herself up
to indigo, or red. If we can barely even speak

to each other, living so separately,
how can we all die the same?
I used to take the train to the hospital
and sometimes the only empty seats
would be the ones that face backwards.
I'd sit there and watch where I'd been

waver and blur out, and finally
I liked it, seeing what you've left
get more beautiful, less specific.
Maybe her light was all that gabardine
and flannel, khaki and navy
and silks and stripes. If you take everything,

you've got to let everything go. Dying
must take more attention than I ever imagined.
Just when she'd compose herself
and seem fixed on the work before her,
Mother would fret, trying to help her
just one more time: *Look for the light.*

Until I took her arm
and told her wherever I was in the world
I would come back, no matter how difficult
it was to reach her, if I heard her calling.
Shut up, Mother, I said, and Annie died.

Nominated by Lynda Hull and David Wojahn

"BY LOVE POSSESSED"

fiction by LORNA GOODISON

from CALLALOO

SOMETIMES, SHE USED to wake up and just look at him lying asleep beside her; she would prop herself up on one elbow and study his face. He slept like a child, knees drawn up to his stomach, both hands tucked between his thighs. His mouth was always slightly open when he slept, and his mouth water always left a damp patch on the pillowcase; no matter how many days after, it seems the patch would always be damp and every time she washed it, she would run her finger over the stain and her mind would pick up the signal and move back to the image of him lying asleep. When the radio next door began to play the first of the morning church services, she would know that it was time to begin to get ready to go to work. From Monday to Saturday, every day, her days began like this. She would go to the kitchen to prepare his breakfast, then she would leave it covered up on top of the stove over a bowl of hot water. Then she would go to the bathroom, bathe in the cold early morning water and then get dressed. Just before she left, she always placed some money on the top of the bureau for his rum and cigarettes, then she would say to his sleeping form, "Frenchie, ah gone, take care till I come back." Dottie sometimes wondered how she was so lucky to be actually living with Frenchie. He was easily the best looking man in Jones Town, maybe in the whole of Jamaica and she, ten years older than him, tall and skinny and 'dry up'. She had never had luck with men and she had resigned herself to being an old maid a long time ago. She was childless, 'a mule' as really unkind people would say. She worked hard and saved her money, and she kept a good house. Her two rooms in the big yard were spotless. She had a big trunk bed, that was always made up with pretty chenille spreads, a lovely mahogany bureau, a big wardrobe with good quality glass (mirrors) and in the front room, in pride of place, her China Cabinet. Nobody in the yard, maybe in Jones Town, maybe in the whole of Jamaica, had a China Cabinet so full of beautiful things. Dottie had carefully collected them over the years and she never used them. Once a year when she was fixing up her house at Christmas, she would carefully take them out, the ware plates, cups and saucers, tureens, glasses, lemonade sets, serving dishes and teapots, and she would carefully wash them. This took her nearly a whole morning. She washed them in a pan of soapy warm water, rinsed them in cold water, then dried them with a clean towel. Then she would rearrange them artistically in the Cabinet. On that night, she would sometimes treat herself to a little drink of Porto Pruno wine, sitting by herself in her little living room and would gaze on her China Cabinet enjoying the richness within, the pretty colours and the lights bouncing off the glasses. Her sister always said that she worshipped her possessions; maybe she did, but what else did she have? Till she met Frenchie.

There was one other thing that Dottie really liked, she liked the movies and that is how she met Frenchie. She was in the line outside the Ambassador theatre one Saturday night, waiting to get into a hot triple bill when she struck up a conversation with him. He was standing in the line behind her and she remembered feeling so pleased that a man as good looking as this was talking to her. They moved up in the line till they got to the cashier, and she being ahead of him, took out ten shillings to pay for herself. It was the easiest most natural thing in the world for her to offer to pay for him when he suddenly raised an alarm that his pocket had been picked. If she had been seeing straight, she would have noticed that some people were laughing when he raised the alarm. But she didn't see anything but the handsome brown skin man with 'good hair', straight nose and a mouth like a woman's. It was the best triple bill Dottie ever watched. He had walked her home. All the way home they talked about the movie . . . His favourite actor was Ricardo Montalban, she liked Dolores Del Rio, for that is how she would like to have looked, sultry and Spanish, for then she and Frenchie would make a striking couple, just like two movie stars. As it was she

420

looked something like Popeye's girlfriend Olive Oyl and he was probably better looking than Ricardo Montalban.

Frenchie did not work. He explained that he used to have a job at the wharf but he got laid-off when his back was damaged unloading some cargo. She sympathized with him and some nights she would rub the smooth expanse of his back with wintergreen oil. He said he liked how her hands felt strong. Frenchie moved in with Dottie about two weeks after they met. At first, she was a little shy about having a man living in her room, then she began to be very proud of it. At least she was just like any other woman in the yard. As a matter of fact, she was luckier than all of them, for Frenchie was so good looking. "She mind him. Dottie buy down to the very drawers that Frenchie wear," said her sister, "not even a kerchief the man buy for himself". The people in the yard would laugh at her behind her back, they wondered if Frenchie kept women with her. Winston her nephew said, "Cho, Rum a Frenchie woman, man, you ever see that man hug up a rum bottle?"

Now that was true. Frenchie loved rum and rum loved him, for he never seemed to get drunk. As a matter of fact, every day he spent a good eight hours like a man going to work, in Mr. Percy's bar at the corner. After Dottie had gone to work at the St. Andrew House where she did domestic work for some brown people, Frenchie would wake up. He would bathe, eat the breakfast that Dottie had left for him and get dressed, just like any man going to work. He always wore white short sleeved shirts which Dottie washed whiter than 'Pelican shit'; he favored khaki pants, so she ironed both shirt and pants very carefully.

He would get dressed very, very carefully; put some green brilliantine in his hair and brush it till it had the texture of a zinc fence, or as one of the men in the yard said, "Everytime I see you hair Frenchie, I feel sea-sick". Frenchie would laugh showing his gold crown on his front teeth, run his hand over his hair and say, "Waves that behaves, bwoy, waves that behaves." When his toilette was over, he would walk leisurely up the road to the bar. The one thing which made you realize that he could not have been going to work like any other decent man was his shoes: he always wore backless brown slippers. Frenchie would sit in the bar and make pronouncements on matters ranging from the private life of the Royal Family (Princess Margaret was a favourite topic), to West Indian Cricket (he always had inside knowledge on these matters), general world affairs and most of all the movies.

Everybody was in awe of Frenchie, he was just so tough, handsome and in control of life. His day at the bar usually ended around 5:00 p.m., just like any other working man. Then he would walk home and join the Domino game which went on constantly in the yard. Usually Dottie would find him at the Domino table, when she burst in through the gate, always in a hurry, anxious to come home and fix his dinner. She always said the same thing when she came through the gate, "Papa, ah come" and he looking cool and aloof, eyes narrowed through the cigarette smoke, would say, "O, yu come." Dottie always experienced a thrill when he said that, it was a signal of ownership, the slight menace in his voice was exciting, you knew it gave the right to say, "Frenchie vex when I come home late . . ."

She would hurry to fix his dinner and set it on the table before him. She hardly ever ate with him, but sat at the table watching him eat. "Everyday Frenchie eat a Sunday dinner," Winston would say. It was true, Dottie cooked only the best for Frenchie, he ate rice and peas at least three times per week unlike everybody else who only ate it on Sunday . . . Dottie would leave the peas soaking overnight and half boil them in the morning, so that they could finish cooking quickly, when she hurried home in the evenings. He also had beef steak at least twice a week and 'quality fish' and chicken, the rest of the week.

Dottie lived to please Frenchie. She was a character in a film, 'By Love Possessed.' Then one day in Mr. Myers' bar, the movies turned into real life . . . Frenchie was sitting with his usual group of drunkalready friends talking about a movie he had seen, when a stranger stepped into the saloon, actually he was an ordinary man. He had a mean and menacing countenance, because he was out of work and things were bad at home. He walked into the bar and ordered a white rum and sat on a barstool scowling, screwing up his face everytime he took a sip of the pure 100% proof cane spirit, and suddenly Frenchie's incessant talking began to bother the stranger. The more Frenchie talked, the more it bothered him. He looked at Frenchie's pretty boy face and his soft looking hands and he hated him.

Then Frenchie reached a high point of the story he was telling. He was painting a vivid picture of the hero, wronged by a man who doubted his integrity and Frenchie was really into it . . . he became the wronged hero before everyone's eyes, his voice trembled, his eyes widened in disbelief as the audience gazed spell-bound at him . . . "Then the star boy say," said Frenchie, him say, "What kind of man do you think I am?" The stranger at the bar never missed a beat . . . he replied, "A batty Man." And the bar erupted. The laughter could be heard streets away, the barmaid laughed till they had to throw water on her to stop her from becoming hysterical, all the people who had ever wanted to laugh at Frenchie, laughed at him, all the people who envied him, his sweet boy life, laughed at him, everybody was laughing at him. The uproar didn't die down for almost half an hour and people who heard came running in off the streets to find out what had happened. One man took it upon himself to tell all the newcomers the story, over and over again. Frenchie was sitting stunned, he tried to regain face by muttering that the man was a blasted fool . . . but nobody listened.

Finally, the self-appointed raconteur went over to him and said, "Cho Frenchie, you can't take a joke?" Then he lowered his voice, taking advantage of the fallen hero and said, "All the same yu know everybody must wonder bout you, how a good looking man like you, live with a mawgre dry up ooman like Dottie, she fava man, she so flat and crawny . . ." Upon hearing this, Frenchie got angrier and funnily enough, he wasn't angry at the man, he was angry at Dottie. It was true, she didn't deserve him, she was mawgre and crawny and dry up and really was not a woman that a handsome sexy man like him should be with . . . No wonder the blasted ugly bwoy coulda facety with him. He understood what the hero meant in the movies when he said he saw red . . . Frenchie felt like he was drowning in a sea of blood . . . he wanted to kill Dottie! He got up and walked out of the bar to go home. When Dottie hurried in through the door that evening, saying breathlessly, "Papa ah come," she was met with the following sight. Frenchie was standing at the door of her front room with her best soup tureen in one hand and four of her best gold rimmed tumblers stacked inside each other in the other hand, and as soon as he saw her he flung them into the street. He went back inside and emerged with more of the precious things from her China Cabinet and he flung them into the street where they broke with a rich full sound on the asphalt. After a while, he developed a steady rhythm, he began to take what looked like the same amount of steps each time he went into the house, then he'd

emerge with some crockery or glass, walk to the edge of the veran-
dah taking the same amount of steps and with an underarm bowling
action, fling the things into the street. Dottie screamed, she ran up
the steps and clutched at him, he gave her a box which sent her
flying down the steps. Everybody screamed, the men kept saying
that he had gone rass mad . . . nobody tried to restrain him for he
had murder in his eyes . . . and he never stopped till he had broken
all of Dottie's things and then he walked out of the yard.

"Frenchie bad no rass bwoy . . . You see when him just fling the
things, chuh." Frenchie's name became a great legend in the neighborhood, nobody ever seen anybody 'mash it up' like that, so nobody had ever seen anybody in such a glorious temper, "mash up
the place to blow wow" . . . Nobody remembered him for "What
kind of man do you think I am?" Even poor broken Dottie remembered him for his glorious temper . . . She would have forgiven him
for breaking her precious things, she would have liked to have told
the story of how bad her man was and the day he broke everything
in her China Closet and boxed her down the steps . . . But he
didn't give her a chance. She kept going to the Sunday night triple
bills at the Ambassador, but she never saw him again and after that,
she took a live-in job and gave up her rooms in the Yard.

Nominated by Ted Wilentz

IMAGINING THE OCEAN

by JENNIFER ATKINSON

from THREEPENNY REVIEW

OUR ENGLISH class met outside on the temple steps in the thin shade of its brightly painted entrance. The glossy Tibetan tiger crouched on the lintel, the birds and vines that swooped and scrolled around the doors and portico posts, were the subjects of all our sentences. "The tiger lives on the mountain." "The tiger was sleeping under the tree." "The tiger ate the green bird." My students, most of them under ten, never tired of tiger stories, and though they were all Buddhist and wearing robes of Buddhist schoolboys, they especially reveled in our tiger's violence. That, they thought, was the real story. When asked where the tiger was going, they'd tell me "he was hunting the man." When asked to make up a sentence with "likes to," they'd rush to tell me what and who "the tiger likes to eat." I tried to interest them in the vines of painted flowers or the real gardenias that grew beside the steps, whose scent was stronger even than the gardenia room-spray my fourth-grade teacher had used to freshen our classroom's air, but my students hardly noticed. They'd indulge me with a word or two—"pretty" or "bees liking," but they cared as little for those sweet flowers as I had for Mrs. Wilkinson's gardenias-in-a-can.

As the weeks went by and the days grew steadily hotter, it seemed their interest in the adventures of that hungry tiger just would not fade. I, however, finally came to the end of my tiger imagination. There was nothing left to say about its stripes, its roar, its cleverness, or even its voracious appetite. I was all out of sentences—especially of the kind one teaches to Buddhist boys.

The temperature that day was up past a hundred in the shade. The boys sat half-dizzy on the floor, too hot to even elbow one another. Our class met from one to two-thirty, right after dinner, and though we'd had tea with our meal, all of us were thirsty again. There had been no rain for weeks. Down valley through the leafless frangipani tree I could see the villagers' rice, brassy in the sun. No one was working. It was far too hot. Just one black water buffalo was plowing head-down through the dust.

At the foot of our temple steps stood a statue of Tara, the female incarnation of Buddha, beloved for her generosity. The reflecting pool before her was nearly dry, because the boys and I had used her water gradually cup by cup, doling it out to the okra we'd helped plant under the mangoes and to the blue morning glories twined around the fig tree. I only hoped no one had gotten thirsty enough to drink that water, unboiled.

Probably half of us were suffering from dysentery that day. Weeks earlier, after my first bout, a Kathmandu doctor told me most Nepali people live with dysentery—the weakness, the thirst, and the pain. They take that reality for granted. Our school was fortunate to receive donations for antibiotics, but even so our students were often quite sick. Unless they were in real pain, however, they would not complain, but instead just sit there, dull in the sun.

It was July. I imagined my parents back at home in Connecticut, under an orange-striped beach umbrella, the smell of tide-exposed muck and rotting seaweed, sunlight focused on the water. I thought of children bridging sandcastle moats with splayed blue-mussel shells. And I thought of myself years before, bikini straps down to cancel out the white shadows across my body, *Stairway to Heaven's* nervous treble jangling on the AM radio. Over and over all summer long.

It occurred to me then that my students (some of them already drowsing) had never seen an ocean or even a lake large enough to form its own horizon. They knew the mountains, of course. Many of them came from the Namché Bazaar-Mount Everest region, so they'd seen wide vistas all right, miles of snow peaks which at dawn are entirely uncluttered with fog—a sight I'd come across two oceans to see. But they had never seen or heard the ocean.

They *had* seen a drawing of the Owl and the Pussycat at sea in a pea-green boat; they'd looked at illustrations of Winken, Blinken, and Nod throwing nets in a sea of stars; they knew the pale blue background on the map was supposed to represent water, but they didn't believe it. They had no feel for the sea. It was as if for them the water were space—emptiness—as impossible to truly imagine as it was for me to conceive of the Buddhist Void.

Their Tibetan-Sherpa culture and their mountain-locked nation were worlds away from the coast. One of the Temple's most precious possessions was the conch which was blown to call us all to services. As much as the boys loved to touch that shell's smooth, furled bone, flushed pink inside like the mouth of a flower, they could not believe there were hundreds just like it buried somewhere deep in saltwater. They preferred to believe their conch was singular, irreplaceable, magic. And it was. It was a natural trumpet borne first over the Hindu Kush to Tibet on pony-back, and then years later packed across the mountains to Nepal with Tibetans escaping the Chinese invasion. So when my students held that shell to their ears, they heard no sound of the sea. They heard the history they knew: wind gusting across snowy upland plateaus. Or the sound of Absolute Reality, an empty, imageless Void.

Yet out of the Void arises beauty. Every day, as part of the daily cycle of prayer and meditation, each student made a "mandala offering"—the symbolic offering-back of a wholly purified world, the imagined mandala. To form it, they would recite the names of things: moonflowers, shells, sandalwood, nectar, turquoise and garnets, stars, circular lakes and cool refreshing seas. By chanting and so revisualizing a perfect, symbolic world, they could make the whole world become theirs and then give it back. The boys were taught that the words of the chant were as real as the things themselves, and more powerful. With those words the world itself could be re-imagined, re-created into a simple elegant order.

In this world, there was a central symmetrical peak, Meru, the Tibetan mountain of Paradise, around which spoked four continents divided by four symbolic oceans. Those were the only oceans my students really knew. And although they knew them intimately, their knowing was incomplete. In contrast to the other parts of their imagined worlds, the boys had no sensuous connection with *ocean* except through the conch, which they had only seen on a shelf beside the altar. I certainly had no desire to adulterate their silvery mythic seas or to educate them to a textbook truth, but I was sure that talking about the wide real ocean would only make the mythic one more miraculous. After all, our stylized, painted tiger hadn't

427

suffered from the tales we'd told. Even after the hunts, leaps, and lurid feasts were over, there he crouched, still just as unrealistic tiger-lily orange and unforeshortened.

So why not gloss their imagined picture of the ocean? We were all thirsty and limp with sickness or its aftermath, and needed some kind of relief from the drought and dulling heat. It was far too hot to work repetitive sentences. So (though the headmaster wouldn't have liked the idea) I decided to tell the children stories about the sea. But not of Davy Jones's locker or Sinbad's sails over the bounding main. Mere description would be strange and magical enough for an expanse of water they knew lapped the shores of Paradise. Even so I began—so they would understand—in the conventional language of storytelling:

Faraway down, farther than Namché,
As far as Lhasa, as far as the clouds,
There's a kingdom we call the sea.
It's all water, always moving
Up and down and frothy
Like cream in the churn before butter.
Sometimes the ocean is blue like my eyes.
Other times it has nothing to do
With any of us, and it's all different colors
Like the back of a hard-shell beetle.
When it's as sunny as this, the water shines
Like all the spoons in the school together.
But the sea is useless water.
You can't drink it or wash clothes,
Since there's a hundred hundred bowls
Of salt stirred in—one for every fish
That lives there, fish that look like stars
Or flowers or green parrots flying . . .

The rhythm of my voice began to lull the boys to sleep. Usually when they dozed, I'd have them run to Tara and back to wake them up, but today I thought I'd let them drift back and forth from dream to story. It would get us through the afternoon. At least they were quiet. I droned on. I told of whales bigger than the whole school, and redtide creatures so small you can see them only when there are thousands washed up together—like blood in the water—and so powerful they kill much larger fish. The children still awake were intrigued by that power. They couldn't believe something so small could kill. I reminded them of dysentery and the mighty little animals that swam around in our well-water. They couldn't believe it. "Not seeing," they said, meaning that unless they saw those amoebas, they refused to believe, despite the pain in their guts and evidence of their own blood. And despite the hypocrisy, then, of their prayers. Even for Buddhist children, apparently, seeing is believing.

They asked me if I'd ever seen amoebas. I said I'd only seen pictures in a doctor's book (they weren't pleased to hear that) but that I *had* seen a whale as big as their dormitory. They liked that. That they wanted to believe. They wanted to know how to spell *whale*.

I printed the word on our blackboard, a plywood sheet flimsier than the one we used to play school with when I was a child. Then I too would believe whatever was written there—even if only a play-teacher had scrawled it. The word was there, like a provable sum, true and existing in white and black. Next, just as I had in school and in playing school, my class and I spelled *whale* out loud together. And I drew a child's outline of a whale—a hollow black vessel filled with the same black space that surrounded it. Just a white line on the blackboard, and I think they understood. *Whale*, I said, pointing to my crude drawing. Then to fuse the word, the picture, and the thing into something apprehensible, I led them in the "spelling chant."

Traditionally, Tibetan children learn by memorization. They memorize by sing-song meters. My elementary school boys spent at least an hour a day memorizing scripture by chanting. Each boy learned as much per day as he could. One of my students learned by heart over fifteen lines of difficult text every day. I loved to watch them at their work, chanting and pacing back and forth along the dusty paths. The song and pace kept time. Both drove the words home. Those kids (still kids, pinching each other as they paced past) literally learned by heart and by lungs and by body, incorporating Buddhist ideas of selflessness into their very flesh and physical lives.

They learned everything to the tune of that same chant. It made the words somehow ring true. It made the words rhyme with the things they named. I learned the power of the chant quickly. My first day as their teacher, not knowing what else to ask, I asked if they knew the English alphabet. Immediately, as if on cue, they all began to chant: A-P-P-L-E, APPLE, B-I-R-D, BIRD. They chanted right through to ZEBRA. Naturally, they hadn't the slightest idea what a zebra was, but they knew zebra existed because they could see and hear it: Z-E-B-R-A, ZEBRA. There's nothing so odd in that. I spent years with alphabet books myself, and to this day have no particular other reason to believe in the mysterious G-N-U, NEW.

I wrote *ocean* on the board next. We chanted it together, and it too became more comprehensible. I wondered if by hearing all that they learned in the same meter, they would hear and remember the world in harmony and whole—at once both idea and material, imagined and real. I hoped so.

The world of my childhood was split between stories and storybooks, on the one hand, and lessons and textbooks, on the other— but only because the teachers constantly reminded us of the cute falsity of the first and the hard facts of the second, as if they were mutually exclusive. I wanted to believe in both. I knew the teachers at school were right and I also knew the stories felt more true than the texts. After all, the wind my father called *northern*, the one that made my eyes cry when I wasn't even sad, was the same North Wind my storybook said whisked children back behind it to the cold land of the dead. And after all, though the teacher had said quite firmly that there was no such thing, I with my own bare feet had felt the slimy seaweed touch of sea serpents under the waves of the Long Island Sound. I was afraid and not afraid. I knew what I felt was true; and I also knew perfectly well the whole time it was not.

I knew a lot about the ocean, because I loved it and because I lived near the beach. I knew the moon folded back the ocean like a bed quilt to reveal the shiny ugly muck underneath. But the metaphor of a cloth ocean didn't obscure my knowledge of what lay under it—rotten fish, mussels open in the heat and steaming with gnats, gull-smashed clamshells bleaching on the rocks. And neither did that harsh low-tide vision undermine my other knowledge of deep-sea treasure and Jonah locked in the belly of a whale—a whale I believed was white because of the library's *Illustrated Moby Dick*.

I believed in that whale before I ever saw or touched the rubbery-smooth, barnacle-starred whale at Marineland. I believed because the story was beautiful and scary, and because of the sound of the words. For the same reasons I believed in Eden, and even, as my

430

students described it, Mount Meru. And when I learned the mandala chant that recreates the world and holds it pure in the space of the mind, sometimes I believed in that—almost.

It looked as if I'd put all my students to sleep by now. When I stopped talking I could hear them breathe, it was so quiet. Down in the village someone clanked a temple bell. Inside the temple, where the intermediate class met, I could hear the children chant verb conjugations: blow, blew, blown: fly, flew, flown . . . I thought again of the Connecticut shore, the wind and the gulls, the feel of the sun tanning my back. Since my students were asleep, it didn't matter what I told them as long as I told them something. If I stopped talking long, the headmaster might notice the class had dissolved in sleep and the children would be punished. So I kept talking. I told a story for myself or whoever might wake up. I said: "When I was ten years old, my father and I went fishing. We were in a small boat. I caught a big fish, a shark. The shark had big, long teeth and I was scared it would bite us. But my father killed the fish. Then he took his knife and cut the fish open so we could see everything inside. In the shark's stomach, I saw another smaller fish just lying there, wet and whole. I looked at it a long time, but then my father threw it away. Sharks are no good to eat."

That *was* what happened. But telling the narrative so baldly took away all its emotional depth. I had reported the facts about fishing that day with my father, but I hadn't told the real story—the remembered, the re-imagined story.

Sitting in front of my sleepy students and waiting for the two-thirty bell to ring, I thought again of that summer day. I remembered drop-line fishing with my father and what it was really like when late in the afternoon, I hauled up a heavy two-foot fish . . . my biggest ever! But when my father called my proud catch *shark*, I yelped, and felt not just afraid but also ashamed, as if by dragging the shark up from the darkness I had partly caused its cruel existence. My hook was set in its mouth. The heavy drop-line bound us together. But the fish was more frightened than I. It flopped around our little rented boat, frantic, sides heaving, unable to breathe. I hated that shark, and I hated my part in its life and its death. My father grabbed it by the tail and knocked it dead against the hull— twice. The sand shark hung limp in his hands. I touched its rough sides: sandpaper. It felt so ordinary that ordinary things like scuffed leather and the rough cement of the gym walls at school would now

431

feel shark-like, untrustworthy—implicated by touch. My father unsheathed his knife, yanked it up the shark's belly, and splayed the body open to show me a small whole fish in the core. I saw it held secure like that, surrounded completely. I looked and looked. The waves rocked and jostled our skiff. But I couldn't tell my father that I wanted to be held whole. I couldn't smile back or look up even. He must have taken my silence for revulsion, because too quickly he threw the fish over the side. I remembered my father's face flushed red under the shadow of his weekend beard, the ocean mottled gray-red behind us as the fish and its guts came loose in the water; and we pulled anchor.

A bell rang to mark the end of class. My students and I all revived enough to sing a Tibetan hymn to wisdom and compassion and to go join the rest of the school under the shade of the fig tree. My next-to-youngest student, Thubten Mindul, whose greatest pleasures were fairy tales, penmanship, soccer, and chocolate, brought me a big blue cup of boiled water. Mindul's family lived ten days' walk across the mountains. He hadn't been home in over a year. When I asked how he liked the story, he said he didn't believe about little fish in the well, but he liked the part about whales. If we caught a whale, all the boys in the school could eat meat for a week! That would be a good story, he told me. How do you catch a whale?

Nominated by Marjorie Sandor

FREEZE

fiction by DAVID JAUSS

from NEW ENGLAND REVIEW/BREAD LOAF QUARTERLY

AT FIRST Freeze Harris thought Nam was a crazy nightmare, an upside-down place where you were supposed to do everything that was forbidden back in the world, but after a while it was the world that seemed unreal. Cutting ears off dead NVA had become routine; stocking shelves at Kroger's seemed something he'd only dreamed. Then, on a mission in the Iron Triangle, Freeze stepped on a Bouncing Betty that didn't go off and nothing seemed real anymore. It was like he'd stepped out of Nam when he stepped on the mine. And now he wasn't anywhere.

The day after Freeze stepped on the mine, the new brown-bar reported for duty. His name was Reynolds, and from the moment he arrived at Lai Khe, he had it in for Freeze. Freeze had just come in off the line that morning, and he was stumbling drunk outside the bunny club, wearing only his bush hat, sunglasses, and Jockey shorts. He had a bottle of Carling Black Label in one hand and a fragmentation grenade in the other. He was standing there, swaying back and forth, when Reynolds came up to him, his jungle fatigues starched and razor-creased, and stuck his square, government-issue jaw into Freeze's face. "What the fuck are you doing, soldier?"

Freeze looked at the brown bar on Reynolds' collar and saluted with the grenade. "Drinking, sir. Beer, sir."

"I'm not blind, Private. I'm talking about the frag."

Freeze looked at the grenade. He had pulled the pin after his first sixpack. If he let go of the firing lever, he'd have only four and a half seconds to make out his will. *I, Mick Harris, being of unsound mind and body. . . .* He laughed.

433

There were red blotches on the lieutenant's white face now. "What's so funny, hand job?"

Freeze laughed again. He closed his eyes, woozy, and shrugged his shoulders. "You," he said. "Me."

Reynolds stiffened. "I'm ordering you to dispose of that frag immediately and safely."

"Can't," Freeze said. "Beer tastes like piss without it." He raised the bottle to his lips.

When he lowered it, the lieutenant had disappeared. Freeze looked around but didn't see him anywhere. Maybe he'd never been there. Maybe he'd imagined it all. He took another long drink from the bottle, concentrating on his sweaty fingers gripping the firing lever. His hand was starting to go numb. It was almost like it was dissolving, disappearing. When he finished his drink, he looked at his hand. It was still there.

As he tilted the bottle back to take another drink, he heard someone say, "Here's the son of a bitch." He squinted toward the voice. The brown-bar was back, a sneer on his face. There was another face too, but this one was grinning. It was an MP. He had a harelip that made his grin look like it was splitting his face. Freeze imagined his face cracking like an egg and laughed.

Then the MP lunged at Freeze, grabbing his hand and twisting it behind his back. The sudden pain made Freeze groan and drop the beer in his other hand. While he looked down at the bottle foaming on the red dirt, the MP pried his fingers open. Then the pain was gone and Freeze looked up. The MP stuck the grenade in Freeze's face and grinned. "My turn to play with this," he said.

Reynolds said, "Cut that shit. Just toss the frag out on the perimeter, then take this soldier to the stockade and let him sleep it off. I'll deal with him in the morning." Then he turned and strode away.

Frigging brown-bar, Freeze thought, and imagined him stepping on a mine and blowing into a hundred pieces.

Only later, after the harelip had hauled him to the stockade and asked him his name, company, platoon, and squad, did Freeze find out that the brown-bar was his new platoon leader. "Your ass is gonna be grass come morning," the MP said, laughing. "Reynolds, he's your new LT." But Freeze didn't care. What could the bastard do to him? Send him to Nam? All he wanted to do was sleep. Sleep and dream. When he woke up, everything would be clear again, everything would be back to normal.

But the next morning he felt worse. He'd been dreaming about a mummy he'd seen in a museum when he was a kid. The mummy was the color of caramel, and in his dream he'd broken off one of the toes and taken a bite. Then a gum-chewing guard woke him, and for a moment he thought the guard had taken a bite too. "Get up and get dressed," the guard said, and tossed some wrinkled fatigues onto Freeze's cot.

Freeze groaned. "What for?"

"What do you think?" the guard said. "You're going to a party." Then he told Freeze that Reynolds had put him and Konieczny on shit-burning detail, and they were to report to the privies by 0700.

Freeze sat up slowly, his head heavy and aching. "*Konieczny?*" he said. Konieczny was the big, red-haired recruit just off the bus from Bien Hoa. It was bad enough to put Freeze in the stockade but to treat him like a twink. . . . He'd spent ten months in country—ten fucking months—and he'd walked point for the first three. Nobody in his company had walked point that long, and they gave him a badge just for having survived. And now this new brown-bar was treating him like a twink.

"That's right, asshole. Now chop chop," the guard said, then went back to chewing his gum.

Freeze grinned as he watched the guard chew. *Eat death*, he thought. *Chew that gristle.*

But when he tried to stand, his head was pounding so hard he sat back on the cot with a moan. He stayed there, dizzy, until he felt he could get up. Then he stood slowly and dressed. Each movement made his head throb.

When Freeze finished tying his boots, the guard escorted him back to barracks. It was already so hot that by the time they reached the barracks his shirt had soaked through. The guard said, "You're on your own from here. Have fun at the party," and left. Freeze opened the screen door and went inside. It wasn't much cooler in the hootch. All of the men were shirtless, but their chests were still wet with sweat. Some of them had pulled their footlockers out into the middle of the wooden plank floor and were sitting on them playing cards and drinking Cokes or smoking joints. A few were lying on their racks talking and laughing about some photograph they were passing around. When they looked up and saw Freeze, they went quiet for a moment. Then Crazy Carl put down his cards and said, "You okay, man?"

That's what he'd said after Freeze had stepped on the mine. He'd come up to him, put his hand on his shoulder, and said, "Hey man, you okay?" Over and over, "Hey man, you okay?" When Freeze could finally answer, he told Carl to fuck off, he was all right, leave him alone. But Carl didn't back off. None of them did. For the rest of the patrol, they all stayed close to him, thinking they were safe if they were around him. He had the magic, they said, the luck. He wasn't going to get greased. The mine had proved that. So they stuck close to Freeze until finally he turned his M-16 on them and said he'd shoot the next mother who came near.

Now Freeze looked at Carl, then the others. Once he had been closer to these guys than to anybody in his whole life. But ever since he had stepped on the mine they had seemed like strangers. He felt like he'd walked into someone else's barracks, someone else's life.

"Yeah," he said to Carl, then crossed over to his rack and pulled off his drenched shirt. He knelt down and started to dig through his bamboo footlocker.

"I hear you and Konieczny are going to a party," Clean Machine said, then laughed. "Some people have all the luck."

Freeze looked at him, but he didn't say anything.

Duckwalk sat down on Freeze's rack. "I hope you're doing all right," he said. "We been worried about you, bro."

Freeze didn't answer. He was trying to remember what he was looking for in his footlocker. Then it came to him: cotton. He found some in the neck of an aspirin bottle and tore off two chunks. Then he stood and turned to Konieczny, who was waiting in front of his rack, smiling uneasily. "What're you laughing at, twink?" he said. Konieczny just stood there, looking confused.

"Ain't nobody laughing," High Noon said, and pushed his Stetson back on his head. "Ain't nothing funny here." Then he looked at Crazy Carl. "You want to finish this hand, pardner? 'Cause if you don't I'll be plenty happy to pick up that pot."

Crazy Carl looked at Freeze, his forehead creased. "You all right?" he asked. "You still with us?"

"What's it to you?" Freeze said.

Crazy Carl looked down and shook his head, then he picked up his cards and turned back to the game.

Freeze went outside then and stood in the heat, his head pounding. He wanted to go back to sleep. Maybe when he woke up he would be Mick again, not Freeze, and the mine would be just a bad dream.

In a moment, Konieczny joined him and they marched in silence up the hill to the latrine, each of them humping a can of diesel fuel. When they got there, Freeze stuffed the cotton up his nostrils, glaring at Konieczny all the while. Then they lifted the shelter off its blocks, exposing the fifty-five gallon drums cut in half, and started to soak the shit with fuel.

"Jesus," Konieczny said. "This is number ten."

Freeze didn't say anything; he was thinking how much he hated Reynolds for making him do this. If the son of a bitch was here right now, he'd throw him into the shit barbecue. Lieutenant Crispy Critter. He smiled as he poured the fuel into the latrine.

"Make that ten thousand," Konieczny said, his hand over his nose and mouth.

Though it was still early, the day was so hot and humid that the air seemed too thick to breathe. Freeze was breathing through his open mouth because of the cotton in his nose, and it felt like he was suffocating. His head throbbed and his stomach felt queasy. Then, as he finished pouring the fuel into the latrine, the smell of the diesel fumes and the shit suddenly penetrated the cotton and made him drop to his knees. With a noise like a bark, he vomited onto the red dirt between his trembling palms.

"You all right?" Konieczny asked, leaning over him.

Freeze wiped his mouth and looked up at Konieczny's face, its freckles and peachfuzz and acne. The twink would be lucky if he lasted a week in the bush. Freeze could see him tripping a mine and blowing into the air, his body cut in half. He remembered how Perkins had looked after he triggered the Bouncing Betty. He'd had his wet intestines in his hands, and he was trying to put them back in. Or had Freeze just dreamed that?

He looked away, squinting in the sun. "Fuck you," he answered.

"Just trying to help," the kid said. He shrugged his shoulders and turned back to the work.

Freeze stood, his legs trembling. He thought about saying he was sorry, but then he'd have to explain and he didn't know how to explain or even what to explain. So they finished soaking the shit without talking, then dropped matches on it. Black smoke curdled out of the pit, and the stench made them gag. Standing there beside the blaze, his eyes burning, head swimming, Freeze almost threw up again. And later, back in the hootch, he lay on his rack, the stink of the burning shit still thick in his nostrils, and heaved his guts into a C-rats can. His heart was beating fast, like it did when they were in a fire fight. What had happened? He'd been a strack soldier for ten months, an assistant squad leader—leader of the first fire team—for the past four, ever since C. B. got zapped. And now he was a shit-burner. God, how he hated that frigging brown-bar.

Hating the lieutenant made him feel better than he had since he'd stepped on the mine. It made things seem more real, more understandable. He stoked his hate, made it grow. Everything was Reynolds' fault. Reynolds was the evil heart of it all. If it weren't for him, he'd be happy now, he'd be one of the guys again, nothing would have changed. The bastard was worse than Charlie.

Lying there on the canvas cot, Freeze imagined Reynolds walking point through knee-high brush. Then he saw him stop dead. He'd felt something under his boot. For a second, stupidly, Reynolds thought it was a scorpion, or a rock, but then he felt the pin sink and he knew it was the metal prong of a Bouncing Betty. Before he could move, or even think, the mine flew up out of the ground with a pop. Reynolds closed his eyes and covered his head with his hands, and for a moment, a moment that stretched out until it was outside of time, he waited for the explosion of light, the thundering roar, the hail of shrapnel. Then the moment ended and the Bouncing Betty fell back at his feet, dead. The main charge hadn't gone off. Reynolds opened his eyes and stood there for several minutes, panting hard, the sweat rolling off his face and dripping onto the mine, his eyes staring into ozone. *Hey*, his men would say later, *you should have seen the brown-bar freeze.*

Freeze planned his revenge all afternoon. Then, an hour or so before dusk, he saw Reynolds go into the officers' club. After waiting a few minutes to be sure he wasn't coming back out, he snuck into Reynolds' quarters. He had planned to fire a single pistol shot into his pillow and leave, but once he was there, that plan seemed too dangerous, even crazy. He had to do something, though, so he stole the two officer-grade steaks Reynolds had in his refrigerator. He stuffed them inside his shirt and left, almost giddy. He could just see the look on Reynolds' face when he saw the steaks were missing.

Back in the hootch, Freeze put the smaller steak up for auction. He stood on his footlocker and dangled the slab in front of his squad. "What am I bid for this hunk of heaven?" he said.

Duckwalk was sitting on his rack, cleaning an AK-47 he'd souvenired from an NVA. He shook his head. "The LT's gonna fuck you, Freeze," he said.

"You'll have his steaks for supper, but he'll have your ass for breakfast," Crazy Carl agreed. "He's gonna know you swiped his meat." He took another drag on his joint and went back to playing solitaire on his footlocker.

Everybody was trying to act uninterested, but Freeze knew better. He knew how long it had been since anybody'd had a steak. To them, even the warm Cokes they got every stand-down were bennies.

"Let's start the bidding at a bag of el primo no-stem, no-seed, shall we?" he said and grinned. He was having fun. He had crossed over the edge of hatred and now he was having fun. He could barely keep from laughing.

"Are you nuts?" said McKeown. "We buy that hot cow and we're in as much trouble as you."

"Smoke my pole," High Noon said.

"Shit," Clean Machine said. "I wouldn't give one joint for your sister and your mother both."

But before long, McKeown offered a pack of Park Lanes and soon they were all bidding. When it was over, Clean had shelled out four packs of Park Lanes and a handful of military payment certificates for the steak. Freeze stashed his loot under the floorboard beneath his rack, then ditty-bopped out to the perimeter where nobody could see him and hunkered down in some brush to broil his steak. He lit a tin of Sterno and set over it a little stove he'd made by puncturing an empty C-rats can. Then he started to broil the steak on a steel plate he'd ripped off the back of a claymore mine.

Smelling the steak browning on the plate, he forgot the stench of the burning shit for the first time that day. He leaned back on one elbow, lit a Park Lane, and inhaled deeply, holding the smoke in his lungs. As he smoked, he looked out over the brush at the lead-colored sky and tried to daydream about going back to the world. He imagined he was back in Little Rock, lying on a lounge chair beside his apartment pool, catching some rays and checking out the talent. But the daydream began to unravel as soon as it started. First he

439

couldn't remember what his pool had looked like. Then he wasn't even sure whether or not he'd had a pool at Cromwell Court or if that was earlier, at the Cantrell Apartments. And the girls that strolled by in their bikinis were faceless, vague. He tried to remember Mary Ellen, the girl he'd dated the fall before he enlisted, but nothing would come to him. He wasn't sure of the color of her eyes or hair, the sound of her voice. He laughed. Then he listened to himself laugh. It was such a strange sound. He wondered why he'd never noticed how strange it was. He tried to remember Mary Ellen's laugh, but it was no use. Ever since he'd come to Nam he'd been forgetting things, and now almost everything was gone. And what he did remember seemed more like something he'd overheard in a bar, some dim, muffled conversation. He couldn't have seen Perkins holding his plastic yellow guts, or C. B.'s brains in his mouth, the top of his skull turned to pulp. He couldn't have seen these things. It was impossible. Wasn't Perkins transferred to another company? Hadn't C. B. gone back to the world?

When Freeze finally remembered to turn over the steak, it was burned black.

After lights out, a heavy monsoon rain began to beat against the ponchos nailed on the outside of the hootch. The wind whipped the water against the green plastic, battering the hootch like incoming.

Then it *was* incoming. Duckwalk sat up in the rack next to Freeze's. "You hear that?" he asked.

Freeze sat up, his poncho liner wrapped around him.

"Not tonight, Charlie," Crazy Carl moaned. "I'm having me a wet dream."

They listened as the mortars walked in closer and closer. At first there was only a distant pop, then a closer thud. Then they heard the whistling of a round and the roar of the explosion.

"Shit," Freeze said. And he and the rest of the men scrambled out of their racks, grabbing their M-16s, and double-timed in their skivvies out into the cold pounding rain. Through the rain's thick odor of rot, they could smell the sharp scents of gunpowder and cordite. On the perimeter of the camp, M-79 grenade launchers and mortars were thumping into a sky green with star flares, punctuating the nonstop sentence of an M-16 on rock-'n'-roll.

In the platoon bunker, they huddled behind the wet sandbags, shivering, staring out at the dark. Konieczny was next to Freeze.

"Are they gonna come through the wire?" he asked. When a star flare burst, his face turned green, a Martian's, and Freeze felt the urge to laugh. Then he heard the whistle of an incoming round. He ducked and waited for the burst. It seemed to take forever. Looking around, he saw that everyone was still, as if they'd been frozen. He remembered the game he'd played as a kid back in Arkansas. Statues. It was like they were playing Statues.

Then the shell exploded nearby, raining shrapnel into the bunker, and everybody came alive again. Somebody started screaming.

Reynolds stood up at his end of the bunker. "Who's down?"

Everybody looked around. But no one was hurt. Then the screaming started again. It was coming from outside the bunker.

"I'm dying!" the man yelled. "Help me!"

Before anyone could say anything, Reynolds had crawled out of the bunker and started to run in a crouch toward a man lying in the mud halfway between the second platoon hootch and bunker. Under the light of the star flares, Freeze watched the brown-bar drag the man to the bunker. He's bucking for Eagle Scout, he thought. The bastard.

The moment Reynolds made it back, they heard the whistle of another mortar and ducked, holding their breaths until it exploded. Then they looked up.

Someone shined his flashlight on the man. "Jesus H. Christ," Reynolds said then, and turned away, disgusted. The man was all right. He hadn't been hit at all. Still, he was moaning like he was dying.

"Save me," the soldier pleaded. "Don't let me die. I don't want to die." It was clear that he wasn't talking to anybody there. He was staring up at the sky, his eyes blank as milk glass, and whimpering. And he wasn't even a twink. He'd been in the bush long enough to get a bad case of jungle rot. It had invaded his face, and though he'd tried to hide it by growing a scruffy beard, it made his skin look raw.

They told him he was okay, but he kept on moaning and crying. Even after the mortars stopped falling and the machine guns faded to random bursts, he would not stop.

The rest of the men looked away, embarrassed, but Freeze couldn't take his eyes off him.

The next morning, the other soldiers were laughing about the man who thought he was wounded, calling him a snuffy, a wuss, and

441

praising Reynolds for risking his butt to save him. They even had a nickname for Reynolds now. "Man, did you see the look he gave that poge?" Crazy Carl had said. "It was righteous rabid." And it stuck. All the while they prepared for inspection, the men talked about Righteous Rabid and the Wuss. A week before, Freeze would have joined in. But he wasn't one of them anymore.

At inspection, Reynolds stopped in front of Freeze and poked him in the gut with his finger. "Private Harris," he said, "you look like you've put on a couple of pounds since yesterday." He looked Freeze in the eye. "Maybe you had an extra helping of ham and mothers? Or maybe the entire platoon gave you their cookies?"

Freeze stood there a moment. For some reason he was suddenly sleepy. He wanted to lie down and go to sleep right there on the floor of the hootch.

"I'm talking to you, Private," Reynolds said.

Freeze just stood there. He felt very tired; he didn't even have the energy to lie.

"So you did do it," Reynolds said. Then he put his face in Freeze's. "I'm going to report this little incident to Captain Arnold, and I'm going to recommend that you get an Article 15. If I have my way, he'll bust your ass to E-1." Reynolds sneered. "But until then I've got a little working party for you. How does filling sandbags sound?"

A mortar shell had blasted through the first layer of sandbags during the attack and ripped into the second layer, spilling sand like guts. It would take hours to fill enough sandbags to repair the bunker, and it was going to be another hundred and ten degree day. Already the sun was burning off the puddles formed by the rain.

Freeze stared at the blue vein that popped out on Reynolds' forehead, between his eyes, a perfect target. "It sounds like shit," he heard someone say. It was a second before he realized that he had said it.

Reynolds stiffened.

"What did you say, poge?"

Freeze said, "Cut me some slack."

Reynolds' eyes narrowed. "Maybe one Article 15 isn't enough for you, Harris. Maybe you'd like another."

Freeze stared at him. He was trying to hate him, trying to re-capture the way he'd felt when he stole the steaks, but he couldn't

442

get it back. He wanted it back desperately, but it wouldn't come. After a moment he looked down.

"No, I didn't think you'd want any more," Reynolds said then, stepping back and smiling. "I figured you'd had enough."

The rest of that morning, Freeze filled sandbags in the dizzying heat, his back and shoulders aching, while a fatass MP named Jorgenson stood by the bunker, throwing his walnut baton into the air and catching it. He was trying to see how many times he could spin the baton and still catch it. So far his record was six revolutions. Whenever he dropped the baton, he'd say "Uncle fucking Ho" and spit. Freeze stood, stretching his stiff back, and watched the MP fling the baton. He shook his head. He'd come halfway around the world to watch a man toss a baton into the air and try to catch it. And the MP had made the same trip to watch a man shovel sand. Freeze wanted to tell him how crazy it was, maybe suggest they go get a beer, but the MP caught the baton and said, "*Seven*. A new record! Let's hear it for the boy from Brooklyn." Freeze turned back to his work.

He finished repairing the bunker just before noon. He thought the brown-bar was done with him then, but after lunch, Reynolds gave him more scut work to do. He mopped the barracks, unloaded ammo crates from a deuce-and-a-half truck, and then helped carry the wounded from medevac helicopters, humping stretchers down the metal ramp to the deck, where medics sorted the living from the dead. He was so exhausted from working in the heat that he could barely stand in the prop wash of the helicopters. He staggered in the hot wind, gravel swarming around him, stinging like hornets, and felt his hatred for Reynolds rise almost to madness. He knew Reynolds was just making an example of him, using him to prove to the others that he was in charge and wasn't going to take any shit, and he knew he'd back off as soon as he felt he'd made his point. But Freeze didn't care. He still hated him. The bastard had treated him like a dead man's turd. He'd embarrassed him in front of his best friends, he'd turned them against him. He could hear the men now, talking and laughing about Righteous Rabid and Freeze. Well, he'd give them something to talk about. When they got out into the bush, he'd pay the son of a bitch back. Then everything would be clear again, and he could think straight.

As soon as Freeze decided to frag Reynolds, he began to feel calm, even happy, but almost instantly his happiness turned to sympathy for Reynolds and everything was as confused as a dream again. He saw Reynolds lying dead on the jungle floor, his eyes open to nothing, his face mottled with shadows cast by the sunlight flickering through the trees, but he was wearing Freeze's fatigues and he was smiling. Grinning. Almost laughing. Freeze stood there in the prop wash until his partner yelled from the chopper's cargo bay for him to hurry up and give him a hand.

About ten minutes later, as he bent to pick up his end of a stretcher, he saw that one of the grunt's legs had been blown off just below the knee and that the other was terribly mangled. Someone had laid the severed leg on top of him. He had his arms around it, holding it to his chest, and he was staring off somewhere, a slight smile frozen on his lips, as if he'd just heard something mildly funny.

"Heavy fucker, ain't he?" Freeze's partner said, as they hoisted the stretcher.

The next day the stand-down ended and the company was sent back out on line. They stood inspection, marched to the airfield, climbed aboard the choppers and flew north over the jungle, finally setting down in the brush and bamboo of Tay Ninh province. Freeze was glad to be back in the bush; he'd rather be in the shit, where all you had to worry about was someone shooting you, than in camp, where poge officers like Reynolds policed your every move. He figured that Reynolds would let up on him now, but if he didn't Freeze would pick his moment and frag his ass.

Reynolds didn't let up. The first day after they'd finished carving Fire Base Molly out of the jungle, stripping the foliage down to the bare red dirt, digging bunkers, and stringing coils of concertina wire around the perimeter, he dispatched Freeze, Konieczny, and Clean to secure a helicopter supply drop for a tank column—three men to defend thousands of gallons of diesel fuel and tons of ammo.

"One dink with a hand grenade could blow the whole damn drop to Saigon," Freeze complained, though he didn't really care.

Reynolds looked at him. "The tank column is expected at 1900 hours. Saddle up." Then he turned and walked away.

Freeze raised his hand and sighted down his index finger at the lieutenant's back. *Bang.*

Duckwalk turned to him, his thumbs hooked behind the silver buckle of the NVA belt he'd souvenired from a sniper. "Relax, bro," he said. "He's just the Army. What you expect him to do? Be your friend?"

Freeze didn't say anything. He shouldered his pack and headed out for the supply drop with Konieczny and Clean. When they got there, Konieczny sat on one of the crates and radioed back to Reynolds. Freeze broke open another crate. "Chocolate milk," he said, taking out a carton and shaking his head. "Chocolate fucking milk."

"What's your problem, Freeze?" Clean said. "I'm getting sick of this shit. We're all getting sick of it."

Freeze looked at Clean. Then he opened the carton and took a drink. When he finished, he wiped his mouth with his hand. "Whatever you do," he said, "don't let this milk fall into enemy hands."

Then he turned and humped off into a stand of bamboo a couple hundred yards away and crawled down into a crater left by a mortar shell. He lay there, smoking a Park Lane, and thought about greasing Reynolds. He would have shot him already if he'd had the chance. He didn't know why he'd ever felt sorry for the bastard. It wouldn't bother him at all to shoot him now. The only thing he worried about was getting caught. He had just fifty-four days and a wake-up left before he could fly the freedom bird home, and if he got caught they'd put him in Long Binh Jail. But even that might be worth it. He imagined Reynolds face-down on the ground, his brains leaking out his open mouth. As soon as Reynolds was dead, he could rest. Everything would make sense again and he'd be at peace. He took out another joint and smoked it. The sun bore down on him, the heat like a heavy weight, and soon he fell asleep.

He didn't wake until he felt the ground tremble and heard the steel rumble of the tanks. The sun was hovering over the edge of the horizon, staining the countryside a dusty red. Climbing out of the crater, he sauntered back to the supply drop. He came up to Konieczny and Clean just as the tanks rolled over the rise.

Clean looked at him. "Thanks for your fucking help."

Konieczny looked down the road and didn't say anything.

Freeze didn't know Clean had reported him until the next day, when Reynolds led the platoon on a reconnaissance-in-force. They humped through the jungle all day, sweating under their packs;

then, toward mid-day, they smelled shit cooking in the heat. It had to be a NVA camp. Through a stand of bamboo, they spotted a row of bunkers. Reynolds ordered Freeze's fire team to go in first, and they approached in a cloverleaf pattern. But the camp was abandoned. Bombers had attacked it, probably no more than a week before, and there were tank- sized craters everywhere. In a few places, the ground was still white from the phosphorous the spotter plane had dropped to give the B-52s their target. There was no sign of the NVA anywhere. Still, Reynolds ordered Freeze to check out a bunker that hadn't been caved in by the bombs.

"It's crawling with fire ants," Freeze said. "There's no gooks in there."

"I said check it out, Harris."

"Why me?" Freeze said.

Reynolds glared at him. "Yesterday I gave you a direct order, and you subverted it. It will not happen again."

Freeze looked at Konieczny, then at Clean. Clean crossed his arms on his chest and looked back.

So he climbed down and checked the bunker out, and when he came scrambling out a moment later, the ants were all over him. He jumped up and down, swatting and swiping at the red sons of bitches, while the men laughed at him.

"You bastard," Freeze said to Reynolds. "You motherfucking bastard. I'm not going to eat any more of your shit."

"Oh, yes, you will," Reynolds said. "You'll eat it. You'll lick your plate clean, and you'll like it."

Freeze stood there, breathing hate, and stared at Reynolds, an animal snarl on his face. He hated him more than he'd ever hated the NVA. He hated him more than the heat and the jungle, the leeches and mosquitoes, the monsoon rains, the smells of sulfur and shit and death, more than his sixty-pound pack, the blisters on his shoulders, the wet socks, the jungle rot and immersion foot, more than the lizards that cried *fuck you, fuck you* in the night, the thump of mortars, the booby traps, more even than the mine that hadn't gone off.

"That's a negative," Freeze said, and before Reynolds could move, he snapped the bolt of his M-16, chambering a round, and shoved the flash suppressor into his belly, just under this ribs. The blood was drumming in his temples.

Reynolds sucked in a breath. The men steppped back. "Holy shit," Konieczny said.

"Take it easy, bro," Crazy Carl said. "Everybody's looking. You don't want to do nothing when everybody's looking."

Freeze ignored him. He stared at Reynolds. Reynolds opened his mouth to say something, but no words came out. He closed and opened it again. Sweat began to bead on his upper lip. Freeze focused on one of the beads, and waited for it to slide down his lip and break. But it didn't move. It hung there, as if time had stopped, as if there were no more time.

Then everything went out of Freeze. What was he so angry about? It didn't mean anything anymore. It didn't seem real. Nothing seemed real. The drop of sweat. The circle of men staring at him like he was a gook. Reynolds. He looked around at the craters that surrounded them. They could be on the moon. He lowered his rifle and sat down in the red dust, suddenly dizzy. His hands were trembling.

Then Reynolds blinked and swallowed hard. He looked around him and finally found words. "Konieczny," he said, his voice shaking slightly, "get on the horn to HQ. We need to call in a chopper to remove Private Harris to the stockade."

Konieczny said, "Yes, sir" and began to call headquarters.

Reynolds looked down at Freeze. Then he squared his shoulders and said, in a voice that shook now more with anger than fear, "Get this son of a bitch out of my sight. Get him out of here before I kill him."

But Freeze didn't hear him. He wasn't there. He had stepped on the mine and he was rising into the air, twisting and turning in the bursting light for one last peaceful second.

Nominated by Philip Booth, Philip Dacey and David Wojahn

SEQUENCE

by LYNN NELSON

from NEW VIRGINIA REVIEW

HIS MOTHER

For months the letters from his mother came,
that first year of our lawful wedded life.
She didn't even want to know my name,
much less what I was like, his nightmare wife.
He wouldn't read them to me, but I knew
her letters told him that she'd been betrayed
by his transgression of her worst taboo.
She begged him to renege the vows he'd made.
Dumbstruck with pain, he struggled toward a choice
between love for his mother and for me,
turning from both of us without a voice
to ask either of us for sympathy.
Its tongue cut out by my guilt and his loss,
our love hung silent on his mother's cross.

HOW DID I LOVE HIM?

I loved him with a passion put to use
in childhood's longing for identity.
I loved him for his detailed and profuse
remembered past: It gave a past to me.
I loved him for the thin potato soup,
the push-meat sandwiches after the war,

his mother's sneaking up on him, to swoop
him up and wrestle him to the floor.
I loved his college and his army days,
his trips to capitols I'd never seen;
the operas and concerts, films and plays
I saw as he described them, with a keen
and narcissistic vision: With what grace
I bent to kiss his sky, and saw my face!

FROGS

That spring I dreamed incessantly of frogs,
Their silly croaking lulled me every night;
sometimes they swam through me as polliwogs
or sperm bearing the chromosome for blight.
They wanted me to kiss their ugliness,
beseeching me with staring, swollen eyes.
Caught in the dream, I had to acquiesce:
My children, in dream-logic's weird disguise,
they wanted me to love them and conceive.
In autumn when the test read positive,
he told me if I had it, he would leave
I loved him: That's the thing I can't forgive.
Feet in the stirrups, riding on my back,
I loved him. Even as my world went black.

THE CIRCUS

The woman whom I hoped to make my friend
invited us to meet her and her kids
three hours' drive away, so we could spend
an evening at the circus. There, amid
the awe and shouts of laughter, I forgot
how miserable I'd been an hour before.
Like Guinevere in love in Camelot,
I was enchanted by the lions' roar,
the trained pigs, and this woman's youngest son
whose giggle was a melody of bells

which shivered joy through every ganglion
of my unhappy body, made me swell
almost to bloom. Then he said he'd prefer
if I drove her kids home: He'd ride with her.

WHAT I KNEW

The clash of cultures—of my ignorance
and his clear, European intellect—
embarrassed and enraged me. What a dunce
I thought I was. My fledgling self-respect
disintegrated daily. He was shocked
by my miseducation, so I'd shrink
when he made any overture to talk,
because I was afraid of what he'd think.
The insecurity I'd felt at school—
where I got A's, I thought, for being black
when all the time I knew I was a fool—
and deeply buried in myself, came back.
My habit of surrender grew so strong
he never knew when I knew he was wrong.

EVERYDAY

I never felt the ordinary rage
my friends confess to over coffee cups.
I never had to go on a rampage
as they do, when their husbands won't clean up
the bathroom, when they don't take out the trash,
when they leave dirty laundry on the floor.
My husband whipped up dinners with panache;
he gladly tackled any household chore.
We went for months without an argument,
without a missed beat in our clockwork life,
with nothing to take ill, or to resent:
my perfect husband and his perfect wife.
For months, I could have nothing to complain
to him about, except my constant pain.

450

SISTERS

The schoolbus drove us home from highschool, where
we got off in the Negro neighborhood
and several times a week there was a fight:
One sister called another sister "hoe,"
pulled out black handfuls of her straightened hair,
clawed at her face and hands, and ripped her shirt.
I walked home. I believed in sisterhood.
I still do, after thirty years, although
I'll never understand why several white
sisters walked on me as if I was dirt.
We were all sisters, feminists, I thought,
forgetting what those cat-fights should have taught.
I was too well brought-up, too middle class
to call a heifer out, and whup her ass.

BY THE TRACK

We came home to our lives, and home to all
the friends we'd half-forgotten. Home to her.
She was unhappy; at midnight, she'd call
to talk with him. I listened: a voyeur.
I saw her notes to him, counted her gifts,
and plotted routes by which I could escape.
It wasn't her fault: She'd been set adrift,
and had no sextant other than her shape.
One day, we walked beside the railroad track.
I thinking *murder, lawyers, money, death.*
He reached his goal, decided to turn back,
and mused, "I think, before my fortieth
birthday, I might like to have a child . . ."
He didn't understand why I ran wild.

COLOR

For him, I gave away my father's name.
He gave away his mother's love for me.

So each of us was partially to blame
for the other's lost, and found identity.
I tried to find myself, in our old car,
by looking at his profile as he drove
to see if we were somehow similar,
had more in common than the kitchen stove
and our Breughel print, which only shared a room.
I asked him once what he was thinking of;
I should have known his answer spelled our doom,
for nothing I could think of sounded duller:
He said, "Of Goethe's writings about color."

RECURRENT DREAM

My father came back regularly, to see
how I was doing, long after he died.
He came in dreams in which he lovingly
explained that he'd returned to be my guide
through the important shadows. I awoke
and all day saw day's light intensified.
The last time, in an aureole of smoke
that somehow shone, he stood outside the door.
I didn't open it. Instead, I spoke:
"I'm grown up; I don't need you any more."
He smiled and nodded, saying, "Yes, I know."
Last night I had another visitor:
Love's ghost, as though compelled by need, as though
it knew the way. My love, I'm grown. Let go.

Nominated by Rita Dove

THE RAIN OF TERROR

fiction by FRANK MANLEY

from THE SOUTHERN REVIEW

"MY NAME IS Oletta Crews."

It sounded like a public announcement.

"This is James Terry Crews, my husband." She indicated the old man on the sofa beside her. He was dressed in khaki trousers and six-inch workboots. The woman had on a print dress, a bold floral pattern like slashes. She wore no shoes.

James Terry Crews gestured silently, acknowledging himself.

"Don't act like an idiot," Oletta Crews said, and the man dropped his hand.

"Just sit there." She turned away from him.

"This is James Terry Crews, my husband." She spoke in a powerful voice, lifted like a singer's from her diaphragm. "He's retired. We're both retired," she added significantly. "Him from work and me from housework. I got a bad heart, and I'm stout besides. You can see that. Doctor says I'm hundreds of pounds overweight, shortening my life with every bite of food I take. But what if I didn't. You think that'd help?"

She leaned forward and spoke confidentially. "There's more dies of hunger than does of the other."

She leaned back and gestured toward her husband again. "He helps me," she said. "He does what he needs to."

James Terry Crews sat beside her and stared straight ahead. He looked afraid.

"Listen to me," Oletta Crews said.

James Terry Crews started to get up, but she held out a hand and restrained him.

"Sit there," she ordered.

"Listen," she said. "I live here alone all by myself, a poor old woman, except for him. He lives here, too. Both together."

There were one or two aluminum windows, an aluminum door, a dinette set, strings of laundry overhead, a scattering of shoes and other debris on the floor, aluminum cans, some in plastic sacks, some loose, piled in the corner. The feeling was that of a cave or a nest—the secret bestial place.

"This is a trailer, you notice that?"

James Terry Crews corrected her. "Mobile home."

"Same damn thing." She was suddenly angry. "I told you that. Pay attention."

James Terry Crews ignored her. "Trailer's something you trail after you," he explained. "That's what it means, trailer. You hitch it on the back of a car and hit the trail."

"And mobile home's mobile," Oletta Crews shouted. "That means it moves."

It seemed like an argument they had had before, the lines already memorized, the positions taken not only well-known but entrenched and fortified.

"Tell them about the rain of terror."

"The rain of terror," Oletta Crews said, repeating the words, savoring them. She turned to James Terry Crews. "They don't want to hear about mobile homes. They want to hear about the rain of terror." She bugged her eyes as she said *the rain of terror*. The effect was not comic. Her eyes were filled with something other than fear.

"It was at night."

"Two nights ago." James Terry Crews sounded incredulous.

"It was two nights ago," Oletta Crews said. "And it was dark. James Terry was already home soaking wet from the weeds where he'd been and changed his clothes already to dry them. He was picking aluminum cans. I'm too stout to get out and help or else I'd be there driving the truck, but I can't even drive no more. It's bad on my heart, and the pedals are too close anyway. They're all underfoot. It's hell to be old." She leaned forward. "If I was you, I'd die before I got there." She laughed silently, baring her gums.

"I used to be a house painter," James Terry Crews announced suddenly. "Twenty-eight years and every day sober on the job."

"That don't matter," Oletta Crews shouted. "They don't want to hear about that. You're retired. He sells aluminum cans," she explained. "That's what he does now. They got a yard in town buys them. Beer cans and such as that."

"I didn't always do it," James Terry Crews said. "I used to paint with the best of them."

"That was then. This is now. I'm telling this," Oletta Crews said, picking up where she had left off. "He came in sopping wet from the rain of terror where he been out in the weeds all day looking for beer cans, and I told him what I saw on TV so he don't fall too far behind. And he was changing his socks. I can close my eyes and still see him sitting right there." She pointed across the room at an overstuffed chair that matched the sofa. The arms were shiny and greasy with wear. The seat was piled high with clothes, the upper layers of which had toppled over onto the floor. "Sitting in that chair right there changing his socks, when I heard this knocking at the door."

"What did you think?"

"I thought, Who's that?"

"Me, too," James Terry Crews said. "I thought, Who's that?"

"I thought, Who's that knocking on the door in the dark? I knew it wasn't nobody I knew. His children are gone, and I don't have none, and all my kinfolks are dead before me."

"Tell them about the news."

"I don't generally watch the news if I can help it," Oletta Crews said. "But this night was special. The good Lord led me to it this night. It's like I almost heard this voice said, 'Don't touch the TV. I got something on the news.' I was too tired to get up, and it said, 'Don't do it then. I got something better for you to do than get up and change the channel. I got something to show you right here on this one you're watching.' It's like I almost heard this voice beside the still waters, leading me on in the valley of the shadow of death where I fear no evil for thou art with me. Thy rod and staff they comfort me."

"And you were afraid."

"Of course I was afraid after hearing what I heard and knowing it was some kind of message delivered on TV special for me. Of course I was afraid. Who wouldn't be? I knew he'd protect me like he done. That's why I'm alive and the other one's dead because I could walk through the valley of the shadow of death and fear no evil. So the answer is no. No, I wasn't afraid. But I *was* interested. When I heard how he escaped from the work camp and killed two men, and it wasn't more than five miles down the road and was coming this way, I wasn't afraid, but I *was* interested."

"She heard the knock," James Terry Crews explained.

"I heard the knock and wondered, Who is it? But I already knew. I said, 'It's him.' "

"And I said, 'Who?' "

"Let me tell it," Oletta Crews shouted. "You weren't even there when it happened. I'm telling it. Listen," she said. "This is how it happened. I heard the knock, and I said, 'It's him,' and James Terry looked up from his sock and said, 'Who you mean?' and I said, 'The one on TV when you wasn't here escaped from the work camp and killed two men. It's him at the door,' and he put on his sock," indicating her husband, "and said, 'What you want to do?' And I said, 'Go get it. He might have some money hid.' "

"And I said, 'Money? What you mean money?' "

"Where he hid it after he stole it," Oletta Crews said. "I thought he might have some, and I said, 'Let him in. He might have some money hid.' And James Terry went to the door, one shoe on and one in his hand, and it was him. I was sitting right here where I always sit on this side of the sofa, and I saw him standing in the door soaking wet where it was raining outside in the dark as far as the eye could see. Looked like silver knives. And he said, 'Can I come in? I'm awful wet.' And I yelled, 'I can see you are, honey. Let him in, James Terry. Let him in to get dry.' And he came in, and I said, 'Get him a towel.' And James Terry got him a towel and sat down and put on his shoe. And I said to him, 'I know who you are.' "

"She knew who he was."

"I told him I saw his picture on TV, and I knew who he was, thanks to God, and what he was there for."

"What was that?" James Terry Crews asked.

"You were there. Don't ask things you already know. He was there to rob us. He came there to rob us."

"Your life was in danger."

"My life was in danger. As soon as I saw him, I knew I might not live."

She paused, staring at something in the distance.

"Go on."

"I told him his name. I said, 'You're Q. B. Farris, escaped from the work camp.' And he said, 'Yes Ma'am. I can't fool you, I can see that.' And I said, 'That's right. There's many a one better than you tried all my life, and they didn't do it so why should you?' And he laughed. He was good-hearted. I can say that for him. He might have been mean, but he was good-hearted. He didn't care."

"I liked him," James Terry Crews said.

"Then he said, 'You know who I am? You know what I done?' And I said, 'Some. I know the most recent.' And I told him he killed two men. And he said that was exaggerated. And I said, 'It's on TV.' And he said he didn't care. It was exaggerated. And I said, 'Don't kill me. I'm just a poor old woman. It won't help to kill me. I don't know where your money's hid.' And I saw him looking at James Terry where he just finished putting on his shoe, and I knew what he was thinking. I said, 'Don't kill him either. He got to help me. I'm retired.' And he laughed like he done and said, 'What you retired from, momma?' And I said, 'Don't call me momma. I ain't your momma. I ain't nobody's momma.' And he said, 'You look like you ought to be. You got a kind face and a big bosom.' And I thought then, He's going to rape me. Been in prison with men too long."

"His name was Duke," James Terry Crews explained.

"Q. B. Farris. He said his name was Duke. He said, 'Call me Duke. I don't know who Q. B. is.' "

"And I said, 'What's the Q. B. stand for?' " James Terry Crews said. "And you know what he said? He said, 'Queer Bastard.' I didn't know what to make of that."

"Except he wasn't queer," Oletta Crews said. "Else he wouldn't have wanted to rape me."

"Unless he was both."

"I'm telling this," Oletta Crews shouted. "We already agreed on that." She looked straight ahead. "That's the kind of person he was, full of useless jokes like that. He didn't care. You know what he said when I said don't kill me? He said, 'I wouldn't kill you or him either, momma. I got a momma of my own.' "

"What did you think about that?"

"I thought, Well where is she? I said, 'You say you got a momma, where is she?' I figured she might have the money. And he said, 'Oconee, Tennessee—in the graveyard,' and looked at me and laughed. And I said, 'You laughing because she's dead or you laughing because you broke her heart?' That straightened him out. He

457

quit laughing and said, 'Neither one. I loved my momma. She's the only one I trust.' And I said, 'I reckon. I'd trust her too, state she's in now.' That's when he hit me."

"He hit you?" James Terry Crews glanced at her, then turned away.

"He tried to," Oletta Crews said. "Then he looked at me and said, 'She died when I was still in prison. I never got to go to the funeral because it was out of state.' Said if it'd been in the state, they'd have let him, but she was buried in Tennessee, and that's a whole other system. And I thought, So what? She wouldn't know if you were there or not—chained like a wild dog at a funeral. 'They all die. That's a common fact,' I told him. 'She'd have died if you were in jail or not.' And he said it wasn't the dying he minded. It was they wouldn't let him out to be there. That's what he hated. And that's when he told me about the nine years. He said, 'I ain't been my own man in nine years and nine more to go.' And I thought, Whose fault is that? Don't come crying on my shoulder. You should have thought about that when you decided what you wanted to be."

"What do you mean?"

"What do I mean? I mean a robber—steals money and hides it somewhere. And I said, 'Your momma's house still standing? That where you going?' And he said no, he liked it here. And I said, 'I don't got no money. You might want to go and get yours.' And he said, 'Mine?' like he didn't know what I was talking about. He said, 'I don't got no money. What are you talking about?' And I said, 'That money you got hid you come out of jail to get.' And he said, 'I don't got no money hid. I come out because I couldn't stand to stay in,' and laughed like he done so I knew he was lying. I said, 'Where's your home at in Oconee? You from town?' I figured that's where he hid the money. And he said, 'Oconee? I ain't from Oconee. I'm from right here.' He was born and raised in this county. Reason his momma died in Oconee, she was living with her sister, and they buried her there. That's when I knew he had it on him. All the money he stole and buried, it was right there beside me. Only difference was he had it, not me, and he was fixing to leave if he could."

"I didn't know what that meant," James Terry Crews explained, "but she said it was stolen already and buried nine years, and besides they're all dead anyway. . . ."

458

"I said I'd tell it," Oletta Crews said, each word heavy with its own weight.

James Terry Crews did not look at her. He did not answer.

"And that's when he said, 'How about some supper?' He was looking at me. And I said, 'You talking to me?' And he said, 'I was. I ain't now,' and laughed like it was some kind of joke. He said, 'You look like you might be hungry. How about you and me eating something?' And I said, 'I ain't hungry.' And he said, 'Well then why don't you rustle up something for me?' And I said, 'I don't cook. I'm retired.' And he said, 'Retired? What are you retired from?' And I said, 'The human race.' That took him back. And he said, 'Lord God, I thought you had to be dead for that.' And I said, 'Some do. Your momma maybe.' And he said, 'Don't talk about my momma. She's some kind of saint in heaven when you rot in hell.' And I said, 'I don't believe in saints.' And he said he didn't care, he knew her, I didn't, and he started doing these things on his head like he was beating up on himself. And I said, 'What's that?' "

She turned to her husband. "Show how he done."

James Terry Crews looked surprised. He took off his glasses and slapped at his forehead, then at his ears. First with one hand, then with the other.

"I saw Duke do that," Oletta Crews said. "I said, 'What you do that for?' And he said it was something he learned in prison. Means you're sorry for what you done. And I said, 'What for?' And he said, 'Whatever. It works for all.' "

"I thought he was crazy," James Terry Crews said.

"Me too. I figured he was going to kill us both or else stay there and keep us for ransom."

"What she means is hostages."

"That's right. Stay with us here till he was safe and then kill us as soon as he walked out that door going to California."

"She wants to die in California," James Terry Crews explained.

"That's right. I'm a poor old woman. That's my only hope, to see California and die happy there. That's all I want."

"That's all she wants."

"They got the Pacific Ocean out there. I got a picture in the bathroom from *National Geographic*. You ever see that one on California? That picture I got's the best one in it. I see that picture, I get all smooth inside. The jitters fall off like leaves off a tree. Shows the ocean and the sun going down, smooth and calm as far as the eye can see. Another thing—it don't ever rain. There ain't no rain of terror out there. Nature is mild. They got orange trees, bloom all year, and you want an orange, you pick it yourself."

"They got retirement," James Terry Crews said.

Oletta Crews turned and stared at him. James Terry Crews fell silent.

"What he was saying is they take care of you out there even if you don't got no children."

"I got a daughter."

"There ain't no minimum social security," Oletta Crews said. "No matter how much you made, they fix it up so you live like a prince. It ain't like here. They care about you in California. All it takes is getting out there. You got a bus ticket to California, you got a ticket to the Garden of Eden. It's like what they call your Heart's Desire. 'Lay up for yourselves treasure in heaven, where neither moth nor rust doth corrupt, and where thieves do not break through nor steal. For where your treasure is, there will be your heart also.' "

"They know all that," James Terry Crews said. "Tell them what happened."

"That's what I'm trying to do. He was going to California, and we stopped him, that's all." Oletta Crews stopped suddenly as though slamming a door. "We already told the police."

"That was yesterday. This is today," her husband explained.

"What do I care? I'm old." She paused. "I said, 'Fix your own supper, I'm too old.' "

"I fixed it for him."

"He fixed it."

"I told him I'd fix it. I said, 'I generally fix the meals around here.' "

"And he said, 'You know how to cook?' " Oletta Crews turned to her husband. "I'm telling this."

James Terry Crews stared straight ahead as in an old photograph. He gave no sign of having heard. He looked as though he might have been dead the last twenty or thirty years.

"All right," Oletta Crews said, leaning forward. "Listen to this. Duke said, 'You know how to cook?' like he was surprised at a man cooking. And I said, 'How you think you ate in prison?' And he said 'With my hands.' And I said, 'What?' And he said, 'I ate with my hands. Haw haw.' And I said, 'I thought you might have used a spoon.' That straightened him up. And then I said, 'He learned in the army,' " meaning James Terry Crews. "He was in the Second World War and cooked for generals when he wasn't killing folks."

"I cooked for General Eisenhower." The memory seemed to stir the ashes in James Terry Crews. "I cooked steaks and eggs for breakfast, and he drank whiskey. He didn't touch a drop of coffee. He said, 'I'll have whiskey, Cookie. You got some bourbon?' And I said, 'Damn right. I'll make it myself.' I didn't even know what I was talking about. He was the most famous man in the world. This was overseas in France."

"They don't want to hear about that," Oletta Crews shouted. "That's too long ago, and he's dead anyway. They want to hear about Q. B. Farris."

"He's dead, too."

"He died more recent."

James Terry Crews turned away.

"Now, where was I?" Oletta Crews asked.

"Cooking supper," James Terry Crews replied.

"You were out cooking supper. I was entertaining him. I asked what he robbed to get in the work camp for eighteen years. I figured it must have been a bank. And he said, 'Robbed? Who told you that?' And I said, 'I don't need nobody to tell me nothing. I can figure it out by myself.' And he said, 'Then in that case you tell me.' And I said, 'A bank. I figure you for robbing a bank.' And he looked up quick under his hair. Had this hair over his eyes. And that's when it came to me. If he robbed a bank, there must have been a lot of money. Where was the suitcase? I said, 'You got a car?' And he said, 'Not yet. I'm fixing to.' And I said, 'How'd you get here then?' And he said, 'Through the woods. I walked.' And that's when I knew he had it on him, thousands of dollars wrapped up in plastic inside his pocket. And I said, 'You going to California?' And he said, 'Not if I can stay with you, momma. I love you too much to go off and leave you.' "

"Then we ate supper," James Terry Crews said, "and I told him about the army. He said it sounded a lot like prison, and I told him he was wrong about that. 'There's a world of difference between them,' I said."

"They just talked about this and that," Oletta Crews said. "Most of it him and the other one. I didn't listen. I was thinking about what comes next. And then I asked him, 'Are we prisoners?' And he said, 'Not any more than I am.' And I said, 'What's that supposed to mean?' "

"That was what you might call a threat," James Terry Crews explained.

"A threat?"

"Meaning we were hostages."

"That's right," Oletta Crews said. "We were hostages. It was a threat."

"Then we finished supper."

"We finished supper," Oletta Crews said. "And he said, 'Here, let me help you.' And I said, 'Help what?' And he said, 'Clean up. Don't you clean up the dishes? You let them stay dirty or you got dogs?' And I said, 'Dogs? What dogs got to do with it?' And he said, 'A joke.' He was joking. He was a jokey fellow, he said. That's one thing I got to get used to. And I said, 'What for?' And he said, 'What for? To understand what I'm saying. That's what for. To get the good out of me.' And I said, 'I don't see nothing funny about dogs.' And he said he meant lick the dishes. Clean them that way. And I said, 'James Terry does the dishes. And besides that I never had a dog in my life. Dogs unclean. It says in the Bible.' Then I told him, 'They don't have dogs in California.' And he looked surprised at that and said, 'California? You ever been out to California?' And I said, 'Not yet. I'm fixing to.' "

"As soon as she can sell this place," James Terry Crews explained. "She's been talking about it ever since she retired. 'Going to California,' I told him. 'That's where she want to go and die happy.' "

"And he laughed at that," Oletta Crews shouted. "I said, 'What are you laughing at? That some kind of joke like dogs?' And he said, 'No ma'am. I was thinking about dying happy.' That struck him funny. He said, 'I can't figure that one out.' And I didn't even look at him. I told my husband, I said, 'You better clean up the dishes before he calls in some dogs to do it.' And he laughed and made like he was going to hug me, but I flung him off. And he said, 'That's why I like you, momma. You're so fast and full of jokes.' "

"Then we went and washed the dishes," James Terry Crews said. "He called me dad."

"Same way he called me momma," Oletta Crews shouted. "He didn't mean it. I told him, 'I ain't your momma. Your momma's dead. I wouldn't have a son in the work camp.' And he said, 'It'd break your heart. It'd break your heart, wouldn't it, Momma?' And I told him it'd kill me for sure if I had a child and he ended up in the work camp for eighteen years. And he said, 'Nine'—like he was setting me straight. He laughed and said, 'I stayed for nine. I ain't fixing to stay for the rest. That way I'm ahead.' He didn't care."

"Tell them about the dictionary."

Oletta Crews reached under the sofa and pulled out a book. The covers were torn off, the pages dirty and dog-eared. She held it up for inspection.

"This is the dictionary," Oletta Crews announced. It was like an exhibit, a piece of evidence. "I was reading it."

"Reads it all day, that and the Bible, when she ain't watching television," James Terry Crews explained. "That's what she does. She does that to pass the time."

"It's all in there, everything you need to know," Oletta Crews said. "One's the head and the other's the heart. I got something to figure out, I read the dictionary till I find what it is."

"The Bible's the heart," James Terry Crews explained. "She reads it to ease her heart."

"When it gets too full," Oletta Crews said. "When I get to suffering too much. It puts my weary heart to rest. But I couldn't find it. It was there, but I couldn't find it."

"Find what?"

Oletta Crews looked at her husband as though she could not believe he was stupid enough to have asked such a question.

"What comes next," she said. "And then it came to me. I was in the bathroom, and I heard them washing dishes and talking like bees in the wall, and I was looking out at the ocean, that picture I told you about of the water. And that's when it came to me."

"That's when she decided," James Terry Crews explained.

"I didn't decide. Something told me."

"Something told her."

"Like a voice in California. I got up and flushed the toilet and went back and sat down and turned it over in my mind."

Oletta Crews held up her hand. "Listen to me," she said. "This is the main part. I knew what he was fixing to do, and he knew I knew. He already killed two men to get here. I heard that where God led me this far on TV, and now he was telling me what to do next."

"God," James Terry Crews explained. It was like nailing a pelt on a wall. "The voice she heard. It was God."

Oletta Crews looked at him with contempt. "They know that. Who else got a voice? Of course it was God. Speaks in your heart just like he led me on TV to know who it was came to the door in the rain of terror. And he opened it," indicating her husband, "and I looked out and knew who it was like in a mirror he looked so familiar."

"You were afraid."

"Yes."

"You killed him because you were afraid."

"Yes," And then, "I didn't kill him."

"I killed him."

"Don't listen to him," Oletta Crews shouted. "Listen to me. He don't know nothing."

"I don't know nothing."

"He just did it. I heard the voice."

"She heard the voice. I'm the one murdered him."

"It wasn't a murder. Police say that. Police say, 'You shoot whoever you want to, Lady, breaks in your house and keeps you hostage.' "

"Damn right, wouldn't you? She was afraid he might kill her."

"And I was afraid he might kill him, too," Oletta Crews said, indicating her husband. "I need him to help me. Besides I heard the voice. It spoke in my heart." She stopped as though reflecting. " 'You can't serve two masters.' That's what it said. 'No man can serve two masters: for either he will hate the one, and love the other; or else he will hold to the one and despise the other.' "

"That's right. Then what?"

"I thought how to do it."

"How to kill him."

"I thought of ways of how to do it. Like roach tablets. Putting them in his grits at breakfast. And then I thought, What if they don't work? What if they just work on roaches? Then I thought of rat poison. But what if he tastes it? Drano. That's too strong. Lysol and Clorox. He might have to drink a gallon. Poison is out."

"I told her about the nail."

"That was later, when he went to bed."

"You were still thinking about it."

"Not that way I wasn't."

"In the ear . . ." James Terry Crews began.

"Let me tell it," Oletta Crews shouted. "I'm telling this. It was all over by then. I already figured it out. He said, 'What about a nail?' And I said, 'A nail?' And he said, 'I read about it in the paper.' "

"No, I didn't. It was in the *Police Gazette*. In the Charlotte, North Carolina bus station. I was there waiting, and I went to the newsstand and picked up the magazines like you do, looking for pictures. . . ."

"They got pictures of half-naked women where they been raped in the *Police Gazette*," Oletta Crews said. "That's what he was looking at."

"No I wasn't. I was just looking, waiting for the time to pass till I got my bus, and I picked up the *Police Gazette*, and the first thing I turned to, that was it. Nail Murder. All about how this farmer in Kansas and this girlfriend he got killed her husband by driving a thirty-penny nail in his ear." James Terry Crews glared about him in triumph. "They killed him by driving a nail in his ear." He leaned forward. "You know why they did that?"

"So it wouldn't be a wound," Oletta Crews shouted. "They know that. The nail went in, and they wiped up the blood and burned the rag and called the doctor and said, 'He rose up in the bed and shouted and fell over dead.' And the doctor didn't even look in the ear. Said, 'Must have been a heart attack.' And they almost got away with it except for the farmer. He went crazy and confessed it all. Otherwise, they'd have joined the farms, his and the one she got from the murder, and made a million dollars by now selling it off for shopping centers."

"You ever hear anything like that?" James Terry Crews said proudly. "That's what you call a perfect crime except he went crazy."

"That's where he went wrong," Oletta Crews said. "That's why it ain't perfect. So I told him the nail was out." She lowered her voice. "I even thought of cutting his throat. Waiting till he was asleep and then creep in the light at the end of the hall shining in so we could see the vein in his neck beating and then pull the razor across it. But what if it's too deep? What if the gristle is too hard to cut through? I ain't that strong, and I knew he couldn't do it," indicating her husband. "He can talk about nails all he wants to, but I knew he couldn't even hold it still. He's too soft. He might look at him and feel sorry for him. I couldn't chance it. I didn't want Duke getting up, throat flapping open from ear to ear where I cut at it and him not dead. Ain't no telling what he might do bleeding like that, bubbling and shouting. He'd kill me for sure. That's when I knew James Terry would have to shoot him."

"I had to. You heard her."

"Hold on," Oletta Crews shouted. "Don't rush ahead. They ain't finished the dishes yet. I got out of the bathroom, and they came in and sat down, and James Terry said, 'Duke's been telling me about all the good times they had in the work camp. He liked it there.' And I said, 'If he liked it so much, why didn't he stay? Why come around here bothering us?' And then Duke says. 'What's on TV?' And I say, 'Nothing.' And he says, 'They got Monday Night Football.' And I say, 'I don't watch it. I don't know the rules.' And he says, 'What about you, old dad?' speaking to my husband, James Terry Crews."

" 'I don't watch it either,' I said. And he said, 'Why not? You don't know the rules?' And I said, 'I know them. I just don't watch it.' " He glanced at his wife. "It's too rough."

"That's right," Oletta Crews said. "I told him that game's all right for the work camp. I said, 'Rough men done worse than that to each other every day of their lives, but it ain't all right for women and children. It's too rough. Besides which,' I told him, 'it ain't Monday night.' And he said, 'Not Monday?' And I said, 'That's right. Yesterday was Monday. This is Tuesday.' And he laughed and said, 'Lord God,' and grinned like he just ate something he shouldn't."

"He had this kind of shit-eating grin," James Terry Crews explained.

"It was attractive, I don't mean that," Oletta Crews said, "but it's like he been eating something he shouldn't. And he said, 'I can keep up with it in the work camp. It's when I get out, that's when I lose track.' And I said, 'How many times you get out?' And he said every chance he got. That and Monday Night Football's his only pleasure, he said. That and beating up on folks to get in the work camp in the first place. 'And grinning,' I said. 'You left out grinning.' And he laughed and said, 'That's right, momma. That's the only pleasure I got, that and being here with you. What about going to bed?' And I thought, This is when the raping commences. And I said, 'Not me. I don't go to bed and get raped.' And you know what he did? He laughed. He fell on the floor like he couldn't stand up and kicked his feet in the air pretending. Looked like the devil come up through the floor from hell. And he said, 'Momma, you ever think you going to get raped, you know what I'd do?' But I didn't answer. I was too ashamed. And he laughed and said he'd stay up instead. 'I'd stay up all night before I'd go to bed and get raped,' and so on like that. But I didn't look at him. I heard him scrabbling around down there, but I didn't dare cast my eyes on him to see what nasty thing he was doing."

"He was getting up," James Terry Crews explained.

"I didn't want to see what it was for fear it might be something I didn't want to see. That's how he was. He didn't care. Then I felt him lean over me, grinning and mocking, and say what he meant was for me to go to one bed and him to another and sleep this time if that was all right with me. And that's when I knew there wasn't no way. Even if I could have saved him before, I knew I couldn't after that. I was a prisoner in my own house."

"He trusted us," James Terry Crews explained. "He said, 'I sleep light, but I trust you anyway, old dad. I know you don't want me to go back to the work camp for nine more years.' And he said to Mrs. Crews, 'Wake me for breakfast, you hear me, momma? Don't let me oversleep my welcome. I'm just going to rest a minute. Then I'm going to have to leave you, much as you hate to see me go.' "

"And I thought, To California. He's going to California without me," Oletta Crews shouted, "and leave me alone and take all the money. And that's when I told James Terry to kill him. I said, 'Go get your gun.' "

"I got this single barrel shotgun," James Terry Crews said. "First gun I ever owned."

"They don't want to hear about that."

But James Terry Crews turned on her. "Let me talk," he said. "This is interesting. I got that gun in Fayetteville when I was a boy. Walked in and slapped down seven dollars and said, 'I'll take that Stevens single-barrel,' and Mr. Robert reached up and got it out of the cradle. Had this cradle made out of deer hoofs, and he said, 'This squirrel gun?' And I said, 'Squirrel gun? I could bring you down with it if I had some buckshot.' That's the way I was then. I didn't take no smart talk from nobody. I said, 'This gun cost too much to waste on squirrels.' And he said, 'What you fixing to shoot with it, if you don't shoot me?' And I said, 'I don't know,' like I was still thinking about it. I said, 'I ain't made up my mind yet.' And then I said, 'Give me some buckshot' and looked right at him. That got his attention. Buckshot'll blow a hole in a man big as a melon. I was a man when I was fourteen, when I first went to work for the sawmill. I worked there till I hurt myself and moved to Atlanta and got married and went to painting. But I kept that gun. I had others, but it was my favorite. It reminded me."

"That's beside the point," Oletta Crews said. "The point is I could say, 'Go in there and do it,' and James Terry would go in there, and I'd feel it shake where he shot at him—once, twice, three times maybe—in the head or in the back, wherever it hit him. But what then? He was laying in my bed, and he'd bleed on it and ruin the mattress."

"Not to mention the shot," James Terry Crews said. "She didn't even think about that. I had to tell her. I said, 'Blood ain't nothing. Blood washes off. But buckshot—buckshot'll blow a hole in a man as big as a melon right through him and the mattress both. Might even blow a hole in the floor.' " His face lit up. "I ever tell you about the time we were moving, and there was a copperhead in the house, and I had the gun, but the shells were packed up somewhere in boxes?"

"Don't be an idiot."

"I shot a hole in the floor," James Terry Crews shouted, hurrying to finish while he still had the chance. "I found the shells and shot the floor clean out. Snake with it." He looked at his wife. "Ever see buckshot hit a melon?"

"Hush up," Oletta Crews said. "You're talking too much."

James Terry Crews said, "It explodes. You can't even find the pieces. It just lifts and disappears. Same way with heads."

"I knew I'd smell it," Oletta Crews said. "Whenever I put my face to it, I knew I'd smell it in my sleep no matter how good I washed it. The police would come and take off the body, but they'd leave all the blood in the mattress and on the sheets and on the rug across the floor where it runs out when they carry him off, and I'd have to clean it up. He can't clean," indicating her husband. "All he can do is paint."

"I say paint it. If it's dirty enough to wash it, it's dirty enough to paint it, I say."

"Only trouble is you can't paint sheets and mattresses where all the blood ran out." She leaned forward and spoke confidentially. "If it wasn't drinking, it was talking. All his life. He'd get to painting a house and talk himself right off the job. Couldn't even climb the ladder or mix the paint, he talked so much. Folks don't like that. They run him off. And it wasn't even drinking sometimes. It's what he calls high spirits."

James Terry Crews looked at her balefully. "High spirits," he said.

"Besides which I thought of something else," Oletta Crews said, rocking forward again. "What about Q. B. Farris?" She bugged her eyes as someone else might simulate fright. "Where was his gun? And then I thought about the money. What if he had it in his pocket and James Terry shot it all full of holes? Would they still take it? What do they do with money like that?"

"They don't do nothing," James Terry Crews replied. "Because it blows away just like a melon. If he had that money in his pocket, you couldn't even find the pieces."

"That's what I thought. Besides which he can't even see in the day time let alone in the dark at night. He might point it at his head and hit the wrong place, where the money is, and just wound him, and he'd come crawling out at me."

"That's why I picked up two other loads," James Terry Crews explained. "In case I missed. I ain't never shot a man before."

"He said he might miss the first but not the second. But I told him, 'No. It's too dangerous. There's some other way.' And he said, 'I can't think of it.' And I said, 'I know. I wasn't expecting you to. Give me a minute.' " She paused and then spoke in an altered voice. " 'Even though I walk through the valley of the shadow of death, I fear no evil, for thou art with me.' And then it said, 'It ain't your death. That's why it's a shadow. If it was your death, it'd be real. But killing him's only a shadow.' And as soon as I heard that, I knew who it was, and all my fear fell off me like sweat, and I dried up, it's like I was reborn. I knew what was promised. And I said to James Terry, 'Let it go. Don't shoot him now. Wait till later.' And he said, 'When?' And I said, 'When he's fixing to kill us.' "

"And I said, 'What if it's too late? What if he beats me to it?' And she said, 'Then you don't have to worry. You'll already be dead by then.' That don't make no sense to me."

"And I said, 'It won't come to that. Just get it loaded. I'll give you a sign—like this.' " She winked her eye and waved her hand.

"And I said, 'What if I'm tying my shoe and don't see you do it?' " James Terry Crews said. " 'What if I get up and go to the bathroom?' "

"We heard him rattling around in there," Oletta Crews said. "And I said, 'Get ready. He's fixing to kill us.' And James Terry said, "What do I do?' And I said, 'Sit here.' " She patted the cushion beside her. " 'Sit down here and hide the gun under the sofa where you can get at it.' "

"And I said, 'That's too slow. He'll shoot us both before I get to it.' And she said, 'That's good. In that case you don't got nothing to worry about.' "

"All my fear dried up like sweat."

"And I cocked it and put it under the sofa. There ain't no safety on a single-barrel Stevens," James Terry Crews started to say, but his wife interrupted him.

"They don't want to hear about that. We were sitting on the sofa waiting."

"Not me, I was thinking about what if he kills me. That worried me. I knew what she said, but it still worried me."

"And always will," Oletta Crews said. "That's what's wrong with you." She paused suddenly "We heard him stirring and singing, and then he came in tucking James Terry's shirt in his pants where he hid the gun and stopped and fell back all of a sudden like he was surprised and said, 'I didn't see you sitting there. You almost scared me to death sitting there side by side. You know what you look like?' But I ignored him. And he said, 'Two cats. You look like two cats lined up waiting for dinner. Ever see that?'—grinning and laughing to show he was lying. He tried to hug me, but I pushed him off. And then he said, 'I got to go, much as I hate to leave you, momma.' "

"And I said, 'Why don't you stay then? What's your hurry?' " James Terry Crews said. "I didn't mind him so much. He wasn't too bad except he might kill us. He had a good heart. Then I saw her look at me, and I felt my bowels tighten up. They were feeling loose. . . ."

Oletta Crews ignored him. "And then Duke said, 'I'd sure like to stay, old dad. It feels just like home.' And I said, 'Home? It ain't your home. I don't want children. I never had them.' And he laughed at that and said, 'I know. I'd have guessed it at how you kept your figure even if you hadn't told me about it. You sure look good for a woman your age'—laughing and grinning so I didn't know if he meant it or not. And I tried to hit him. I said, 'Go on. Don't talk like that, my husband sitting right here beside me.' "

"And I said, 'Don't mind me. I think she's pretty good-looking myself.' "

"And then he said, 'They'll be along directly looking for me. Don't tell them I been here. I'd rather be dead than go back to the work camp the rest of my life. How would you like it?' And I said, 'I wouldn't. But I wouldn't deserve to.' That straightened him up. And he said, 'Well, I got to go. Much obliged for the company. It ain't often I get to have such high old times.' "

"And I said, 'Me neither,' " James Terry Crews said. " 'I enjoyed it,' I said. 'Come back. You ever get where they ain't looking for you, come back. You know where it's at. Come back and stay. We'd like to have you. You're good company.' "

"I didn't say nothing," Oletta Crews said. "And he said, 'How about you? You want me to come back too, momma?' And I said, 'I won't be here. I'm fixing to go to California.' Then he got serious all of a sudden. His face fell, and he looked old. He said, 'I sure do wish you luck,' reaching over to shake James Terry by the hand. And he said to me, 'I know how you feel wanting to go someplace like that, even if it's only to go there and die. That's one thing I learned in the work camp.' "

"Then he slapped me on the shoulder," James Terry Crews said, "and hugged me like that and backed off and said, 'I might buy this place myself if I had the time.' "

"That's how I knew he had the money," Oletta Crews said. "He wasn't lying."

"He'd have done it if he had the time."

"And the money," Oletta Crews said, "That's when I told him I might see him out there. And he said, 'Where?' And I said, 'California.' And he grinned and said, 'You might do it.' Then he looked at me. He looked me right in the eye and said, 'I'll see you in California, momma.' And I knew then I was right. He's fixing to walk right out that door and shut it behind him and stomp his feet down the steps like he's going somewhere and then creep back when we're sitting here side by side on the sofa thinking he's gone now, the danger is over, our lives are safe in our own hands again, praising God and weeping for joy we ain't dead, he didn't kill us, when all of a sudden the door flings open, and there he is standing there grinning and laughing like a devil from hell because it's a joke, don't you see, pretending to leave and then coming back and shooting us

471

both right on the sofa side by side, one after the other—bang, bang, bang—till it wasn't even a sofa no more, just a hole in the floor and us in it, bits and pieces mixed with the stuffing."

"That's a shotgun," James Terry Crews explained. "You're talking about a twelve-gauge shotgun."

"That was his plan," Oletta Crews said. "I saw it as clear as I'm seeing you, and I knew I was right. It's just like him, I thought to myself—kill us like we were some kind of joke. You ain't got no will if you're a hostage. It's like you get tired. You can't even move. You got to sit there and wait."

"Unless you kill him first. That's right, ain't it, Letta?"

"It's like you can't move. You ain't got no will of your own."

"That's what I mean. That's why I killed him. No matter how good a heart he had, he was conceited."

"Listen to this," Oletta Crews shouted. She held up her hand again. "I said, 'Ain't you scared?' And he said, 'What for?' I didn't know if he was joking or not. I said, 'There's a posse of police out there waiting.' And he said, 'What for?' like he didn't know what I was talking about and went to the door and stuck his head out like he was trying to see who was out there. And I said, 'Because you don't care. You joke too much. You ain't serious.' "

"He was conceited. I could see that."

"I made the sign. And James Terry reached under and got the shotgun, and Duke turned around and looked at James Terry, and James Terry looked at Duke, and then his head lifted off. If it weren't for the roaring in my ears and the light and the smoke and the shaking on the sofa beside me where James Terry shot it off, I'd have thought it busted or something, like a balloon. One minute it was Duke Farris, the next minute it was gone like it went out the door. It was still raining, and I thought to myself, It ain't there. It ain't out there. You can look all you want to, but there ain't even bits and pieces. It lifted clean off. That head exploded."

She paused. "I was glad the door was open. That way it went right out. It didn't blow a hole in the wall, and there wasn't nothing left to clean up. I said, 'Here. Help me up.' But he didn't move. I got up and went over there, and you know what he had in his pockets? A ring snap off an aluminum can. He didn't even have a wallet. If he was hit by a car on the highway and killed on the spot, you wouldn't have even known who he was. I searched everywhere, and I told my husband, I said, 'James Terry, I can't find the money.' I couldn't believe it. And he said, 'What money?' He didn't even know what I was talking about. And I said, 'That money he's going to California with. The money he hid and come out to dig up.' And James Terry said, 'Where is it?' And I said, 'I don't know. You shot him too soon.' "

"He didn't even have a gun," James Terry Crews explained.

"He didn't have nothing except a ring snap off an aluminum can,"Oletta Crews said. "But how was I to know that? The police said, 'Don't worry. You shot him on your own property.' And I said, 'My own property? I shot him in my own house. How was I to know?' And they said, 'No way. He might have had a gun to kill you.' "

"That's probably even my ring snap off an aluminum can," James Terry Crews said. "He had on my trousers. There wasn't nothing in his at all."

"Police said it was self-defense," Oletta Crews continued. "Said, 'You killed him to save yourself. That's only natural.' "

"Ain't a jury in the land convict you of that."

"I couldn't move it," Oletta Crews said. "I sat down on the floor beside it and tried to push it out with my feet. I wanted to close the door. It was still raining. I said to James Terry, 'I can't move it by myself. Get up and help.' And he got up. Then I saw him lift an arm and start to drag him out. A leg slid by me and then a foot, and then I was free. The door was open, and I looked out and saw the rain. The floodlight was still on. It went on in the yard like a room and lit up the rain. I could see it coming down like knives. It was all silver, and in the tree, it was all silver like ice—like the whole world turned to ice. And James Terry started to come in, and I said, 'Get the light.' And he got the light, and it was dark. It was dark out there as far as the eye could see, and I could still hear it raining. It was like it was moving, like a great wind lifting and heaving. And I said to James Terry, 'Close the door. Close the door on it.' And he closed the door."

"He wasn't so bad," James Terry Crews said as though in eulogy. "I don't care what they say he done. He had a good heart. Lots of folks rob banks got better hearts than the people that own them. He was what you might call a godsend. I thought that. I thought to myself, Q. B. Farris—Duke, you're what you might call some kind of godsend."

"We were hostages," Oletta Crews shouted. "He took our will."

"I mean before that."

"There wasn't no before that. As soon as he came and knocked at that door, he took our will."

"I mean when we were doing the dishes. I thought to myself, He's some kind of a godsend. I wouldn't be here laughing and talking and cutting the fool if he wasn't here. I'm grateful to him. I'm grateful he's here. He reminded me of when I was working." He paused. "Robbing banks. . . . Robbing banks ain't so bad. I might have done that myself if I hadn't got hurt and moved to Atlanta and got married. It's a whole other way of doing—a whole other kind of life."

"Listen to me," Oletta Crews shouted. "I know about godsend. As soon as I heard that knock on the door, I felt it knocking in my heart, and I said to myself, It's God knocking at the door of my heart, asking me to open up and let him come in and change me, change my whole life." She paused. "There's a better place than this, and I thought I was going. But I know better now, even if he don't," indicating James Terry Crews. She lowered her voice, increasing its intensity. It sounded like someone else speaking inside her: " 'For even Satan disguises himself as an angel of light. His end shall be according to his deeds.' And his shows that," Oletta Crews said, "when James Terry shot him and there wasn't no money."

"And no gun."

"And nothing to show except mockery. All my hopes mocked and bleeding half in and half out the door where I couldn't even shut it myself, and he dragged it out where it'd been killed, I felt like something inside me was dead."

"Me, too. It felt like something inside me was dead too. I didn't know what it was."

"I did. I sat on the floor where I'd been looking for money and thought to myself, 'You can't serve two masters.' Satan appeared as an angel of light and killed all my hopes, took my will and killed all my hopes. But I'm still alive. I ain't dead, and I ain't changed. I'm just like I was."

Nominated by The Southern Review

THE FAMILY IS ALL THERE IS

by PATTIANN ROGERS

from TRIQUARTERLY

Think of those old, enduring connections
found in all flesh—the channeling
wires and threads, vacuoles, granules,
plasma and pods, purple veins, ascending
boles and coral sapwood (sugar-
and light-filled), those common ligaments,
filaments, fibers and canals.

Seminal to all kin also is the open
mouth—in heart urchin and octopus belly,
in catfish, moonfish, forest lily,
and rugosa rose, in thirsty magpie,
wailing cat cub, barker, yodeler,
yawning coati.

And there is a pervasive clasping
common to the clan—the hard nails
of lichen and ivy sucker
on the church wall, the bean tendril
and the taproot, the bolted coupling
of crane flies, the hold of the shearwater
on its morning squid, guanine
to cytosine, adenine to thymine,

fingers around fingers, the grip
of the voice on presence, the grasp
of the self on place.

Remember the same hair on pygmy
dormouse and yellow-necked caterpillar,
covering red baboon, thistle seed
and willow herb? Remember the similar
snorts of warthog, walrus, male moose
and sumo wrestler? Remember the familiar
whinny and shimmer found in river birches,
bay mares and bullfrog tadpoles,
in children playing at shoulder tag
on a summer lawn?

The family—weavers, reachers, winders
and connivers, pumpers, runners, air
and bubble riders, rock-sitters, wave-gliders,
wire-wobblers, soothers, flagellators—all
brothers, sisters, all there is.

Name something else.

Nominated by Reginald Gibbons

SPECIAL MENTION

(The editors also wish to mention the following important works published by small presses last year. Listing is alphabetical by author's last name)

ESSAYS

Cultural Conservatism and Democratic Education—Benjamin Barber (Salmagundi)

The Grace of Indirection—Robert Bly (Painted Bride Quarterly)

Demystifying The Mayas—Omar S. Castaneda (Rollins Record)

Recoleta—Judith L. Elkin (Michigan Quarterly Review)

Chekhov's Anger—Robert Hass (Threepenny Review)

The Interesting Case of Nero, Chekhov's Cognac and a Knocker—Seamus Heaney (Shenandoah)

The Menil Collection—Richard Howard (Gettysburg Review)

to Q—Mahnaz Ispahani (The Quarterly)

Seven Moons—Cynthia Kadohata (Grand Street)

Into The Light—Judith Kroll (American Voice)

Never Live Above Your Landlord—Phillip Lopate (Columbia Magazine)

Compassion—Cameron Macauley (North American Review)

Growing Up With Jo—Gail Mazur (Boston Review)

Beginnings—Joyce Carol Oates (Michigan Quarterly Review)

Outside In—Sam Pickering, Jr. (Texas Review)

Baptie In Her Homeland—David Schmahmann (Yale Review)

After-Images:Autobiographical Sketches—W. D. Snodgrass (Salmagundi)

Intrusions In Ice—Marilyn Stablein (Wash n' Press)

One Step Enough—Keith Waldrop (Conjunctions)

FICTION

1940:Fall—Alice Adams (Shenandoah)

What Do I Know?—Kim Addonizio (Fiction Network)

Ladies' Luncheon—Paulette Bates Alden (*Feeding the Eagles*, Graywolf)

Paco Real—Elizabeth Alexander (American Voice)

Sea Girls and Men With Hands—Jennifer Allen (The Quarterly)

The Unfinished Minaret—Tony Ardizzone (Gettysburg Review)

In Sight of Josephine—Carol Ascher (Witness)

Sometimes Pain Waits—Yolanda Barnes (Ploughshares)

Mexico—Rick Bass (Antaeus)

I Am A V-I-S-U-A-L-E-X-M-I-N-S-T-E-R—Erik Belgum (Chicago Review)

Holding Together—Madison Smartt Bell (Boulevard)

Lives of the Saints—Gina Berriault (ZYZZYVA)

Recognizable At A Distance—Stephanie Bobo (Missouri Review)

Living To Be A Hundred—Robert Boswell (Iowa Review)

The Devil and Irv Cherniske—T. Coraghessan Boyle (Antioch Review)

Questions From A Foreigner—Maria del Carmen Boza (Bilingual Review)

The Guardian—Peter Bricklebank (Mid-American Review)

The Boys In Their Bicycles—Harold Brodkey (The Quarterly)

The English And Their Dogs—Jerry Bumpus (Greensboro Review)

Psycho In Buckingham Palace—Richard Burgin (Mississippi Review)

Chinchilla—Dan Chaon (Crazyhorse)

Discussions With the Embryo—Ken Chowder (Boulevard)

Columbia—Michelle Cliff (American Voice)

Maps To Anywhere—Bernard Cooper (Grand Street)

From The Adventures of Lucky Pierre—Robert Coover (Witness)

Room 601—Mark Costello (Shenandoah)

German—Moira Crone (American Voice)

The Curate—Timothy Dekin (TriQuarterly)

Ghost Story—Leslie Dick (City Lights Review)

The Visit—Stephen Dixon (Confrontation)

Highway Trade—John Domini (Southwest Review)

The Dark Snake—Michael Dorris (Georgia Review)

The Official and Final Version—John Dranow (Galileo Press)

Tolstoy In Maine—Jay Neugeboren (New Letters)
The Apple—Josip Novakovich (Ploughshares)
Stroke—Joyce Carol Oates (Malahat Review)
Jealous-Hearted Me—Nancy H. Packer (Southern Review)
The Sky-Writing School—Max Phillips (Threepenny Review)
The Beginning of Sorrows—Constance Pierce (New Virginia Review)
Retrieval—Joe Ashby Porter (Raritan Review)
Player In The Symphony—Stanford Pritchard (NER/BLQ)
Ghirlandaio—Francine Prose (Tikkun)
Switzerland—Ann Pyne (The Quarterly)
Bizarre Births—Diana Reed (Georgia Review)
Doing That Outside Dance—William Reid (Gargoyle Magazine)
Waffles—Kurt Rheinheimer (Chattahoochee Review)
Fishboy—Mark Richard (The Quarterly)
Monkeygirl—Paul Rovina (Chelsea)
Mountain Flashes—Jean Rukkila (Quarterly West)
Ned Jumper—Tom Russell (Georgia Review)
The Farther You Go—Richard Russo (Shenandoah)
Twenty Minutes—James Salter (Grand Street)
A Gordon Milk Suite—Scott Russell Sanders (Gettysburg Review)
The Bonbon Man—Marjorie Sandor (Shenandoah)
Before Sewing One Must Cut—Jeanne Schinto (NER/BLQ)
Black Hole—Helen Schulman (Arete)
The Melting Pot—Lynne Sharon Schwartz (Pequod)
Arrival of the Snake Woman—Oliver Senior (Callaloo)
The Summy—Robert Shapard (Prism International)
The Letter Writer—M. T. Sharif (Agni Review)
Pinks—Lisa Shea (Columbia)
The Island of the Mapmaker's Wife—Marilyn Sides (Yellow Silk)
Skirts—Rachel Simon (Quarterly West)
A Window On The Bath—Laurie Skiba (Shenandoah)
Baptism of Desire—Ingrid Smith (Southern Review)
Gulf Weather—Jim Smith (Black Ice)
At Night, On the Island, In the Dark—Debra Spark (Madison Review)
Caressing Mine Idol's Pillow—Dorothy Speak (Ontario Review)
The Skater—Elizabeth Spencer (North American Review)
The Letter—Mark Spencer (Gambit)
The Key—George Staples (Antaeus)

Bronx Fighter—Michael Stephens (Ontario Review)
The Box—Susan Straight (TriQuarterly)
Yesterday Was Not Tru—Melanie Sumner (Story Quarterly)
Poor Helen—Jean Thompson (Carolina Quarterly)
Winterkill—Ronald Tobias (Chelsea)
Rumplestiltskin—Dennis Vannatta (Colorado North)
Original Sin—Katherine Vaz (Black Ice)
King Ortega—David Veloz (Quarterly West)
Scintillant Orange—William T. Vollmann (Conjunctions)
Colors—Sylvia Watanabe (Hawaii Review)
Keeping House With Freud—Gloria Whelan (Gettysburg Review)
Family Knots—Meredith Sue Willis (Kalliope)
Grandpa's Growth—Margaret Young (Southern Review)

POETRY

Frousanda Mahrad—Damia Abbas Amara (Pigiron Press)
Rexroth As He Appeared to Exist March 28, 1968 9 pm—Antler
(Nada Press)
For The Missing In Action—John Balaban (Ploughshares)
Continental Drift—Catharine H. Beyer (Crab Creek Review)
Dies Irae—Maureen Bloomfield (Cincinnati Poetry Review)
1957—Marianne Boruch (Prairie Schooner)
Inupiaq—Joseph Bruchac (Abraxas)
The Parrots—Ernesto Cardenal (*Flights of Victory*, Curbstone)
Essay On Death—Hayden Carruth (American Poetry Review)
The Narrow Roads of Oku—Marilyn Chin (Iowa Review)
Little World—Richard Cecil (Crazyhorse)
Running My Fingers Through My Beard on Bolton Rd—Mark Cox
(Ampersand)
A Question—Michael Cuddihy (Pequod)
What's Left Unsaid, Or the Dodo's Joy—Tom Disch (Boulevard)
William Carlos Williams—Cornelius Eady (William & Mary Re-
view; State Street Press)
The Rabbit Story—Russell Edson (Willow Springs)
The First Few Hours, Alone After Prison—Steve Fisher (TriQuar-
terly)
Angus, The One-Legged Duckling—Barbara Ganzel (Georgia Re-
view)

Gold/Silk—Albert Goldbarth (Southwest Review)

Silent Movie Theater—Laurence Goldstein (Iowa Review)

Sue Ellen: A Change of Circumstance—Jana Harris (Plainswoman)

Stretch Marks—Roald Hoffmann (Negative Capability)

Adagio—Lynda Hull (Gettysburg Review)

Blue Monk—Lawson Inada (Caliban)

Winter Retreat: Homage To Martin Luther King—Rodney Jones (Missouri Review)

Three Songs At The End of Summer—Jane Kenyon (Poetry)

Naming The Elements—Michael Klein (James White Review)

Sleeping With Animals—Maxine Kumin (Ontario Review)

The Whole of It—Carol Jean Logue (America's Review)

Time and Its Double—Robert Long (*What Happens*, Galileo Press)

Mediterranean—Thomas McGrath (*Selected Poems 1938-88*, Copper Canyon)

Devolution of the Nude—Lynne McMahon (Pacific Review)

The Wound—Robert McNamara (Kansas Quarterly)

The Highway—Dian Million (Mr. Cogito)

Snow, Red Wine, and Intelligent Gray Eyes—Leonard Nathan (NER/BLQ)

Stick Seller—Steven Nesheim (Artful Dodge)

Taking A Message—Bin Ramke (Poetry)

I Say, Not Here, Not There, So Where?—Patricia Reeves (*Returning The Question*, Cleveland St. University)

Pedestrian Pastoral—Michael Ryan (TriQuarterly)

The Pig—David Silverstein (America's Review)

Fence—R. T. Smith (The Journal)

The Woman on The Dump—Elizabeth Spires (Georgia Review)

A Flow Behind The Walls—Robert Stewart (*Plumbers*, Bk Mk)

The World And What We Know—Elizabeth Thomas (Outerbridge)

Galang—Susan Tichy (Beloit Poetry Journal)

Chanel No. 5—Chase Twichell (Ohio Review)

Snow Landscape, In A Glass Globe—Jean Valentine (*Home Deep Blue* Alice James)

American Manhood—Robert Wrigley (Poetry)

PRESSES FEATURED IN THE PUSHCART PRIZE EDITIONS (1976–1989)

Acts
Agni Review
Ahsahta Press
Ailanthus Press
Alcheringa/Ethnopoetics
Alice James Books
Amelia
American Literature
American PEN
American Poetry Review
American Scholar
The American Voice
Amnesty International
Anaesthesia Review
Another Chicago Magazine
Antaeus
Antioch Review
Apalachee Quarterly
Aphra
The Ark
Ascent
Aspen Leaves
Aspen Poetry Anthology
Assembling
Barlenmir House
Barnwood Press
The Bellingham Review

Beloit Poetry Journal
Bennington Review
Bilingual Review
Black American Literature
    Forum
Black Rooster
Black Scholar
Black Sparrow
Black Warrior Review
Blackwells Press
Bloomsbury Review
Blue Cloud Quarterly
Blue Unicorn
Blue Wind Press
Bluefish
BOA Editions
Bookslinger Editions
Boulevard
Boxspring
Brown Journal of the Arts
Burning Deck Press
Caliban
California Quarterly
Callaloo
Calliopea Press
Canto
Capra Press

Cedar Rock
Center
Chariton Review
Charnel House
Chelsea
Chicago Review
Chouteau Review
Chowder Review
Cimarron Review
Cincinnati Poetry Review
City Lights Books
Clown War
CoEvolution Quarterly
Cold Mountain Press
Columbia: A Magazine of Poetry
    and Prose
Confluence Press
Confrontation
Conjunctions
Copper Canyon Press
Cosmic Information Agency
Crawl Out Your Window
Crazyhorse
Crescent Review
Cross Cultural Communications
Cross Currents
Cumberland Poetry Review
Curbstone Press
Cutbank
Dacotah Territory
Daedalus
Decatur House
December
Domestic Crude
Dragon Gate Inc.
Dreamworks
Dryad Press
Duck Down Press
Durak
East River Anthology
Ellis Press
Empty Bowl
Epoch

Exquisite Corpse
Fiction
Fiction Collective
Fiction International
Field
Firelands Art Review
Five Fingers Review
Five Trees Press
Frontiers: A Journal of Women
    Studies
Gallimaufry
Genre
The Georgia Review
Gettysburg Review
Ghost Dance
Goddard Journal
David Godine, Publisher
Graham House Press
Grand Street
Granta
Graywolf Press
Green Mountains Review
Greenfield Review
Greensboro Review
Guardian Press
Hard Pressed
Hermitage Press
Hills
Holmgangers Press
Holy Cow!
Home Planet News
Hudson Review
Icarus
Iguana Press
Indiana Review
Indiana Writes
Intermedia
Intro
Invisible City
Inwood Press
Iowa Review
Ironwood
Jam To-day

The Kanchenjuga Press
Kansas Quarterly
Kayak
Kelsey Street Press
Kenyon Review
Latitudes Press
Laughing Waters Press
L'Epervier Press
Liberation
Linquis
The Little Magazine
Living Hand Press
Living Poets Press
Logbridge-Rhodes
Lowlands Review
Lucille
Lynx House Press
Magic Circle Press
Malahat Review
Manroot
Massachusetts Review
Mho & Mho Works
Micah Publications
Michigan Quarterly
Milkweed Editions
Milkweed Quarterly
The Minnesota Review
Mississippi Review
Missouri Review
Montana Gothic
Montana Review
Montemora
Mr. Cogito Press
MSS
Mulch Press
Nada Press
New America
The New Criterion
New Directions
New England Review and Bread
    Loaf Quarterly
New Letters
New Virginia Review

North American Review
North Atlantic Books
North Dakota Quarterly
North Point Press
Northern Lights
Northwest Review
O. ARS
Obsidian
Oconee Review
October
Ohio Review
Ontario Review
Open Places
Orca Press
Oyez Press
Painted Bride Quarterly
Paris Review
Parnassus: Poetry In Review
Partisan Review
Penca Books
Pentagram
Penumbra Press
Pequod
Persea: An International Review
Pipedream Press
Pitcairn Press
Ploughshares
Poet and Critic
Poetry
Poetry East
Poetry Northwest
Poetry Now
Prairie Schooner
Prescott Street Press
Promise of Learnings
Quarry West
The Quarterly
Quarterly West
Raccoon
Rainbow Press
Raritan A Quarterly Review
Red Cedar Review
Red Clay Books

485

Red Dust Press
Red Earth Press
Release Press
Revista Chicano-Riquena
River Styx
Rowan Tree Press
Russian *Samizdat*
Salmagundi
San Marcos Press
Sea Pen Press and Paper Mill
Seal Press
Seamark Press
Seattle Review
Second Coming Press
The Seventies Press
Sewanee Review
Shankpainter
Shantih
Sheep Meadow Press
Shenandoah
A Shout In The Street
Sibyl-Child Press
Small Moon
The Smith
Some
The Sonora Review
Southern Poetry Review
Southern Review
Southwest Review
Spectrum
The Spirit That Moves Us
St. Andrews Press
Story Quarterly
Streetfare Journal
Stuart Wright, Publisher
Sulfur
Sun & Moon Press
Sun Press
Sunstone
Tar River Poetry
Telephone Books

Telescope
Temblor
Tendril
Texas Slough
13th Moon
THIS
Thorp Springs Press
Three Rivers Press
Threepenny Review
Thunder City Press
Thunder's Mouth Press
Tombouctou Books
Toothpaste Press
Transatlantic Review
TriQuarterly
Truck Press
Tuumba Press
Undine
Unicorn Press
University of Pittsburgh Press
Unmuzzled Ox
Unspeakable Visions of the
    Individual
Vagabond
Virginia Quarterly
Wampeter Press
Washington Writers Workshop
Water Table
Western Humanities Review
Westigan Review
Wickwire Press
Wilmore City
Word Beat Press
Word-Smith
Wormwood Review
Writers Forum
Xanadu
Yale Review
Yardbird Reader
Y'Bird
ZYZZYVA

CONTRIBUTING SMALL PRESSES

(These presses made or received nominations for this edition of *The Pushcart Prize*. See the *International Directory of Little Magazines and Small Presses*, Dustbooks, Box 1056, Paradise, CA 95969, for subscription rates, manuscript requirements and a complete international listing of small presses.)

A.

AWP Newsletter, Assoc. Writing Programs, Old Dominion University, Norfolk, VA 23529

Abattoir Editions, Annex 22, University of Nebraska, Omaha, NE 68182

ABBEY, 5360 Fallriver Row Court, Columbia, MD 21044

Abraxas, see Ghost Pony Press

ACTS, 514 Guerrero St., San Francisco, CA 94110

Aerial, P.O. Box 25642, Washington, DC 20007

Agni, Boston University Creative Writing Prog., 236 Bay St., Boston, MA 02215

Ahsahta Press, English Dept., Boise State University, Boise, ID 83725

Akwesasne Notes, P.O. Box 223, Hagansburg, NY 13655

Alabama Literary Review, English Dept., Troy State University, Troy, AL 36082

Alaska Quarterly Review, English Dept., University of Alaska, Anchorage, AK 99508

The Albany Review, 4 Central Ave., Albany, NY 12210

Albatross, 4014 S.W. 21 Rd., Gainesville, FL 32607

Algamut Press, P.O. Box 2293, Edison, NJ 08818

alicejamesbooks, 33 Richdale Ave., Cambridge, MA 02140

All American Press, P.O. Box 20773, Birmingham, AL 35216

Alternative Fiction & Poetry, 7783 Kensington Lane, Hanover Park, IL 60103

Ambergris, P.O. Box 29919, Cincinnati, OH 45229

Amelia, 329 "E" St., Bakersfield, CA 93304

The American Book Review, Box 188, Cooper Sta., New York, NY 10003

The American Voice, 332 W. Broadway, Ste. 1215, Louisville, KY 40202

Americas Review, P.O. Box 7681, Berkeley, CA 94707

Ampersand Press, Creative Writing Prog., Roger Williams College, Bristol, RI 02809

Amy's, P.O. Box 1718, Fort Myers, FL 33902

Another Chicago Magazine, Box 11223, Chicago, IL 60611

Antietam Review, 82 W. Washington St., Hagerstown, MD 21740

The Antioch Review, P.O. Box 148, Yellow Springs, OH 45387

Apalachee Quarterly, P.O. Box 20106, Tallahassee, FL 32316

Appalachian Heritage, Berea College, Berea, KY 40404

Appletree Alley, Press of,-P.O. Box 608, Lewisburg, PA 17837

Applezaba Press, P.O. Box 4134, Long Beach, CA 90804

Arbiter Press, 1285 Roma Court, Orlando, FL 32825

Arete, Forum for Thought, P.O. Box 27789, Escondido, CA 92027

Aristos, P.O. Box 1105, Radio City Sta., New York, NY 10101

Art Papers, P.O. Box 77348, Atlanta, GA 30357

Artemis, P.O. Box 8147, Roanoke, VA 24014

Artful Dodge, English Dept., College of Wooster, Wooster, OH 44691

Ascent, English Dept., University of Illinois, 608 S. Wright St., Urbana, IL 61801

Asylum, P.O. Box 3307, Greensboro, NC 27402

AURA Literary/Arts Review, P.O. Box 76, University Center, Univ. Sta., Birmingham, AL 35294

Aviva Press, P.O. Box 1357, Brookline, MA 02146

B

The Bad Henry Review, P.O. Box 45, Van Brunt Sta., Brooklyn, NY 11215

Bank Street Press, 24 Bank St., New York, NY 10014

The Barnwood Press, RR #2, Box 11-C, "Riverhouse", Daleville, IN 47334

Bay Windows, 1523 Washington St., Boston, MA 02118

The Beacon Review, Box 15945, Seattle, WA 98115

la bella figura, P.O. Box 411223, San Francisco, CA 94141

Bellflower Press, 20 Laurel Court, Moreland Hills, OH 44022

Beloit Poetry Journal, RFD 2, Box 154, Ellsworth, ME 04605

Between C & D, 255 East 7 St., New York, NY 10009

Biblio Press, 22 W. 28th St., Rm. 1001, New York, NY 10011

The Bieler Press, University of California, Research Annex, 3716 S. Hope St., Los Angeles, CA 90007

Big Cigars/The P.O.N. Press, 1625 Hobart St., NW, Washington, DC 20009

Bilingual Review/Press, Hispanic Research Center, Arizona State University, Tempe, AZ 85287

Bits Press, English Dept., Case Western University, Cleveland, OH 44106

Bitterroot, P.O. Box 489, Spring Glen, NY 12483

BkMk Press, 5216 Rockhill Rd., Rm. 204, Kansas City, MO 64110

Black Buzzard Review, 4705 S. 8th Rd., Arlington, VA 22204

Black Ice, P.O. Box 49, Belmont, MA 02178

Black River Review, 855 Mildred Ave., Lorain, OH 44052

Black Warrior Review, P.O. Box 2936, Tuscaloosa, AL 35487

The Bloomsbury Review, 1028 Bannock St., Denver, CO 80204

Blue Light Red Light, 496A Hudson St., Ste. F42, New York, NY 10014

The Blue Sky Journal, 1710 Decker Rd., Malibu, CA 90265

Blue Unicorn, 22 Avon Rd., Kensington, CA 94707

Blueline, Blue Mountain Lake, NY 12812

The Boston Review, 33 Harrison Ave., Boston, MA 02111

Bothomos Enterprises, Box 74109, Metairie, LA 70033

Bottom Dog Press, Firelands College, 901 Rye Beach Rd., Huron, OH 44839

Boulevard, 2400 Chestnut St., 3301, Philadelphia, PA 19103

Bowman Books, see Greenfield Review Press

Box Turtle Press, 184 Franklin St., New York, NY 10013

Branch Redd Books, 4805 "B" St., Philadelphia, PA 19120

Brick, Box 537, Sta. Q, Toronto, Ont., M4T 2M5, CANADA

Burning Deck, 71 Elmgrove Ave., Providence, RI 02906
Byline, P.O. Box 130596, Edmond, OK 73013

C

Cadmus Editions, Box 687, Tiburon, CA 94920
Cafe Solo, 222 Chaplin, San Luis Obispo, CA 93401
Calapooya Collage, The Monmouth Institute, West Oregon State College, Monmouth, OR 97361
Caliban, c/o L. R. Smith, ed., P.O. Box 4321, Ann Arbor, MI 48106
Calliope, see Ampersand Press
Calyx Inc., P.O. Box B, Corvallis, OR 97339
The Camel Press, HC80, Box 160, Big Cove Tannery, PA 17212
Canadian Fiction Magazine, P.O. Box 946, Sta. F, Toronto, Ont. M4Y 2N9, CANADA
Candle Publishing Co., P.O. Box 5009-136, Sugar Land, TX 77478
Caprice, 229 No. Fountain, Wichita, KS 67208
Carriage House Press, Carriage Lane, Barnes Landing, East Hampton, NY 11937
Catalyst, 1665 Havilon Dr., SW, Atlanta, GA 30311
The Cathartic, P.O. Box 1391, Ft. Lauderdale, FL 33302
Central Park, P.O. Box 1446, New York, NY 10023
The Chariton Review, Northeast Missouri State University, Kirksville, MO 63501
The Chattahoochee Review, Dekalb College, 2101 Womack Rd., Dunwoody, GA 30338
Chelsea, Box 5880, Grand Central Sta., New York, NY 10163
Chicago Review, Faculty Exchange Box C, University of Chicago, Chicago, IL 60637
Chicory Blue Press, East Street North, Goshen, CT 06756
Chimera Connections, 3712 NW 16th Blvd., Gainesville, FL 32605
Cimarron Review, English Dept., 205 Morrill Hall, Oklahoma State University, Stillwater, OK 74075
Cincinnati Poetry Review, English Dept. 069, University of Cincinnati, Cincinnati, OH 45221
Cinco Puntos Press, 2709 Louisville, El Paso, TX 79930
City Lights, 261 Columbus Ave., San Francisco, CA 94133
Cleis Press, P.O. Box 8933, Pittsburgh, PA 15221

Cleveland State University Poetry Center, English Dept., R.T. 1834, Cleveland, OH 44115

Clinton Street Quarterly, P.O. Box 3588, Portland, OR 97208

Clockwatch Review, English Dept., Illinois Wesleyan University, Bloomington, IL 61702

Clyde Press, 373 Lincoln Pkwy, Buffalo, NY 14216

Colorado-North Review, University of No. Colorado, Greeley, CO 80639

Columbia, 404 Dodge, Columbia University, New York, NY 10027

Commonweal, 15 Dutch St., New York, NY 10038

Concourse Press, Box 28600, Overbrook Sta., Philadelphia, PA 19151

Conditions, Box 159046, Van Brunt Sta., Brooklyn, NY 11215

Confluence Press, Lewis Clark State College, 8th Ave. & 6th St., Lewiston, ID 83501

Confrontation, English Dept., C. W. Post Campus, Brookville, NY 11548

Conjunctions, 33 West 9th St., New York, NY 10011

Copper Canyon Press, P.O. Box 271, Port Townsend, WA 98368

Cottonwood Review Press, Box J, Student Union, Lawrence, KS 66045

Coydog Review, P.O. Box 2608, Aptos, CA 95001

Crazy Quilt Literary Quarterly, 3341 Adams Ave., San Diego, CA 92116

Crazyhorse, English Dept., University of Arkansas, Little Rock, ARK 72204

Cream City Review, P.O. Box 413, University of Wisconsin, Milwaukee, WI 53201

Creeping Bent, 433 W. Market St., Bethlehem, PA 18018

Crescent Review, P.O. Box 15065, Winston-Salem, NC 27113

Cross Currents, Mercy College, Dobbs Ferry, NY 10522

Croton Review, P.O. Box 277, Croton-On-Hudson, NY 10520

Crystal Rainbow, 340 Granada Dr., Winter Park, FL 32789

Cumberland Poetry Review, P.O. Box 120128, Acklen Sta., Nashville, TN 37212

Curbstone Press, 321 Jackson St., Willimantic CT 06226

CURRENT,; An Arts Tabloid, P.O. Box 247, Walla Walla, WA 99362

CUTBANK, Univ. of Montana, Missoula, MT 59812

D

John Daniel & Co., Publishers, P.O. Box 21922, Santa Barbara, CA 93121

Dawn Valley Press, P.O. Box 58, New Wilmington, PA 16142

Day's Eye Press, Box 709, La Honda, CA 94020

Denotations, 11919 Moss Point Lane, Reston, VA 22094

Denver Quarterly, University of Denver, Denver, CO 80208

Desert Sun Press, 344 Barbara St., Perris, CA 92370

The Devil's Millhopper, Box 26, University of South Carolina, 171 University Pkwy, Aiken, SC 29801

Devon Publishing Co., 2700 Virginia Ave., NW, Washington, DC 20037

Druid Press, 2724 Shades Crest Rd., Birmingham, AL 35216

The Dunery Press, P.O. Box 116, Harbert, MI 49115

E

Earth's Daughters, P.O. Box 41, Central Park Sta., Buffalo, NY 14215

The Elephant-ear, School of Humanities, Irvine Valley College, Irvine, CA 92720

The Eleventh Muse, P.O. Box 2413, Colorado Springs, CO 80901

Ellipsis Press, 1176 E. Campbell Ave., Campbell, CA 95008

Epiphany Journal, P.O. Box 14727, San Francisco, CA 94114

Epoch, 251 Goldwin Smith Hall, Cornell University, Ithaca, NY 14853

Event, P.O. Box 2503, New Westminster, B.C. CANADA V3L 5B2

Exile Press, 765 Sunset Pkwy, Novato, CA 94947

Exit 13, c/o Tom Plante, 22 Oakwood Ct., Fanwood, NJ 07023

Expresso Tilt, 737 Wharton, Philadelphia, PA 19147

Exquisite Corpse, English Dept., Louisiana State University, Baton Rouge, LA 70803

F

Farce, see The Paper Plant

Fell Swoop, 1521 N. Lopez St., New Orleans, LA 70119

Fiction Collective, English Dept., Brooklyn College, Brooklyn, NY 11210

Fiction International, English Dept., San Diego State University, San Diego, CA 92182

Fiction Network, 870 Market St., Ste. 921, San Francisco, CA 94102

Field, Rice Hall, Oberlin College, Oberlin, OH 44074

Fine Madness, P.O. Box 15176, Seattle, WA 98115

Firebrand Books, 141 The Commons, Ithaca, NY 14850

5 A.M., 1109 Milton Ave., Pittsburgh, PA 15218

Five Fingers Review, 553-25th Ave., San Francisco, CA 94121

The Florida Review, English Dept., University of Central Florida, Orlando, FL 32816

Folio, Dept. of Lit., American University, Washington, DC 20016

Footwork, Passaic Co. Community College, College Blvd., Paterson, NJ 07509

Formations, P.O. Box 327, Wilmette, IL 60091

Forum, Ball State University, English Dept., Muncie, IN 47306

FORUM, KCAC, 201 Wyandotte, Kansas City, MO 64105

FRANK, 6 rue Monge, 75005 Paris, FRANCE

Frontiers, Women Studies, CB 246, University of Colorado, Boulder, CO 80309

G

Gambit, c/o J. Somerville, ed., P.O. Box 1122, Marietta, OH 45750

GAMUT, 1216 Rhodes Tower, Cleveland State University, Cleveland, OH 44115

Gargoyle, P.O. Box 30906, Bethesda, MD 20814

Georgia Review, University of Georgia, Athens, GA 30602

J. B. Gerald & J. Maas, P.O. Box 252, Moody, ME 04054

The Gettysburg Review, Gettysburg College, Gettysburg, PA 17325

Ghost Pony Press, 2518 Gregory St., Madison, WI 53711

Gilmore Gazette, 419a SW Coast Hwy., Newport, OR 97365

Gingko Press, P.O. Box 531, Old Chelsea Sta., New York, NY 10011

Gorilla Press, 9269 Mission Gorge Rd., Ste. 229, Santee, CA 92071

Graham House Review, Box 5000, Colgate Univ., Hamilton, NY 13346

The Grand Valley Review, Grand Valley State Univ., Allendale, MI 49401

The Gray Moose Press, 19 Elmwood Ave., Rye, NY 10580

Graywolf Press, P.O. Box 75006, St. Paul, MN 55175

Great Elm Press, RD 2, Box 37, Rexville, NY 14877

Great Lakes Publishing Co., P.O. Box 321, Emmet, MI 48022

Green Mountains Review, Johnson State College, Johnson, VT 05656

The Green Street Press, P.O. Box 1957, Harvard Sq., Cambridge, MA 02238

Greenfield Review Press, 2 Middle Grove Rd., Greenfield Center, NY 12833

The Greensboro Review, English Dept., University of North Carolina, Greensboro, NC 27412

H

Half tones to Jubilee, English Dept., Pensacola Jr. College, Pensacola, FL 32504

Hanging Loose, 231 Wyckoff St., Brooklyn, NY 11217

Harmony, Box 210056, San Francisco, CA 94121

Hayden's Ferry Review, Student Publications, Matthews Ctr., Arizona State University, Tempe, AZ 85287

Heaven Bone Press, P.O. 486, Chester, NY 10918

Helicon Nine, P.O. Box 22412, Kansas City, MO 64113

High Plains Literary Review, 180 Adams St., Ste. 250, Denver, CO 80206

Hob-Nob, 994 Nissley Rd., Lancaster, PA 17601

Hobo Jungle, Roxbury, CT 06783

Hohm Press, P.O. Box 25839, Prescott Valley, AZ 86312

The Hollins Critic, P.O. Box 9538, Hollins College, VA 24020

Hot Wire, 5210 N. Wayne, Chicago, IL 60640

Hutton Publications, P.O. Box 1870, Hayden, ID 83835

Hydraulic Press, 1436 Grant Ave. #5, San Francisco, CA 94133

I

Ice River, 953 North Gale, Union, OR 97883

Indiana Review, 316 N. Jordan Ave., Bloomington, IN 47405
Interim, English Dept., University of Nevada, Las Vegas, NV 89154
Iowa Review, 308 EPB, University of Iowa, Iowa City, IA 52242
Iowa Woman, P. O. Box 680, Iowa City, IA 52244
Ironwood, P.O. Box 40907, Tucson, AZ 85717
Ithaca House Books, see Greenfield Review Press

J

Jeopardy, West Washington Univ., Hum. 350, Bellingham, WA 98225
The Journal, English Dept., Ohio State University, Columbus, OH 43210

K

Kaleidoscope, 326 Locust St., Akron, OH 44398
Kalliope, FCCJ, 3939 Roosevelt Blvd., Jacksonville, FL 32205
Kansas Quarterly, English dept., Kansas State University, Manhattan, KS 66506
Kentucky Poetry Review, Bellarmine College, Newburg Rd., Louisville, KY 40205
The Kenyon Review, Kenyon College, Gambier, OH 43022
Kindred Spirit, Rte. 2, Box 111, St John, KS 67576

L

La Jolla Poets Press, P.O. Box 8638, La Jolla, CA 92038
Lactuca, P.O. Box 621, Suffern, NY 10901
Lake Effect, Box 315, Oswego, NY 13126
Lake Street Review, Box 7188, Powderhorn, Sta., Minneapolis, MN 55407
Landscape, P.O. Box 7107, Berkeley, CA 94707
Lapis Press, 589 No. Venice Blvd., Venice, CA 90291
Late Knocking, P.O. Box 336, Forest Hill, MD 21050
Latin American Literary Review Press, 2300 Palmer St., Pittsburgh, PA 15218

Laughing Waters Press, 864-18th, Boulder, CO 80302

Laurel Review, English Dept., Northwest Missouri State University, Maryville, MO 64468

Lesman, P. R. Ltd., Publishers, P.O. Box 367, Woolwich, ME 04579

Liberty, P.O. Box 1167, Port Townsend, WA 98368

Lintel, Box 8609, Roanoke, VA 24014

LIPS, P.O. Box 1345, Montclair, NJ 07042

Lomakatsi, Box 633, 1377 K St., NW, Washington, DC 20005

Loom Press, Box 1394, Lowell, MA 01853

Loonfeather, 426 Bemidji Ave., Bemidji, MN 56601

Lorien House, P.O. Box 1112, Black Mountain, NC 28711

Lost & Found Times, Luna Bisonte Prods., 137 Leland Ave., Columbus, OH 43214

Lost Roads Publishers, P.O. Box 5848, Providence, RI 02903

Lotus Press, Inc., P.O. Box 21607, Detroit, MI 48221

Lynx House Press, 915 Sunrise Dr., Emporia, KS 66801

M

The MacGuffin, Schoolcraft College, 18600 Haggerty Rd., Livonia, MI 48152

The Madison Review, English Dept., University of Wisconsin, Madison, WI 53706

The Mage, Student Assoc., Colgate University, Hamilton, NY 13346

Malahat Review, University of Victoria, P.O. Box 1700, Victoria, BC CANADA V8W 2Y2

Maledicta, 331 So. Greenfield Ave., Waukesha, WI 53186

Man Root Press, Box 762, Boyes Hot Springs, CA 95416

Manhattan Review, 440 Riverside Dr., #45, New York, NY 10027

Mankato Poetry Review, Box 53, English Dept., Mankato State University, Mankato, MN 56001

Maryland Poetry Review, Drawer H, Catonsville, MD 21228

The Massachusetts Review, Memorial Hall, University of Mass., Amherst, MA 01003

McFarland & Co., Inc., Publishers, Box 611, Jefferson, NC 28640

Memphis State Review, Eng. Dept., Memphis State Univ., Memphis, TN 38152

Metropolitan, see Omega Cottonwood Press

Micah Publications, 255 Humphrey St., Marblehead, MA 01945

Michigan Quarterly Review, University of Michigan, 3032 Rackham Bldg., Ann Arbor, MI 48109

Mid-American Review, English Dept., Bowling Green State University, Bowling Green, OH 43403

Midland Review, English Dept., Oklahoma State University, Stillwater, OK 74078

Mildred, P.O. Box 9252, Schenectady, NY 12309

Mind in Motion, P.O. Box 1118, Apple Valley, CA 92307

The Mind's Eye, Box 656, Glenview, IL 60025

Minnesota Review, English Dept., SUNY, Stony Brook, NY 11794

Mississippi Review, Southern Sta., Box 5144, University of So. Mississippi, Hattiesburg, MS 39408

Mississippi Valley Review, English Dept., Western Illinois University, Macomb, IL 61455

Modern Haiku, P.O. Box 1752, Madison, WI 53701

Mr. Cogito, Box 627, Pacific University, Forest Grove, OR 97116

N

NRG, 6735 S.E. 78th St., Portland, OR 97206

Nada Press/Big Scream, 2782 Dixie SW, Grandville, MI 49418

Nebraska Review, ASH 215, Univ. of Nebraska, Omaha, NE 68182

Negative Capability, 62 Ridgelawn Dr. East, Mobile, AL 36608

New American Writing, 1446 W. Jarvis, #3D, Chicago, IL 60626

The New Criterion, 850 Seventh Ave., New York, NY 10019

New England Review & Bread Loaf Quarterly, Middlebury College, Middlebury, VT 05753

New Formalist Press, 288 3rd Ave., Westwood, NJ 07675

New Letters, UMKC, 5100 Rockhill Rd., Kansas City, MO 64110

New Orleans Review, Loyola Univ., Box 195, New Orleans, LA 70118

New Poets Series, Inc., 541 Piccadilly Rd., Baltimore, MD 21204

The New Renaissance, 9 Heath Rd., Arlington, MA 02174

New Rivers Press, 1602 Selby Ave., St. Paul, MN 55104

New Victoria Publishers, P.O. Box 27, Norwich, VT 05055
New Virginia Review, 1306 E. Cary St., Richmond VA 23219
Night Roses, P.O. Box 393, Prospect Heights, IL 60070
Nightmares of Reason, 107 Brighton Ave., Allston, MA 02134
Nimrod, Arts & Humanities Council, 2210 Main, Tulsa, OK 74114
No Trees, Englewood Ave., Buffalo, NY 14214
North American Review, Univ. of Northern Iowa, Cedar Falls, IA 50614
North Country Books, 18 Irving Place, Utica, NY 13501
North Dakota Quarterly, P.O. Box 8237, Univ. of North Dakota, Grand Forks, ND 58202
Northeast, 1310 Shorewood Dr., LaCrosse, WI 54601
Northeastern University Press, Huntington Plaza, Ste. 272, Boston, MA 02115
The Northern Review, Rm 018 LRC, University of Wisconsin, Stevens Point, WI 54481
Northwest Review, 369 PLC, University of Oregon, Eugene, OR 97403
Nostoc Magazine, Box 162, Newton, MA 02168
Notus, 2420 Walter Dr., Ann Arbor, MI 48103
Now and Then, Box 19180A, E. Tennessee State University, Johnson City, TN 37614
Nuestro, P.O. Box 75418, Washington, DC 20013

O

Occident, Rhetoric Dept., University of California, Berkeley, CA 94720
The Ohio Review, Ellis Hall, Ohio University, Athens, OH 45701
The Old Red Kimono, Floyd College, P.O. Box 1864, Rome, GA 30163
Olde & Oppenheim, Publishers, P.O. Box 61203, Phoenix, AZ 85082
Ontario Review, 9 Honey Brook Dr., Princeton, NJ 08540
Orchises Press, P.O. Box 20602, Alexandria, VA 22320
Organica Press, 4419 N. Manhattan Ave., Tampa, FL 33614
Osiris, Box 297, Deerfield, MA 01342
The Other Side, 1225 Dandridge St., Fredericksburg, VA 22401
Other Voices, 820 Ridge Rd., Highland Park, IL 60035

Outerbridge, English A323, College of Staten Island, 715 Ocean Terrace, Staten Island, NY 10301

Outrider Press, 1004 E. Steger Rd., Ste. C-3, Crete, IL 60035

Owl Creek Press, 1620 N. 45th St., Seattle, WA 98103

Oxalis, Stone Ridge Poetry Soc., P.O. Box 3993, Kingston, NY 12401

Oxford Magazine, 356 Bachelor Hall, Miami University, Oxford, OH 45056

P

Painted Bride Quarterly, 230 Vine St., Philadelphia, PA 19106

Pandora, 2844 Grayson, Ferndale, MI 48220

The Pandhandler, English Dept., Univ. of W. Florida, Pensacola, FL 32514

Panther Press, see The Cathartic

The Paper Plant, Box 543, Raleigh, NC 27602

Papier-Mache Press, 34 Malaga Place East, Manhattan Beach, CA 90266

Parabola, 656 Broadway, New York, NY 10012

Paragraph/Oat City Press, 1423 Northampton St., Holyoke, MA 01040

Paris Review, 541 East 72nd St., New York, NY 10021

Parnassus: Poetry in Review, 41 Union Sq. W, Rm.804, New York, NY 10003

Partisan Review, 141 Bay State Rd., Boston, MA 02215

Passages North, William Bonifas Fine Arts Ctr., Escanaba, MI 49829

Pentagram Press, 212 No. Second St., Minneapolis, MN 55401

Perivale Press, 13830 Erwin St., Van Nuys, CA 91401

Phanes Press, P.O. Box 6114, Grand Rapids, MI 49516

Phoebe, 4400 University Dr., Fairfax, VA 22030

Piddiddle Press, 1000 Timm Dr., College Sta., TX 77840

Pig Iron Press, P.O. Box 237, Youngstown, OH 44501

Pivot, 250 Riverside Dr., #23, New York, NY 10025

Pocahontas Press, 2805 Wellesley Ct., Blacksburg, VA 24060

Poet & Critic, 203 Ross Hall, Iowa State University, Ames, IA 50011

Poet Lore, 7815 Old Georgetown Rd., Bethesda, MD 20814

Poetalk, BAPC, 1527 Virginia St., Berkeley, CA 94703

Poetpourri, Box 3737 Taft Rd., Syracuse, NY 13220

Poetry Atlanta Press, 614 Page Ave., Atlanta, GA 30307

Poetry East, English Dept., DePaul University, 820 W. Belden Ave., Chicago, IL 60614

Poetry Flash, P.O. Box 4172, Berkeley, CA 94704

Poetry Magic, Box 521, Potterville, MI 48876

Poetry New York, CUNY, 33 W. 42 St., New York, NY 10036

The Poetry Peddler, P.O. Box 250, W. Monroe, NY 13167

Poltroon Press, P.O. Box 5476, Berkeley, CA 94705

Prairie Schooner, 201 Andrews, University of Nebraska, Lincoln, NE 68588

Primavera, 1212 E. 59th St., Chicago, IL 60637

Prism International, E-455-1866 Main Mall, Univ. of B.C., V6T 1W5, CANADA

Profile Press, 3004 So. Grant St., Arlington, VA 22202

Provincetown Arts, P.O. Box 35, Provincetown, MA 02657

Pruett Publishing Co., 2928 Pearl St., Boulder, CO 80301

Pudding House Publications, 60 N. Main St., Johnstown, OH 43031

Puerto del Sol, Box 3E, No. Mexico St. Univ., Las Cruces, NM 88003

Q

The Quarterly, 201 E. 50th St., New York, NY 10022

Quarterly West, 317 Olpin Union, Univ. of Utah, Salt Lake City, UT 84112

R

Raccoon, P.O. Box 111327, Memphis, TN 38111

Raddle Moon, 9060 Ardmore Dr., Sidney, B.C., CANADA V8L 3S1

Raritan, Rutgers University, 165 College Ave., New Brunswick, NJ 08903

Raw Dog Press, 128 Harvey Ave., Doylestown, PA 18901

Readable Heart Publishing, 13 Butterworth Rd., Beverly, MA 01915

The Real Comet Press, 3131 Western Ave., #410, Seattle, WA 98121
Real Fiction, 298 9th Ave., San Francisco, CA 94118
The Reaper, 325 Ocean View Ave., Santa Cruz, CA 95062
Redstart, 229 No. Fountain, Wichita, KS 67208
Reflections, P.O. Box 368, Duncan Falls, OH 43734
Rhododendron, 2058 E. Louise Ave., Salt Lake City, UT 84109
Rhyme Time, see Hutton Publications
River Styx, 14 South Euclid, St. Louis, MO 63108
Riverside Quarterly, P.O. Box 464, Waco, TX 76703
Roadrunner, P.O. Box 25, Ocatillo, CA 92259
Rowan Tree Press, 124 Chestnut St., Boston, MA 02108
Runaway Spoon Press, Box 3621, Port Charlotte, FL 33949

S

S.C. Magazine, P.O. Box 31249, San Francisco, CA 94131
Sachem Press, P.O. Box 9, Old Chatham, NY 12136
Salmagundi, Skidmore College, Saratoga Springs, NY 12866
Samisdat, Box 129, Richford, VT 15476
San Francisco Sentinel, 500 Hayes St., San Francisco, CA 94102
Scoresheet, 491 Mandana Blvd, #3, Oakland, CA 94610
SCREAM Magazine, P.O. Box 10363, Raleigh, NC 27605
The Seal Press, 3131 Western Ave., #410, Seattle, WA 98121
Seems, Lakeland College, P.O. Box 359, Sheboygan, WI 53081
Selene Books, P.O. Box 220-253, El Paso, TX 79913
Seneca Review, Hobart & William Smith Colleges, Geneva, NY
   14456
Sequoia, Storke Publications Bldg., Stanford, CA 94305
The Sheep Meadow Press, P.O. Box 1345, Riverdale-on-Hudson,
   NY 10471
Shenandoah, Box 722, Lexington, VA 24450
Shooting Star Review, 7123 Race St., Pittsburgh, PA 15208
Showcase, 3544 Buck Mountain Rd., Roanoke, VA 24014
Silverfish Review, P.O. Box 3541, Eugene, OR 97403
Singing Horse, P.O. Box 40034, Philadelphia, PA 19106
Singular Speech Press, 10 Hilltop Dr., Canton, CT 06019
Skylark Press, Purdue University, Calumet, 2233 171st St., Ham-
   mond, IN 46323

Slipstream, Box 2071, New Market Sta., Niagara Falls, NY 14301

The Socratic Press, P.O. Box 66683, St. Petersburg Beach, FL 33736

Sojourner, 143 Albany St., Cambridge, MA 02139

Sonora Review, English Dept., University of Arizona, Tucson, AZ 85721

Soundings East, English Dept., Salem State College, Salem, MA 01970

South Coast Poetry Journal, English Dept., California State University, Fullerton, CA 92634

Southern California Anthology, Prof. Writing Prog, WPH 404, University of So. Calif., Los Angeles, CA 90089

Southern Humanities Review, English Dept., SHR, Auburn University, AL 36849

The Southern Review, 43 Allen Hall, Louisiana State University, Baton Rouge, LA 70803

Southwest Review, 6410 Airline Rd., SMU, Dallas, TX 75275

Sou'wester, English Dept., Southern Illinois University, Edwardsville, IL 62026

Space And Time, 138 W. 70th St., Apt. 4-B, New York, NY 10023

Spectrum, Box 72-E, Anna-Maria College, Paxton, MA 01612

The Spirit that Moves Us Press, P.O. Box 1585, Iowa City, IA 52244

Spitball, 6224 Collegeville Pl., Cincinnati, OH 45224

Spoon River Poetry Press, P.O. Box 1443, Peoria, IL 61655

Spoon River Quarterly, English Dept., Illinois State University, Normal, IL 61761

St. Andrew's Press, St. Andrews College, Laurinburg, NC 28352

Stand Magazine, 175 Wingrove Rd., Newcastle-on-Tyne, NE4 9DA, ENGLAND

Star Line, P.O. Box 1764, Cambridge, MA 02238

StarMist Books, Box 12460, 4322 Lake Ave., Rochester, NY 14612

State Street Press, Box 278, Brockport, NY 14420

Stone Country, P.O. Box 132, Menemsha, MA 02552

Story County Books, Box 355, Ames, IA 50010

Story Press, P.O. Box 10040, Chicago, IL 60610

Story Quarterly, P.O. Box 1416, Northbrook, IL 60065

The Sun, 412 W. Rosemary St., Chapel Hill, NC 27516

Sun Eagle Publishing, P.O. Box 33545, Granada Hills, CA 91344

T

Talisman, Box 1117, Hoboken, NJ 07030

Tampa Review, University of Tampa, Tampa, FL 33606

Tar River Poetry, English Dept., East Carolina University, Greenville, NC 27834

The Teitan Press, Inc., 339 W. Barry Ave., Ste, 16B, Chicago, IL 60657

Texas Review, Sam Houston State Univ., Huntsville, TX 77341

Thema, See Bothomas Enterprises

Third Lung Press, P.O. Box 361, Conover, NC 28613

Third World Press, 7524 S. Cottage Grove, P.O. Box 730, Chicago, IL 60619

Thistlerose Publications, 1007 Greenbrier St., St. Paul, MN 55106

Three Continents Press, Inc., 1636 Connecticut Ave. NW, Ste. 501. Wash. DC 20009

Three Tree Press, P.O. Box 10044, Lansing, MI 48901

The Threepenny Review, P.O. Box 9131, Berkeley, CA 94709

Thunder's Mouth Press, 93-99 Greene St., Ste. 2A, New York, NY 10012

TIKKUN, 5100 Leona St., Oakland, CA 94619

TIMBUKTU, P. O. Box 469, Charlottesville, VA 22902

Tioga Publishing Co., 150 Coquito, Portola Valley, CA 94025

Tombouctou Books, Box 265, Bolinas, CA 94924

Townhouse Publishing, 301 N. Harrison St., Bldg. B, Ste. 115, Princeton, NJ 08540

Treetop Panorama, R. Rt. 1, Box 160, Payson, IL 62360

Trestle Crook Review, English Dept., No. Idaho College, Coeur D'Alene, ID 83814

TriQuarterly, 2020 Ridge Ave., Northwestern University, Evanston, IL 60208

Trivia, P.O. Box 606, N. Amherst, MA 01059

Truly Fine Press, P.O. Box 891, Bemedji, MN 56601

Turnstile, 175 Fifth Ave., Ste. 2348, New York, NY 10010

U

Unipress, P.O. Box 689, Brookings, SD 57006

the unspeakable visions of the individual, P.O. Box 439, California, PA 15419

V

Venus in Libra Books, 821 Carroll St., Brooklyn, NY 11215
Verse, English Dept., College of William & Mary, Williamsburg, VA 23185
Visions, 4705 S. 8th Rd., Arlington, VA 22204
Vol. No. Magazine, 24721 Newhall Ave., Newhall, CA 91321

W

Wallace Stevens Journal, Clarkson Univ., Potsdam, NY
Walrus, Mills College, 5000 MacArthur Blvd., Oakland, CA 99613
Washington Writers' Publishing House, P.O. Box 15271, Washington, DC 20003
Water Row Books, Inc., P.O. Box 438, Sudbury, MA 01776
Weber Studies, Weber State College, Ogden, UT 84408
Webster Review, Webster College, Webster Groves, MO 63119
Wesley Press, English Dept., Springfield College, Springfield, MA 01109
West Branch, English Dept., Bucknell University, Lewisburg, PA 17837
Western Humanities Review, Univ. of Utah, Salt Lake City, UT 84112
Wheels, Wheels Verlag, Knauerstrasse 9, 8500 Nurnberg 70, W. GERMANY
Whetstone, BAAC, P.O. Box 1266, Barrington, IL 60011
William & Mary Review, College of William & Mary, Williamsburg, VA 23185
Willow Springs, Publ., P.O. Box 1063, E. Washington University, Cheney, WA 99004
The Windhorse Review, 2995 Eagle Way, 36, Boulder, CO 80301
The Wineberry Press, 3207 Macomb St. NW, Washington, DC 20008
Witness, 31000 Northwestern Hgwy, Ste. 200, Farmington Hills, MI 48010

Wood Thrush Books, 18 N. Winooski, Burlington, VT 05401
Woods Colt Press, P.O. Box 22524, Kansas City, MO 64113
The Worcester Review, 6 Chatham St., Worcester, MA 01609
Wordcraft, see Ice River
The Wormwood Review, P.O. Box 8840, Stockton, CA 95208
Writ, Two Sussex Ave., Toronto, Ont. M5S 1J5, CANADA
The Writers Bar-B-Q, 924 Bryn Mawr, Springfield, IL 62703
Writers' Forum, P.O. Box 7150, University of Colorado, Colorado
    Springs, CO 80933

Y

The Yale Review, P.O. Box 1902A Yale Sta., New Haven, CT 06520
Yarrow, English Dept., Kutztown State Univ., Kutztown, PA 19530
Yellow Silk, P.O. Box 6374, Albany, CA 94706

Z

Z Miscellaneous, P.O. Box 20041, New York, NY 10028
ZYZZYVA, 41 Sutter St., Ste. 1400, San Francisco, CA 94104

INDEX

The following is a listing in alphabetical order by author's last name of works reprinted in the first fourteen *Pushcart Prize* editions.

508

CONTRIBUTORS' NOTES

JENNIFER ATKINSON has poems and essays in recent issues of *The Iowa Review, The Reaper,* and *Fine Madness.* She lives in St. Louis.

JIMMY SANTIAGO BACA won the Before Columbus Foundation Award in 1988. His *Black Mesa Poems* is just out from New Directions.

JULIAN BARNES is the author of five novels, including *Flaubert's Parrot.* He lives in London, England.

CHARLES BAXTER is the author of the story "Harmony of the World" (*Pushcart Prize VII*) which was included in his story collection of the same name (University of Missouri Press). His novel, *Through The Safety Net,* was published by Viking.

PAUL BOWLES is a Founding Editor of The Pushcart Prize series. He is the author of many books and lives in Morocco.

FRANK BURROUGHS teaches at Bowdoin College and is at work on a collection of personal essays.

ROBERT CREELEY has published *Collected Prose* (1984, Marion Boyars) and *Memory Gardens* (1986, New Directions).

LYDIA DAVIS is the author of *Break It Down* (Farrar, Straus and Giroux). She has also done many translations from French Literature. She lives in Port Ewen, New York.

MARK DOTY is the author of *Turtle, Swan* (1987) and the forthcoming *Bethleham in Broad Daylight*, both from Godine. He teaches at Goddard College.

LOUISE GLÜCK's latest book, *Ararat*, is just out from Ecco Press. She lives in Vermont.

LORNA GOODISON is a poet, painter and short story writer. She lives in Jamaica, West Indies and her story collection *Baby Mother and The King of Swords* is forthcoming from Longman Ltd.

MARILYN HACKER's most recent books are *Love, Death, and the Changing of Seasons* (Arbor House) and *Assumptions* (Knopf). She won the National Book Award in 1975.

SAM HAMILL is editor at Copper Canyon Press. His books are published by White Pine Press and Broken Moon Press, where his collection of literary essays, *A Poet's Work*, will soon appear.

DEWITT HENRY is director of *Ploughshares* and teaches at Emerson College. "Witness" is part of a longer work in progress.

BRENDA HILLMAN's second poetry collection, *Fortress*, is due soon from Wesleyan. She lives and teaches in California.

EDWARD HOAGLAND's books include *Heart's Desire, Seven Rivers West, African Calliope, The Courage of Turtles*, and *Notes From The Century Before*. He teaches at Bennington.

SANDY HUSS has published fiction in *River Styx, Rusty Edge* and elsewhere. She lives in Tuscaloosa and teaches at The University of Alabama.

ANGELA JACKSON has published poetry and fiction in *TriQuarterly, Black Quarterly*, and *Open Places*. She lives in Chicago.

DAVID JAUSS edits fiction for *Crazyhorse*. His story collection, *Crimes of Passion*, was published by Story Press in 1984.

DIANE JOHNSON is the author of *Persian Nights* and other works of fiction. She lives in San Francisco.

LI-YOUNG LEE won a Guggenheim award this year. He lives in Chicago and has been concentrating on longer poems.

ALISTAIR MACLEOD's story collection *The Lost Salt Gift of Blood* was published by Ontario Review Press in 1988 and included

"Island." His stories have appeared in *The Southern Review, The Massachusetts Review* and elsewhere. He teaches at the University of Windsor.

FRANK MANLEY teaches at Emory University. His story in this volume is part of a collection, *Within The Ribbons,* just out from North Point Press.

MICHAEL MARTONE lives in Cambridge, Massachusetts. He is the author of two story collections, most recently from Johns Hopkins.

KRISTINA MCGRATH has published in *Paris Review, Woman Poet, Ploughshares* and elsewhere. She lives in San Francisco.

THOMAS MEAGHER lives in Massachusetts. "Strand" is his first published work.

ROBERT MINKOFF is a freelance writer living in New York City. His story is part of a collection in progress titled "The New York Folk Tales."

JUDSON MITCHAM has published in *The Georgia Review, Poetry Northwest* and *Prairie Schooner.* His chapbook, *Notes for a Prayer In June,* was published by State Street.

JIM MOORE is co-editor of *Minnesota Writes: Poetry* (Milkweed Editions). He is also the author of two books and *How We Missed Belgium* (with Deborah Keenan) He lives in St. Paul.

THYLIAS MOSS teaches at Phillips Academy in Andover, Massachusetts Her third collection of poetry, *At Redbone's,* is due soon.

LYNN NELSON (Marilyn Nelson Waniek) teaches at the University of Connecticut. Her books, *For The Body,* and *Mom's Promises,* were published by L.S.U. Press.

SIGRID NUNEZ lives in New York City and is at work on a story collection.

JOYCE CAROL OATES is the author of the novel *American Appetites* (Dutton) and the story collection, *The Assignation* (Ecco Press) which includes "Party."

ALBERTO RIOS teaches at Arizona State University. His first book of poems, *Whispering To Fool The Wind,* won The Walt Whitman prize.

PATTIANN ROGERS was Richard Hugo Poet-In-Residence at The University of Montana last year. Her fourth book of poems, *Splitting and Binding,* is just out from Wesleyan.

SHEILA SCHWARTZ has been a Stegner Fellow and a Jones Lecturer at Stanford. Her stories have appeared in *Atlantic, MSS* and elsewhere.

GERALD STERN is the author of *Lucky Life,* and *Selected Poems,* among other books. He teaches at The Iowa Writer's Workshop.

JOAN SWIFT's most recent book of poems, *The Dark Path of Our Names* (Dragon Gate) won the 1986 Washington State Governor's Award. She lives in Edmonds, Washington.

RON TANNER is a graduate of the Iowa Writer's Workshop, and a 1987 Yaddo Fellow. His work has appeared in *Mid-American Review, Carolina Quarterly, New Orleans Review* and elsewhere.

PETER TYSVER lives in St. Louis and studies at Washington University. This is his first published work.

ELIOT WEINBERGER has frequently appeared in these volumes. He lives in New York City.

BARBARA WILSON is the author of two mysteries, two novels, and the short story collection, *Miss Venezuela.* She is co-publisher of Seal Press.

FOR THE BEST IN PAPERBACKS, LOOK FOR THE 🐧

In every corner of the world, on every subject under the sun, Penguin represents quality and variety—the very best in publishing today.

For complete information about books available from Penguin—including Pelicans, Puffins, Peregrines, and Penguin Classics—and how to order them, write to us at the appropriate address below. Please note that for copyright reasons the selection of books varies from country to country.

In the United Kingdom: For a complete list of books available from Penguin in the U.K., please write to *Dept E.P., Penguin Books Ltd, Harmondsworth, Middlesex, UB7 0DA*.

In the United States: For a complete list of books available from Penguin in the U.S., please write to *Dept BA, Penguin, Box 120, Bergenfield, New Jersey 07621-0120*.

In Canada: For a complete list of books available from Penguin in Canada, please write to *Penguin Books Ltd, 2801 John Street, Markham, Ontario L3R 1B4*.

In Australia: For a complete list of books available from Penguin in Australia, please write to the *Marketing Department, Penguin Books Ltd, P.O. Box 257, Ringwood, Victoria 3134*.

In New Zealand: For a complete list of books available from Penguin in New Zealand, please write to the *Marketing Department, Penguin Books (NZ) Ltd, Private Bag, Takapuna, Auckland 9*.

In India: For a complete list of books available from Penguin, please write to *Penguin Overseas Ltd, 706 Eros Apartments, 56 Nehru Place, New Delhi, 110019*.

In Holland: For a complete list of books available from Penguin in Holland, please write to *Penguin Books Nederland B.V., Postbus 195, NL-1380AD Weesp, Netherlands*.

In Germany: For a complete list of books available from Penguin, please write to *Penguin Books Ltd, Friedrichstrasse 10-12, D-6000 Frankfurt Main I, Federal Republic of Germany*.

In Spain: For a complete list of books available from Penguin in Spain, please write to *Longman, Penguin España, Calle San Nicolas 15, E-28013 Madrid, Spain*.

In Japan: For a complete list of books available from Penguin in Japan, please write to *Longman Penguin Japan Co Ltd, Yamaguchi Building, 2-12-9 Kanda Jimbocho, Chiyoda-Ku, Tokyo 101, Japan*.

FOR THE BEST LITERATURE, LOOK FOR THE 🐧

FOR THE BEST LITERATURE, LOOK FOR THE Ⓟ

☐ **A SPORT OF NATURE**
Nadine Gordimer

Hillela, Nadine Gordimer's "sport of nature," is seductive and intuitively gifted at life. Casting herself adrift from her family at seventeen, she lives among political exiles on an East African beach, marries a black revolutionary, and ultimately plays a heroic role in the overthrow of apartheid.

354 pages   ISBN: 0-14-008470-3   **$7.95**

☐ **THE COUNTERLIFE**
Philip Roth

By far Philip Roth's most radical work of fiction, *The Counterlife* is a book of conflicting perspectives and points of view about people living out dreams of renewal and escape. Illuminating these lives is the skeptical, enveloping intelligence of the novelist Nathan Zuckerman, who calculates the price and examines the results of his characters' struggles for a change of personal fortune.

372 pages   ISBN: 0-14-009769-4   **$4.95**

☐ **THE MONKEY'S WRENCH**
Primo Levi

Through the mesmerizing tales told by two characters—one, a construction worker/philosopher who has built towers and bridges in India and Alaska; the other, a writer/chemist, rigger of words and molecules—Primo Levi celebrates the joys of work and the art of storytelling.

174 pages   ISBN: 0-14-010357-0   **$6.95**

☐ **IRONWEED**
William Kennedy

"Riding up the winding road of Saint Agnes Cemetery in the back of the rattling old truck, Francis Phelan became aware that the dead, even more than the living, settled down in neighborhoods." So begins William Kennedy's Pulitzer-Prize winning novel about an ex-ballplayer, part-time gravedigger, and full-time drunk, whose return to the haunts of his youth arouses the ghosts of his past and present.

228 pages   ISBN: 0-14-007020-6   **$6.95**

☐ **THE COMEDIANS**
Graham Greene

Set in Haiti under Duvalier's dictatorship, *The Comedians* is a story about the committed and the uncommitted. Actors with no control over their destiny, they play their parts in the foreground; experience love affairs rather than love; have enthusiasms but not faith; and if they die, they die like Mr. Jones, by accident.

288 pages   ISBN: 0-14-002766-1   **$4.95**

FOR THE BEST LITERATURE, LOOK FOR THE 🐧

☐ **THE LAST SONG OF MANUEL SENDERO**
Ariel Dorfman

In an unnamed country, in a time that might be now, the son of Manuel Sendero refuses to be born, beginning a revolution where generations of the future wait for a world without victims or oppressors.

464 pages   ISBN: 0-14-008896-2   **$7.95**

☐ **THE BOOK OF LAUGHTER AND FORGETTING**
Milan Kundera

In this collection of stories and sketches, Kundera addresses themes including sex and love, poetry and music, sadness and the power of laughter. "*The Book of Laughter and Forgetting* calls itself a novel," writes John Leonard of *The New York Times*, "although it is part fairly tale, part literary criticism, part political tract, part musicology, part autobiography. It can call itself whatever it wants to, because the whole is genius."

240 pages   ISBN: 0-14-009693-0   **$6.95**

☐ **TIRRA LIRRA BY THE RIVER**
Jessica Anderson

Winner of the Miles Franklin Award, Australia's most prestigious literary prize, *Tirra Lirra by the River* is the story of a woman's seventy-year search for the place where she truly belongs. Nora Porteous's series of escapes takes her from a small Australia town to the suburbs of Sydney to London, where she seems finally to become the woman she always wanted to be.

142 pages   ISBN: 0-14-006945-3   **$4.95**

☐ **LOVE UNKNOWN**
A. N. Wilson

In their sweetly wild youth, Monica, Belinda, and Richeldis shared a bachelor-girl flat and became friends for life. Now, twenty years later, A. N. Wilson charts the intersecting lives of the three women through the perilous waters of love, marriage, and adultery in this wry and moving modern comedy of manners.

202 pages   ISBN: 0-14-010190-X   **$6.95**

☐ **THE WELL**
Elizabeth Jolley

Against the stark beauty of the Australian farmlands, Elizabeth Jolley portrays an eccentric, affectionate relationship between the two women—Hester, a lonely spinster, and Katherine, a young orphan. Their pleasant, satisfyingly simple life is nearly perfect until a dark stranger invades their world in a most horrifying way.

176 pages   ISBN: 0-14-008901-2   **$6.95**

FOR THE BEST LITERATURE, LOOK FOR THE 🐧

☐ **VOSS**
Patrick White

Set in nineteenth-century Australia, *Voss* is the story of the secret passion between an explorer and a young orphan. From the careful delineation of Victorian society to the stark narrative of adventure in the Australian desert, Patrick White's novel is one of extraordinary power and virtuosity. White won the Nobel Prize for Literature in 1973.

448 pages   *ISBN: 0-14-001438-1*   **$7.95**

☐ **STONES FOR IBARRA**
Harriet Doerr

An American couple, the only foreigners in the Mexican village of Ibarra, have come to reopen a long-dormant copper mine. Their plan is to live out their lives here, connected to the place and to each other. Along the way, they learn much about life, death, and the tide of fate from the Mexican people around them.

214 pages   *ISBN: 0-14-007562-3*   **$6.95**